Michael Kidron is a political economist who has written, among other books, *Western Capitalism since the War* and *Foreign Investments in India*. He is the author, with Dan Smith, of *The War Atlas*. He is general editor of Pluto Projects.

Ronald Segal has written many books, including a dictionary of African politics, *Political Africa*; a study of racial conflict in history, *The Race War*; books on the USA and on the Middle East; and a major biography of Trotsky.

The New State of the World Atlas

Michael Kidron & Ronald Segal

A Pluto Press project

Simon & Schuster New York

Published by Simon and Schuster
A Division of Simon & Schuster, Inc.
Simon & Schuster Building
Rockefeller Center
1230 Avenue of the Americas
New York, New York 10020

Artwork for maps by Swanston Graphics, Derby, England
Coordinated by Anne Benewick

Typeset by Rowland Phototypesetting (London) Limited, England
Printed in Hong Kong by Mandarin Offset International (HK) Limited

2 3 4 5 6 7 8 9 10

Library of Congress Cataloging in Publication Data

Kidron, Michael

The New State of the World Atlas

1. Atlases. I. Segal, Ronald, 1932- .II.Title
G1021.K46 912 84-675087

ISBN 0-671-50664-1

Contents

Introduction

The State of the World Atlas was born out of a desire to treat the major issues of our time in an easily accessible and coherent form.

Like its predecessor, this new edition identifies subjects of public concern; provides a frame of reference for the interpretation of events; and explains connections that are obscure in themselves or have been deliberately obscured. And it does so with reference to an underlying structure: the self-perpetuating system of sovereign states preoccupied with their own aggrandisement and with their corresponding fear of one another.

The circumstances in which this edition has been prepared are very different from those of five years ago when we first embarked on the task. The world was then staggering from the impact of the steep rise in the price of oil earlier in the decade. Salvation seemed to lie in industrial 'readjustment' and the 'recycling' of funds from the new oil-rich to the perpetually poor, through the international banks controlled by the established rich. Few saw beyond the fading economic light to the gloom in which so much of the world has since been engulfed.

Now, few people in power dare to believe that economic recovery will come easily or be sustained. And many of them are taking measures, not to lighten the economic prospect, but to adjust their eyes to the dark. We must, it seems, accept as inevitable the violent polarization of wealth and poverty, power and vulnerability, between a minority and majority of states in the world, and between a minority and the majority in each state. We must, it seems, accept as equally inevitable the consequences in conflict within and between societies, which at best makes a mockery of the term 'civilization' and at worst will make an end of us all.

Many people have succumbed to this seeming realism. And while resentment and protest cannot be eradicated in a world as manifestly unjust as ours, they are increasingly dispersed and dissipated within partial or single-focus movements: of women, racial or religious minorities, gays, 'greens' and campaigners against nuclear weapons. Welcome as they are, these movements offer less serious a challenge to the world order than did the broad political coalitions of the past. Moreover, there has been a conspicuous withdrawal from the essentially optimistic political and personal liberalism that flourished in the 1960s and early 1970s, to the bunkers of moral and social disciplinarianism; along with an undeniable spread and intensification of cynicism and apathy.

These manifestations of despair are neither superficial nor capricious. They take sustenance from three mounting threats to the welfare and even survival of humanity. There is the possibility – some even talk now about the probability – of nuclear war by accident or design. There is the course of environmental damage, a sort of global grievous bodily harm, so serious that even governments recently indifferent now express some concern. And there is the pressure of rapidly increasing human redundancy, which is denying to so many hundreds of millions any participation in productive material or cultural activity, and turning them into mere population statistics.

These threats are unmistakeably real. They invade the innermost recesses of social and personal life. But their very existence is a source of hope. For what this atlas ultimately identifies is the clear and consistent irrelevance of conventional solutions to the problems gathering in the world of sovereign states. For increasing numbers of people, such problems, presented with much solemn authority as accidental or manageable, point to a crisis not only within the system, but of the system itself. It is a crisis that can be creatively resolved, in our view, only by a different organization for humanity.

We have refined and updated the atlas in every respect. No topic has been left untouched, and many new ones have been added. While some gaps remain, many, notably those relating to China, have been filled.

We have introduced maps on financial and science power; on complexions of government; on endangered species and unprotected land; on ecological, gay and minority consciousness. Some existing topics have been completely reworked. On unemployment, for example, we have cast aside our conceptual and statistical reservations, and presented such information as we were able to gather, in the belief that a crude and partial picture, state by state, is better than no picture at all.

The first edition of this atlas was accorded a flattering reception. There has been a steady trickle of appreciative – and critical – comment, from students and teachers, from politicians, publicists and the general reading public. Most flattering of all has been the spate of imitations in books, newspapers and on television, confirming the value of our method, even where views very different from our own have been advanced.

We have considerably extended our range of sources. Regrettably, we have to report a definite drop in the standards of the data provided by the United Nations and other international organizations. As such data become more comprehensive, and the relative standings of states become more apparent, the temptation grows for governments to apply information cosmetically: to over- or under-report, to report too late or not at all. With the further effect of recession on the budgets of government statistical offices and those of the international agencies concerned to gather or monitor data independently, there has been a marked decline in the quality of internationally comparable statistics.

For this and other reasons, high quality information is progressively becoming the property of privileged institutions whether business corporations or branches of the state. It is a disquieting and dangerous trend which has compelled us to rely more on private sources: on officials within the data-gathering agencies of international bodies and individual states who have guided us through the maze of often misleading figures; on representatives of pressure groups and non-government organizations whose interest lies in understanding and revealing socially and politically potent information; on those librarians who have gone out of their way to unearth obscure material.

Without these people and their institutions, this atlas could not have been created. We thank them for their generosity, their seriousness of purpose and, where appropriate, their spirit. Those that may be mentioned are recognized on the maps themselves, or in the list of acknowledgements. Those that need or wish to remain unnamed must be satisfied with this blanket expression of indebtedness.

We owe a debt as well to the many people who took seriously the pioneering spirit of the first edition and laced their criticism with positive suggestions for improvement. Some of these we have followed. We are grateful for them all. And we would single out for our appreciation Joe Schwartzberg, of the University of Minnesota.

Many of the strengths of this atlas derive directly from the spirit of Pluto Press. Anne Benewick and Malcolm Swanston are owed particular thanks, as is Nina Kidron, for their several and unique contributions. Above all, this book is a collaboration between authors who have gained through the years an increasingly productive mutual trust and tolerance. We have, therefore, especially each other to thank.

Michael Kidron
Ronald Segal

April 1984

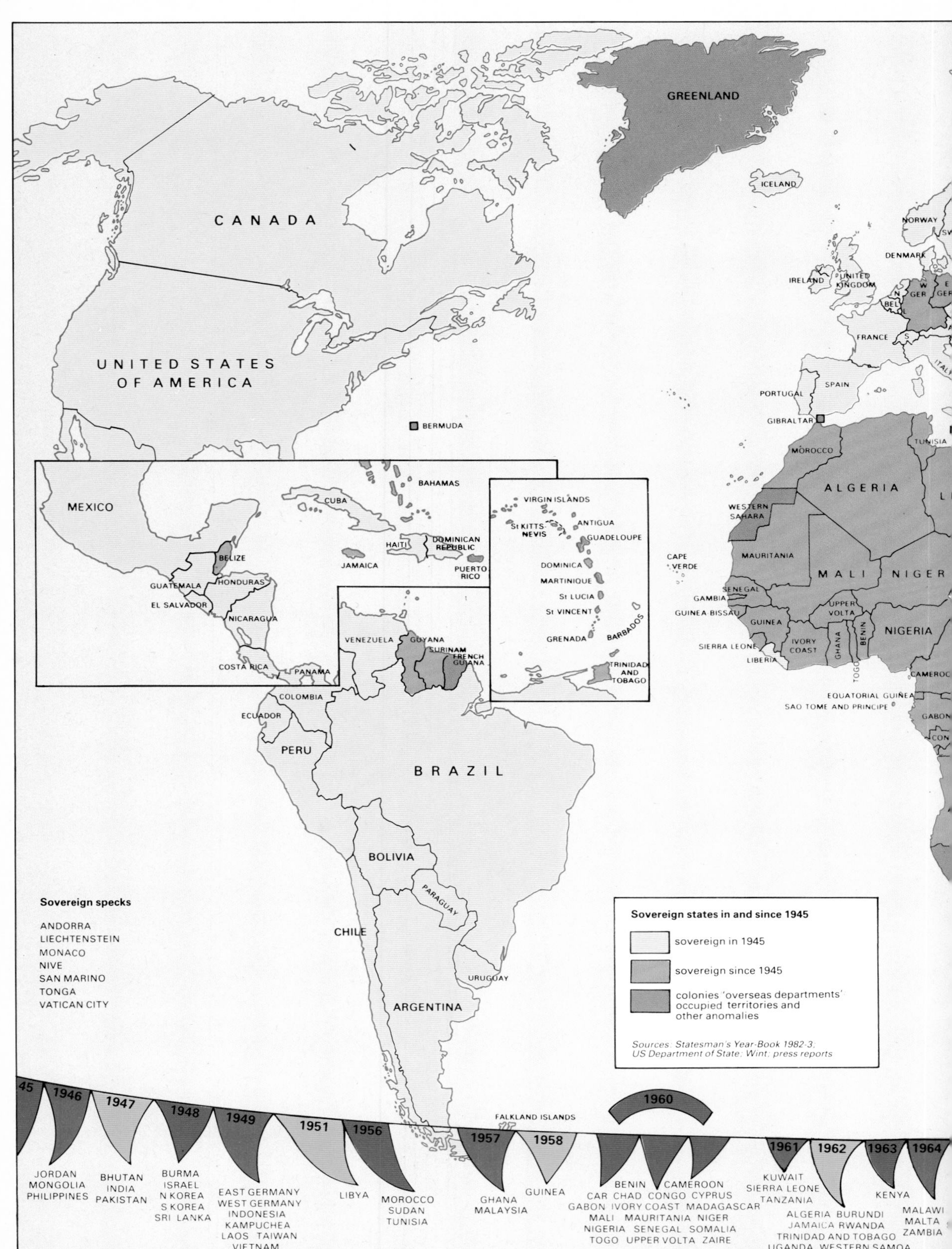

GREENLAND
ICELAND
CANADA
UNITED STATES OF AMERICA
NORWAY
DENMARK
IRELAND
UNITED KINGDOM
N
BEL
W GER
E GER
FRANCE
S
SPAIN
PORTUGAL
GIBRALTAR
BERMUDA
MOROCCO
TUNISIA
ALGERIA
WESTERN SAHARA
MAURITANIA
MALI
NIGER
CAPE VERDE
SENEGAL
GAMBIA
GUINEA BISSAU
GUINEA
UPPER VOLTA
BENIN
NIGERIA
SIERRA LEONE
IVORY COAST
GHANA
LIBERIA
TOGO
EQUATORIAL GUINEA
SAO TOME AND PRINCIPE
GABON
MEXICO
CUBA
BAHAMAS
BELIZE
GUATEMALA
HONDURAS
EL SALVADOR
NICARAGUA
COSTA RICA
PANAMA
JAMAICA
HAITI
DOMINICAN REPUBLIC
PUERTO RICO
VIRGIN ISLANDS
St KITTS-NEVIS
ANTIGUA
GUADELOUPE
DOMINICA
MARTINIQUE
St LUCIA
St VINCENT
GRENADA
BARBADOS
TRINIDAD AND TOBAGO
VENEZUELA
GUYANA
SURINAM
FRENCH GUIANA
COLOMBIA
ECUADOR
PERU
BRAZIL
BOLIVIA
PARAGUAY
CHILE
URUGUAY
ARGENTINA
FALKLAND ISLANDS
Sovereign specks
ANDORRA
LIECHTENSTEIN
MONACO
NIVE
SAN MARINO
TONGA
VATICAN CITY
Sovereign states in and since 1945
sovereign in 1945
sovereign since 1945
colonies 'overseas departments' occupied territories and other anomalies
Sources: Statesman's Year-Book 1982-3; US Department of State; Wint; press reports
1946
JORDAN
MONGOLIA
PHILIPPINES
1947
BHUTAN
INDIA
PAKISTAN
1948
BURMA
ISRAEL
N KOREA
S KOREA
SRI LANKA
1949
EAST GERMANY
WEST GERMANY
INDONESIA
KAMPUCHEA
LAOS TAIWAN
VIETNAM
1951
LIBYA
1956
MOROCCO
SUDAN
TUNISIA
1957
GHANA
MALAYSIA
1958
GUINEA
1960
BENIN CAMEROON
CAR CHAD CONGO CYPRUS
GABON IVORY COAST MADAGASCAR
MALI MAURITANIA NIGER
NIGERIA SENEGAL SOMALIA
TOGO UPPER VOLTA ZAIRE
1961
KUWAIT
SIERRA LEONE
TANZANIA
1962
ALGERIA BURUNDI
JAMAICA RWANDA
TRINIDAD AND TOBAGO
UGANDA WESTERN SAMOA
1963
KENYA
1964
MALAWI
MALTA
ZAMBIA

1. The World of States

Since the Second World War the number of independent states has grown from 72 to 168. The proliferation continues.

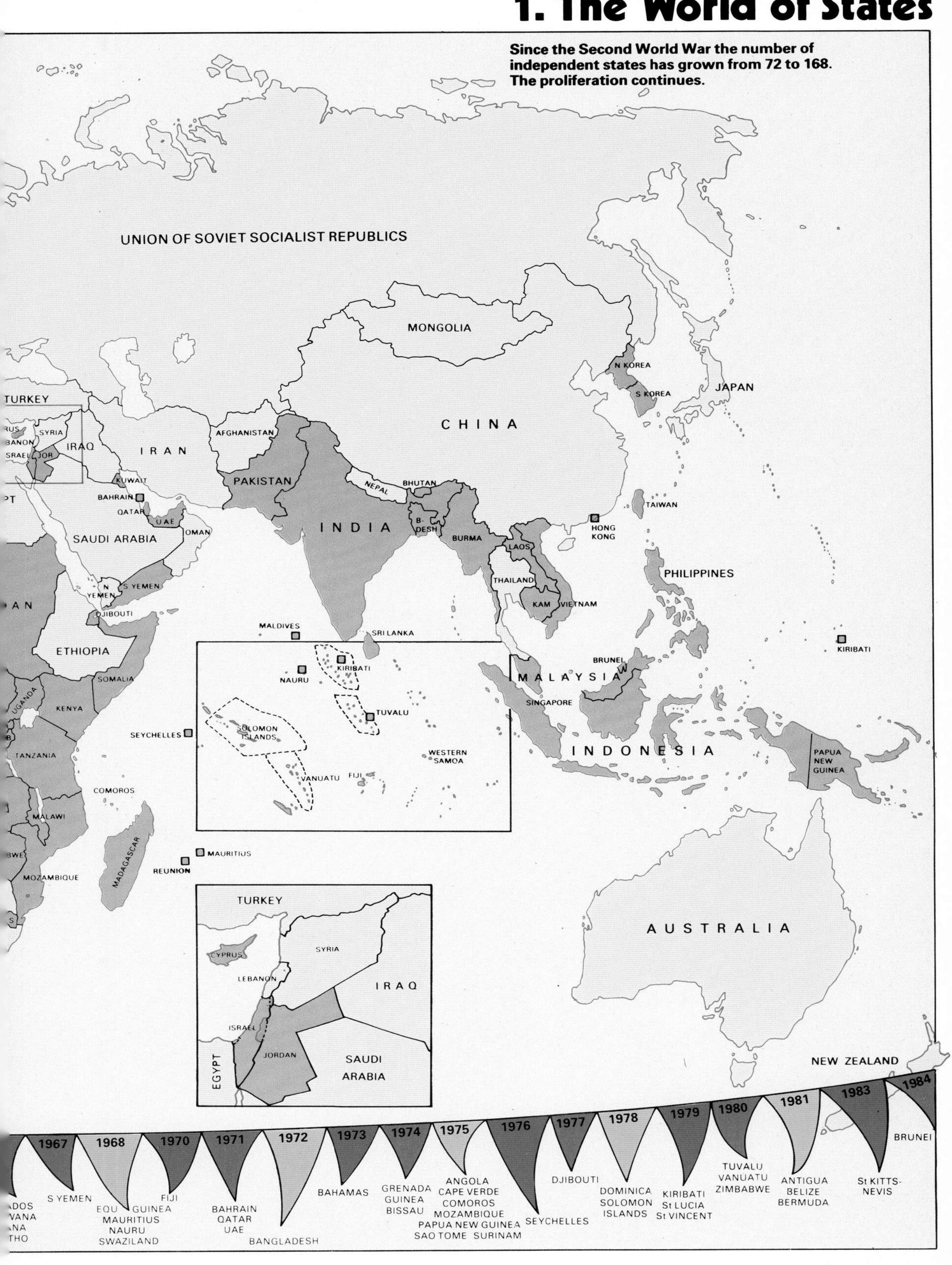

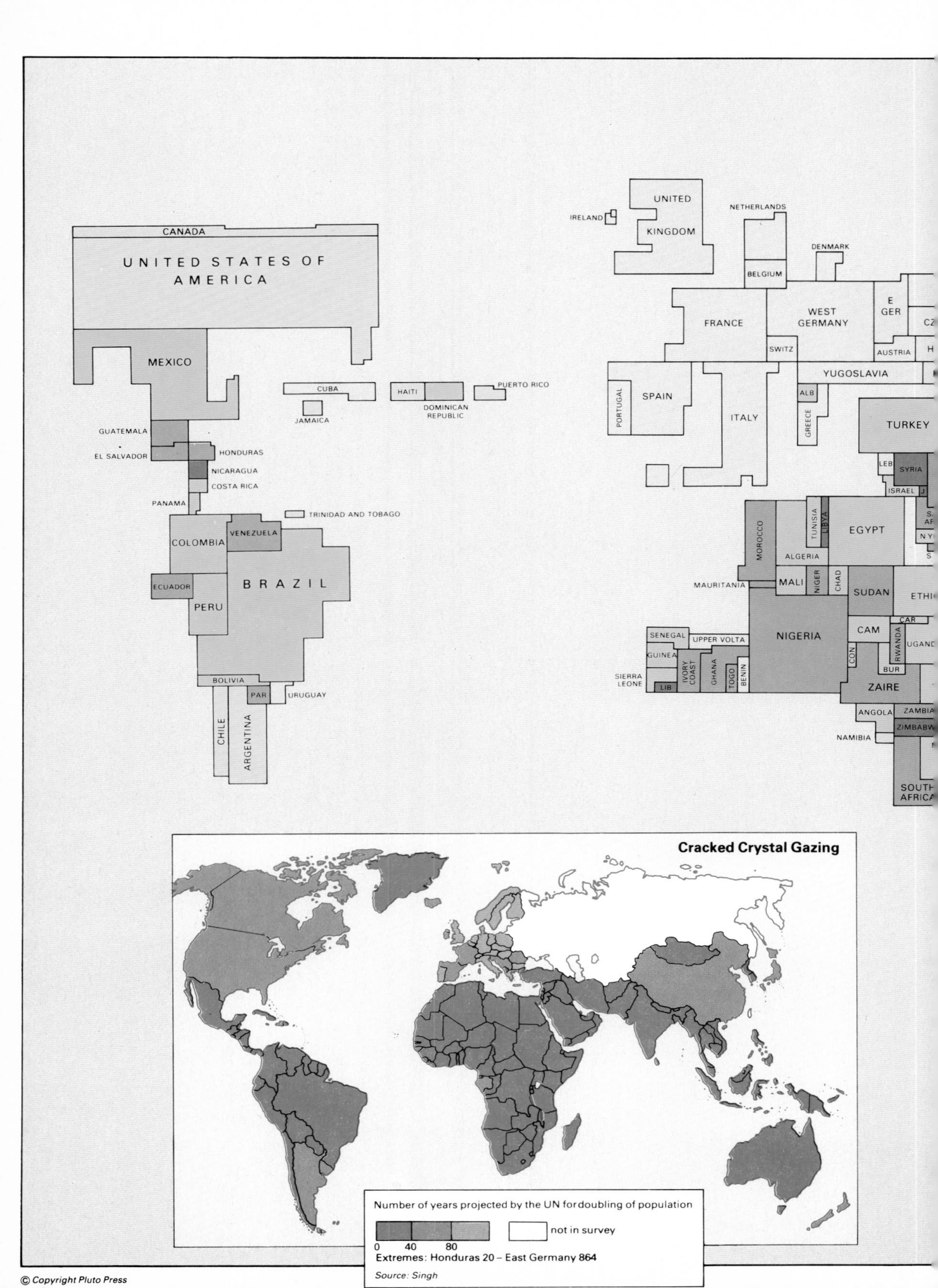

CANADA
UNITED STATES OF AMERICA
MEXICO
GUATEMALA
EL SALVADOR
HONDURAS
NICARAGUA
COSTA RICA
PANAMA
CUBA
JAMAICA
HAITI
DOMINICAN REPUBLIC
PUERTO RICO
TRINIDAD AND TOBAGO
COLOMBIA
VENEZUELA
ECUADOR
PERU
BRAZIL
BOLIVIA
PAR
URUGUAY
CHILE
ARGENTINA
IRELAND
UNITED KINGDOM
NETHERLANDS
BELGIUM
DENMARK
FRANCE
WEST GERMANY
E GER
SWITZ
AUSTRIA
YUGOSLAVIA
PORTUGAL
SPAIN
ITALY
ALB
GREECE
TURKEY
LEB
SYRIA
ISRAEL
MOROCCO
ALGERIA
TUNISIA
LIBYA
EGYPT
MAURITANIA
MALI
NIGER
CHAD
SUDAN
SENEGAL
UPPER VOLTA
GUINEA
SIERRA LEONE
LIB
IVORY COAST
GHANA
TOGO
BENIN
NIGERIA
CAM
CAR
CON
RWANDA
BUR
ZAIRE
ANGOLA
ZAMBIA
NAMIBIA
Cracked Crystal Gazing
Number of years projected by the UN for doubling of population
0
40
80
not in survey
Extremes: Honduras 20 – East Germany 864
Source: Singh

2. The State by Population

By the year 2050 the population of the world will be some 14 billion, or more than three times its present size. The increase will be overwhelmingly among the poor. Yet the poor are poor not because they are many but because resources are disproportionately concentrated among the rich.

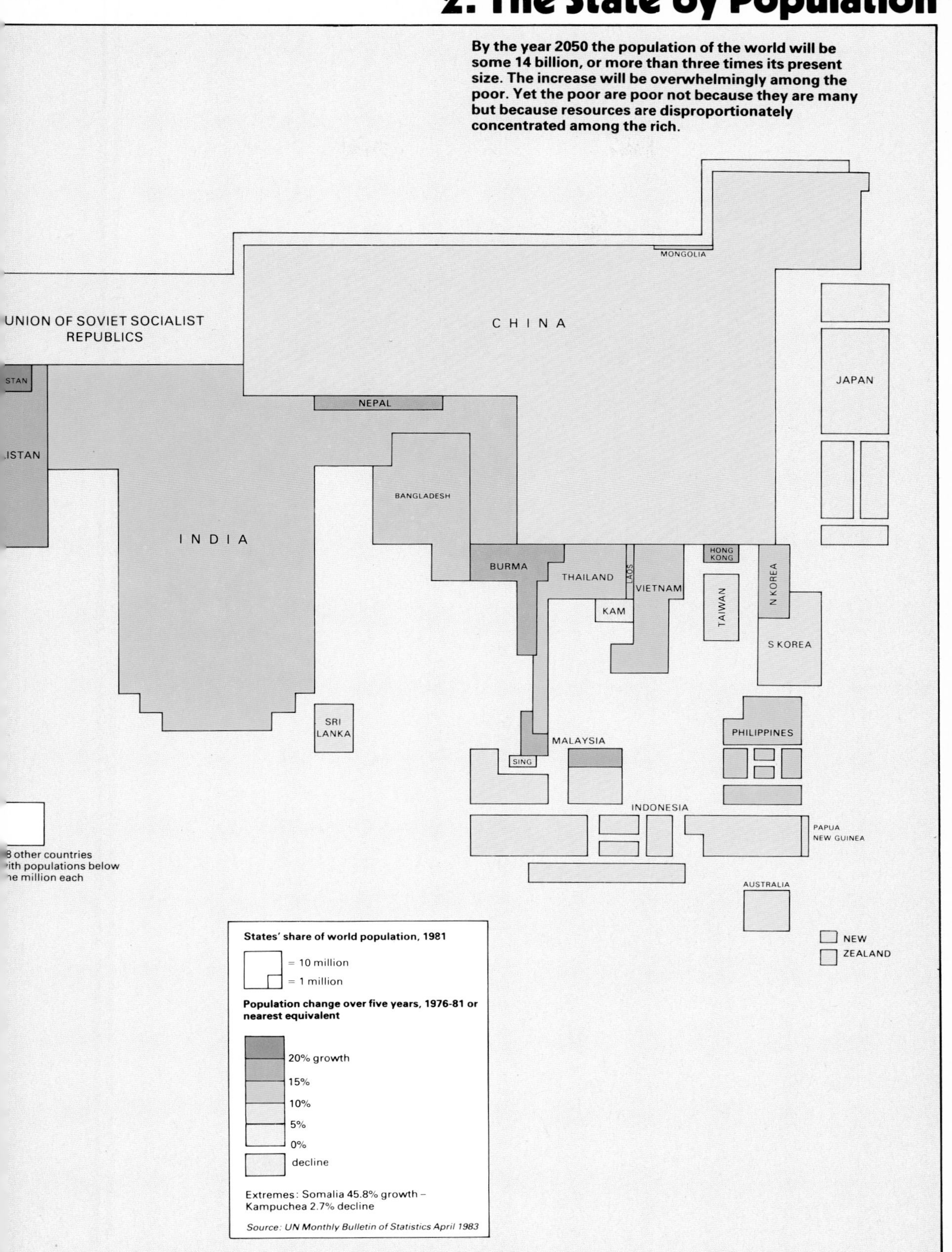

The Lure of Wealth

Antarctica, one hundred million years ago, showing what were until then continuous mountain ranges; the Transantarctic Mountains connected to the Andes in South America; the Central Antarctic Mountains connected to the Rand in South Africa and to mineral rich areas in Australia.
Vast reserves of coal as well as deposits of oil and natural gas are known to exist in Antarctica, though as yet they are uneconomic to exploit.

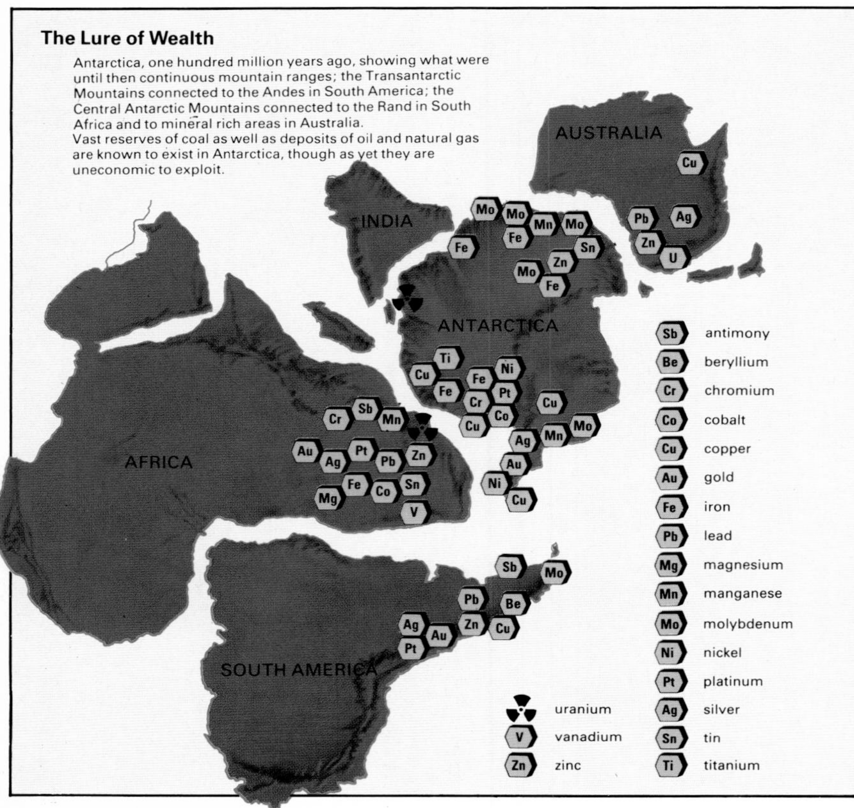

Claimants and Neighbours

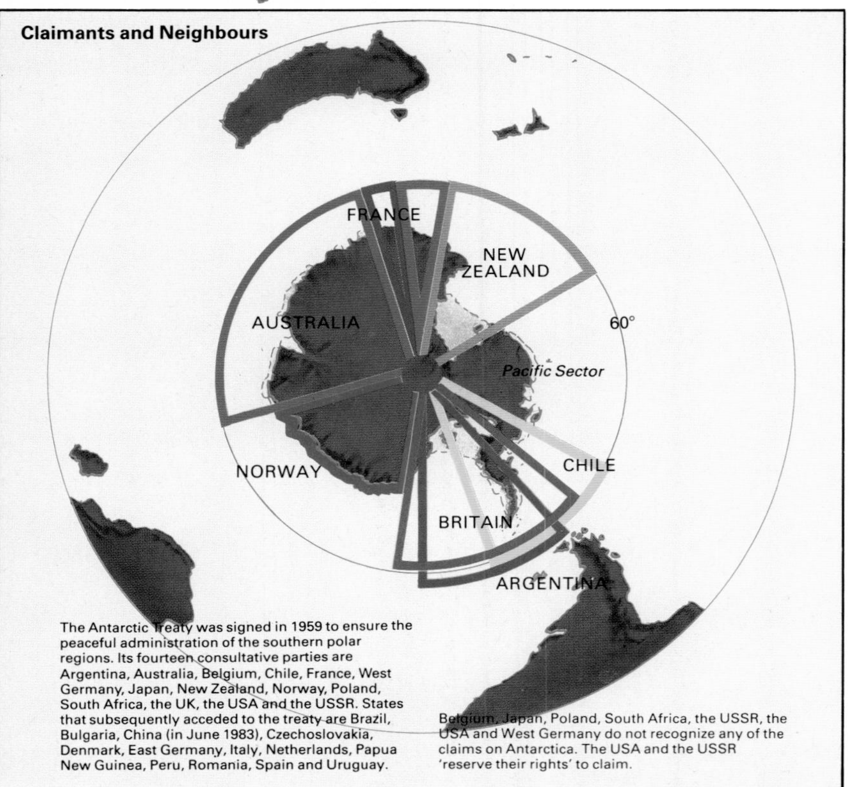

The Antarctic Treaty was signed in 1959 to ensure the peaceful administration of the southern polar regions. Its fourteen consultative parties are Argentina, Australia, Belgium, Chile, France, West Germany, Japan, New Zealand, Norway, Poland, South Africa, the UK, the USA and the USSR. States that subsequently acceded to the treaty are Brazil, Bulgaria, China (in June 1983), Czechoslovakia, Denmark, East Germany, Italy, Netherlands, Papua New Guinea, Peru, Romania, Spain and Uruguay.

Belgium, Japan, Poland, South Africa, the USSR, the USA and West Germany do not recognize any of the claims on Antarctica. The USA and the USSR 'reserve their rights' to claim.

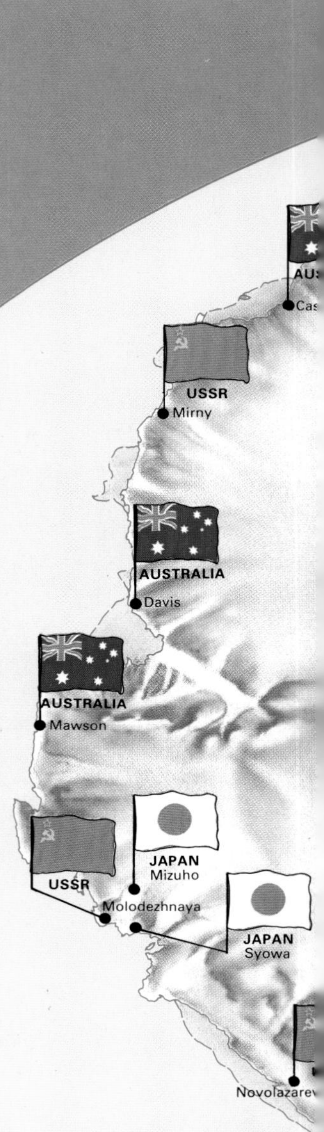

The Settlers

Scientific stations operating south of the 60th parallel, winter 1982-3

Sources: Earthscan; SCAR Bulletin

3. The State Invades Antarctica

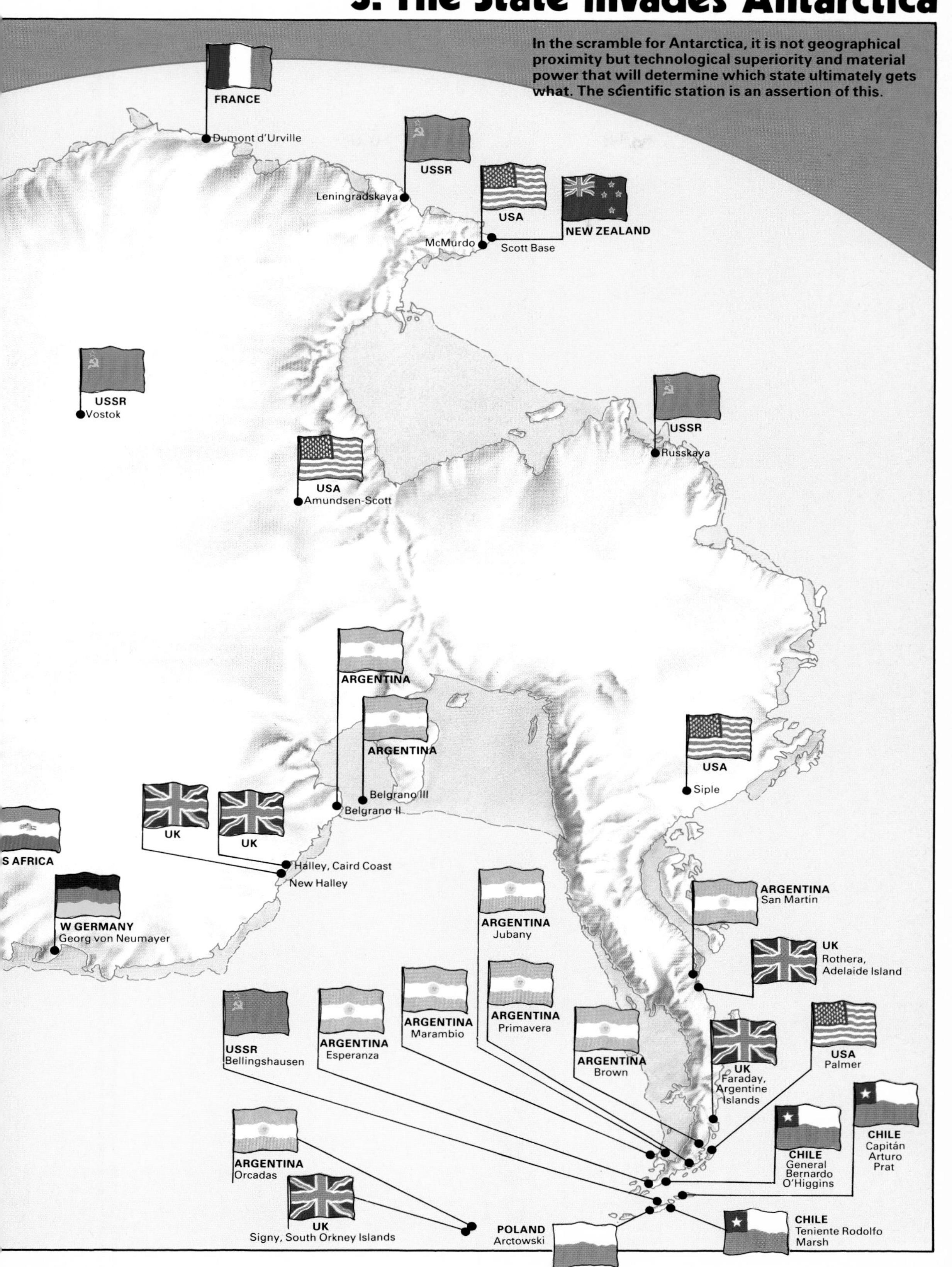
In the scramble for Antarctica, it is not geographical proximity but technological superiority and material power that will determine which state ultimately gets what. The scientific station is an assertion of this.
FRANCE
Dumont d'Urville
USSR
Leningradskaya
USA
McMurdo
NEW ZEALAND
Scott Base
USSR
Vostok
USSR
Russkaya
USA
Amundsen-Scott
ARGENTINA
ARGENTINA
Belgrano III
Belgrano II
USA
Siple
UK
UK
S AFRICA
Halley, Caird Coast
New Halley
W GERMANY
Georg von Neumayer
ARGENTINA
Jubany
ARGENTINA
San Martin
UK
Rothera, Adelaide Island
USSR
Bellingshausen
ARGENTINA
Esperanza
ARGENTINA
Marambio
ARGENTINA
Primavera
ARGENTINA
Brown
UK
Faraday, Argentine Islands
USA
Palmer
CHILE
Capitán Arturo Prat
CHILE
General Bernardo O'Higgins
ARGENTINA
Orcadas
UK
Signy, South Orkney Islands
POLAND
Arctowski
CHILE
Teniente Rodolfo Marsh

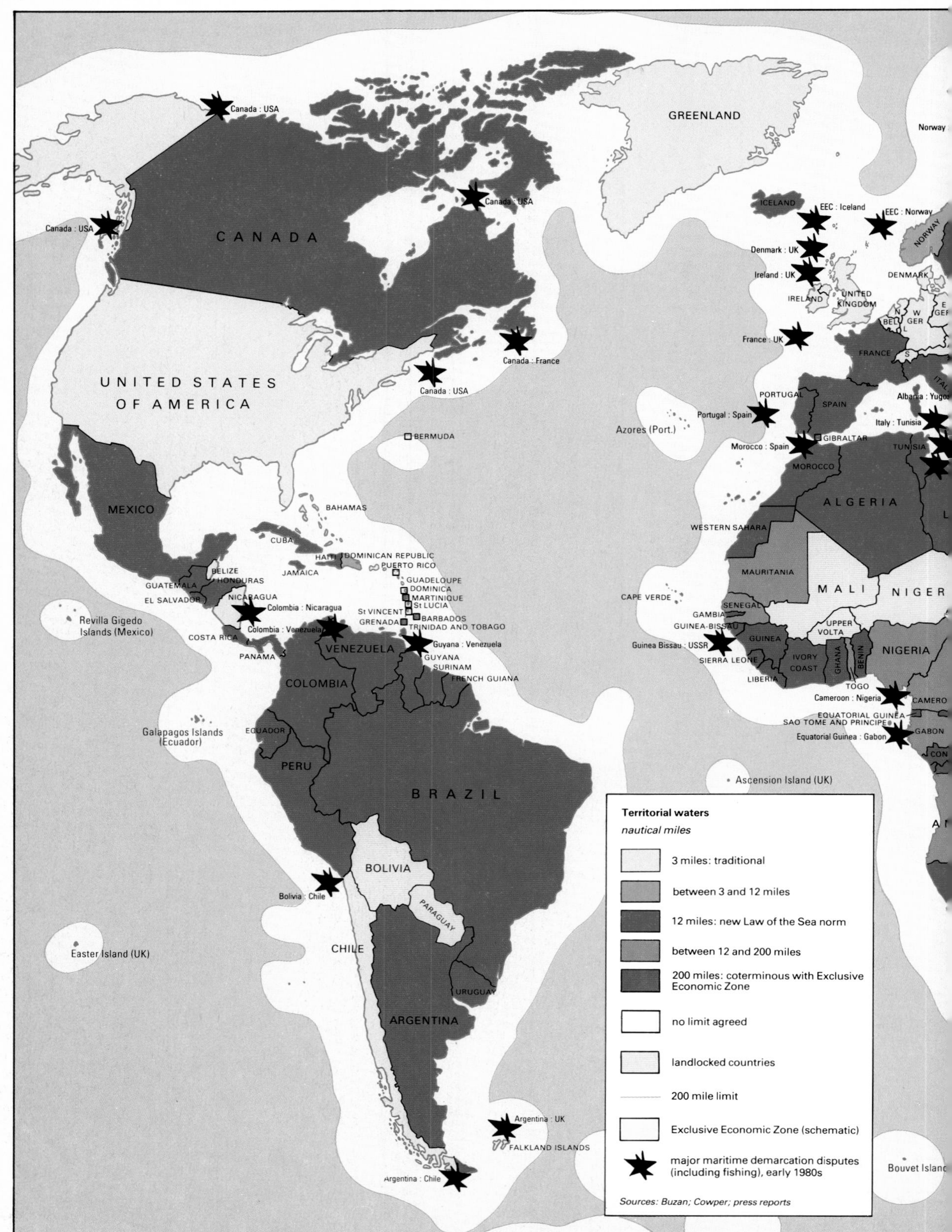

Canada : USA
GREENLAND
Norway
CANADA
Canada : USA
Canada : USA
ICELAND
EEC : Iceland
EEC : Norway
NORWAY
Denmark : UK
Ireland : UK
DENMARK
IRELAND
UNITED KINGDOM
W GER
France : UK
Canada : France
FRANCE
UNITED STATES OF AMERICA
Canada : USA
PORTUGAL
SPAIN
Portugal : Spain
Albania : Yugo
Italy : Tunisia
Azores (Port.)
BERMUDA
GIBRALTAR
Morocco : Spain
TUNISIA
MOROCCO
ALGERIA
MEXICO
BAHAMAS
WESTERN SAHARA
CUBA
HAITI
DOMINICAN REPUBLIC
PUERTO RICO
MAURITANIA
BELIZE
HONDURAS
JAMAICA
GUADELOUPE
DOMINICA
MARTINIQUE
St LUCIA
GUATEMALA
EL SALVADOR
NICARAGUA
Colombia : Nicaragua
St VINCENT
BARBADOS
GRENADA
TRINIDAD AND TOBAGO
MALI
NIGER
CAPE VERDE
SENEGAL
GAMBIA
GUINEA-BISSAU
UPPER VOLTA
Revilla Gigedo Islands (Mexico)
Colombia : Venezuela
COSTA RICA
VENEZUELA
Guyana : Venezuela
Guinea Bissau : USSR
GUINEA
SIERRA LEONE
IVORY COAST
GHANA
BENIN
NIGERIA
PANAMA
GUYANA
SURINAM
FRENCH GUIANA
LIBERIA
COLOMBIA
TOGO
Cameroon : Nigeria
EQUATORIAL GUINEA
SAO TOME AND PRINCIPE
Equatorial Guinea : Gabon
GABON
Galapagos Islands (Ecuador)
ECUADOR
PERU
Ascension Island (UK)
BRAZIL
BOLIVIA
Bolivia : Chile
PARAGUAY
CHILE
Easter Island (UK)
URUGUAY
ARGENTINA
Argentina : UK
FALKLAND ISLANDS
Argentina : Chile
Bouvet Island
Territorial waters
nautical miles
3 miles: traditional
between 3 and 12 miles
12 miles: new Law of the Sea norm
between 12 and 200 miles
200 miles: coterminous with Exclusive Economic Zone
no limit agreed
landlocked countries
200 mile limit
Exclusive Economic Zone (schematic)
major maritime demarcation disputes (including fishing), early 1980s
Sources: Buzan; Cowper; press reports

4. The State Invades the Sea

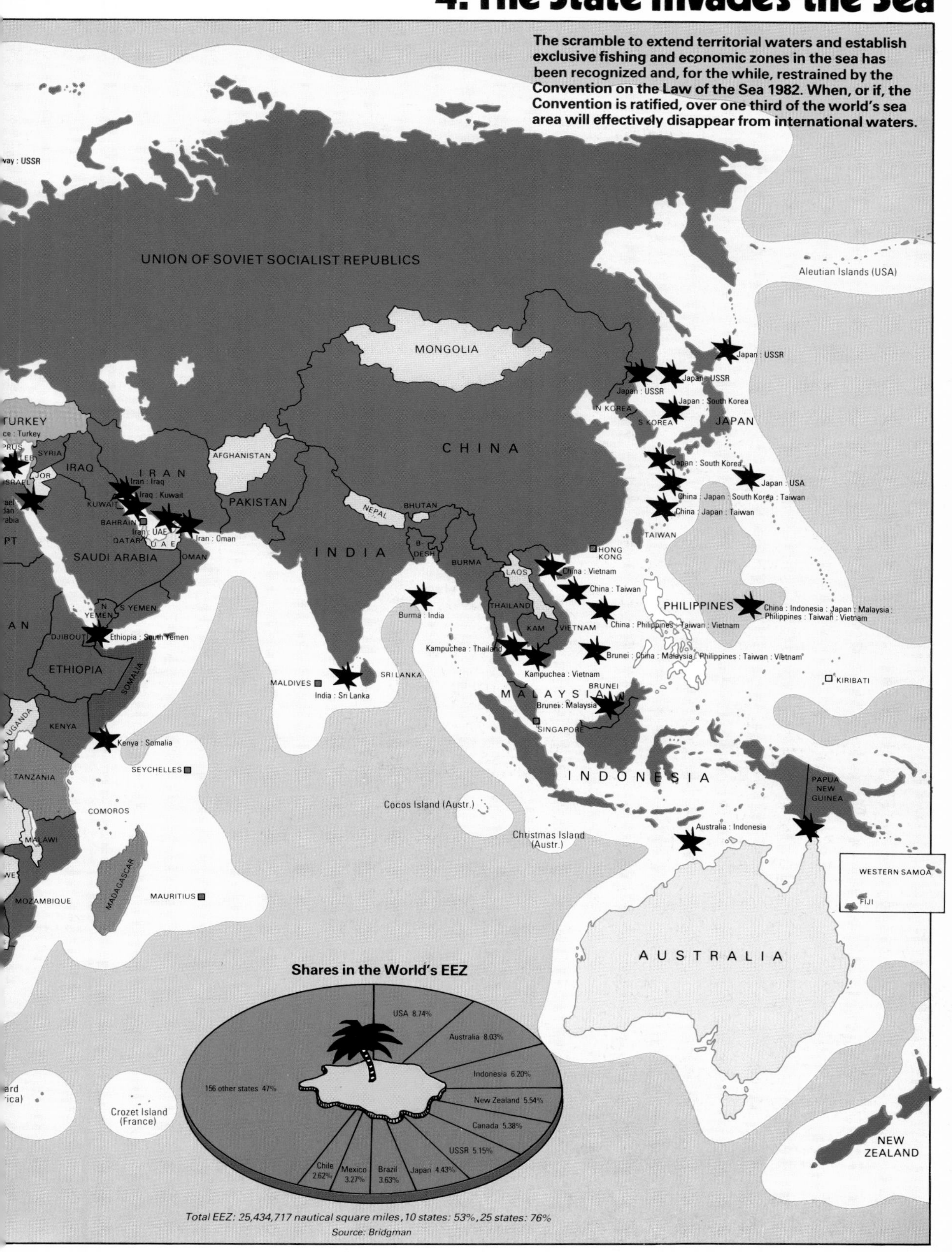

The scramble to extend territorial waters and establish exclusive fishing and economic zones in the sea has been recognized and, for the while, restrained by the Convention on the Law of the Sea 1982. When, or if, the Convention is ratified, over one third of the world's sea area will effectively disappear from international waters.
UNION OF SOVIET SOCIALIST REPUBLICS
MONGOLIA
CHINA
Aleutian Islands (USA)
Japan : USSR
Japan : USSR
Japan : USSR
Japan : South Korea
N KOREA
S KOREA
JAPAN
Japan : South Korea
Japan : USA
China : Japan : South Korea : Taiwan
China : Japan : Taiwan
TAIWAN
TURKEY
SYRIA
IRAQ
IRAN
Iran : Iraq
Iraq : Kuwait
KUWAIT
BAHRAIN
Iran : UAE
QATAR
U A E
Iran : Oman
OMAN
SAUDI ARABIA
AFGHANISTAN
PAKISTAN
NEPAL
BHUTAN
INDIA
B-DESH
BURMA
HONG KONG
LAOS
China : Vietnam
China : Taiwan
THAILAND
KAM
VIETNAM
China : Philippines : Taiwan : Vietnam
PHILIPPINES
China : Indonesia : Japan : Malaysia : Philippines : Taiwan : Vietnam
Burma : India
Kampuchea : Thailand
Kampuchea : Vietnam
Brunei : China : Malaysia : Philippines : Taiwan : Vietnam
BRUNEI
MALAYSIA
Brunei : Malaysia
SINGAPORE
KIRIBATI
S YEMEN
YEMEN
DJIBOUTI
Ethiopia : South Yemen
ETHIOPIA
SOMALIA
SRI LANKA
MALDIVES
India : Sri Lanka
UGANDA
KENYA
Kenya : Somalia
SEYCHELLES
TANZANIA
INDONESIA
PAPUA NEW GUINEA
Cocos Island (Austr.)
COMOROS
Christmas Island (Austr.)
Australia : Indonesia
MALAWI
MADAGASCAR
MAURITIUS
MOZAMBIQUE
WESTERN SAMOA
FIJI
AUSTRALIA
Crozet Island (France)
NEW ZEALAND
Shares in the World's EEZ
USA 8.74%
Australia 8.03%
Indonesia 6.20%
New Zealand 5.54%
Canada 5.38%
USSR 5.15%
Japan 4.43%
Brazil 3.63%
Mexico 3.27%
Chile 2.62%
156 other states 47%
Total EEZ: 25,434,717 nautical square miles, 10 states: 53%, 25 states: 76%
Source: Bridgman

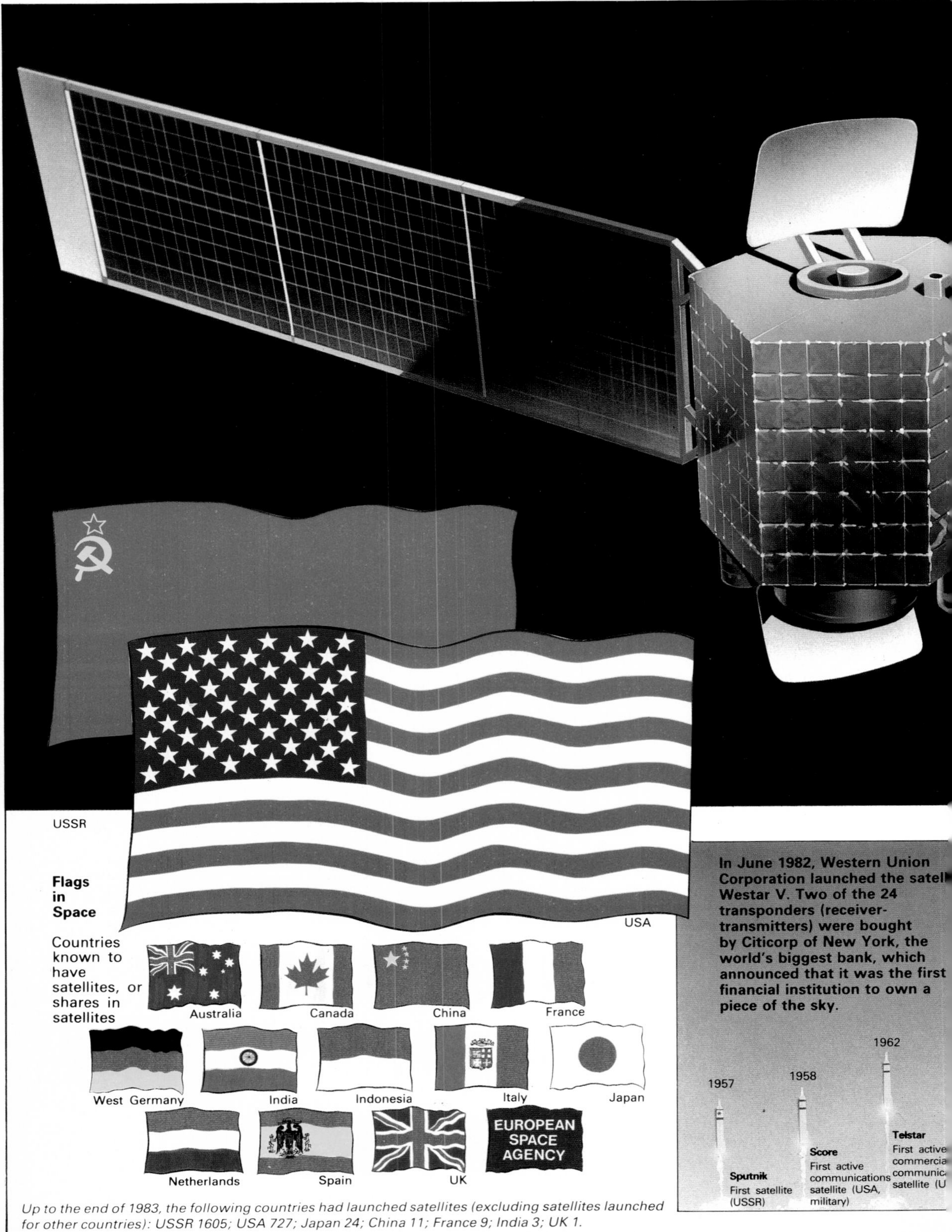

Flags in Space

Countries known to have satellites, or shares in satellites

In June 1982, Western Union Corporation launched the satell Westar V. Two of the 24 transponders (receiver-transmitters) were bought by Citicorp of New York, the world's biggest bank, which announced that it was the first financial institution to own a piece of the sky.

Up to the end of 1983, the following countries had launched satellites (excluding satellites launched for other countries): USSR 1605; USA 727; Japan 24; China 11; France 9; India 3; UK 1.

5. Space Invaders

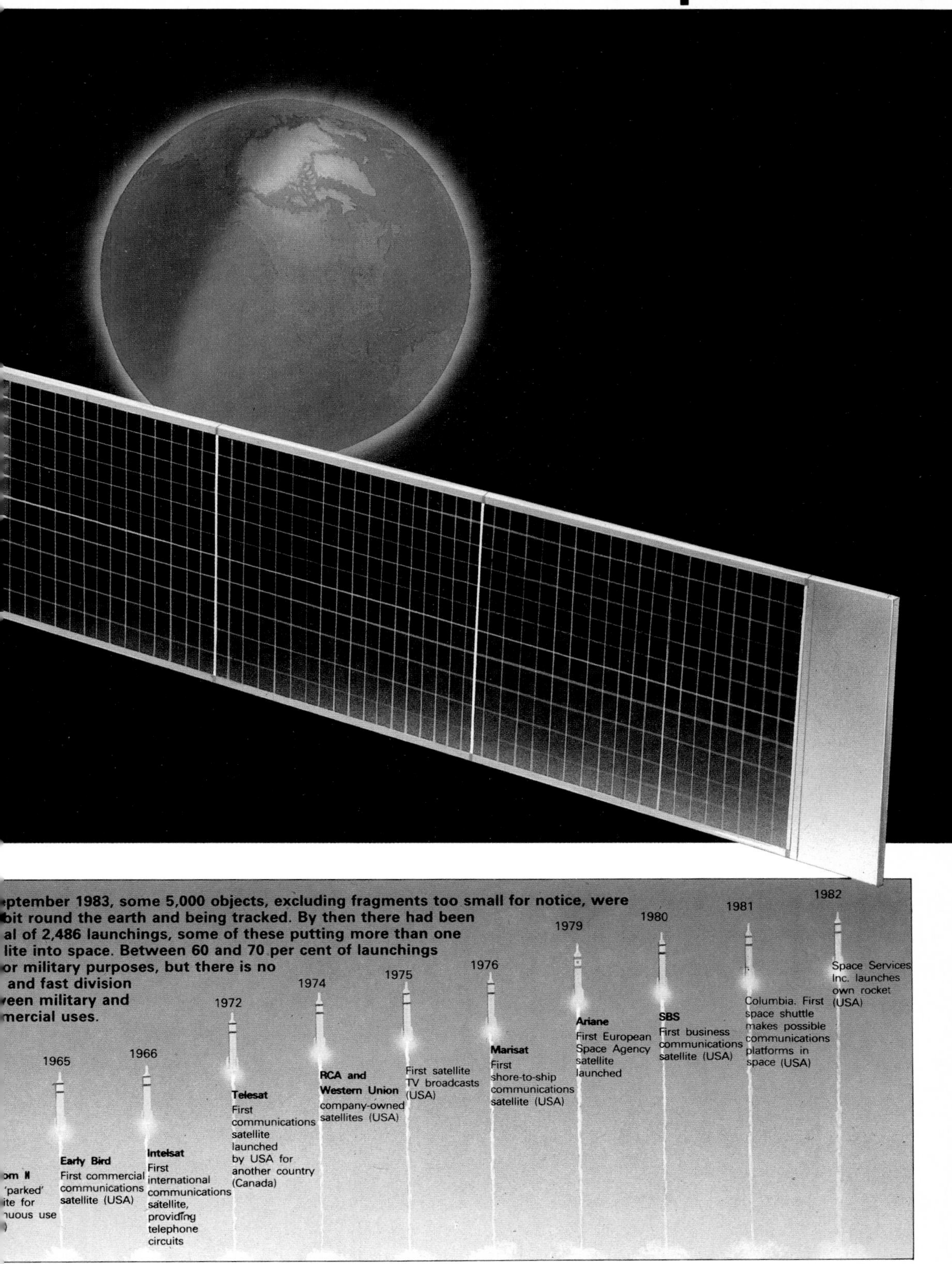

ptember 1983, some 5,000 objects, excluding fragments too small for notice, were
bit round the earth and being tracked. By then there had been
al of 2,486 launchings, some of these putting more than one
lite into space. Between 60 and 70 per cent of launchings
or military purposes, but there is no
and fast division
een military and
mercial uses.
om II
'parked'
ite for
nuous use
1965
Early Bird
First commercial communications satellite (USA)
1966
Intelsat
First international communications satellite, providing telephone circuits
1972
Telesat
First communications satellite launched by USA for another country (Canada)
1974
RCA and Western Union
company-owned satellites (USA)
1975
First satellite TV broadcasts (USA)
1976
Marisat
First shore-to-ship communications satellite (USA)
1979
Ariane
First European Space Agency satellite launched
1980
SBS
First business communications satellite (USA)
1981
Columbia. First space shuttle makes possible communications platforms in space (USA)
1982
Space Services Inc. launches own rocket (USA)

Sources: Kidron & Smith; Royal Aircraft Establishment; press reports

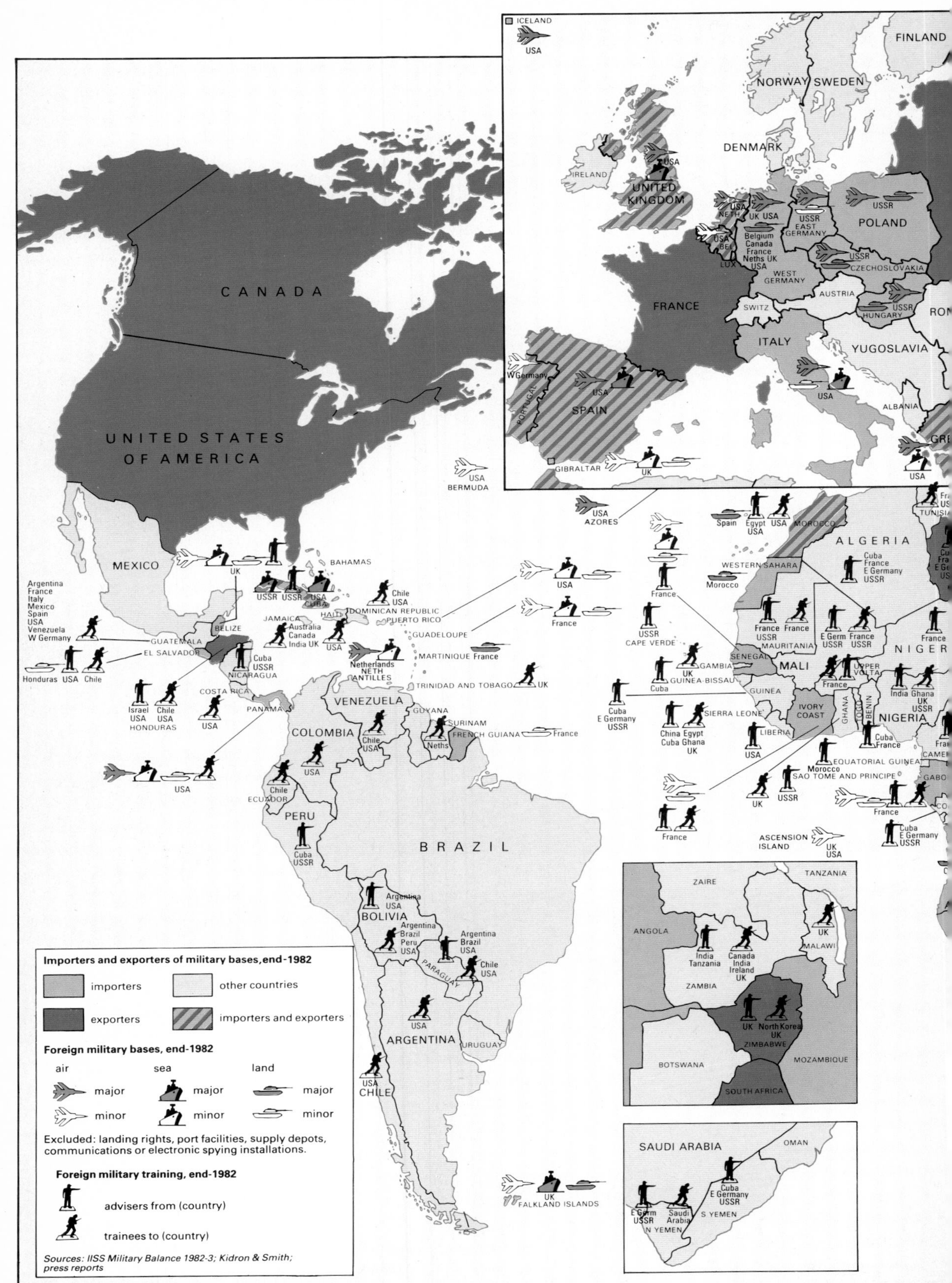

Importers and exporters of military bases, end-1982
importers
other countries
exporters
importers and exporters
Foreign military bases, end-1982
air
sea
land
major
minor
Excluded: landing rights, port facilities, supply depots, communications or electronic spying installations.
Foreign military training, end-1982
advisers from (country)
trainees to (country)
Sources: IISS Military Balance 1982-3; Kidron & Smith; press reports
CANADA
UNITED STATES OF AMERICA
MEXICO
BRAZIL
ARGENTINA
CHILE
PERU
BOLIVIA
COLOMBIA
VENEZUELA
ALGERIA
NIGERIA
FRANCE
SPAIN
ITALY
UNITED KINGDOM
POLAND
YUGOSLAVIA
SAUDI ARABIA

6. Big Brother

The international military order has spawned about 3000 foreign military bases and installations along with innumerable military advisers and trainees.

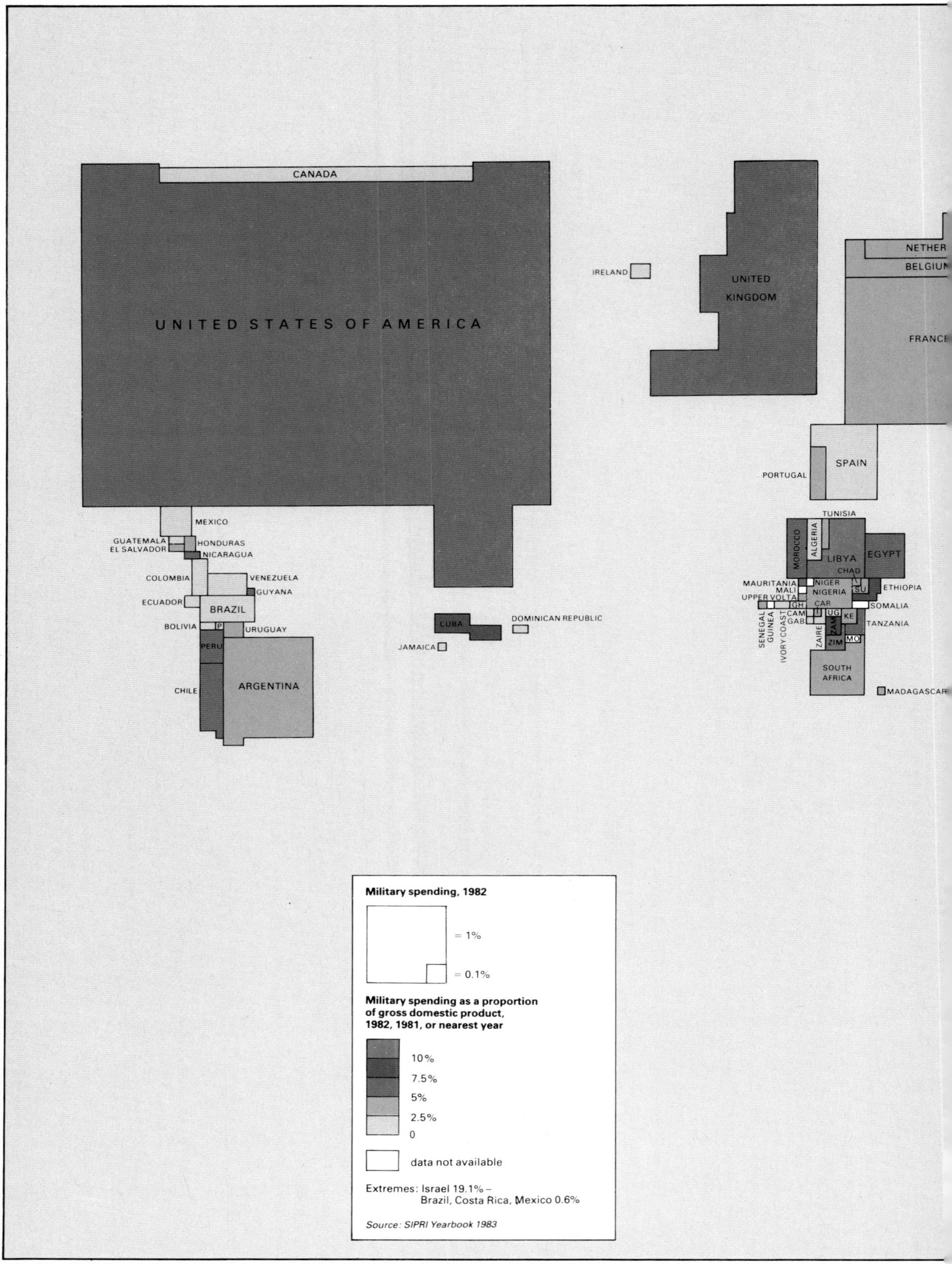

CANADA
UNITED STATES OF AMERICA
MEXICO
GUATEMALA
EL SALVADOR
HONDURAS
NICARAGUA
COLOMBIA
VENEZUELA
GUYANA
ECUADOR
BRAZIL
BOLIVIA
P
URUGUAY
PERU
CHILE
ARGENTINA
CUBA
DOMINICAN REPUBLIC
JAMAICA
IRELAND
UNITED KINGDOM
NETHER
BELGIUM
FRANCE
SPAIN
PORTUGAL
TUNISIA
MOROCCO
ALGERIA
LIBYA
EGYPT
CHAD
MAURITANIA
MALI
NIGER
NIGERIA
SU
ETHIOPIA
UPPER VOLTA
GH
CAR
SOMALIA
SENEGAL
GUINEA
IVORY COAST
CAM
GAB
UG
KE
TANZANIA
ZAIRE
ZAM
ZIM
MO
SOUTH AFRICA
MADAGASCAR
Military spending, 1982
= 1%
= 0.1%
Military spending as a proportion of gross domestic product, 1982, 1981, or nearest year
10%
7.5%
5%
2.5%
0
data not available
Extremes: Israel 19.1% – Brazil, Costa Rica, Mexico 0.6%
Source: SIPRI Yearbook 1983

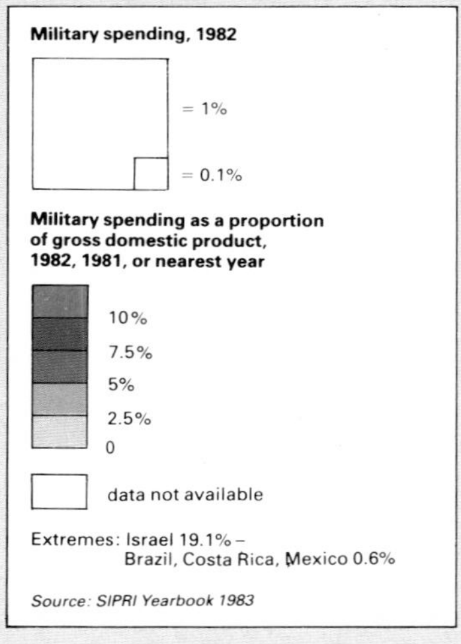

7. Military Spending

Some US $520 billion were spent on the military in 1980, substantially more than all the wealth generated by the 1800 million people living in China, India and Indonesia. The USA and the USSR together account for half of all military spending.

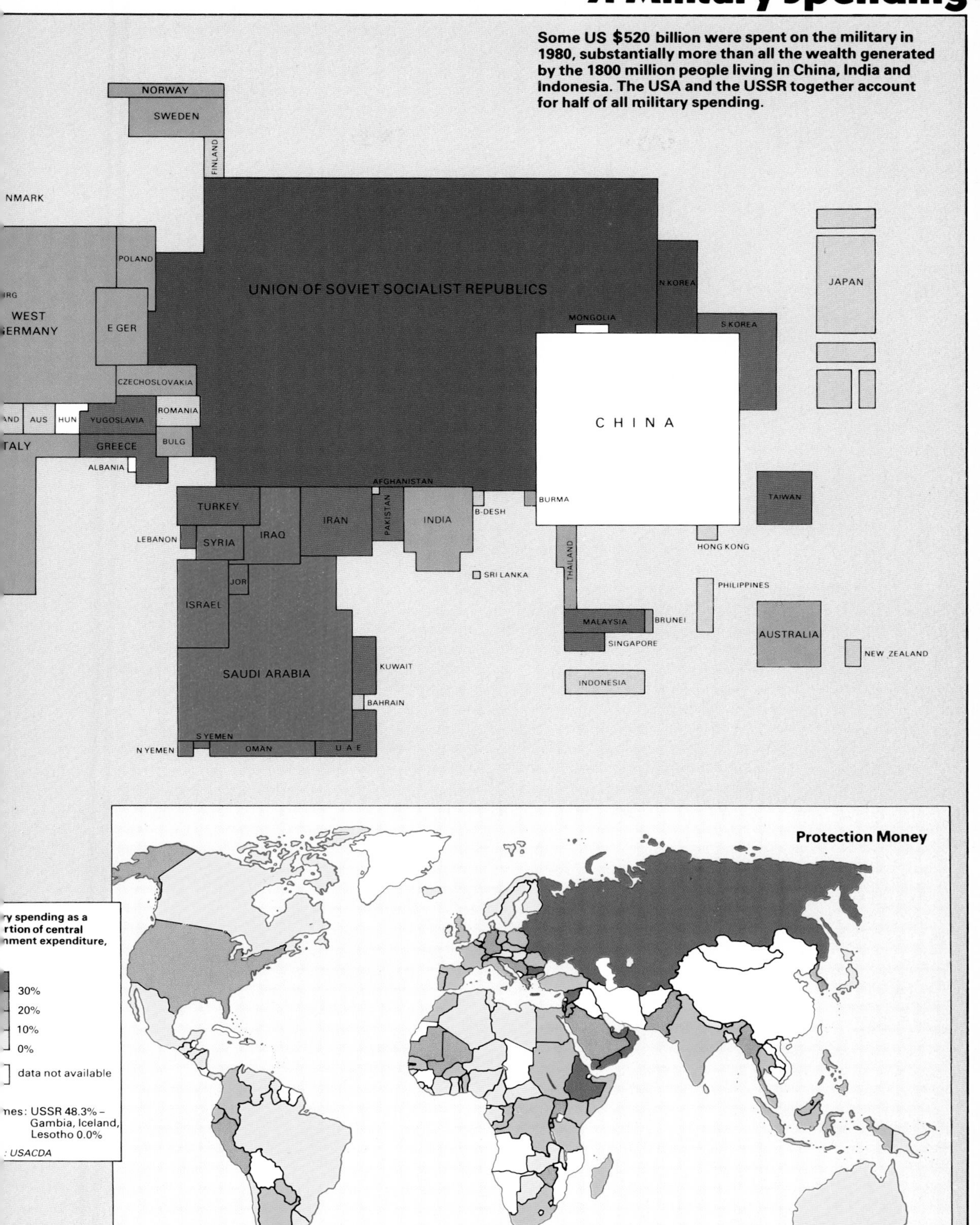

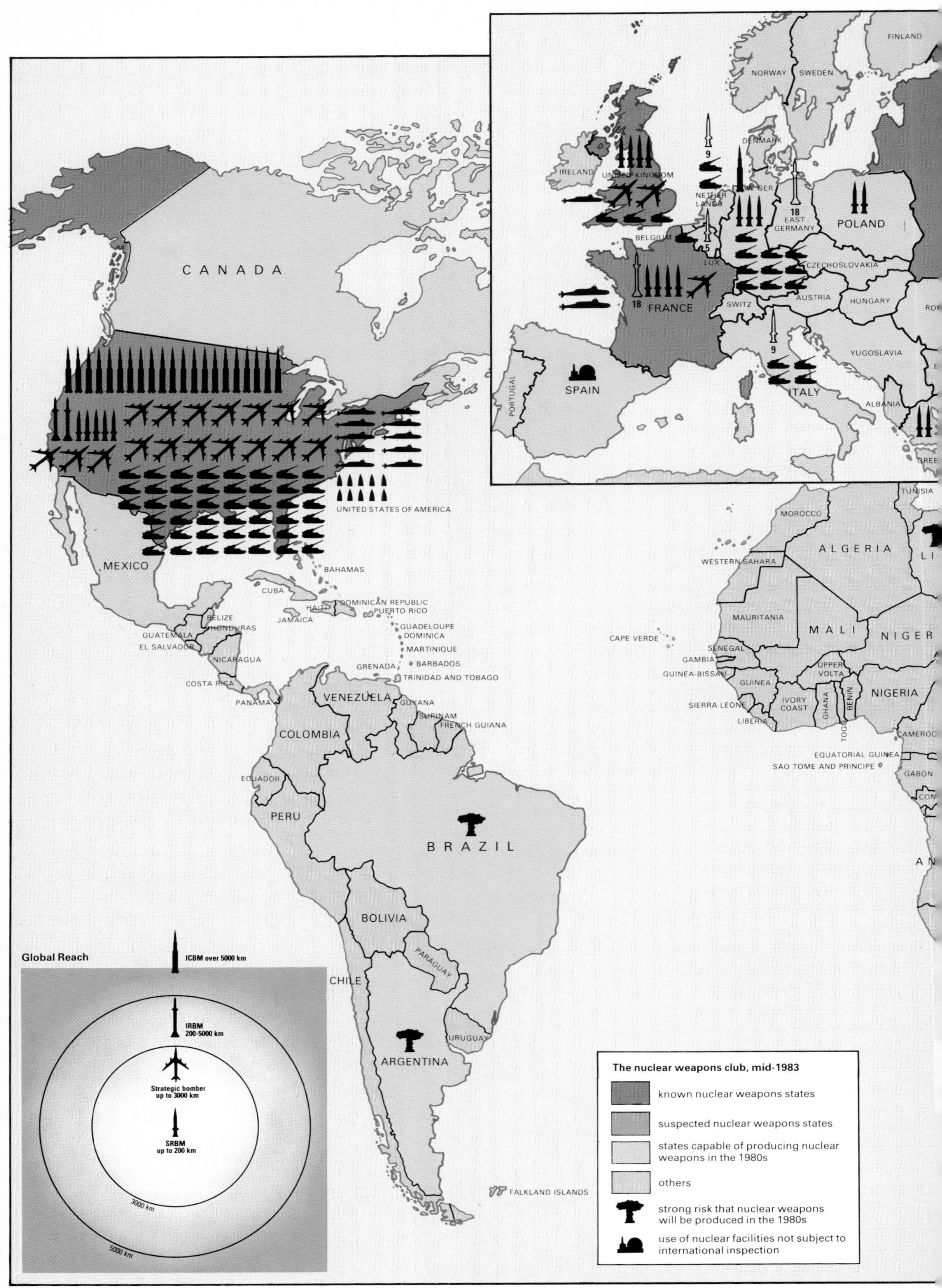
CANADA
UNITED STATES OF AMERICA
MEXICO
BAHAMAS
CUBA
HAITI
DOMINICAN REPUBLIC
PUERTO RICO
JAMAICA
BELIZE
HONDURAS
GUATEMALA
EL SALVADOR
NICARAGUA
COSTA RICA
PANAMA
GUADELOUPE
DOMINICA
MARTINIQUE
GRENADA
BARBADOS
TRINIDAD AND TOBAGO
VENEZUELA
GUYANA
SURINAM
FRENCH GUIANA
COLOMBIA
ECUADOR
PERU
BRAZIL
BOLIVIA
PARAGUAY
CHILE
URUGUAY
ARGENTINA
FALKLAND ISLANDS
FINLAND
NORWAY
SWEDEN
DENMARK
IRELAND
UNITED KINGDOM
NETHERLANDS
EAST GERMANY
POLAND
BELGIUM
LUX
FRANCE
CZECHOSLOVAKIA
SWITZ
AUSTRIA
HUNGARY
YUGOSLAVIA
SPAIN
PORTUGAL
ITALY
ALBANIA
9
18
5
TUNISIA
MOROCCO
ALGERIA
WESTERN SAHARA
MAURITANIA
MALI
NIGER
CAPE VERDE
SENEGAL
GAMBIA
GUINEA-BISSAU
GUINEA
UPPER VOLTA
SIERRA LEONE
LIBERIA
IVORY COAST
GHANA
TOGO
BENIN
NIGERIA
EQUATORIAL GUINEA
SAO TOME AND PRINCIPE
GABON
Global Reach
ICBM over 5000 km
IRBM 200-5000 km
Strategic bomber up to 3000 km
SRBM up to 200 km
3000 km
5000 km
The nuclear weapons club, mid-1983
known nuclear weapons states
suspected nuclear weapons states
states capable of producing nuclear weapons in the 1980s
others
strong risk that nuclear weapons will be produced in the 1980s
use of nuclear facilities not subject to international inspection

8. Shares in the Apocalypse

So far there has been no nuclear war-fighting. But 115 serious accidents involving nuclear weapons are known to have occurred up to the end of 1981.

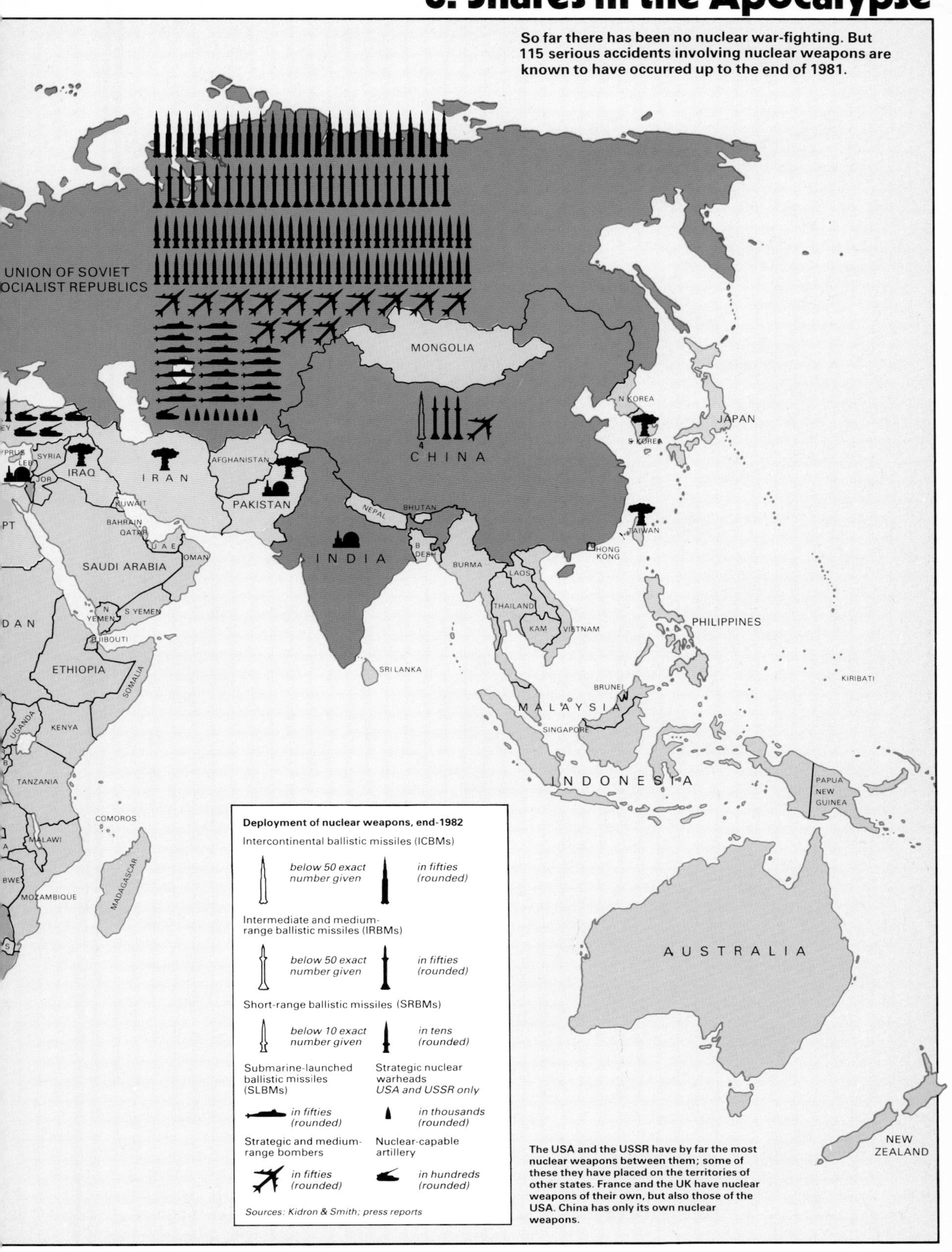

The USA and the USSR have by far the most nuclear weapons between them; some of these they have placed on the territories of other states. France and the UK have nuclear weapons of their own, but also those of the USA. China has only its own nuclear weapons.

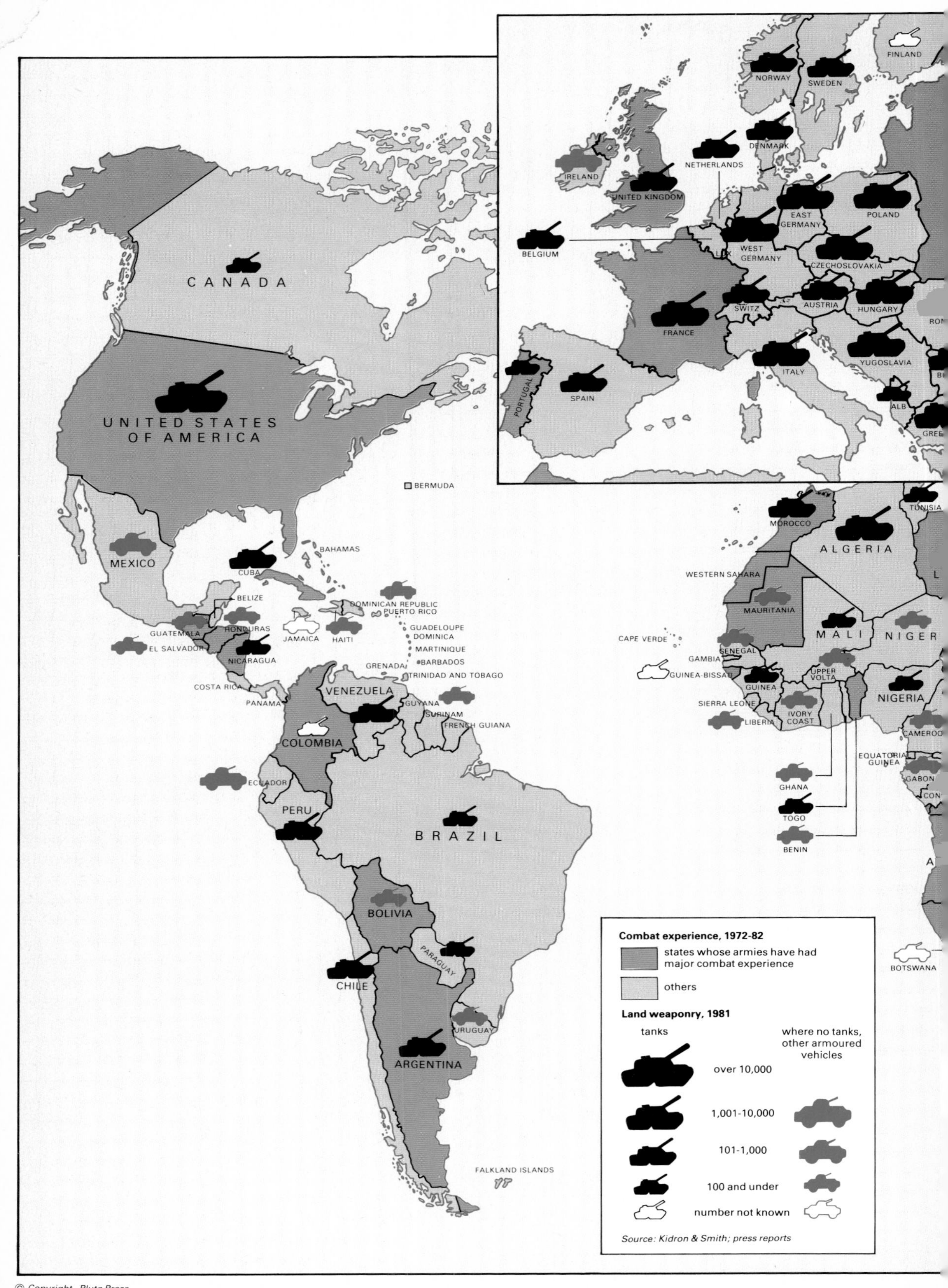
CANADA
UNITED STATES OF AMERICA
MEXICO
CUBA
BAHAMAS
BERMUDA
BELIZE
GUATEMALA
HONDURAS
EL SALVADOR
NICARAGUA
COSTA RICA
PANAMA
JAMAICA
HAITI
DOMINICAN REPUBLIC
PUERTO RICO
GUADELOUPE
DOMINICA
MARTINIQUE
BARBADOS
GRENADA
TRINIDAD AND TOBAGO
VENEZUELA
GUYANA
SURINAM
FRENCH GUIANA
COLOMBIA
ECUADOR
PERU
BRAZIL
BOLIVIA
PARAGUAY
CHILE
URUGUAY
ARGENTINA
FALKLAND ISLANDS
FINLAND
NORWAY
SWEDEN
DENMARK
IRELAND
NETHERLANDS
UNITED KINGDOM
EAST GERMANY
POLAND
BELGIUM
LUX
WEST GERMANY
CZECHOSLOVAKIA
FRANCE
SWITZ
AUSTRIA
HUNGARY
PORTUGAL
SPAIN
ITALY
YUGOSLAVIA
ALB
MOROCCO
TUNISIA
ALGERIA
WESTERN SAHARA
MAURITANIA
MALI
NIGER
CAPE VERDE
SENEGAL
GAMBIA
GUINEA-BISSAU
GUINEA
UPPER VOLTA
SIERRA LEONE
LIBERIA
IVORY COAST
NIGERIA
GHANA
TOGO
BENIN
CAMEROO
EQUATORIA GUINEA
GABON
BOTSWANA
Combat experience, 1972-82
states whose armies have had major combat experience
others
Land weaponry, 1981
tanks
where no tanks, other armoured vehicles
over 10,000
1,001-10,000
101-1,000
100 and under
number not known
Source: Kidron & Smith; press reports

9. Conventional Killing

There are about 26 million people in the military forces of the world; and another 52 million who keep them supplied.

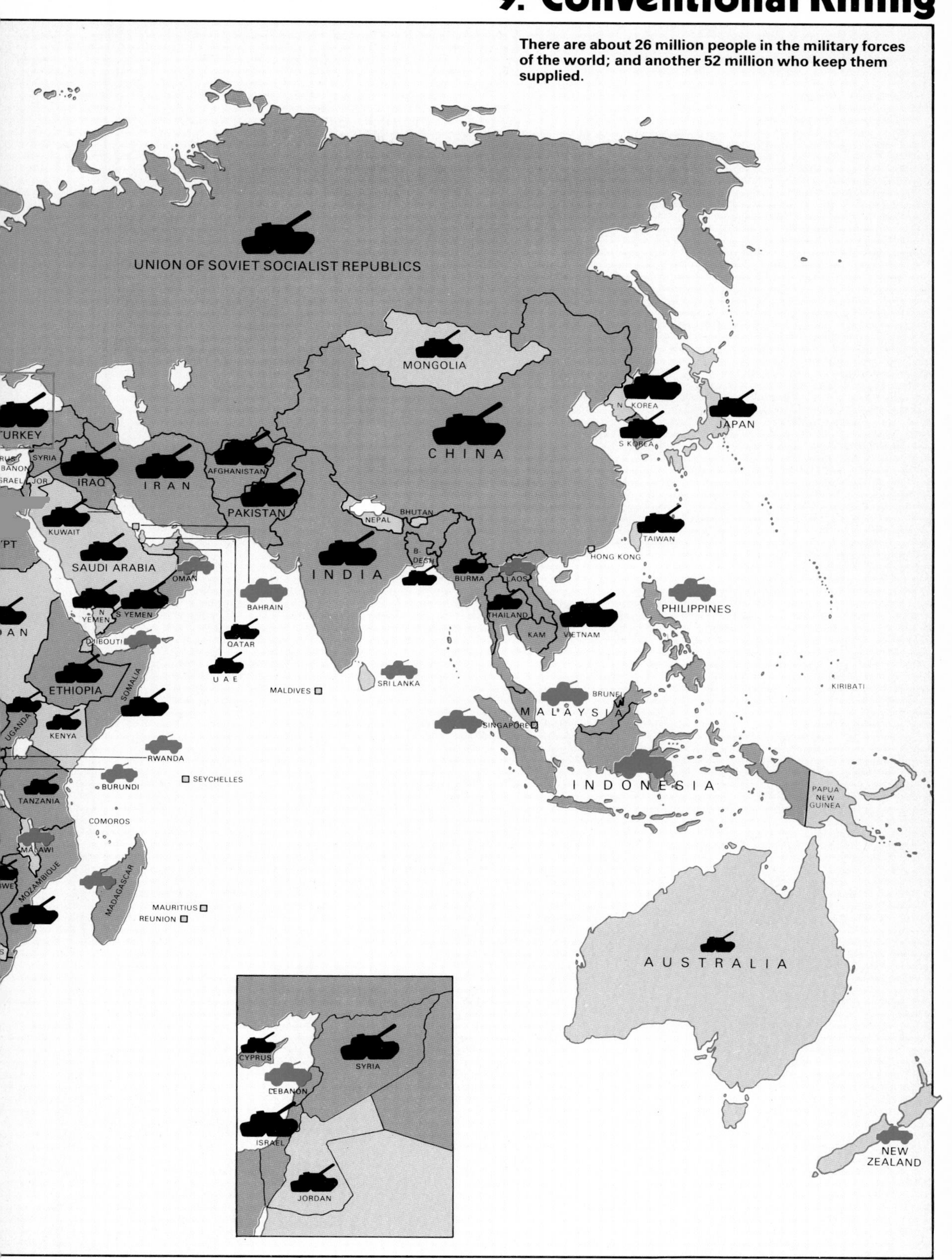

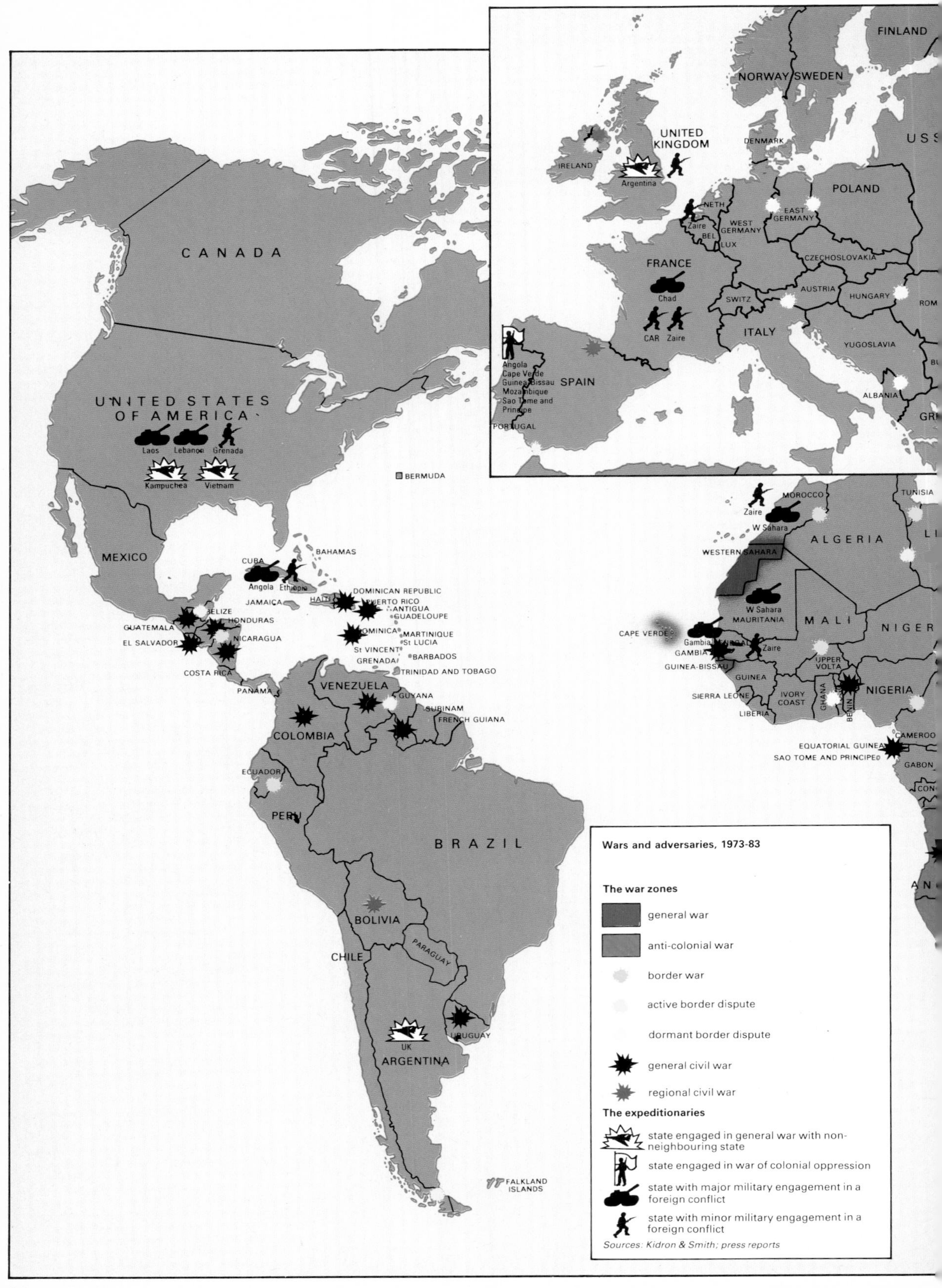
Wars and adversaries, 1973-83
The war zones
general war
anti-colonial war
border war
active border dispute
dormant border dispute
general civil war
regional civil war
The expeditionaries
state engaged in general war with non-neighbouring state
state engaged in war of colonial oppression
state with major military engagement in a foreign conflict
state with minor military engagement in a foreign conflict
Sources: Kidron & Smith; press reports
CANADA
UNITED STATES OF AMERICA
Laos
Lebanon
Grenada
Kampuchea
Vietnam
BERMUDA
MEXICO
CUBA
Angola
Ethiopia
BAHAMAS
DOMINICAN REPUBLIC
JAMAICA
HAITI
PUERTO RICO
ANTIGUA
GUADELOUPE
BELIZE
GUATEMALA
HONDURAS
EL SALVADOR
NICARAGUA
DOMINICA
MARTINIQUE
St LUCIA
St VINCENT
GRENADA
BARBADOS
TRINIDAD AND TOBAGO
COSTA RICA
PANAMA
VENEZUELA
GUYANA
SURINAM
FRENCH GUIANA
COLOMBIA
ECUADOR
PERU
BRAZIL
BOLIVIA
PARAGUAY
CHILE
UK
URUGUAY
ARGENTINA
FALKLAND ISLANDS
FINLAND
NORWAY
SWEDEN
UNITED KINGDOM
DENMARK
IRELAND
Argentina
NETH
Zaire
BEL
WEST GERMANY
EAST GERMANY
POLAND
LUX
FRANCE
CZECHOSLOVAKIA
Chad
AUSTRIA
HUNGARY
SWITZ
CAR
ITALY
YUGOSLAVIA
Angola
Cape Verde
Guinea Bissau
Mozambique
Sao Tome and Principe
SPAIN
PORTUGAL
ALBANIA
MOROCCO
W Sahara
TUNISIA
ALGERIA
WESTERN SAHARA
MAURITANIA
MALI
NIGER
CAPE VERDE
Gambia
GAMBIA
GUINEA-BISSAU
UPPER VOLTA
GUINEA
SIERRA LEONE
IVORY COAST
GHANA
BENIN
NIGERIA
LIBERIA
EQUATORIAL GUINEA
SAO TOME AND PRINCIPE
GABON

10. War in Our Time

The apologists say that expenditure on arms has helped to keep the peace. Some peace!

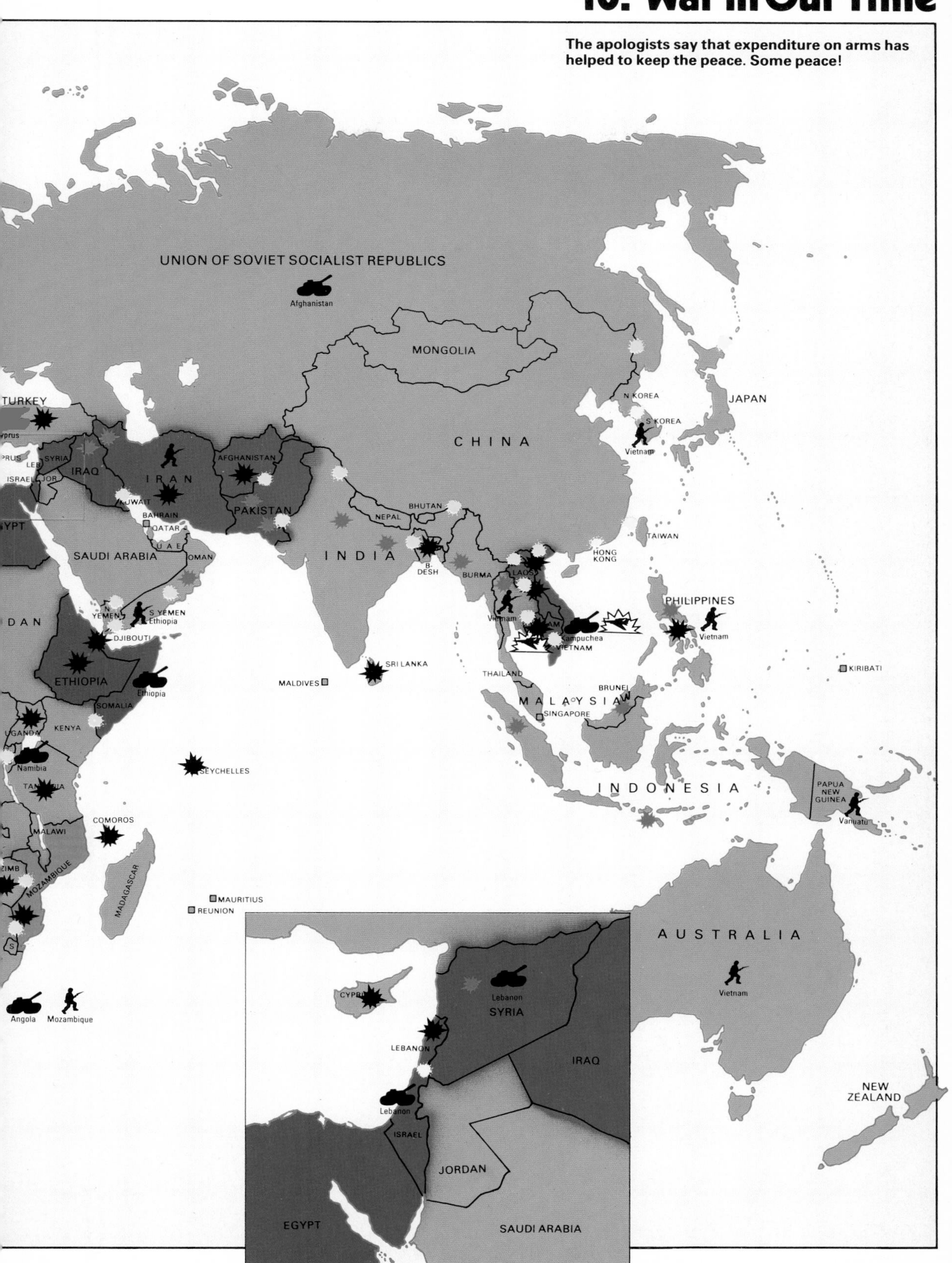

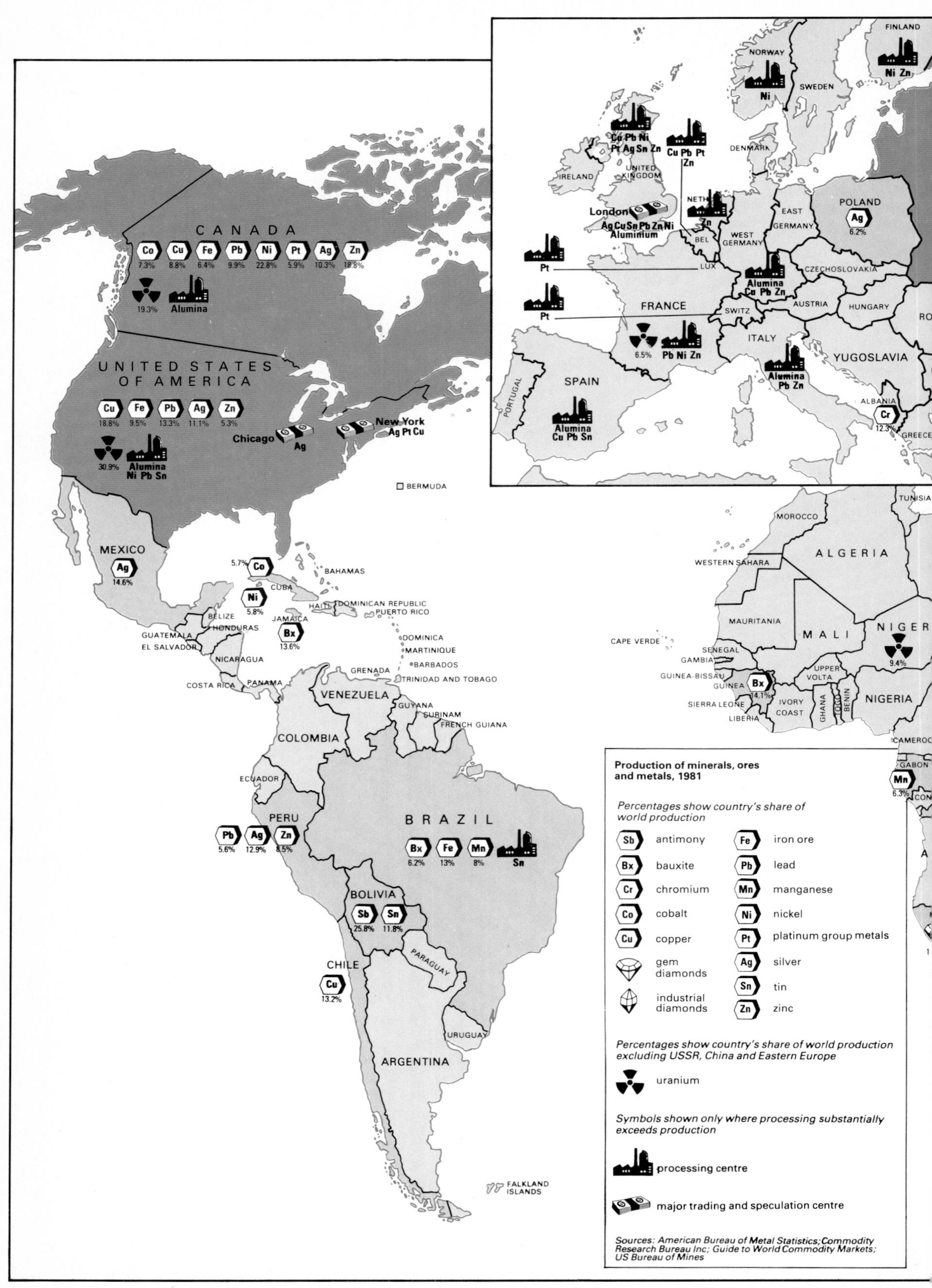

CANADA
Co 7.3% Cu 8.8% Fe 6.4% Pb 9.9% Ni 22.8% Pt 5.9% Ag 10.3% Zn 18.8%
19.3%
Alumina
UNITED STATES OF AMERICA
Cu 18.8% Fe 9.5% Pb 13.3% Ag 11.1% Zn 5.3%
30.9%
Alumina Ni Pb Sn
Chicago Ag
New York Ag Pt Cu
BERMUDA
MEXICO
Ag 14.6%
5.7% Co
Ni 5.8%
BAHAMAS
CUBA
HAITI
DOMINICAN REPUBLIC
PUERTO RICO
JAMAICA
Bx 13.6%
BELIZE
HONDURAS
GUATEMALA
EL SALVADOR
NICARAGUA
COSTA RICA
PANAMA
DOMINICA
MARTINIQUE
BARBADOS
GRENADA
TRINIDAD AND TOBAGO
VENEZUELA
GUYANA
SURINAM
FRENCH GUIANA
COLOMBIA
ECUADOR
PERU
Pb 5.6% Ag 12.9% Zn 8.5%
BRAZIL
Bx 6.2% Fe 13% Mn 8%
Sn
BOLIVIA
Sb 25.8% Sn 11.8%
PARAGUAY
CHILE
Cu 13.2%
URUGUAY
ARGENTINA
FALKLAND ISLANDS
FINLAND
Ni Zn
NORWAY
Ni
SWEDEN
Cu Pb Ni Pt Ag Sn Zn
Cu Pb Pt Zn
DENMARK
IRELAND
UNITED KINGDOM
London
Ag Cu Sn Pb Zn Ni Aluminium
NETH
Zn
BEL
EAST GERMANY
WEST GERMANY
POLAND
Ag 6.2%
Pt
LUX
Alumina Cu Pb Zn
CZECHOSLOVAKIA
Pt
FRANCE
SWITZ
AUSTRIA
HUNGARY
6.5%
Pb Ni Zn
ITALY
Alumina Pb Zn
YUGOSLAVIA
SPAIN
PORTUGAL
Alumina Cu Pb Sn
ALBANIA
Cr 12.3%
GREECE
TUNISIA
MOROCCO
ALGERIA
WESTERN SAHARA
MAURITANIA
MALI
NIGER
9.4%
CAPE VERDE
SENEGAL
GAMBIA
GUINEA-BISSAU
GUINEA
Bx 14.1%
SIERRA LEONE
LIBERIA
IVORY COAST
UPPER VOLTA
GHANA
TOGO
BENIN
NIGERIA
GABON
Mn 6.3%
Production of minerals, ores and metals, 1981
Percentages show country's share of world production
Sb antimony
Bx bauxite
Cr chromium
Co cobalt
Cu copper
gem diamonds
industrial diamonds
Fe iron ore
Pb lead
Mn manganese
Ni nickel
Pt platinum group metals
Ag silver
Sn tin
Zn zinc
Percentages show country's share of world production excluding USSR, China and Eastern Europe
uranium
Symbols shown only where processing substantially exceeds production
processing centre
major trading and speculation centre
Sources: American Bureau of Metal Statistics; Commodity Research Bureau Inc; Guide to World Commodity Markets; US Bureau of Mines

11. Mineral Power

Minerals are the raw material of economic power. States that possess them do not necessarily own them or control their use. Those states that both possess them and exercise such control are major mineral powers.

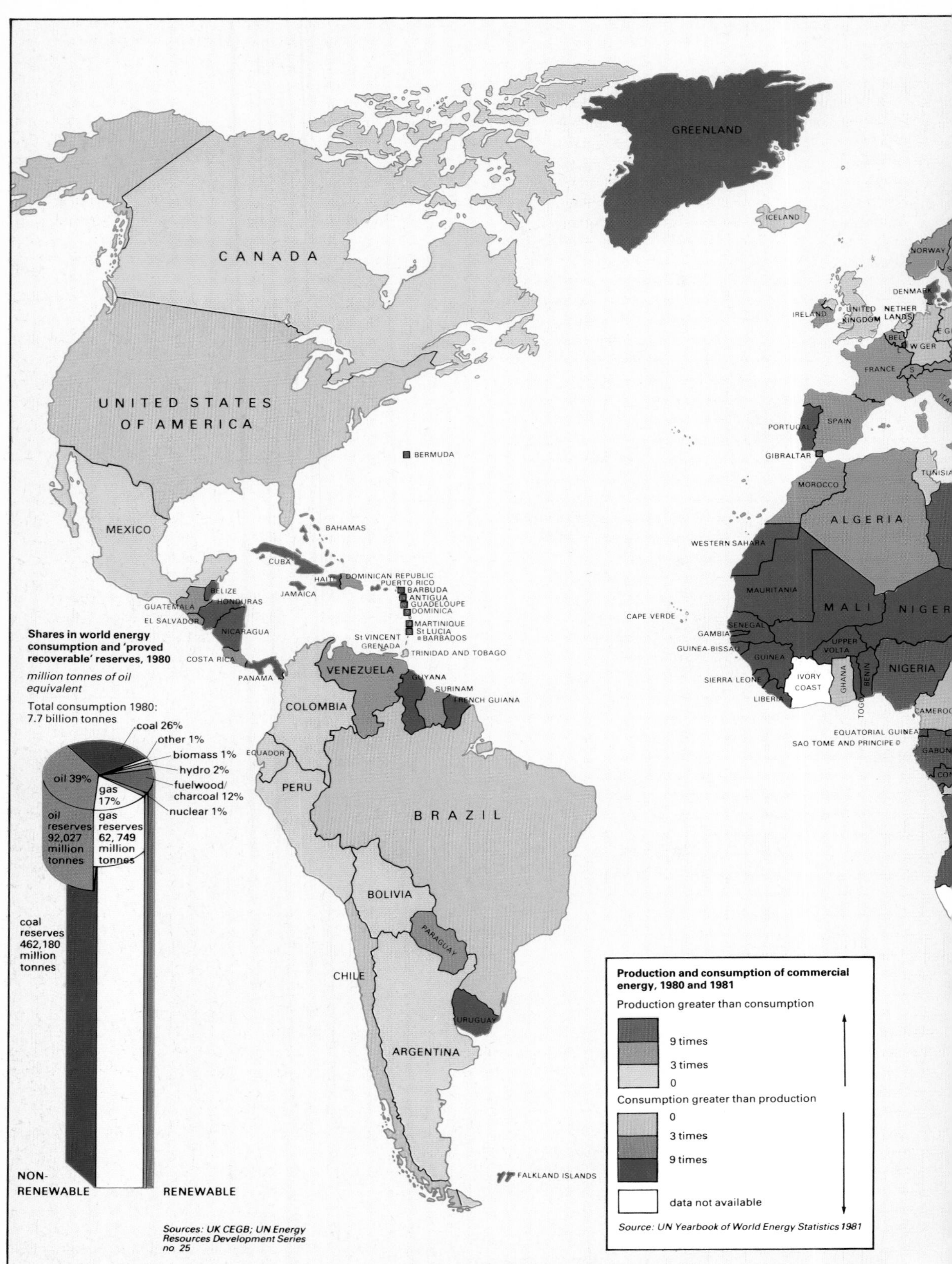

GREENLAND
ICELAND
NORWAY
DENMARK
IRELAND
UNITED KINGDOM
NETHER LANDS
BEL
W GER
FRANCE
S
PORTUGAL
SPAIN
GIBRALTAR
MOROCCO
TUNISIA
ALGERIA
WESTERN SAHARA
MAURITANIA
MALI
NIGER
CAPE VERDE
SENEGAL
GAMBIA
GUINEA-BISSAU
GUINEA
UPPER VOLTA
SIERRA LEONE
LIBERIA
IVORY COAST
GHANA
TOGO
BENIN
NIGERIA
EQUATORIAL GUINEA
SAO TOME AND PRINCIPE
GABON
CANADA
UNITED STATES OF AMERICA
BERMUDA
MEXICO
BAHAMAS
CUBA
HAITI
DOMINICAN REPUBLIC
PUERTO RICO
JAMAICA
BARBUDA
ANTIGUA
GUADELOUPE
DOMINICA
MARTINIQUE
St LUCIA
BARBADOS
St VINCENT
GRENADA
TRINIDAD AND TOBAGO
BELIZE
GUATEMALA
HONDURAS
EL SALVADOR
NICARAGUA
COSTA RICA
PANAMA
VENEZUELA
GUYANA
SURINAM
FRENCH GUIANA
COLOMBIA
ECUADOR
PERU
BRAZIL
BOLIVIA
PARAGUAY
CHILE
URUGUAY
ARGENTINA
FALKLAND ISLANDS
Shares in world energy consumption and 'proved recoverable' reserves, 1980
million tonnes of oil equivalent
Total consumption 1980: 7.7 billion tonnes
coal 26%
other 1%
biomass 1%
hydro 2%
fuelwood/ charcoal 12%
nuclear 1%
oil 39%
gas 17%
oil reserves 92,027 million tonnes
gas reserves 62, 749 million tonnes
coal reserves 462,180 million tonnes
NON-RENEWABLE
RENEWABLE
Sources: UK CEGB; UN Energy Resources Development Series no 25
Production and consumption of commercial energy, 1980 and 1981
Production greater than consumption
9 times
3 times
0
Consumption greater than production
0
3 times
9 times
data not available
Source: UN Yearbook of World Energy Statistics 1981

12. Energy Power

More energy reaches us from the sun than can conceivably be put to human use. Yet many states are energy paupers, and most are energy poor.

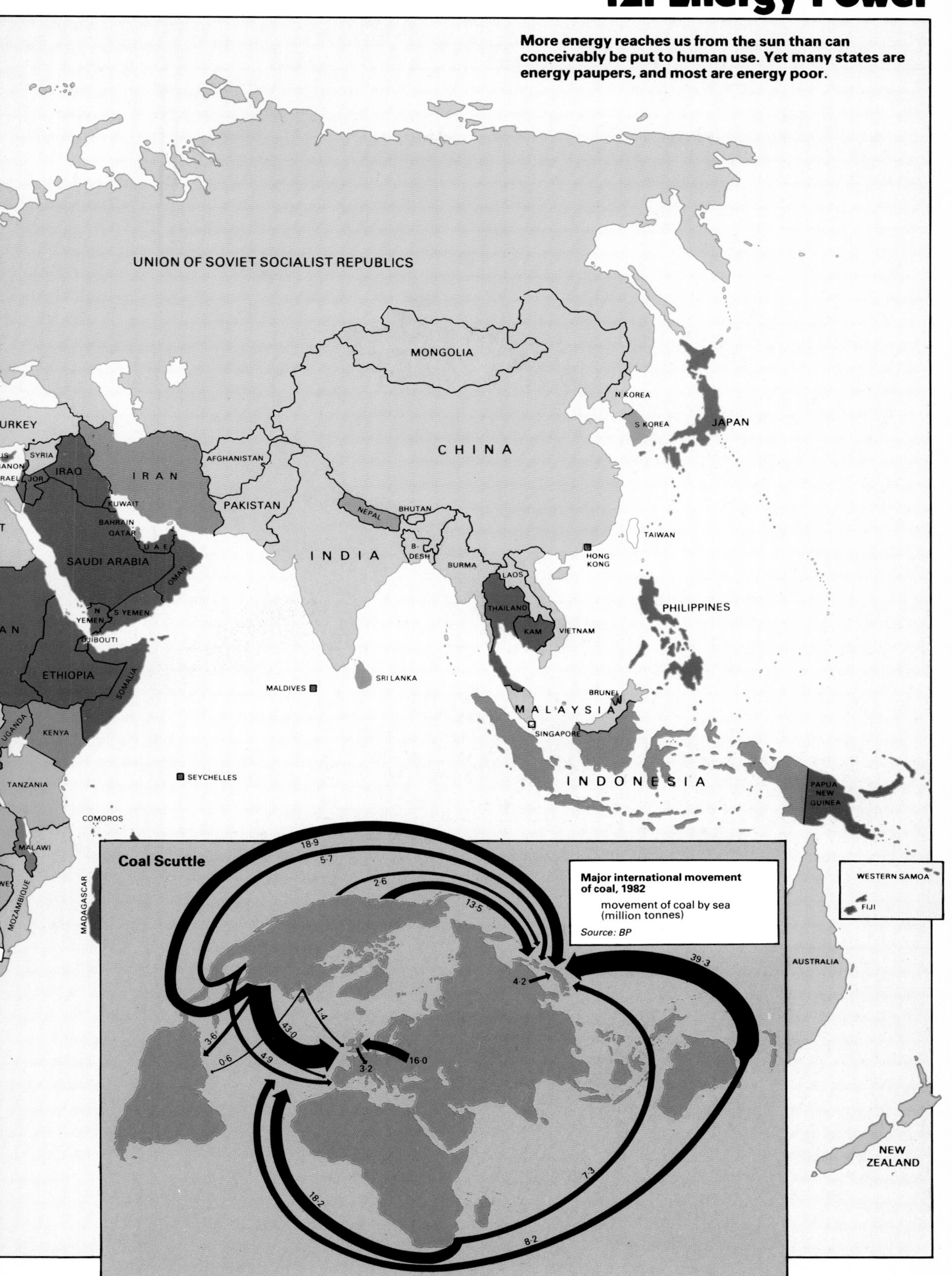

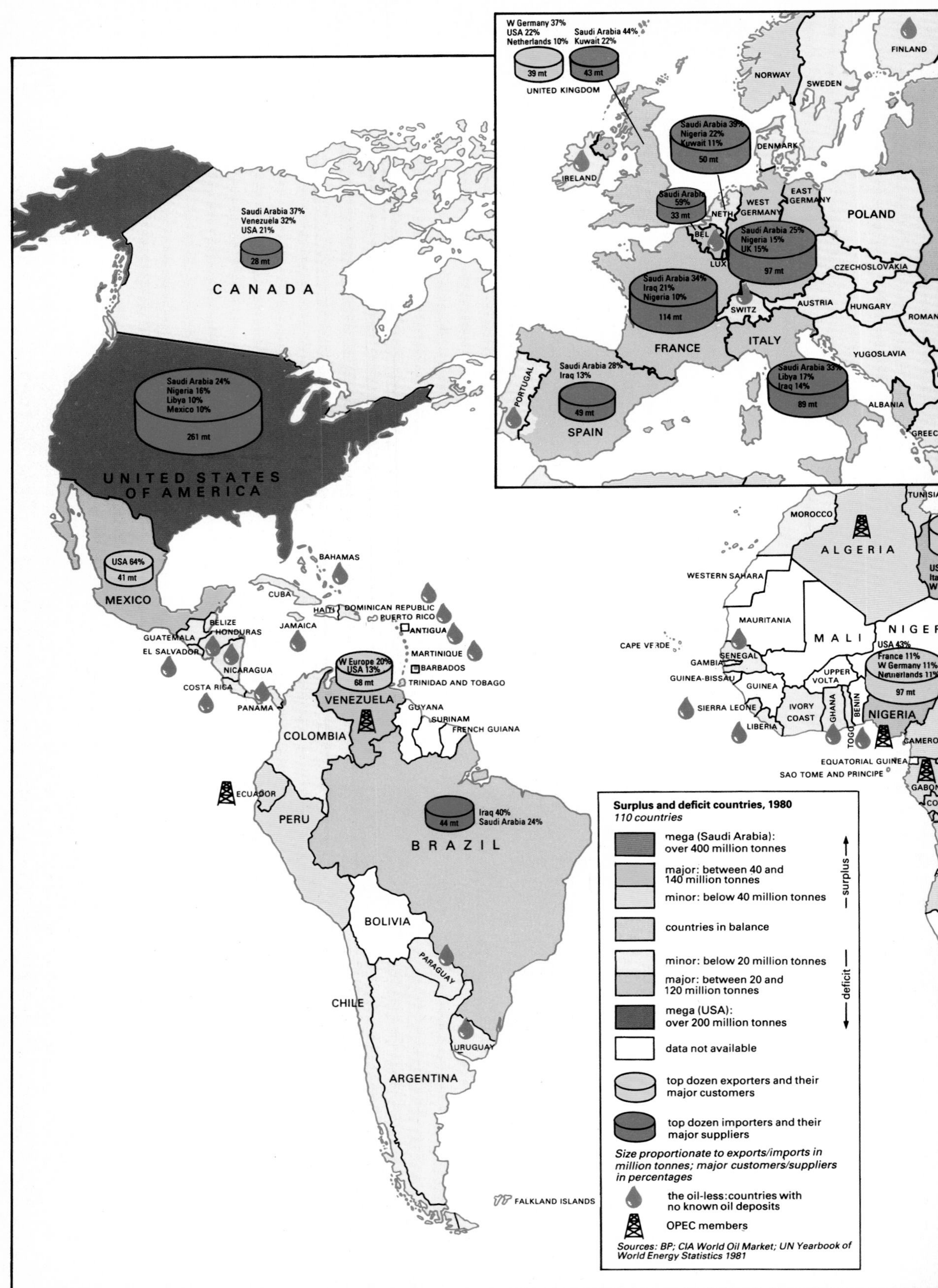
W Germany 37%
USA 22%
Netherlands 10%
39 mt
Saudi Arabia 44%
Kuwait 22%
43 mt
UNITED KINGDOM
FINLAND
NORWAY
SWEDEN
Saudi Arabia 39%
Nigeria 22%
Kuwait 11%
50 mt
DENMARK
IRELAND
Saudi Arabia 59%
33 mt
NETH
WEST GERMANY
EAST GERMANY
POLAND
BEL
LUX
Saudi Arabia 25%
Nigeria 15%
UK 15%
97 mt
CZECHOSLOVAKIA
Saudi Arabia 34%
Iraq 21%
Nigeria 10%
114 mt
SWITZ
AUSTRIA
HUNGARY
FRANCE
ITALY
YUGOSLAVIA
PORTUGAL
Saudi Arabia 28%
Iraq 13%
49 mt
SPAIN
Saudi Arabia 33%
Libya 17%
Iraq 14%
89 mt
ALBANIA
Saudi Arabia 37%
Venezuela 32%
USA 21%
28 mt
CANADA
Saudi Arabia 24%
Nigeria 16%
Libya 10%
Mexico 10%
261 mt
UNITED STATES OF AMERICA
USA 64%
41 mt
MEXICO
BAHAMAS
CUBA
HAITI
DOMINICAN REPUBLIC
PUERTO RICO
ANTIGUA
JAMAICA
BELIZE
HONDURAS
GUATEMALA
EL SALVADOR
NICARAGUA
COSTA RICA
PANAMA
MARTINIQUE
BARBADOS
TRINIDAD AND TOBAGO
W Europe 20%
USA 13%
68 mt
VENEZUELA
GUYANA
SURINAM
FRENCH GUIANA
COLOMBIA
ECUADOR
PERU
Iraq 40%
Saudi Arabia 24%
44 mt
BRAZIL
BOLIVIA
PARAGUAY
CHILE
URUGUAY
ARGENTINA
FALKLAND ISLANDS
TUNISIA
MOROCCO
ALGERIA
WESTERN SAHARA
MAURITANIA
MALI
NIGER
CAPE VERDE
GAMBIA
SENEGAL
GUINEA-BISSAU
GUINEA
UPPER VOLTA
SIERRA LEONE
LIBERIA
IVORY COAST
GHANA
TOGO
BENIN
USA 43%
France 11%
W Germany 11%
Netherlands 11%
97 mt
NIGERIA
EQUATORIAL GUINEA
SAO TOME AND PRINCIPE
GABON
Surplus and deficit countries, 1980
110 countries
mega (Saudi Arabia): over 400 million tonnes
major: between 40 and 140 million tonnes
minor: below 40 million tonnes
surplus
countries in balance
minor: below 20 million tonnes
major: between 20 and 120 million tonnes
mega (USA): over 200 million tonnes
deficit
data not available
top dozen exporters and their major customers
top dozen importers and their major suppliers
Size proportionate to exports/imports in million tonnes; major customers/suppliers in percentages
the oil-less: countries with no known oil deposits
OPEC members
Sources: BP; CIA World Oil Market; UN Yearbook of World Energy Statistics 1981

13. Oil Power

Saudi Arabia accounts for a third of all oil exports. Oil itself constitutes one quarter of the volume of world trade.

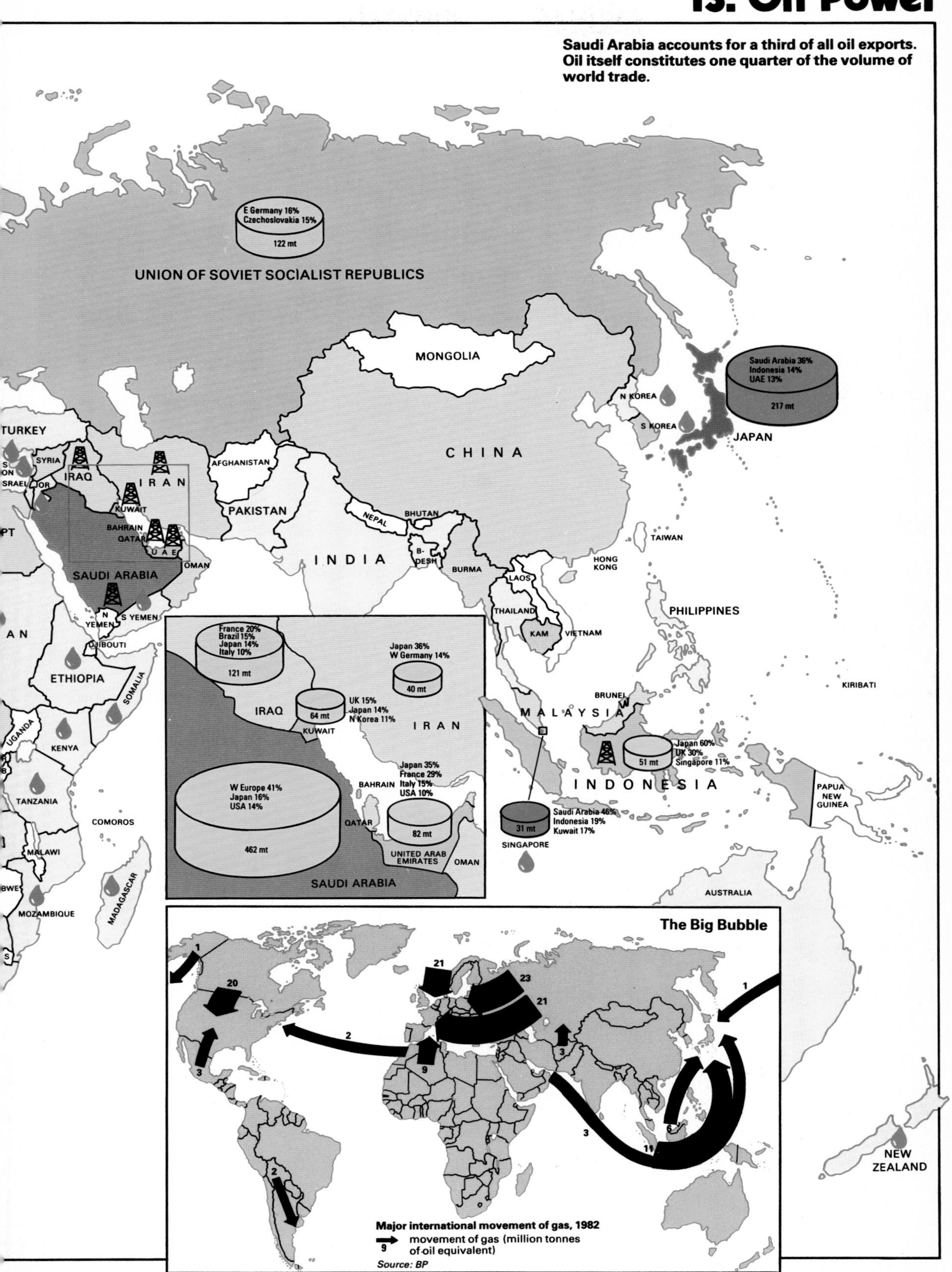

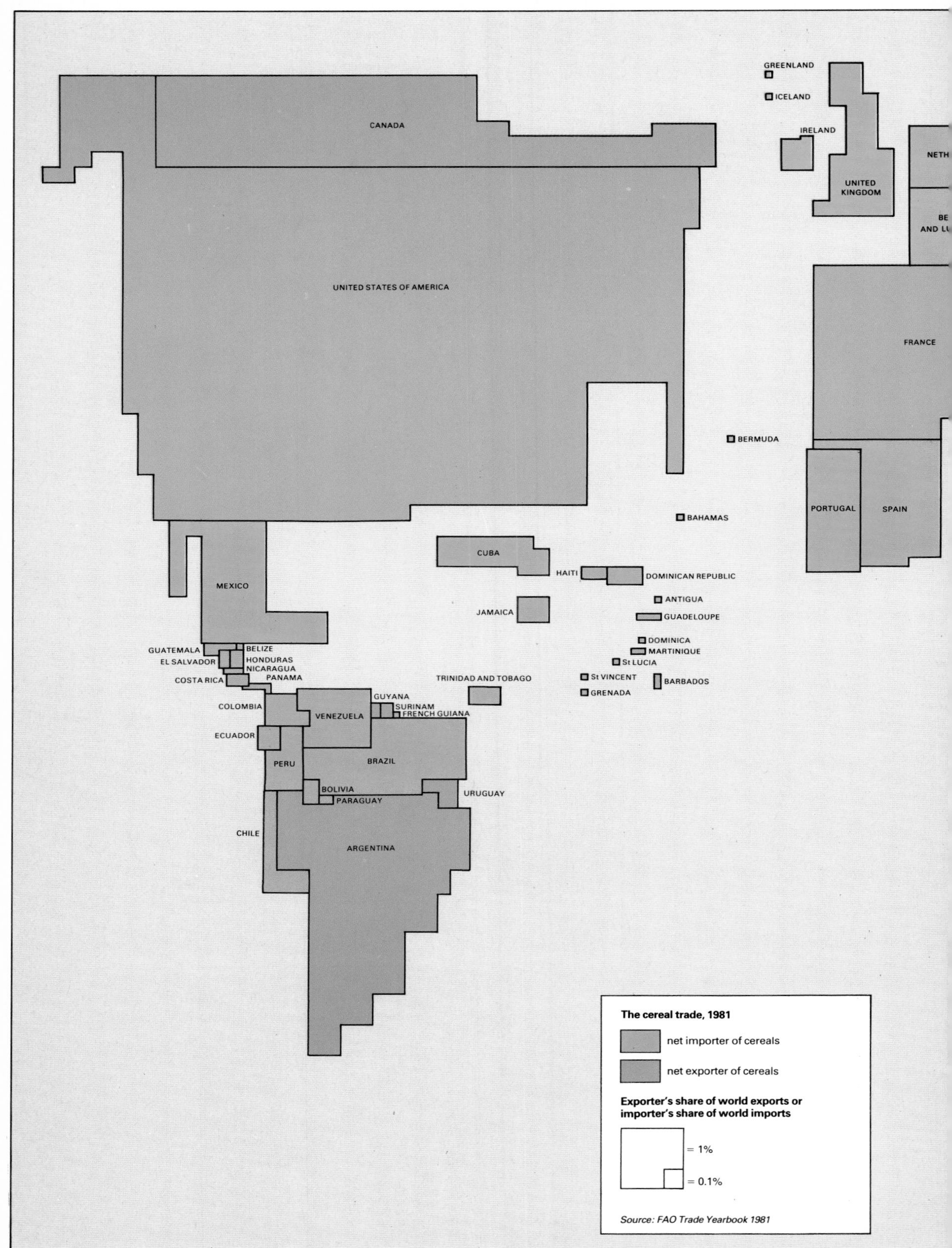
GREENLAND
ICELAND
IRELAND
UNITED KINGDOM
NETH
BE AND LU
CANADA
UNITED STATES OF AMERICA
FRANCE
BERMUDA
PORTUGAL
SPAIN
BAHAMAS
CUBA
HAITI
DOMINICAN REPUBLIC
MEXICO
ANTIGUA
JAMAICA
GUADELOUPE
DOMINICA
MARTINIQUE
St LUCIA
St VINCENT
BARBADOS
GRENADA
GUATEMALA
BELIZE
EL SALVADOR
HONDURAS
NICARAGUA
COSTA RICA
PANAMA
TRINIDAD AND TOBAGO
GUYANA
SURINAM
FRENCH GUIANA
COLOMBIA
VENEZUELA
ECUADOR
PERU
BRAZIL
BOLIVIA
PARAGUAY
URUGUAY
CHILE
ARGENTINA
The cereal trade, 1981
net importer of cereals
net exporter of cereals
Exporter's share of world exports or importer's share of world imports
= 1%
= 0.1%
Source: FAO Trade Yearbook 1981

14. Food Power

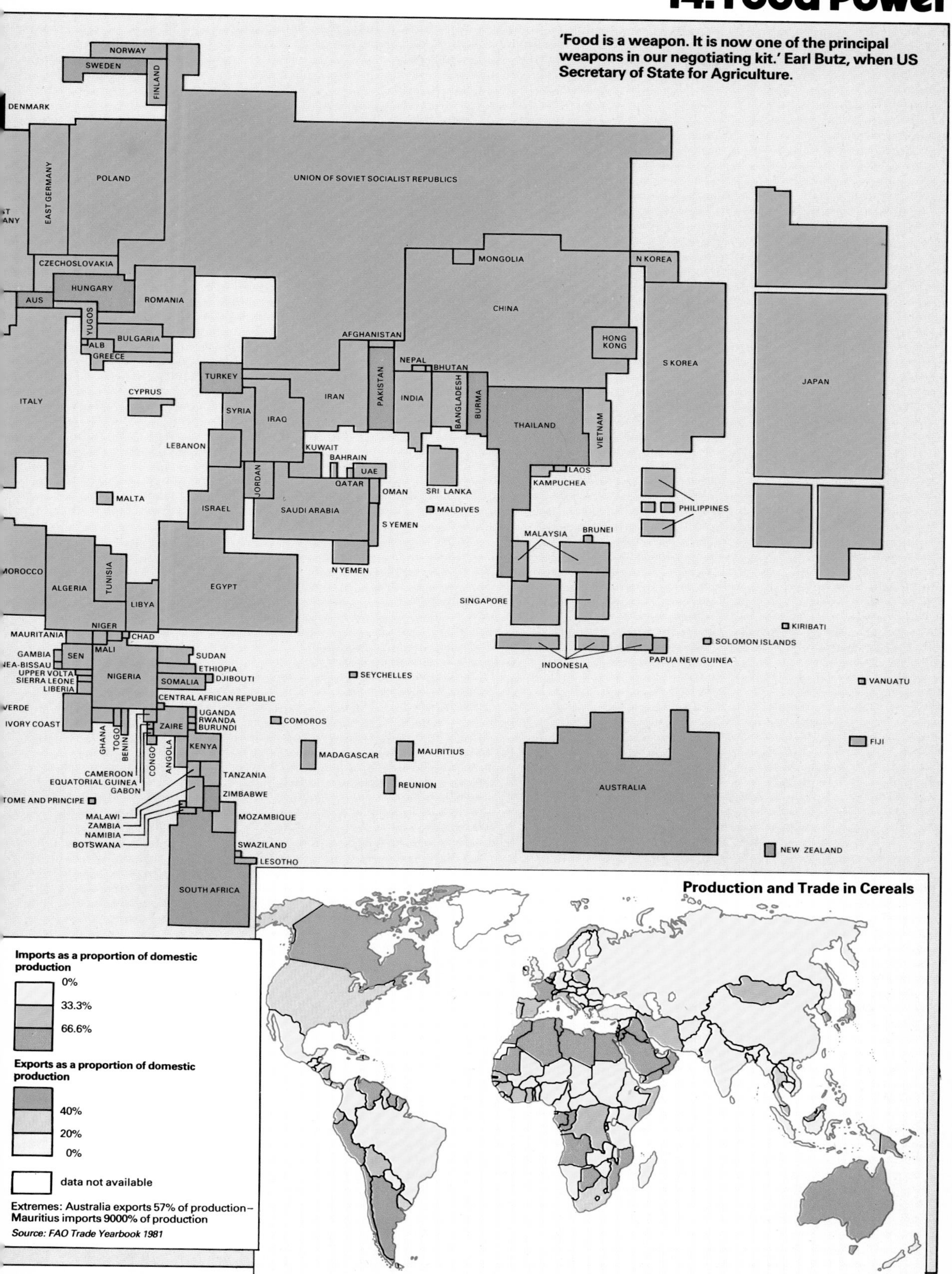
'Food is a weapon. It is now one of the principal weapons in our negotiating kit.' Earl Butz, when US Secretary of State for Agriculture.
NORWAY
SWEDEN
FINLAND
DENMARK
EAST GERMANY
POLAND
UNION OF SOVIET SOCIALIST REPUBLICS
CZECHOSLOVAKIA
HUNGARY
AUS
ROMANIA
YUGOS
BULGARIA
ALB
GREECE
ITALY
CYPRUS
TURKEY
SYRIA
IRAQ
IRAN
AFGHANISTAN
PAKISTAN
NEPAL
BHUTAN
INDIA
BANGLADESH
BURMA
MONGOLIA
CHINA
HONG KONG
N KOREA
S KOREA
JAPAN
THAILAND
VIETNAM
LAOS
KAMPUCHEA
LEBANON
KUWAIT
BAHRAIN
QATAR
UAE
OMAN
SRI LANKA
MALDIVES
JORDAN
ISRAEL
SAUDI ARABIA
S YEMEN
N YEMEN
MALTA
PHILIPPINES
MALAYSIA
BRUNEI
SINGAPORE
INDONESIA
PAPUA NEW GUINEA
KIRIBATI
SOLOMON ISLANDS
VANUATU
FIJI
MOROCCO
ALGERIA
TUNISIA
LIBYA
EGYPT
NIGER
MAURITANIA
CHAD
MALI
GAMBIA
SEN
SUDAN
ETHIOPIA
DJIBOUTI
SOMALIA
NIGERIA
SEYCHELLES
UPPER VOLTA
SIERRA LEONE
LIBERIA
CENTRAL AFRICAN REPUBLIC
IVORY COAST
GHANA
TOGO
BENIN
CONGO
ANGOLA
ZAIRE
UGANDA
RWANDA
BURUNDI
KENYA
COMOROS
MADAGASCAR
MAURITIUS
REUNION
TANZANIA
ZIMBABWE
CAMEROON
EQUATORIAL GUINEA
GABON
TOME AND PRINCIPE
MALAWI
ZAMBIA
NAMIBIA
BOTSWANA
MOZAMBIQUE
SWAZILAND
LESOTHO
SOUTH AFRICA
AUSTRALIA
NEW ZEALAND
Production and Trade in Cereals
Imports as a proportion of domestic production
0%
33.3%
66.6%
Exports as a proportion of domestic production
40%
20%
0%
data not available
Extremes: Australia exports 57% of production – Mauritius imports 9000% of production
Source: FAO Trade Yearbook 1981

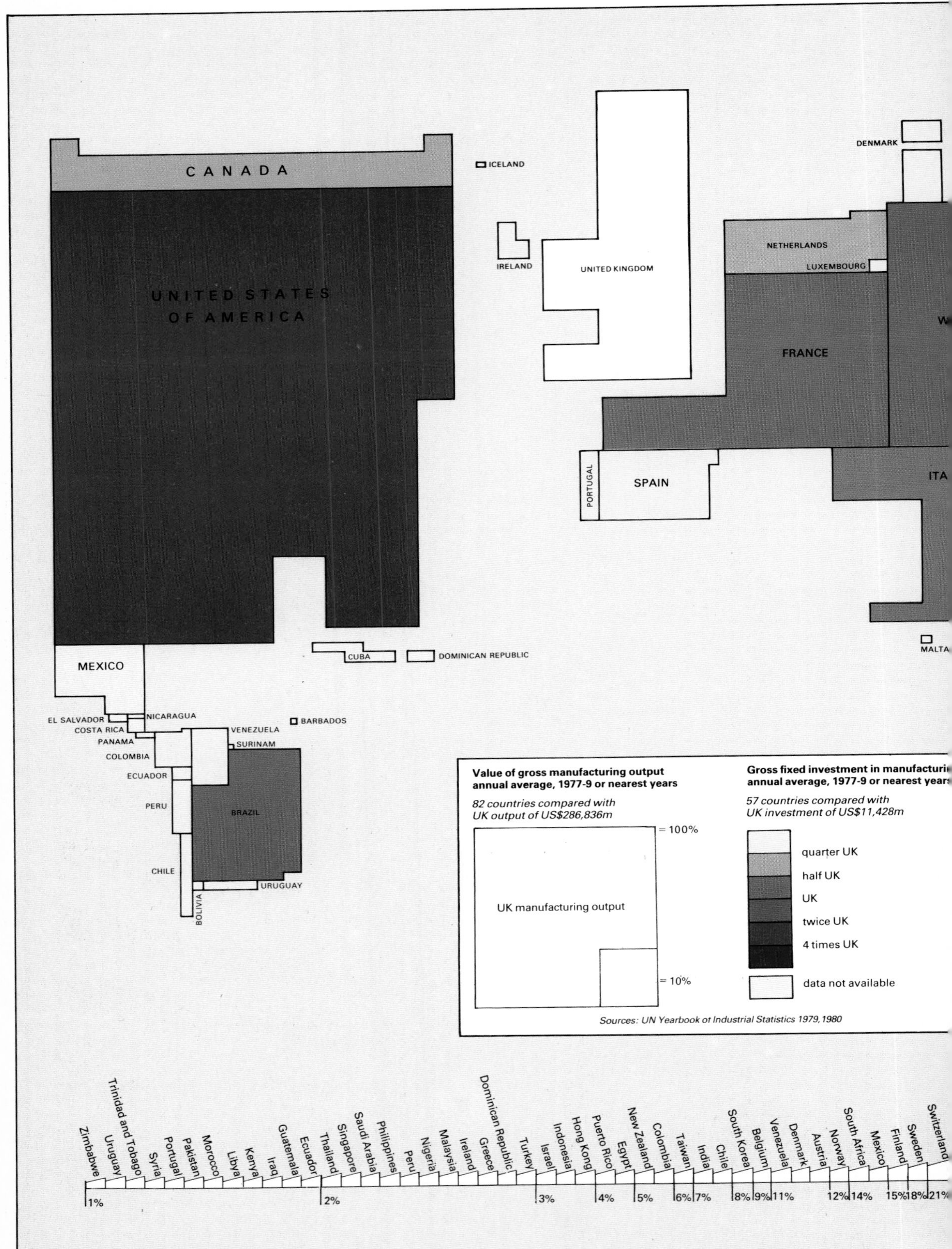

CANADA
UNITED STATES OF AMERICA
ICELAND
IRELAND
UNITED KINGDOM
DENMARK
NETHERLANDS
LUXEMBOURG
FRANCE
PORTUGAL
SPAIN
ITA
MALTA
MEXICO
CUBA
DOMINICAN REPUBLIC
EL SALVADOR
NICARAGUA
COSTA RICA
PANAMA
BARBADOS
VENEZUELA
SURINAM
COLOMBIA
ECUADOR
PERU
BRAZIL
CHILE
URUGUAY
BOLIVIA
Value of gross manufacturing output annual average, 1977-9 or nearest years
82 countries compared with UK output of US$286,836m
= 100%
UK manufacturing output
= 10%
Gross fixed investment in manufacturi
annual average, 1977-9 or nearest year
57 countries compared with UK investment of US$11,428m
quarter UK
half UK
UK
twice UK
4 times UK
data not available
Sources: UN Yearbook of Industrial Statistics 1979, 1980
Zimbabwe
Uruguay
Trinidad and Tobago
Syria
Portugal
Pakistan
Morocco
Libya
Kenya
Iraq
Guatemala
Ecuador
Thailand
Singapore
Saudi Arabia
Philippines
Peru
Nigeria
Malaysia
Ireland
Greece
Dominican Republic
Turkey
Israel
Indonesia
Hong Kong
Puerto Rico
Egypt
New Zealand
Colombia
Taiwan
India
Chile
South Korea
Belgium
Venezuela
Denmark
Austria
Norway
South Africa
Mexico
Finland
Sweden
Switzerland
1%
2%
3%
4%
5%
6%
7%
8%
9%
11%
12%
14%
15%
18%
21%

15. Industrial Power

As the history of the UK in the last century or so illustrates, industry is the basis for the relative power of the modern state and investment a means of achieving or securing it.

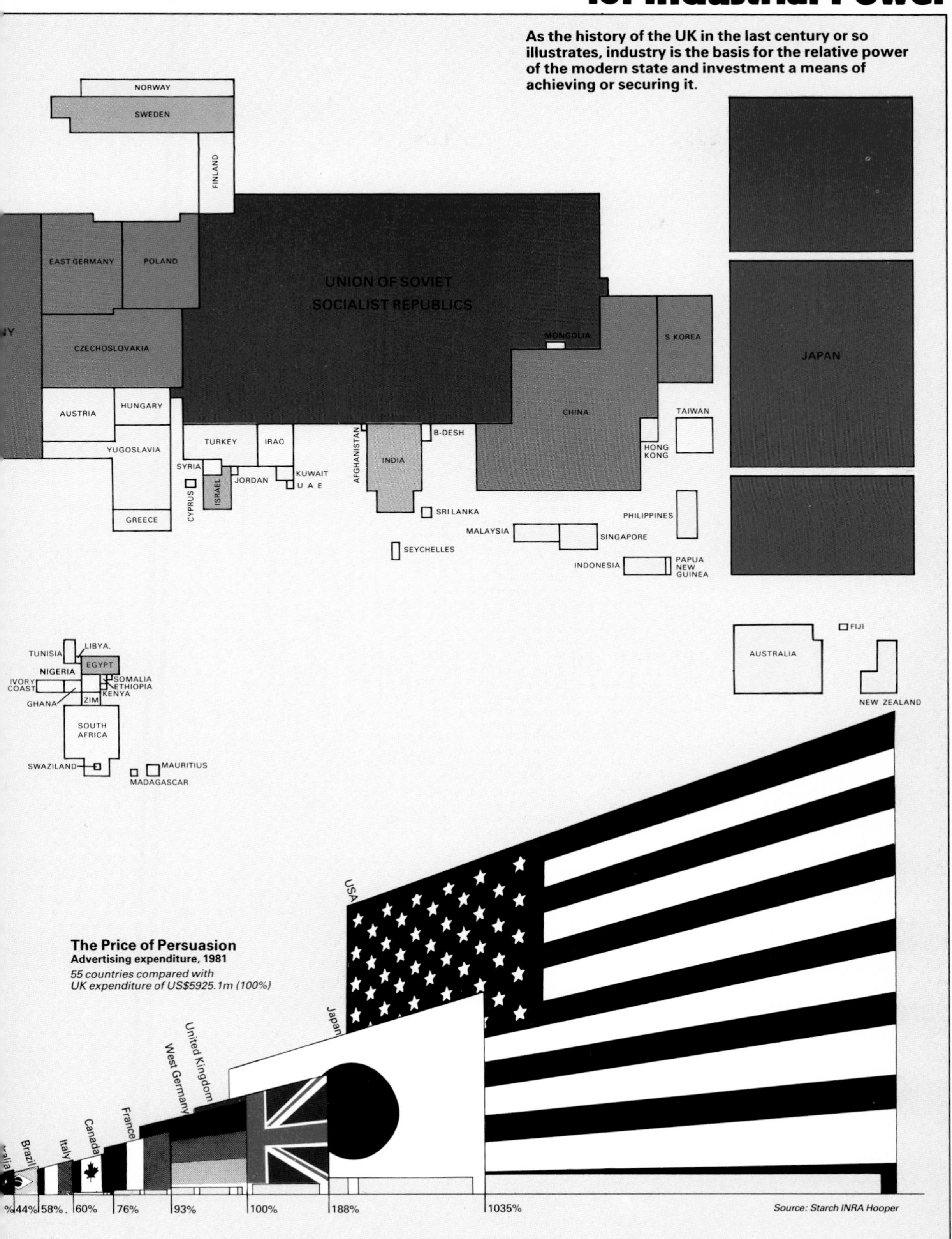

The Price of Persuasion
Advertising expenditure, 1981
55 countries compared with UK expenditure of US$5925.1m (100%)

Source: Starch INRA Hooper

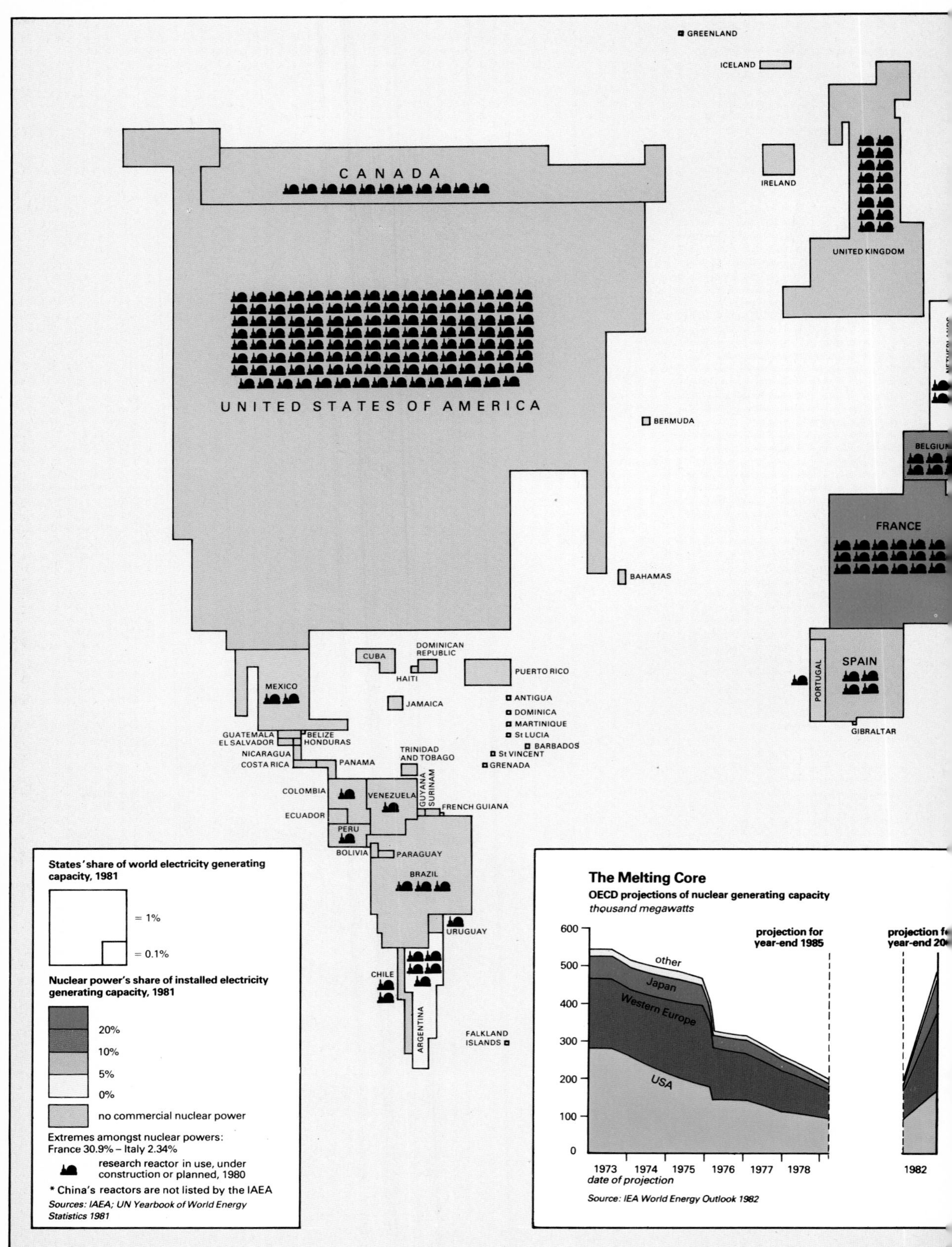
GREENLAND
ICELAND
IRELAND
UNITED KINGDOM
CANADA
UNITED STATES OF AMERICA
BERMUDA
BELGIUM
FRANCE
BAHAMAS
SPAIN
PORTUGAL
GIBRALTAR
CUBA
DOMINICAN REPUBLIC
HAITI
PUERTO RICO
MEXICO
JAMAICA
ANTIGUA
DOMINICA
MARTINIQUE
St LUCIA
BARBADOS
St VINCENT
GRENADA
GUATEMALA
EL SALVADOR
BELIZE
HONDURAS
NICARAGUA
COSTA RICA
PANAMA
TRINIDAD AND TOBAGO
COLOMBIA
VENEZUELA
GUYANA
SURINAM
FRENCH GUIANA
ECUADOR
PERU
BOLIVIA
PARAGUAY
BRAZIL
URUGUAY
CHILE
ARGENTINA
FALKLAND ISLANDS
States' share of world electricity generating capacity, 1981
= 1%
= 0.1%
Nuclear power's share of installed electricity generating capacity, 1981
20%
10%
5%
0%
no commercial nuclear power
Extremes amongst nuclear powers:
France 30.9% – Italy 2.34%
research reactor in use, under construction or planned, 1980
* China's reactors are not listed by the IAEA
Sources: IAEA; UN Yearbook of World Energy Statistics 1981
The Melting Core
OECD projections of nuclear generating capacity
thousand megawatts
600
500
400
300
200
100
0
projection for year-end 1985
other
Japan
Western Europe
USA
1973
1974
1975
1976
1977
1978
date of projection
1982
Source: IEA World Energy Outlook 1982

16. Nuclear Power

Some states use nuclear power; some are nuclear powers. All began with research reactors.

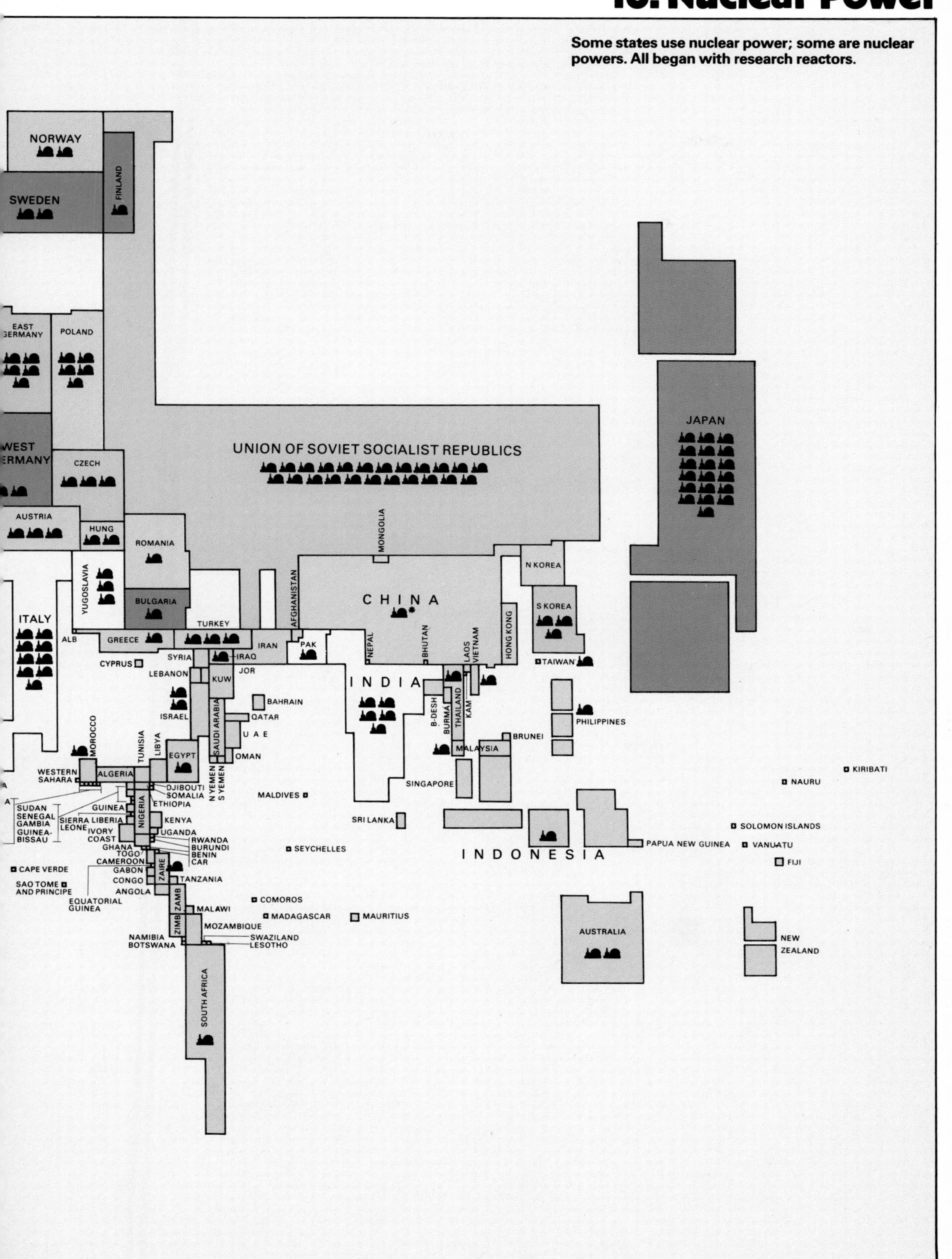
NORWAY
SWEDEN
FINLAND
EAST GERMANY
POLAND
WEST GERMANY
CZECH
AUSTRIA
HUNG
ROMANIA
YUGOSLAVIA
BULGARIA
ITALY
ALB
GREECE
TURKEY
UNION OF SOVIET SOCIALIST REPUBLICS
MONGOLIA
JAPAN
N KOREA
S KOREA
CHINA
AFGHANISTAN
IRAN
PAK
NEPAL
BHUTAN
LAOS
VIETNAM
HONG KONG
TAIWAN
CYPRUS
SYRIA
IRAQ
LEBANON
KUW
JOR
ISRAEL
SAUDI ARABIA
BAHRAIN
QATAR
U A E
OMAN
INDIA
B-DESH
BURMA
THAILAND
KAM
PHILIPPINES
BRUNEI
MALAYSIA
SINGAPORE
MOROCCO
TUNISIA
LIBYA
EGYPT
WESTERN SAHARA
ALGERIA
N YEMEN
S YEMEN
DJIBOUTI
SOMALIA
ETHIOPIA
MALDIVES
SUDAN
SENEGAL
GAMBIA
GUINEA-BISSAU
GUINEA
SIERRA LEONE
LIBERIA
IVORY COAST
NIGERIA
KENYA
UGANDA
RWANDA
BURUNDI
BENIN
CAR
GHANA
TOGO
CAMEROON
GABON
CONGO
ZAIRE
TANZANIA
ANGOLA
EQUATORIAL GUINEA
CAPE VERDE
SAO TOME AND PRINCIPE
ZAMB
ZIMB
MALAWI
MOZAMBIQUE
NAMIBIA
BOTSWANA
SWAZILAND
LESOTHO
SOUTH AFRICA
SRI LANKA
SEYCHELLES
COMOROS
MADAGASCAR
MAURITIUS
INDONESIA
PAPUA NEW GUINEA
KIRIBATI
NAURU
SOLOMON ISLANDS
VANUATU
FIJI
AUSTRALIA
NEW ZEALAND

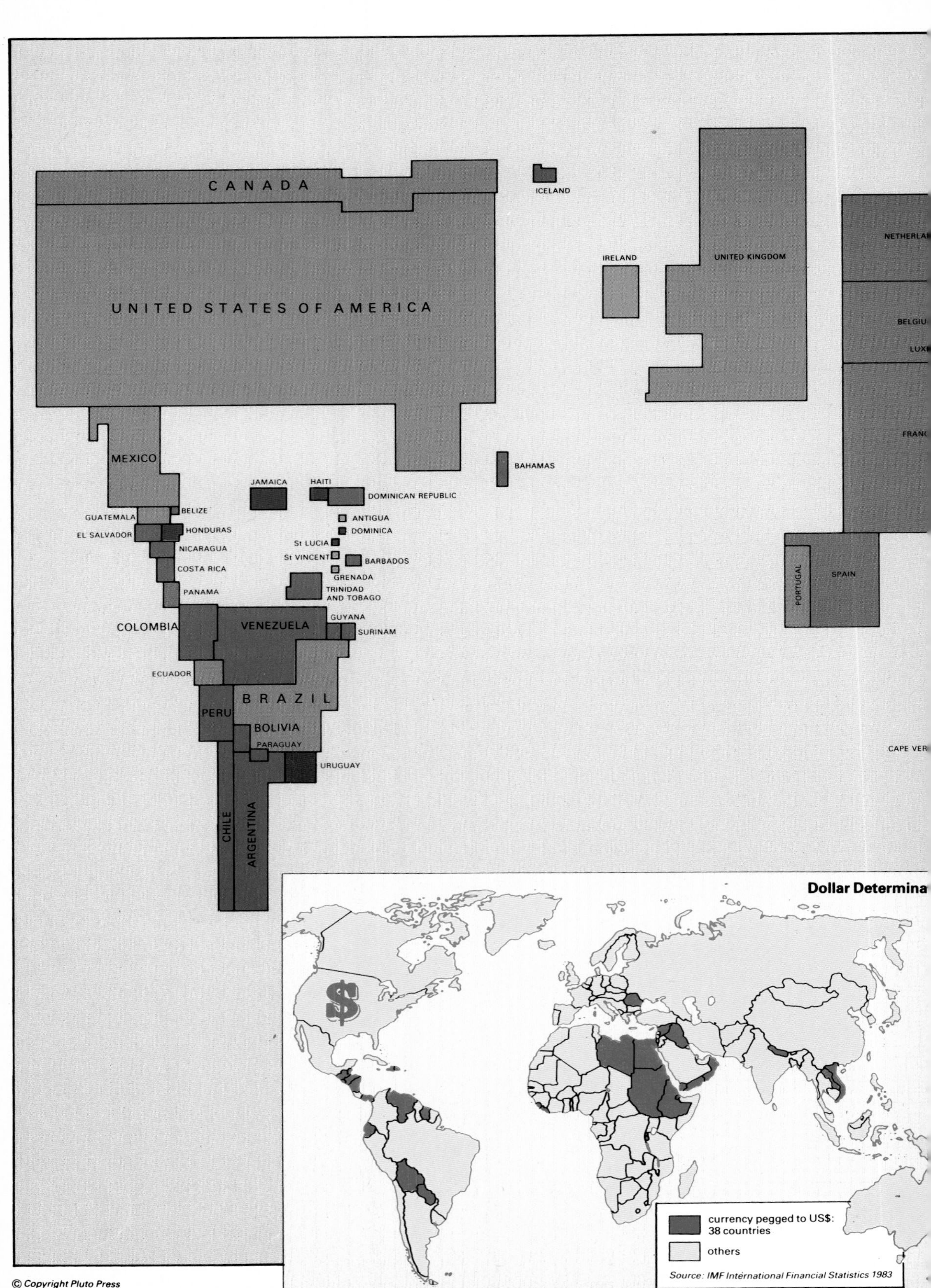
CANADA
UNITED STATES OF AMERICA
ICELAND
IRELAND
UNITED KINGDOM
MEXICO
BAHAMAS
JAMAICA
HAITI
DOMINICAN REPUBLIC
BELIZE
GUATEMALA
HONDURAS
EL SALVADOR
NICARAGUA
COSTA RICA
PANAMA
ANTIGUA
DOMINICA
St LUCIA
St VINCENT
BARBADOS
GRENADA
TRINIDAD AND TOBAGO
COLOMBIA
VENEZUELA
GUYANA
SURINAM
ECUADOR
BRAZIL
PERU
BOLIVIA
PARAGUAY
URUGUAY
CHILE
ARGENTINA
PORTUGAL
SPAIN
Dollar Determina
currency pegged to US$: 38 countries
others
Source: IMF International Financial Statistics 1983

17. Financial Power

The IMF (International Monetary Fund) is the world's leading interstate financial organization. Only a few countries – notably the USSR and Switzerland – do not belong to it.

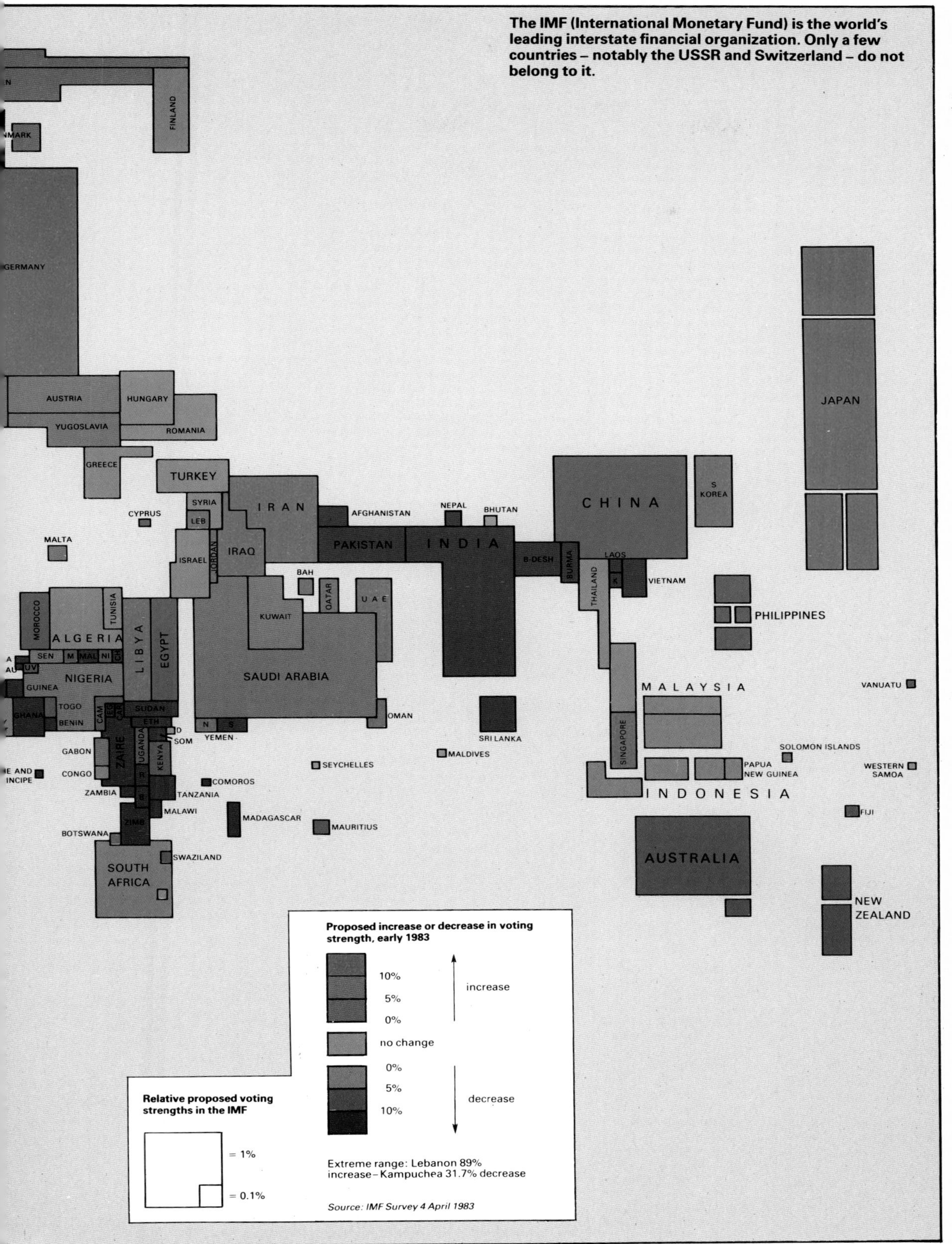

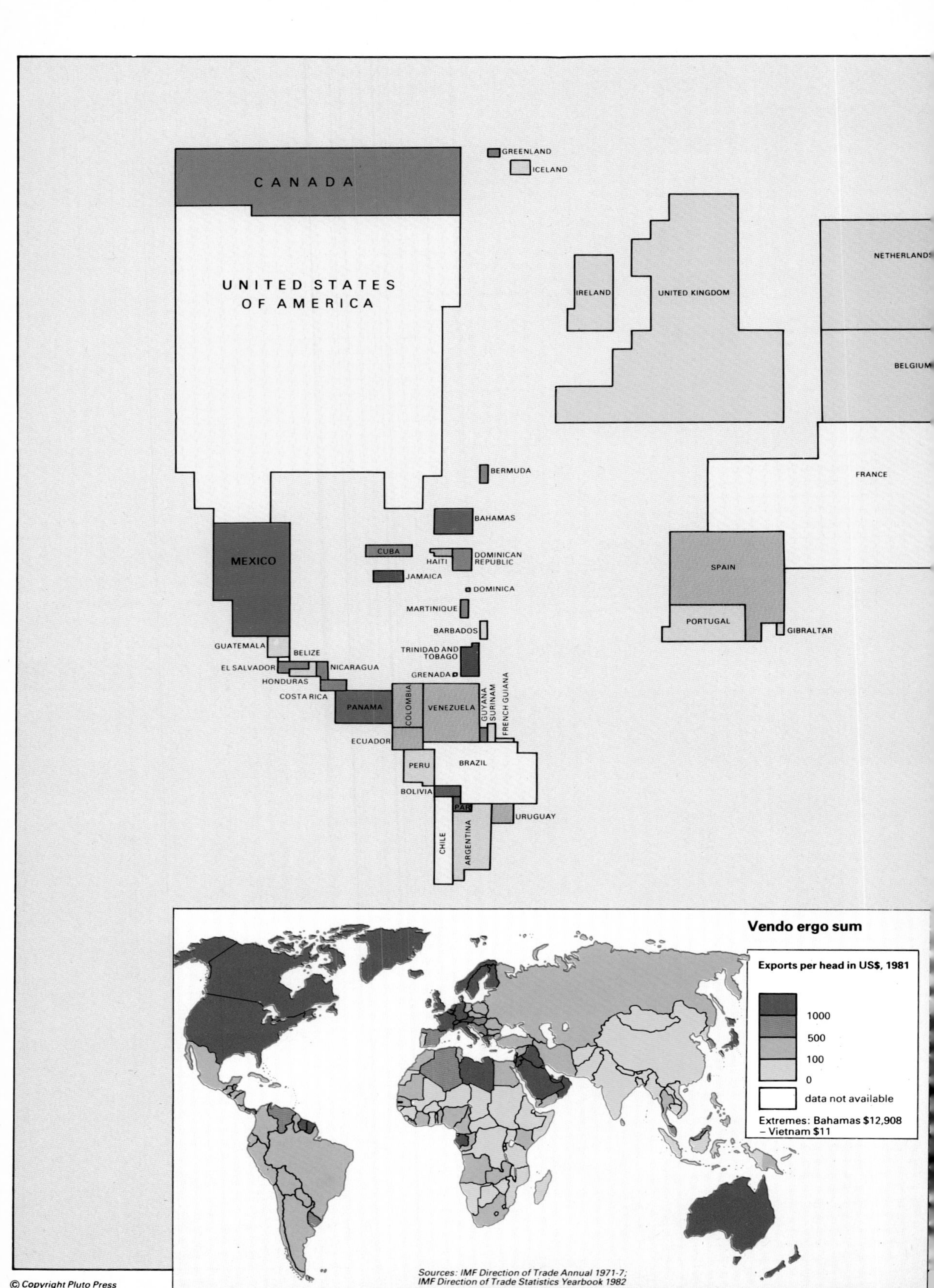
GREENLAND
ICELAND
CANADA
UNITED STATES OF AMERICA
IRELAND
UNITED KINGDOM
NETHERLANDS
BELGIUM
FRANCE
BERMUDA
BAHAMAS
CUBA
HAITI
DOMINICAN REPUBLIC
JAMAICA
MEXICO
DOMINICA
MARTINIQUE
BARBADOS
SPAIN
PORTUGAL
GIBRALTAR
GUATEMALA
BELIZE
TRINIDAD AND TOBAGO
EL SALVADOR
NICARAGUA
HONDURAS
GRENADA
COSTA RICA
PANAMA
COLOMBIA
VENEZUELA
GUYANA
SURINAM
FRENCH GUIANA
ECUADOR
PERU
BRAZIL
BOLIVIA
PAR
URUGUAY
CHILE
ARGENTINA
Vendo ergo sum
Exports per head in US$, 1981
1000
500
100
0
data not available
Extremes: Bahamas $12,908 – Vietnam $11
Sources: IMF Direction of Trade Annual 1971-7; IMF Direction of Trade Statistics Yearbook 1982

18. Trade Power

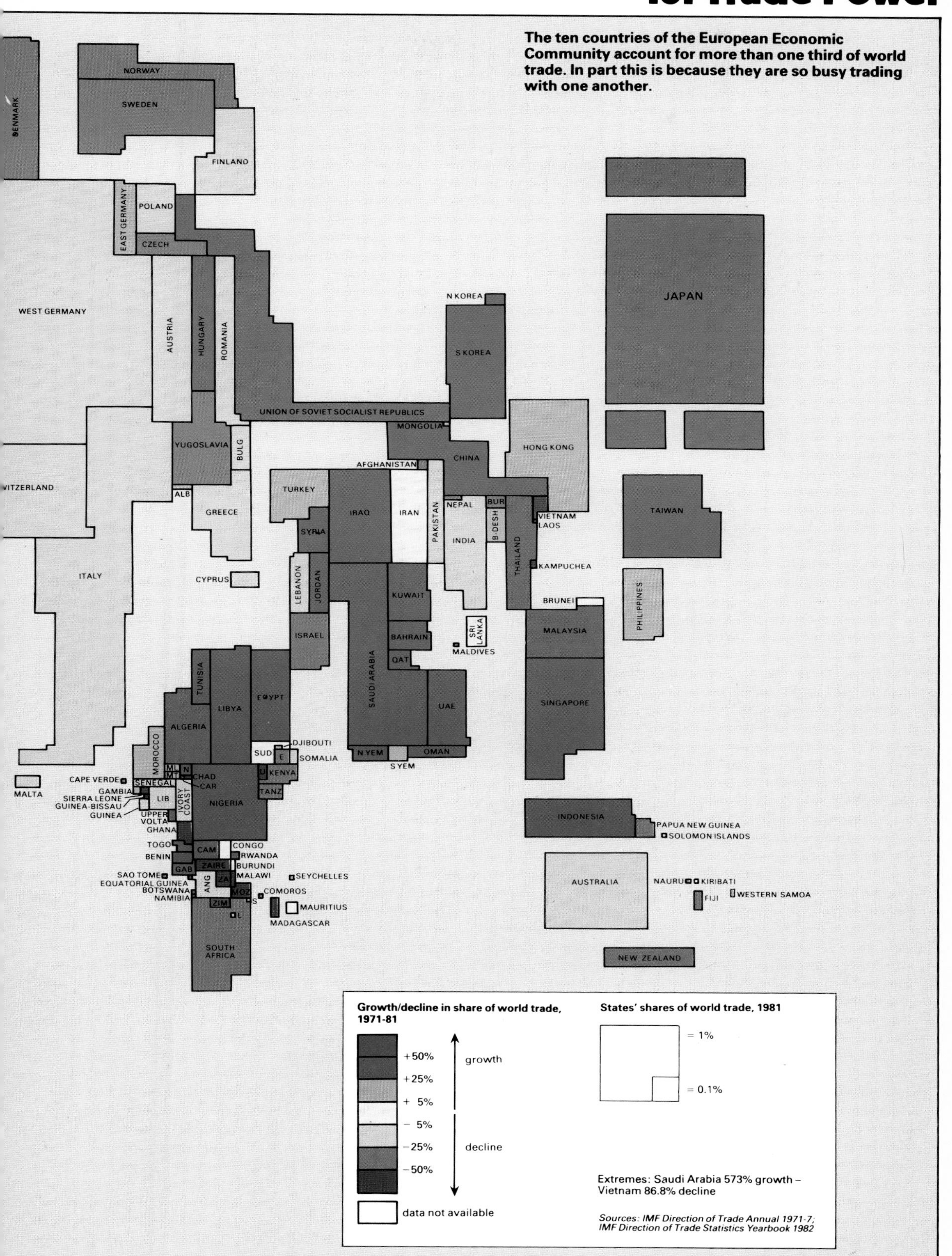

The ten countries of the European Economic Community account for more than one third of world trade. In part this is because they are so busy trading with one another.

DENMARK

NORWAY

SWEDEN

FINLAND

EAST GERMANY

POLAND

CZECH

WEST GERMANY

AUSTRIA

HUNGARY

ROMANIA

SWITZERLAND

YUGOSLAVIA

BULG

ITALY

GREECE

ALB

CYPRUS

MALTA

UNION OF SOVIET SOCIALIST REPUBLICS

N KOREA

S KOREA

JAPAN

MONGOLIA

HONG KONG

CHINA

AFGHANISTAN

TURKEY

TAIWAN

IRAQ

IRAN

NEPAL

BUR

VIETNAM

LAOS

SYRIA

PAKISTAN

INDIA

B-DESH

THAILAND

KAMPUCHEA

LEBANON

JORDAN

KUWAIT

BRUNEI

PHILIPPINES

ISRAEL

BAHRAIN

SRI LANKA

MALAYSIA

QAT

MALDIVES

TUNISIA

SAUDI ARABIA

EGYPT

UAE

SINGAPORE

LIBYA

ALGERIA

MOROCCO

DJIBOUTI

SUD

E

N YEM

OMAN

SOMALIA

S YEM

CAPE VERDE

MLI

N

CHAD

U

KENYA

INDONESIA

PAPUA NEW GUINEA

GAMBIA

SENEGAL

M

CAR

SOLOMON ISLANDS

SIERRA LEONE

LIB

TANZ

AUSTRALIA

NAURU

KIRIBATI

BENIN

ZA

RWANDA

FIJI

WESTERN SAMOA

SAO TOME

GAB

ZAIRE

BURUNDI

EQUATORIAL GUINEA

ANG

MALAWI

SEYCHELLES

BOTSWANA

COMOROS

NAMIBIA

ZIM

MOZ

S

L

MAURITIUS

MADAGASCAR

SOUTH AFRICA

NEW ZEALAND

Growth/decline in share of world trade, 1971-81

+50%

+25% growth

+ 5%

– 5%

–25% decline

–50%

data not available

States' shares of world trade, 1981

= 1%

= 0.1%

Extremes: Saudi Arabia 573% growth – Vietnam 86.8% decline

Sources: IMF Direction of Trade Annual 1971-7; IMF Direction of Trade Statistics Yearbook 1982

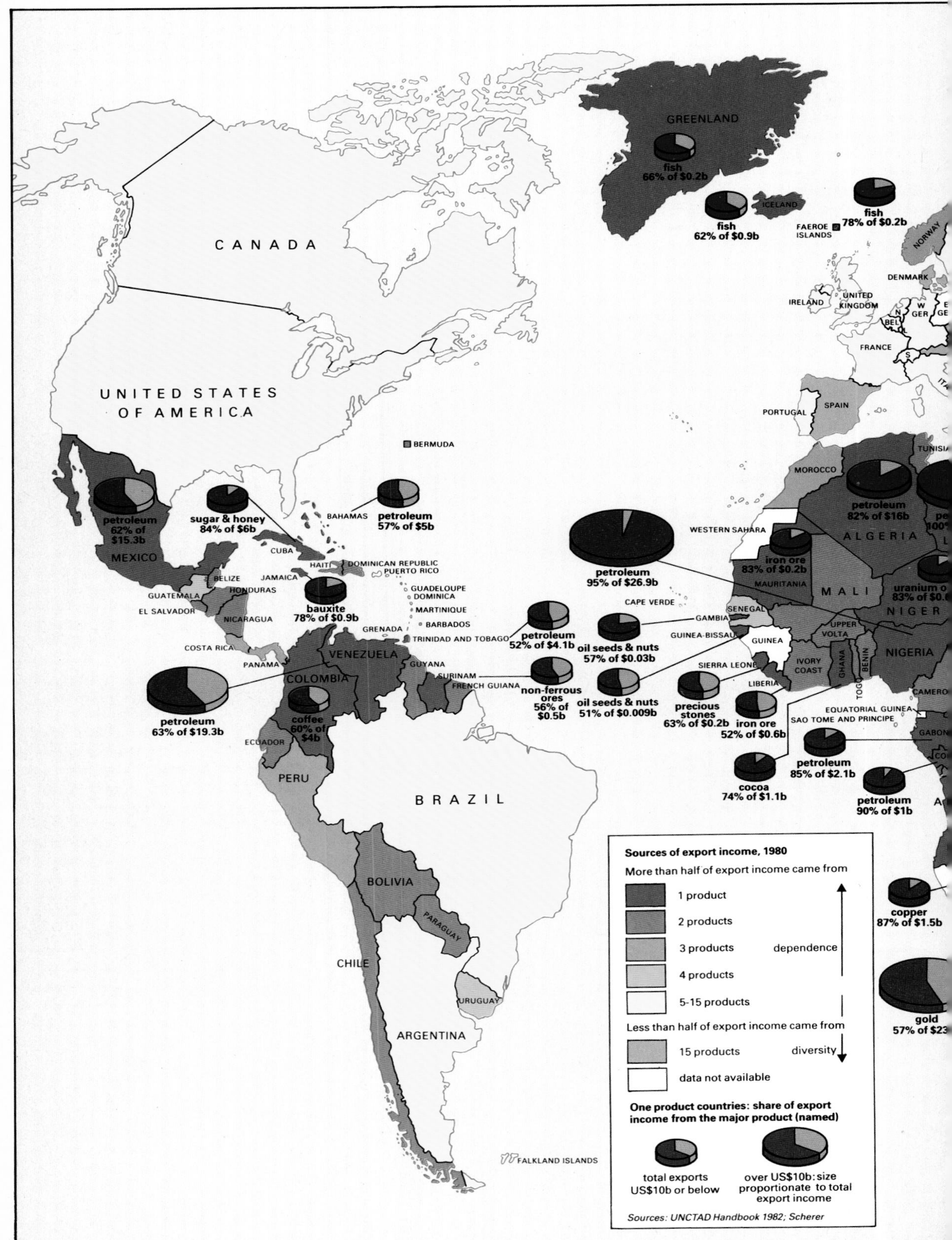
GREENLAND
fish
66% of $0.2b
ICELAND
fish
62% of $0.9b
FAEROE ISLANDS
fish
78% of $0.2b
NORWAY
DENMARK
IRELAND
UNITED KINGDOM
N
W GER
E GER
BEL
L
FRANCE
S
CANADA
UNITED STATES OF AMERICA
PORTUGAL
SPAIN
BERMUDA
TUNISIA
MOROCCO
petroleum
82% of $16b
WESTERN SAHARA
ALGERIA
MEXICO
petroleum
62% of $15.3b
sugar & honey
84% of $6b
BAHAMAS
petroleum
57% of $5b
petroleum
95% of $26.9b
iron ore
83% of $0.2b
MAURITANIA
MALI
NIGER
uranium
CUBA
HAITI
DOMINICAN REPUBLIC
PUERTO RICO
BELIZE
JAMAICA
GUATEMALA
HONDURAS
EL SALVADOR
NICARAGUA
bauxite
78% of $0.9b
GUADELOUPE
DOMINICA
MARTINIQUE
BARBADOS
GRENADA
TRINIDAD AND TOBAGO
petroleum
52% of $4.1b
CAPE VERDE
GAMBIA
SENEGAL
oil seeds & nuts
57% of $0.03b
GUINEA-BISSAU
GUINEA
UPPER VOLTA
NIGERIA
COSTA RICA
PANAMA
VENEZUELA
GUYANA
SURINAM
FRENCH GUIANA
COLOMBIA
petroleum
63% of $19.3b
coffee
60% of $4b
non-ferrous ores
56% of $0.5b
oil seeds & nuts
51% of $0.009b
SIERRA LEONE
precious stones
63% of $0.2b
LIBERIA
iron ore
52% of $0.6b
IVORY COAST
GHANA
TOGO
BENIN
CAMEROON
EQUATORIAL GUINEA
SAO TOME AND PRINCIPE
GABON
ECUADOR
PERU
BRAZIL
cocoa
74% of $1.1b
petroleum
85% of $2.1b
petroleum
90% of $1b
BOLIVIA
PARAGUAY
CHILE
URUGUAY
ARGENTINA
FALKLAND ISLANDS
copper
87% of $1.5b
gold
57% of $23
Sources of export income, 1980
More than half of export income came from
1 product
2 products
3 products
4 products
5-15 products
dependence
Less than half of export income came from
15 products
diversity
data not available
One product countries: share of export income from the major product (named)
total exports US$10b or below
over US$10b: size proportionate to total export income
Sources: UNCTAD Handbook 1982; Scherer

19. Dependence and Diversity

Sixty states depend essentially on a single product for their export income. For more than a third of them that product is oil.

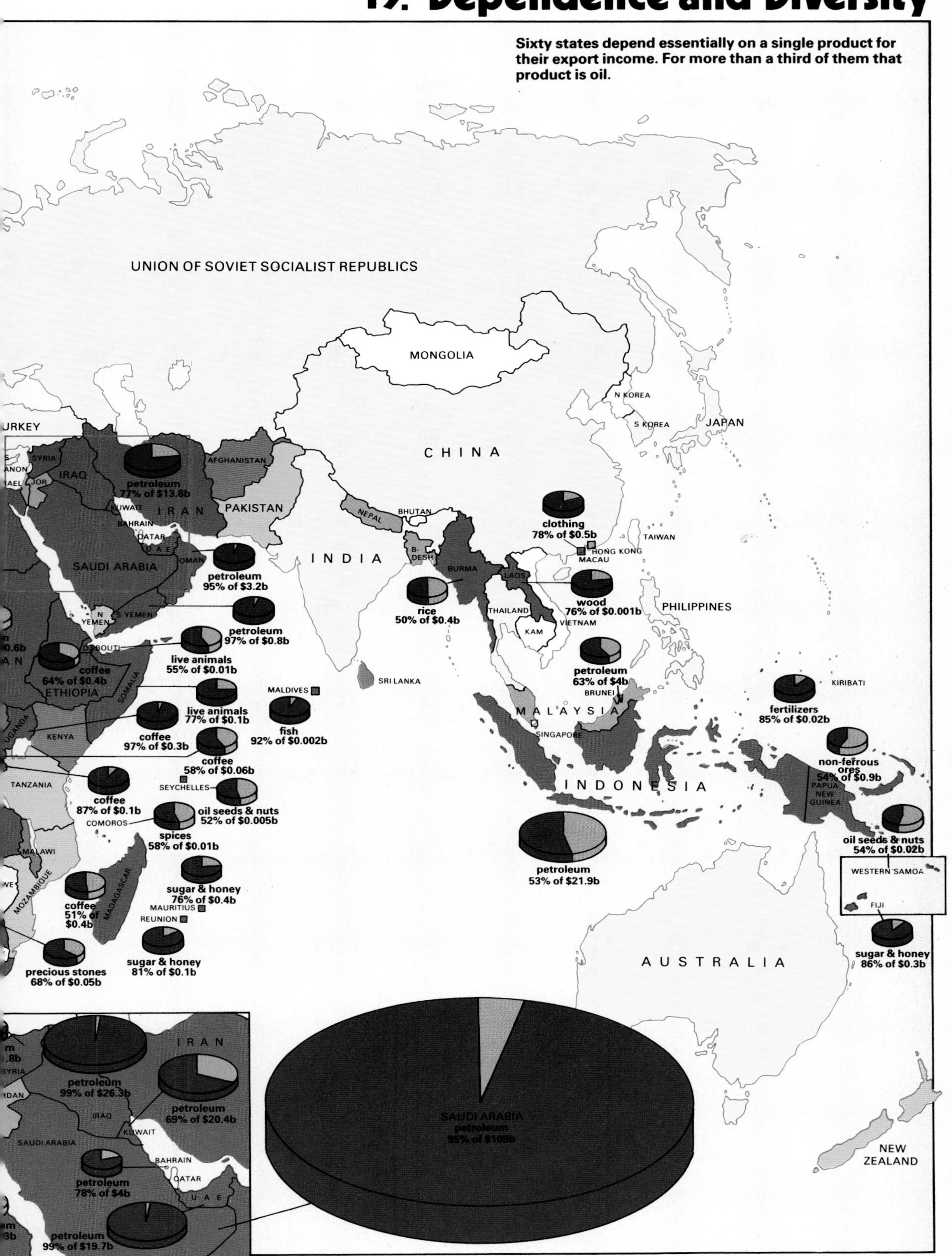

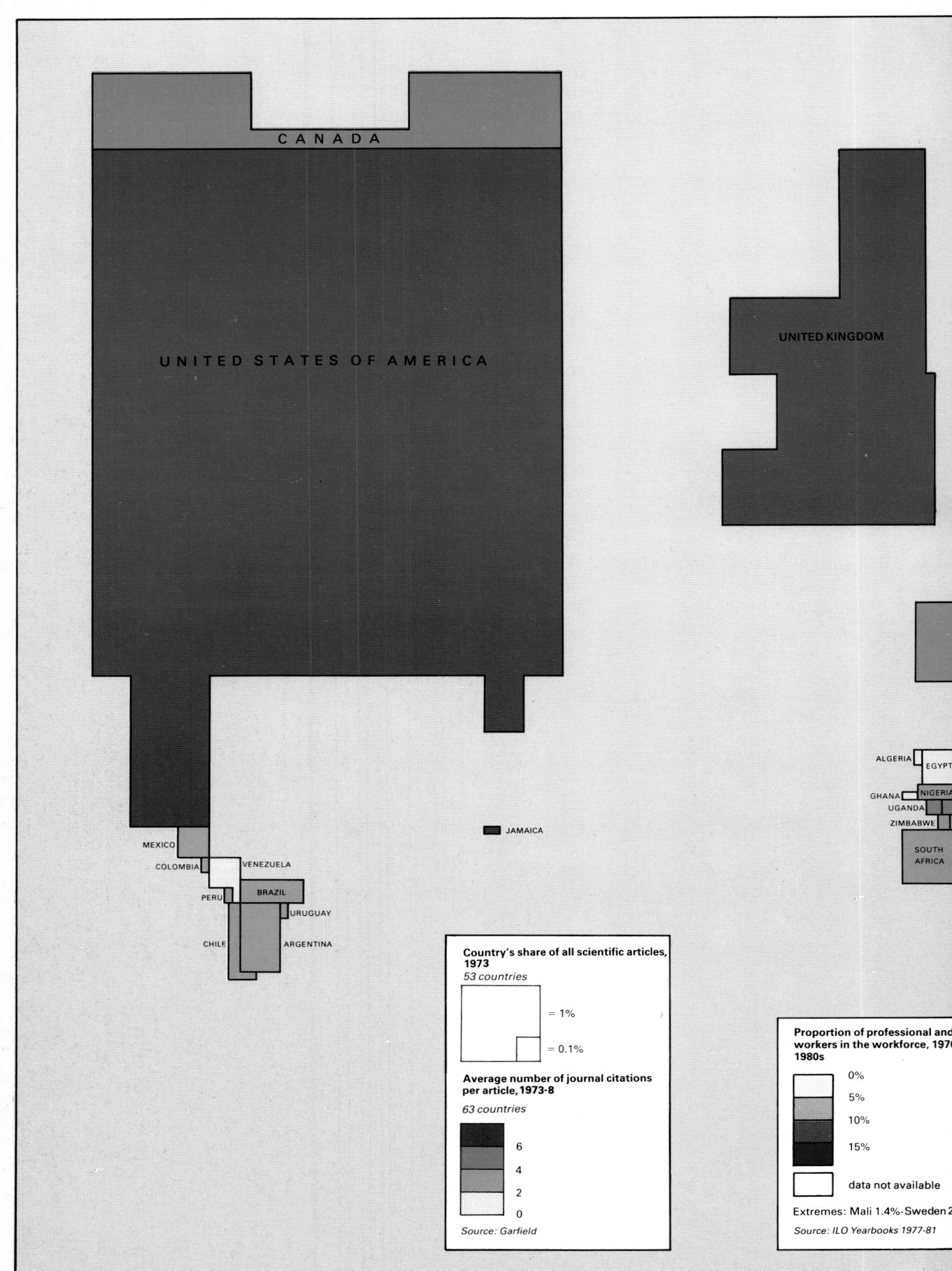

CANADA
UNITED STATES OF AMERICA
UNITED KINGDOM
JAMAICA
MEXICO
COLOMBIA
VENEZUELA
PERU
BRAZIL
URUGUAY
CHILE
ARGENTINA
ALGERIA
EGYPT
GHANA
NIGERIA
UGANDA
ZIMBABWE
SOUTH AFRICA
Country's share of all scientific articles, 1973
53 countries
= 1%
= 0.1%
Average number of journal citations per article, 1973-8
63 countries
6
4
2
0
Source: Garfield
Proportion of professional and
workers in the workforce, 1970
1980s
0%
5%
10%
15%
data not available
Extremes: Mali 1.4%-Sweden 2
Source: ILO Yearbooks 1977-81

20. Science Power

Science is fashioned in very tew countries, and scientific fashions are disseminated by a handful of journals, 80 of which account for one quarter of all citations in science journals.

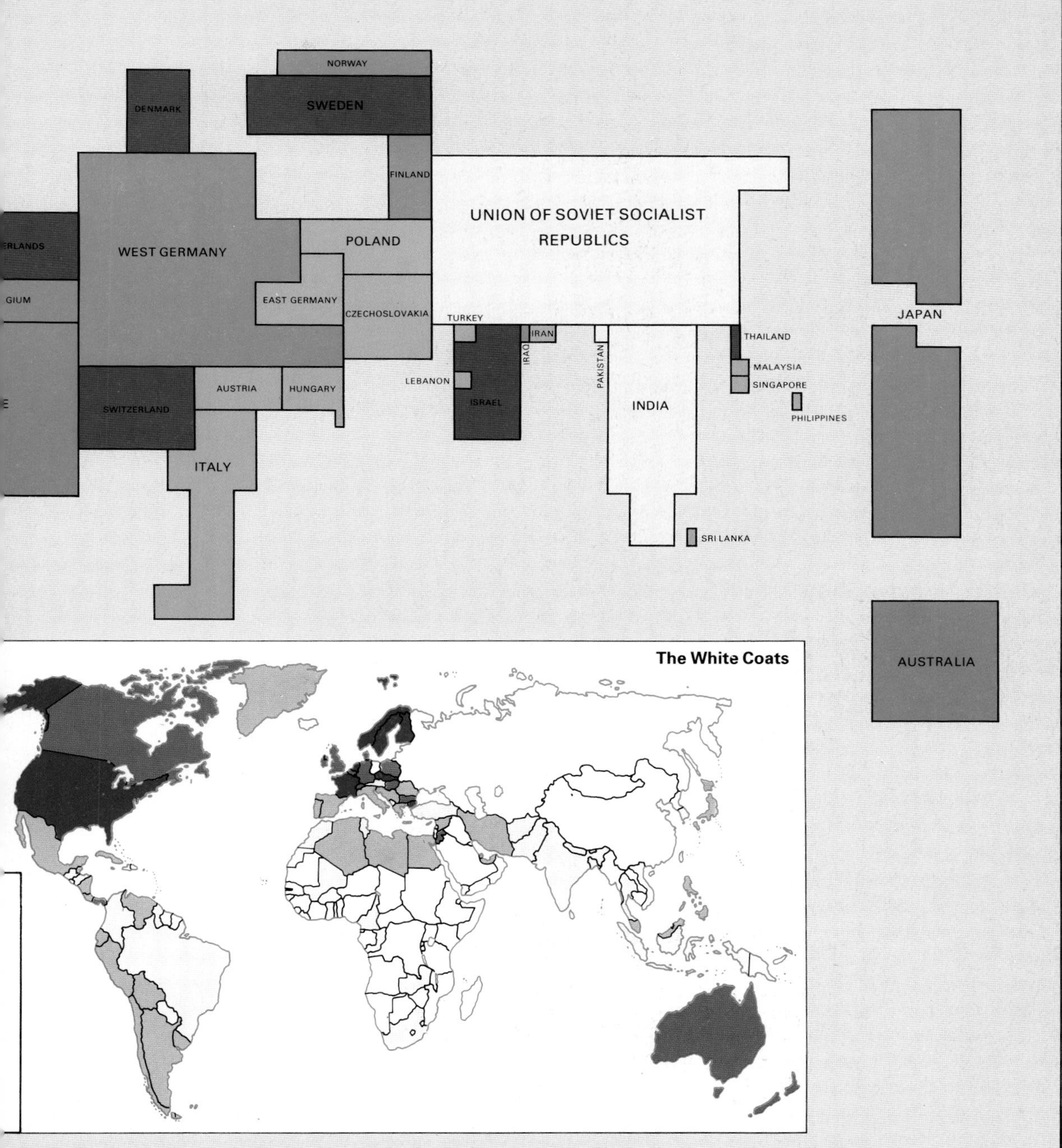

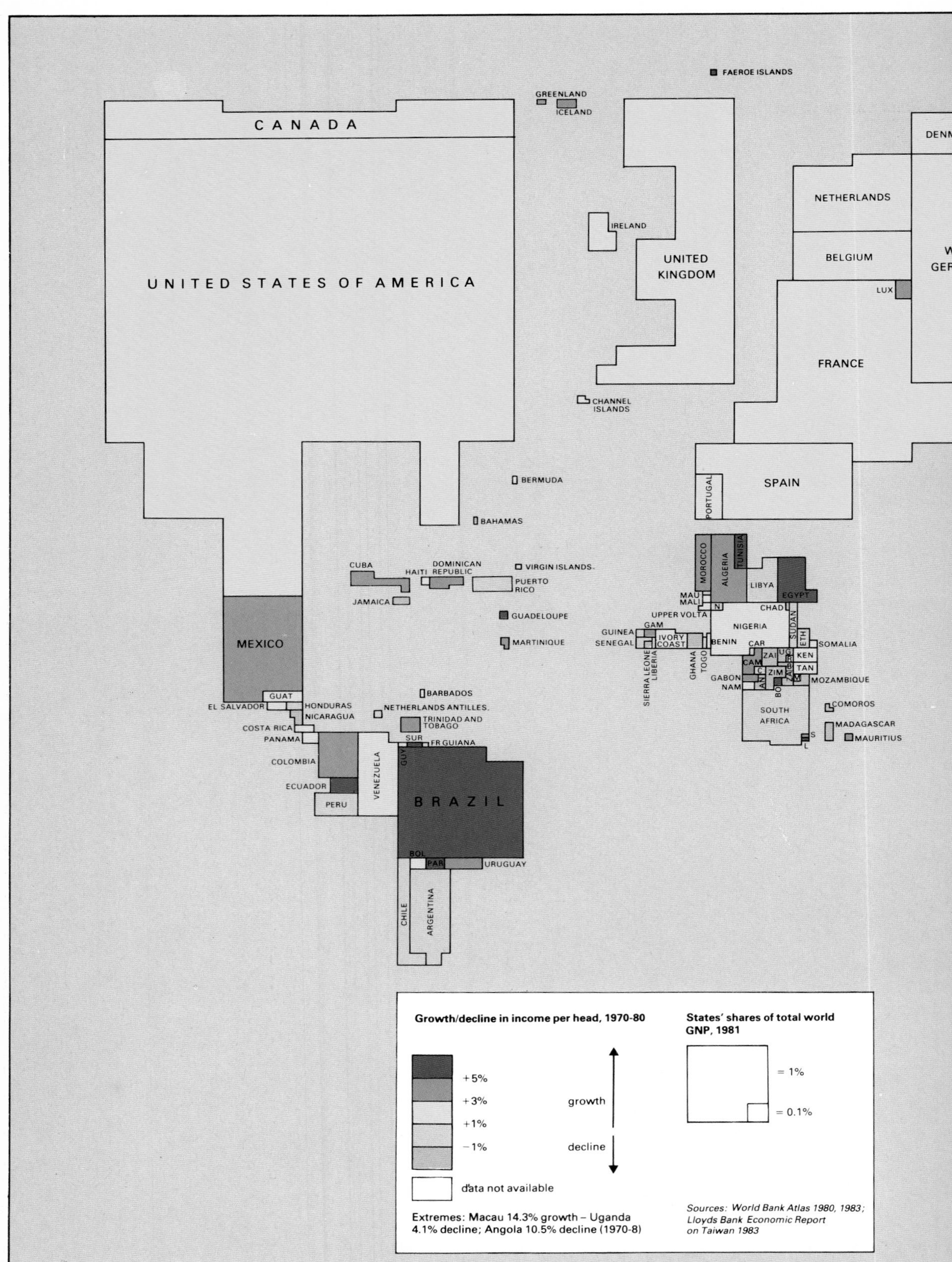
FAEROE ISLANDS
GREENLAND
ICELAND
CANADA
UNITED STATES OF AMERICA
IRELAND
UNITED KINGDOM
CHANNEL ISLANDS
NETHERLANDS
BELGIUM
LUX
FRANCE
SPAIN
PORTUGAL
BERMUDA
BAHAMAS
CUBA
HAITI
DOMINICAN REPUBLIC
VIRGIN ISLANDS
PUERTO RICO
JAMAICA
GUADELOUPE
MARTINIQUE
MEXICO
GUAT
EL SALVADOR
HONDURAS
NICARAGUA
COSTA RICA
PANAMA
BARBADOS
NETHERLANDS ANTILLES
TRINIDAD AND TOBAGO
SUR
FR GUIANA
GUY
COLOMBIA
VENEZUELA
ECUADOR
PERU
BRAZIL
BOL
PAR
URUGUAY
CHILE
ARGENTINA
MOROCCO
ALGERIA
TUNISIA
LIBYA
EGYPT
MAU
MALI
N
CHAD
SUDAN
UPPER VOLTA
GAM
GUINEA
SENEGAL
IVORY COAST
NIGERIA
BENIN
ETH
SOMALIA
CAR
SIERRA LEONE
LIBERIA
GHANA
TOGO
CAM
ZAI
UG
KEN
TAN
GABON
NAM
ZIM
M
MOZAMBIQUE
BO
SOUTH AFRICA
COMOROS
MADAGASCAR
MAURITIUS
S
L
Growth/decline in income per head, 1970-80
+5%
+3%
+1%
−1%
growth
decline
data not available
Extremes: Macau 14.3% growth – Uganda 4.1% decline; Angola 10.5% decline (1970-8)
States' shares of total world GNP, 1981
= 1%
= 0.1%
Sources: World Bank Atlas 1980, 1983; Lloyds Bank Economic Report on Taiwan 1983

21. National Income

The annual income of the USA (230 million people) is more or less equal to the total income of all Asia, Africa and South America (more than 100 states and over 3,000 million people).

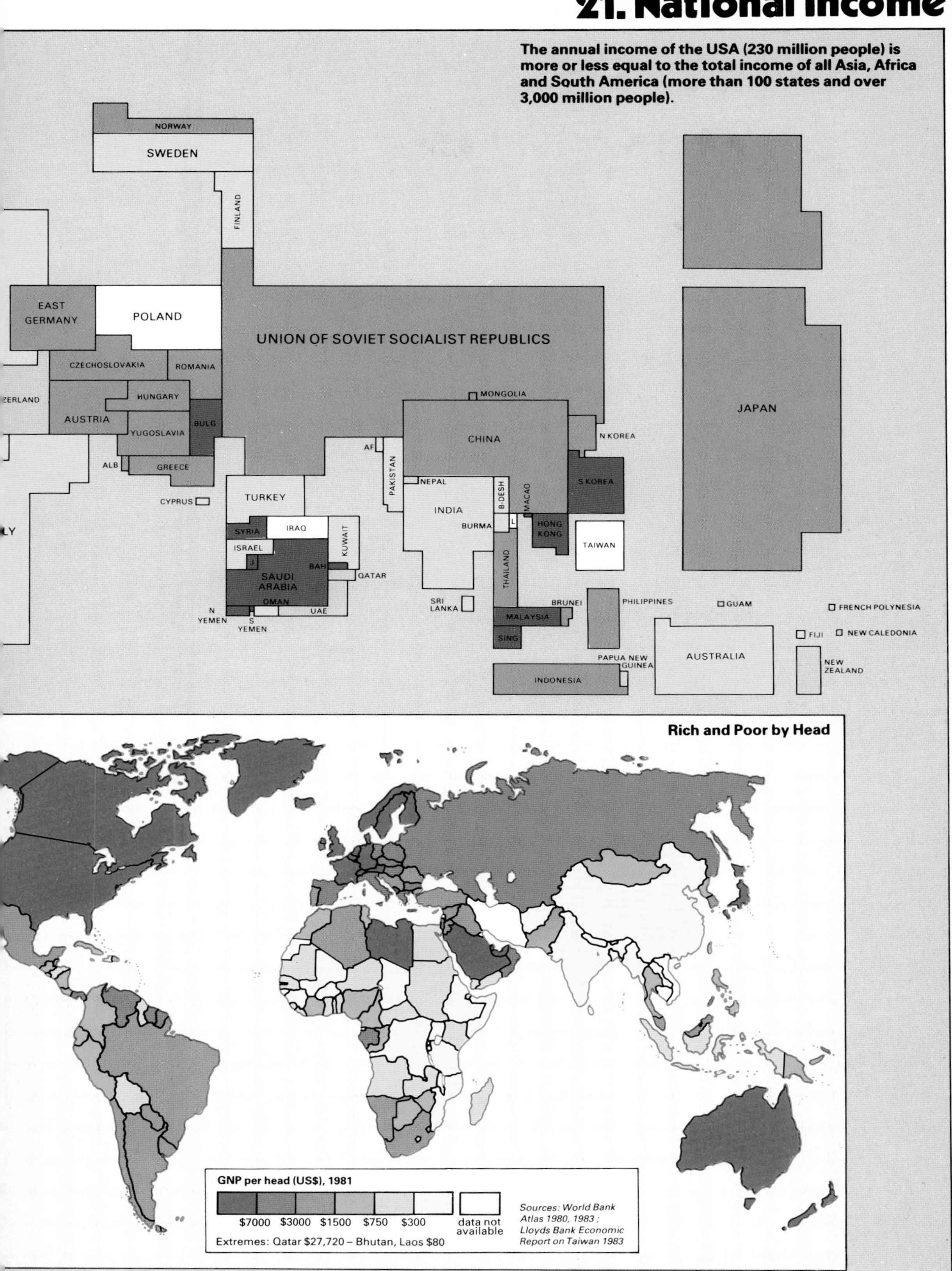

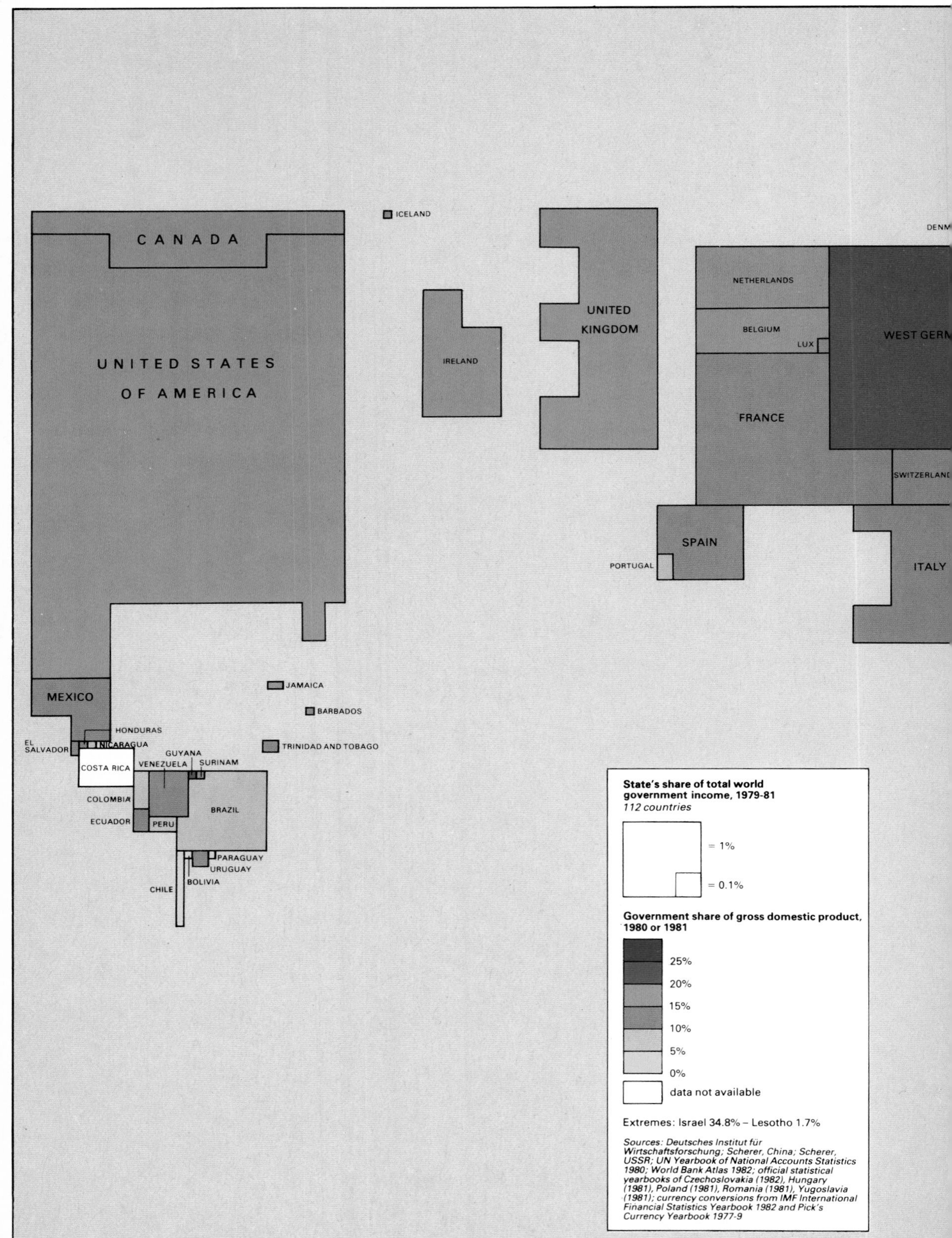

CANADA
UNITED STATES OF AMERICA
ICELAND
IRELAND
UNITED KINGDOM
DENM
NETHERLANDS
BELGIUM
LUX
WEST GERM
FRANCE
SWITZERLAND
SPAIN
PORTUGAL
ITALY
MEXICO
JAMAICA
BARBADOS
TRINIDAD AND TOBAGO
HONDURAS
EL SALVADOR
NICARAGUA
GUYANA
COSTA RICA
VENEZUELA
SURINAM
COLOMBIA
BRAZIL
ECUADOR
PERU
PARAGUAY
URUGUAY
BOLIVIA
CHILE
State's share of total world government income, 1979-81
112 countries
= 1%
= 0.1%
Government share of gross domestic product, 1980 or 1981
25%
20%
15%
10%
5%
0%
data not available
Extremes: Israel 34.8% – Lesotho 1.7%
Sources: Deutsches Institut für Wirtschaftsforschung; Scherer, China; Scherer, USSR; UN Yearbook of National Accounts Statistics 1980; World Bank Atlas 1982; official statistical yearbooks of Czechoslovakia (1982), Hungary (1981), Poland (1981), Romania (1981), Yugoslavia (1981); currency conversions from IMF International Financial Statistics Yearbook 1982 and Pick's Currency Yearbook 1977-9

22. The First Slice of the Cake

A government's wealth does not necessarily reflect the wealth of the people it rules.

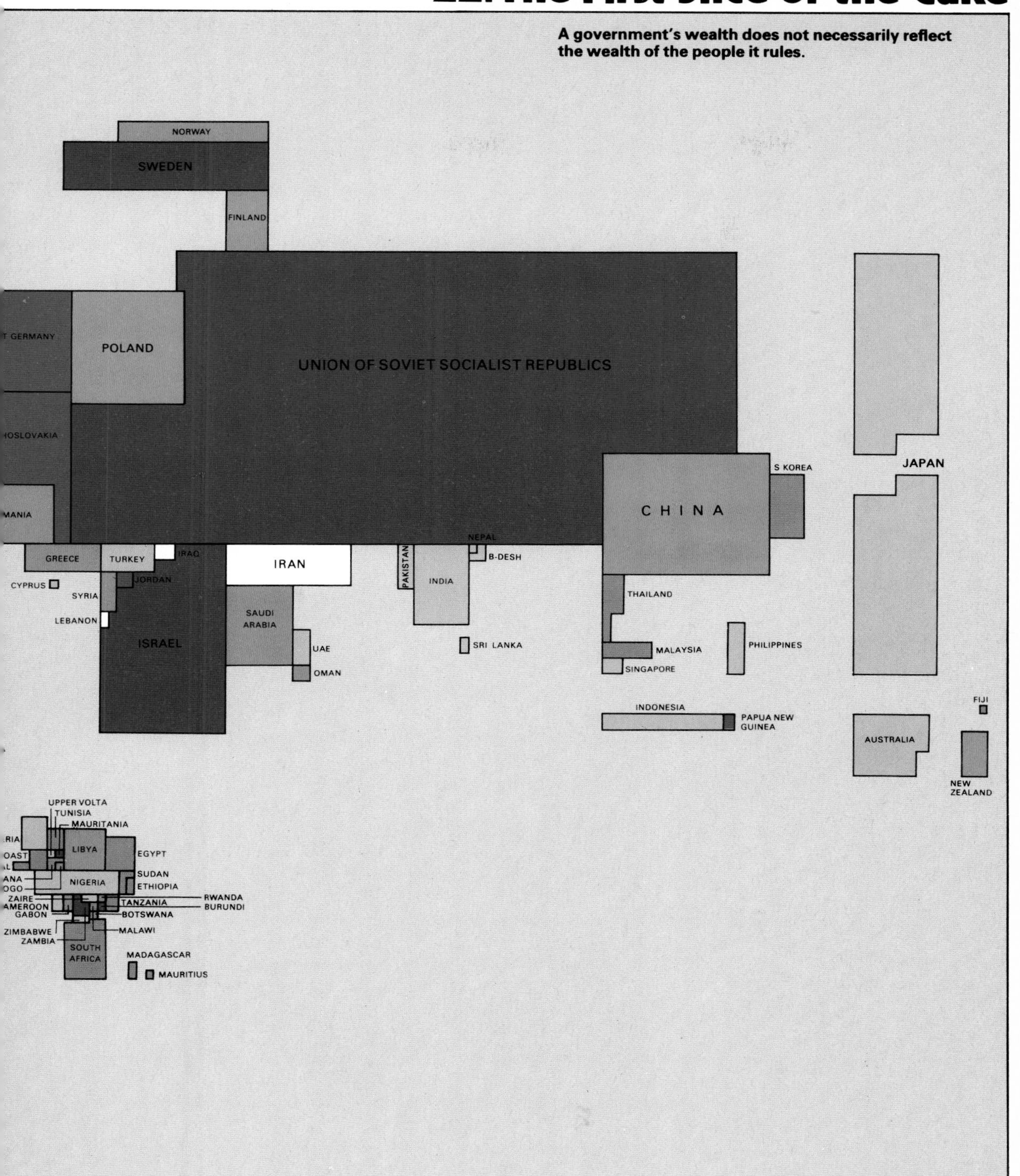

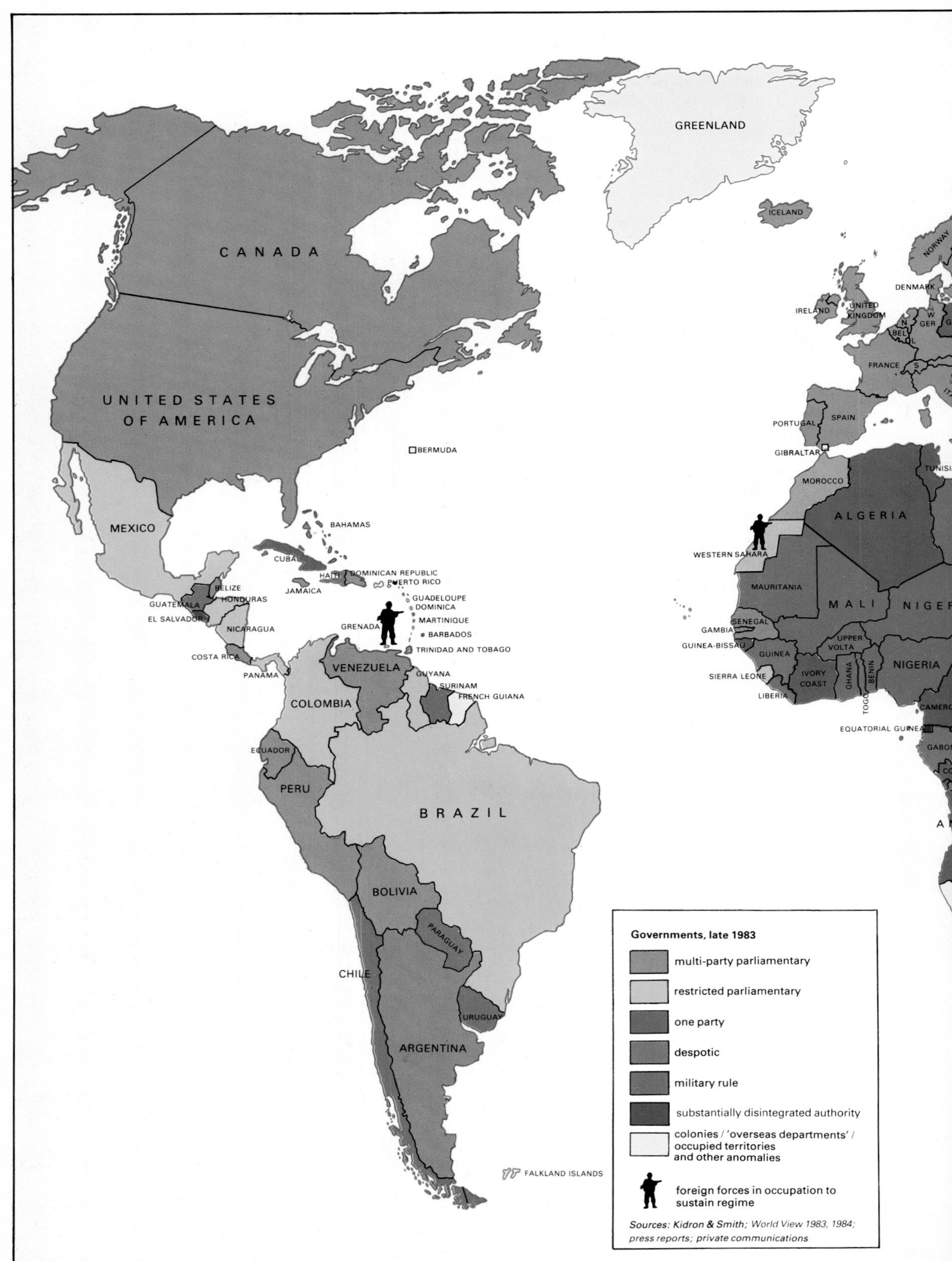

GREENLAND
ICELAND
CANADA
UNITED STATES OF AMERICA
NORWAY
DENMARK
IRELAND
UNITED KINGDOM
N
BEL
L
W GER
FRANCE
S
PORTUGAL
SPAIN
GIBRALTAR
MOROCCO
ALGERIA
WESTERN SAHARA
MAURITANIA
MALI
SENEGAL
GAMBIA
GUINEA-BISSAU
GUINEA
SIERRA LEONE
LIBERIA
IVORY COAST
UPPER VOLTA
GHANA
TOGO
BENIN
NIGERIA
EQUATORIAL GUINEA
BERMUDA
BAHAMAS
CUBA
HAITI
DOMINICAN REPUBLIC
PUERTO RICO
JAMAICA
MEXICO
BELIZE
GUATEMALA
HONDURAS
EL SALVADOR
NICARAGUA
COSTA RICA
PANAMA
GRENADA
GUADELOUPE
DOMINICA
MARTINIQUE
BARBADOS
TRINIDAD AND TOBAGO
VENEZUELA
GUYANA
SURINAM
FRENCH GUIANA
COLOMBIA
ECUADOR
PERU
BRAZIL
BOLIVIA
PARAGUAY
CHILE
URUGUAY
ARGENTINA
FALKLAND ISLANDS
Governments, late 1983
multi-party parliamentary
restricted parliamentary
one party
despotic
military rule
substantially disintegrated authority
colonies / 'overseas departments' / occupied territories and other anomalies
foreign forces in occupation to sustain regime
Sources: Kidron & Smith; World View 1983, 1984; press reports; private communications

23. Complexions of Government

However different governments may be, all are ultimately concerned with the control of the many by the few. In this respect, governments have more in common with one another than with their own citizens.

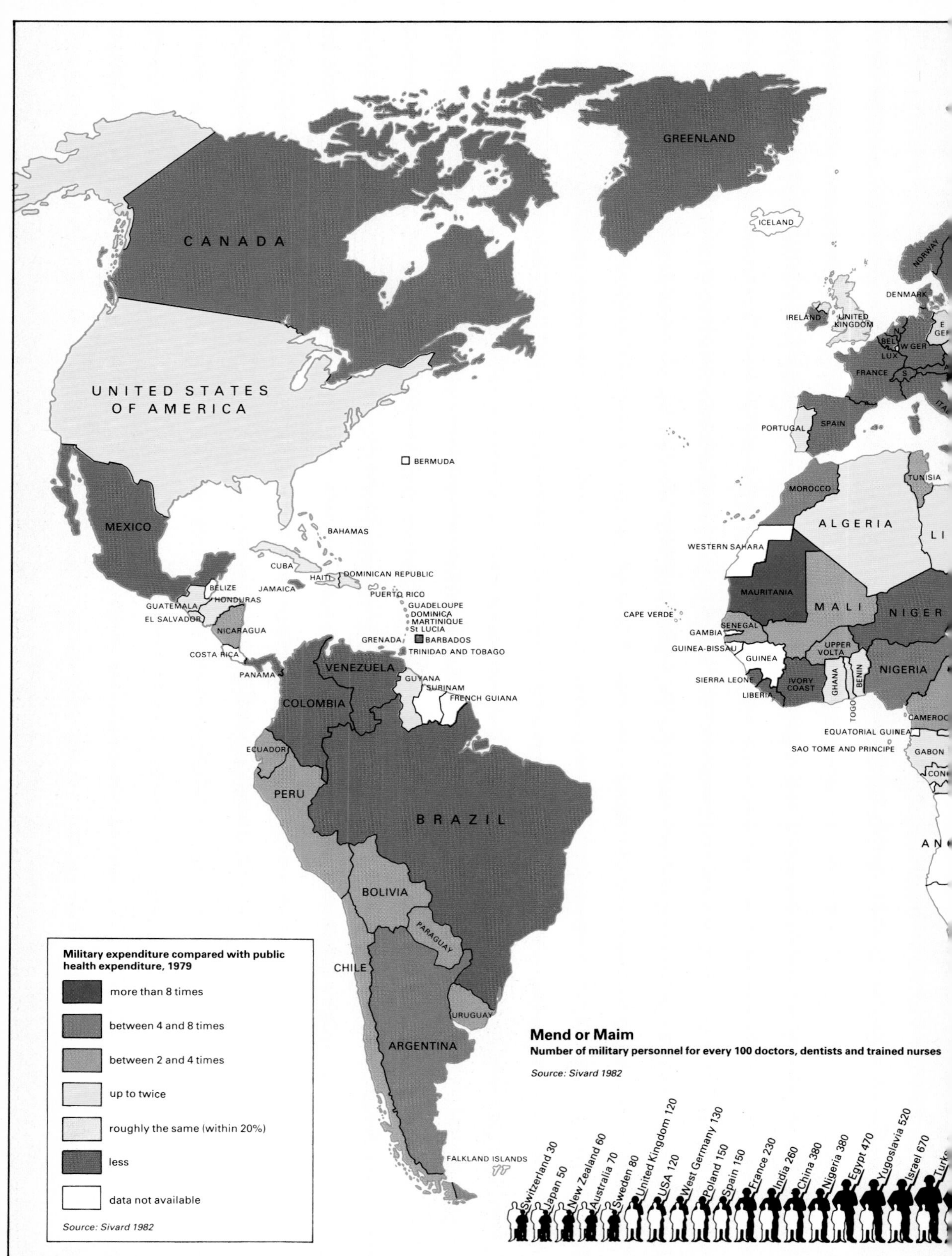

GREENLAND
ICELAND
CANADA
UNITED STATES OF AMERICA
MEXICO
BERMUDA
BAHAMAS
CUBA
HAITI
DOMINICAN REPUBLIC
JAMAICA
BELIZE
HONDURAS
GUATEMALA
EL SALVADOR
NICARAGUA
COSTA RICA
PANAMA
PUERTO RICO
GUADELOUPE
DOMINICA
MARTINIQUE
St LUCIA
GRENADA
BARBADOS
TRINIDAD AND TOBAGO
VENEZUELA
GUYANA
SURINAM
FRENCH GUIANA
COLOMBIA
ECUADOR
PERU
BRAZIL
BOLIVIA
PARAGUAY
CHILE
URUGUAY
ARGENTINA
FALKLAND ISLANDS
NORWAY
DENMARK
IRELAND
UNITED KINGDOM
BEL
LUX
W GER
FRANCE
PORTUGAL
SPAIN
MOROCCO
TUNISIA
ALGERIA
WESTERN SAHARA
MAURITANIA
MALI
NIGER
CAPE VERDE
SENEGAL
GAMBIA
GUINEA-BISSAU
GUINEA
UPPER VOLTA
SIERRA LEONE
LIBERIA
IVORY COAST
GHANA
TOGO
BENIN
NIGERIA
EQUATORIAL GUINEA
SAO TOME AND PRINCIPE
GABON
Military expenditure compared with public health expenditure, 1979
more than 8 times
between 4 and 8 times
between 2 and 4 times
up to twice
roughly the same (within 20%)
less
data not available
Source: Sivard 1982
Mend or Maim
Number of military personnel for every 100 doctors, dentists and trained nurses
Source: Sivard 1982
Switzerland 30
Japan 50
New Zealand 60
Australia 70
Sweden 80
United Kingdom 120
USA 120
West Germany 130
Poland 150
Spain 150
France 230
India 260
China 380
Nigeria 380
Egypt 470
Yugoslavia 520
Israel 670

24. Harmworkers and Healthworkers

There are two-and-a-half times as many military people as health workers in the world; and over a quarter more is spent on supplying them than on health care.

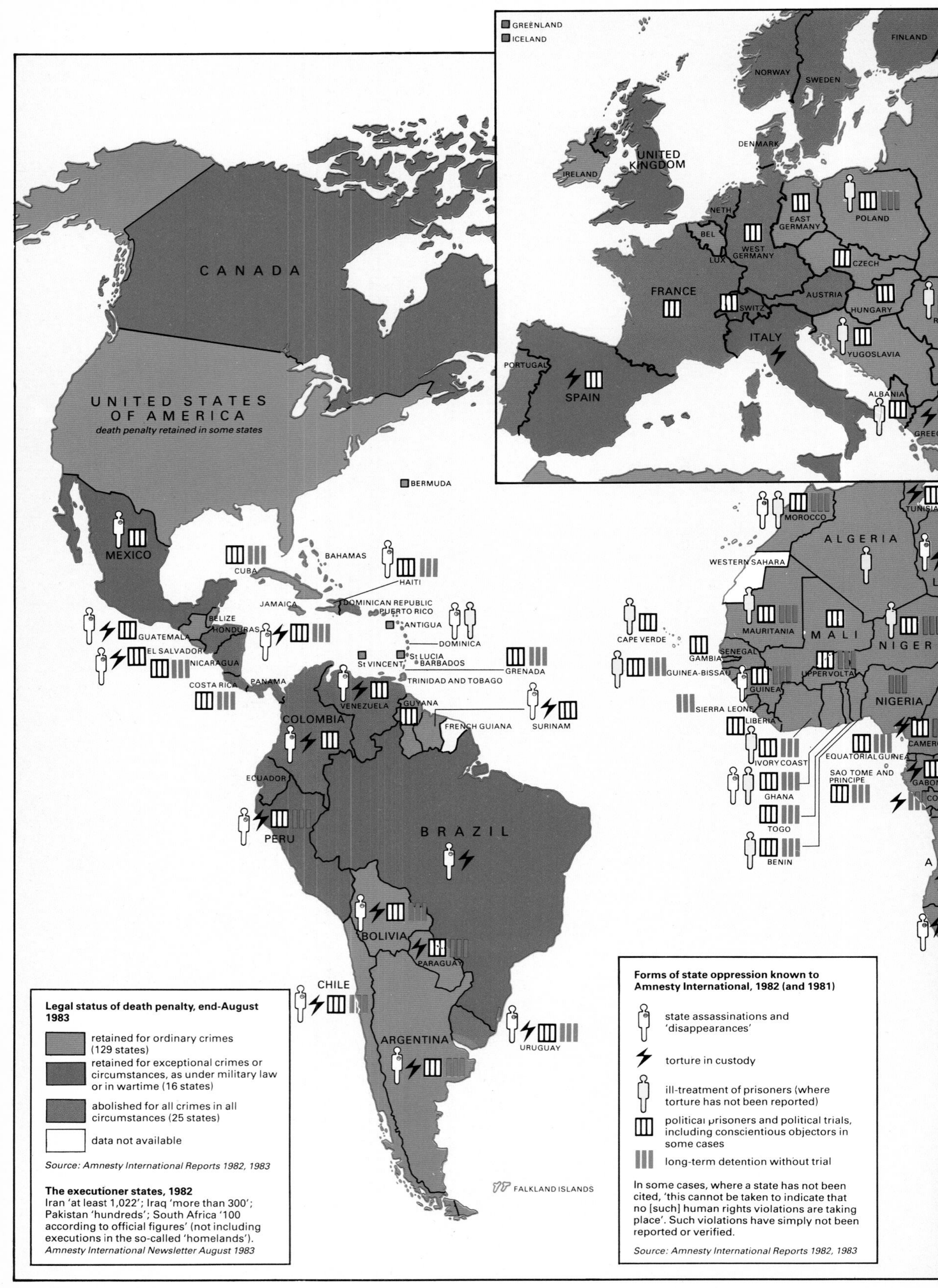
GREENLAND
ICELAND
FINLAND
NORWAY
SWEDEN
DENMARK
UNITED KINGDOM
IRELAND
NETH
BEL
LUX
EAST GERMANY
POLAND
WEST GERMANY
CZECH
FRANCE
AUSTRIA
HUNGARY
SWITZ
ITALY
YUGOSLAVIA
PORTUGAL
SPAIN
ALBANIA
CANADA
UNITED STATES OF AMERICA
death penalty retained in some states
BERMUDA
MEXICO
CUBA
BAHAMAS
HAITI
JAMAICA
DOMINICAN REPUBLIC
PUERTO RICO
ANTIGUA
DOMINICA
St LUCIA
BARBADOS
St VINCENT
GRENADA
TRINIDAD AND TOBAGO
BELIZE
HONDURAS
GUATEMALA
EL SALVADOR
NICARAGUA
COSTA RICA
PANAMA
VENEZUELA
GUYANA
SURINAM
FRENCH GUIANA
COLOMBIA
ECUADOR
PERU
BRAZIL
BOLIVIA
PARAGUAY
CHILE
URUGUAY
ARGENTINA
FALKLAND ISLANDS
MOROCCO
TUNISIA
ALGERIA
WESTERN SAHARA
CAPE VERDE
MAURITANIA
MALI
NIGER
GAMBIA
SENEGAL
GUINEA-BISSAU
UPPER VOLTA
GUINEA
NIGERIA
SIERRA LEONE
LIBERIA
IVORY COAST
GHANA
TOGO
BENIN
EQUATORIAL GUINEA
SAO TOME AND PRINCIPE
GABON
Legal status of death penalty, end-August 1983
retained for ordinary crimes (129 states)
retained for exceptional crimes or circumstances, as under military law or in wartime (16 states)
abolished for all crimes in all circumstances (25 states)
data not available
Source: Amnesty International Reports 1982, 1983
The executioner states, 1982
Iran 'at least 1,022'; Iraq 'more than 300'; Pakistan 'hundreds'; South Africa '100 according to official figures' (not including executions in the so-called 'homelands').
Amnesty International Newsletter August 1983
Forms of state oppression known to Amnesty International, 1982 (and 1981)
state assassinations and 'disappearances'
torture in custody
ill-treatment of prisoners (where torture has not been reported)
political prisoners and political trials, including conscientious objectors in some cases
long-term detention without trial
In some cases, where a state has not been cited, 'this cannot be taken to indicate that no [such] human rights violations are taking place'. Such violations have simply not been reported or verified.
Source: Amnesty International Reports 1982, 1983

25. Scourges of the State

All states are armed against their citizens. Many states use exceptional methods to terrorize them.

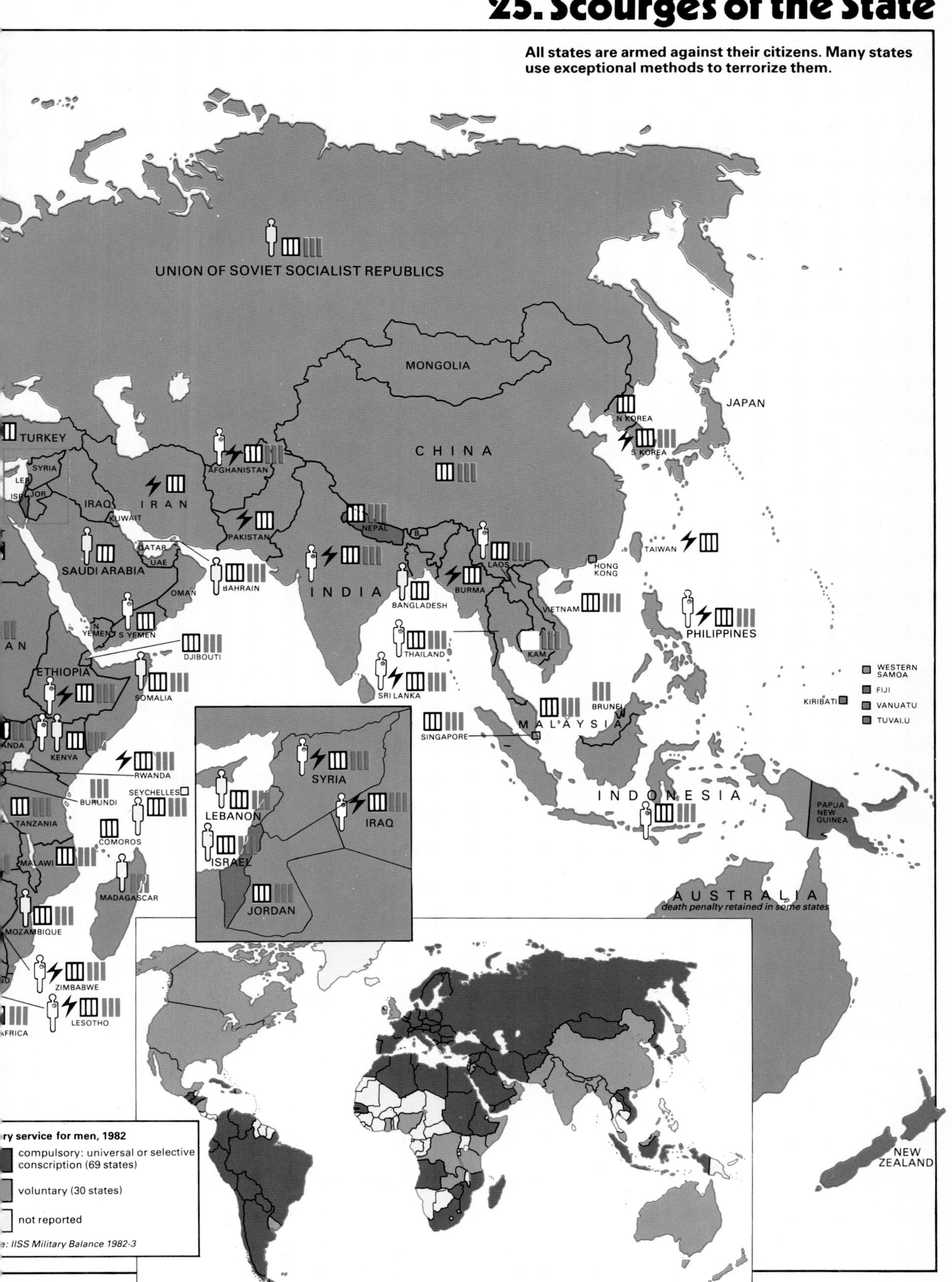

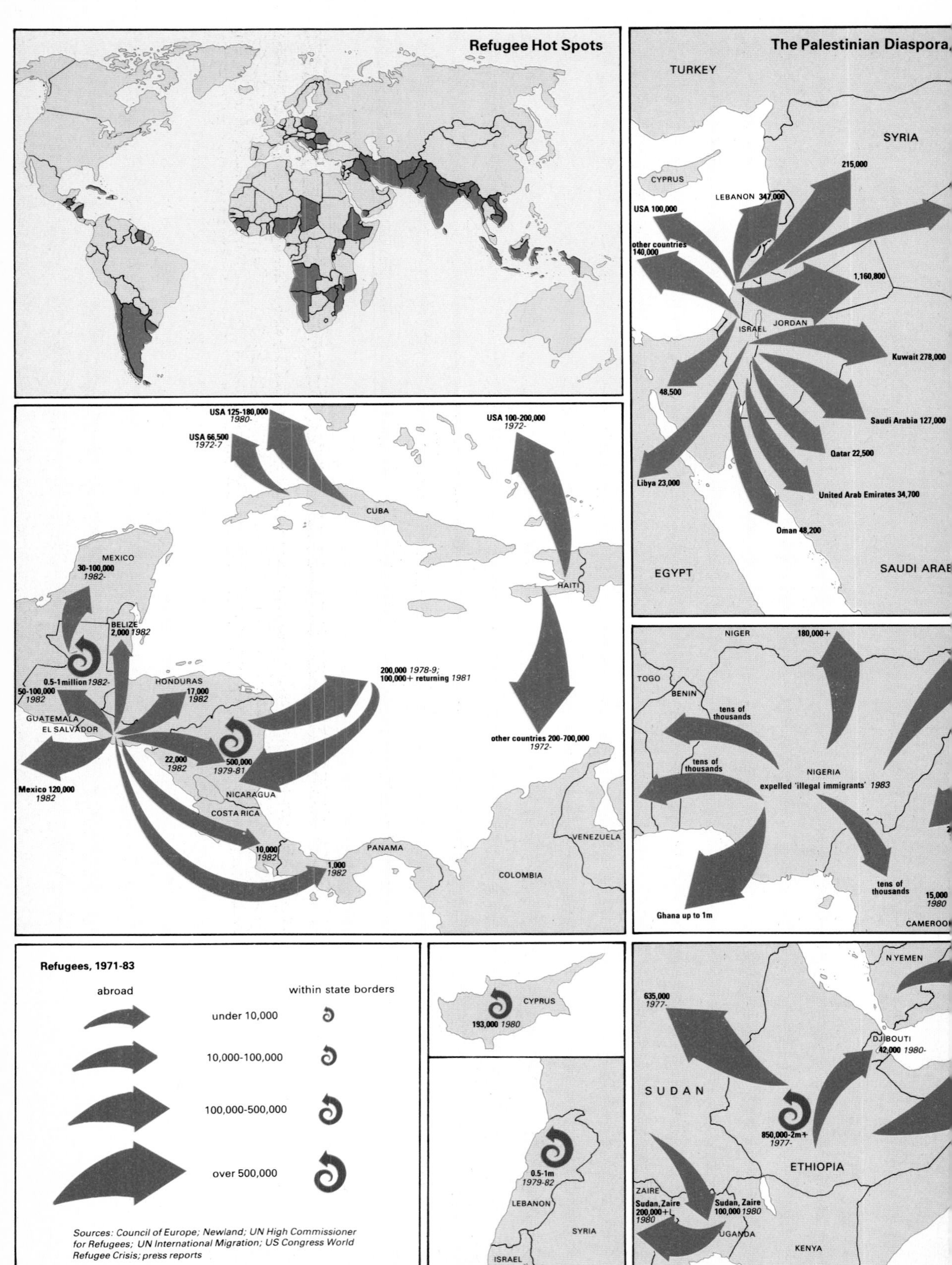
Refugee Hot Spots
The Palestinian Diaspora,
TURKEY
SYRIA
CYPRUS
LEBANON 347,000
215,000
USA 100,000
other countries 140,000
1,160,800
ISRAEL
JORDAN
Kuwait 278,000
48,500
Saudi Arabia 127,000
Qatar 22,500
Libya 23,000
United Arab Emirates 34,700
Oman 48,200
EGYPT
USA 125-180,000 1980-
USA 66,500 1972-7
USA 100-200,000 1972-
CUBA
MEXICO
30-100,000 1982-
HAITI
BELIZE 2,000 1982
0.5-1 million 1982-
50-100,000 1982
HONDURAS
17,000 1982
200,000 1978-9; 100,000+ returning 1981
GUATEMALA
EL SALVADOR
other countries 200-700,000 1972-
22,000 1982
500,000 1979-81
Mexico 120,000 1982
NICARAGUA
COSTA RICA
10,000 1982
PANAMA
1,000 1982
VENEZUELA
COLOMBIA
NIGER
180,000+
TOGO
BENIN
tens of thousands
tens of thousands
NIGERIA
expelled 'illegal immigrants' 1983
tens of thousands
15,000 1980
Ghana up to 1m
Refugees, 1971-83
abroad
within state borders
under 10,000
10,000-100,000
100,000-500,000
over 500,000
Sources: Council of Europe; Newland; UN High Commissioner for Refugees; UN International Migration; US Congress World Refugee Crisis; press reports
CYPRUS
193,000 1980
0.5-1m 1979-82
LEBANON
SYRIA
ISRAEL
N YEMEN
635,000 1977-
DJIBOUTI
42,000 1980-
SUDAN
850,000-2m+ 1977-
ETHIOPIA
ZAIRE
Sudan, Zaire 200,000+ 1980
Sudan, Zaire 100,000 1980
UGANDA
KENYA

26. A Sort of Survival

The world refugee population at the start of 1981 was conservatively estimated at some 14 million people. About 200 private agencies operate assistance programmes.

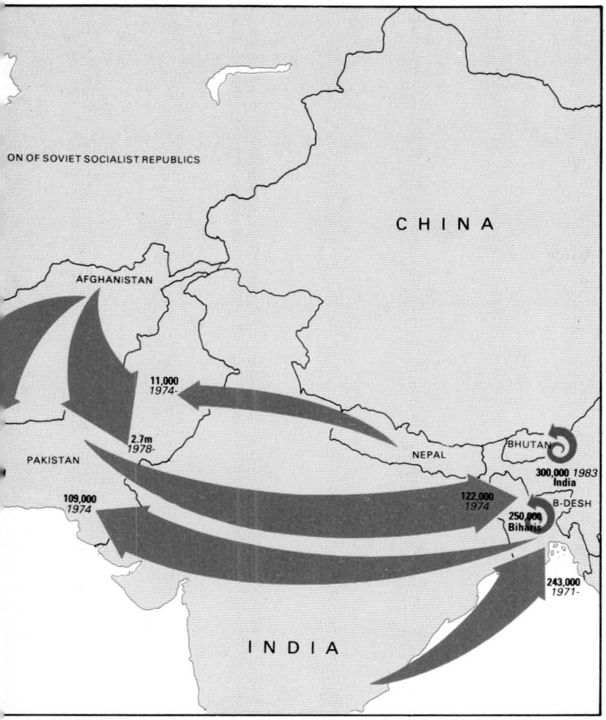

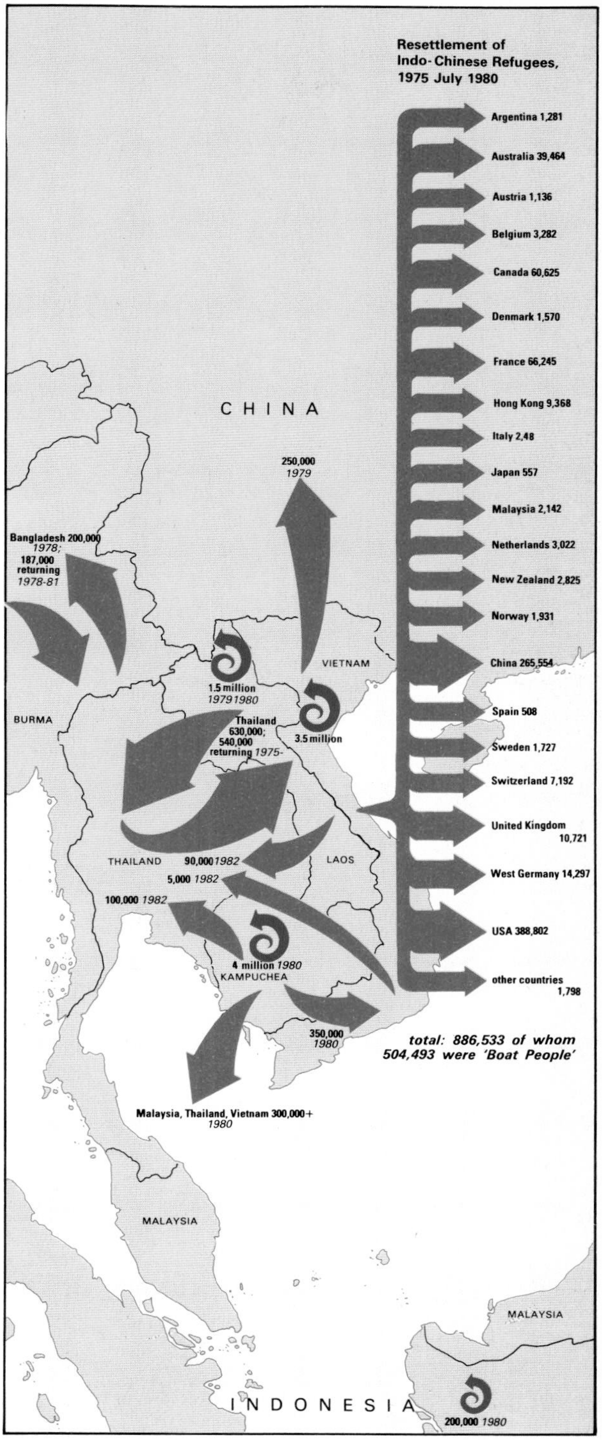

ON OF SOVIET SOCIALIST REPUBLICS
CHINA
AFGHANISTAN
11,000 1974-
2.7m 1978-
PAKISTAN
NEPAL
BHUTAN
300,000 1983 India
109,000 1974
122,000 1974
B-DESH
250,000 Biharis
243,000 1971-
INDIA

CAR
Cameroon 15,000 1980
Sudan, Zaire 200,000+ 100,000 returning
Rwanda-Uganda 100,000 1983 100,000 returning
GABON
CONGO
22,000 1981
UGANDA 100,000+ 1973-
RWANDA
10,000 1973-
500,000 1973 235,000 1981
ZAIRE
BURUNDI
35,000 1973-
Tanzania 150,000+ 1973-
Cape Verde 75,000 1976
Zaire 315,000; 100,000 + returning 1975-
ANGOLA
ZAMBIA
70,000 1981-
700,000 1975-
5,000 1981
2,200 1981
Botswana, Mozambique, Zambia 200,000+ 100,000 returning 1978
ZIMBABWE
1 million 1978
NAMIBIA
BOTSWANA
MOZAMBIQUE
Portugal 120,000+ 1975
SWAZILAND
LESOTHO 10,000 1981
SOUTH AFRICA
Portugal, S Africa 400,000 1975

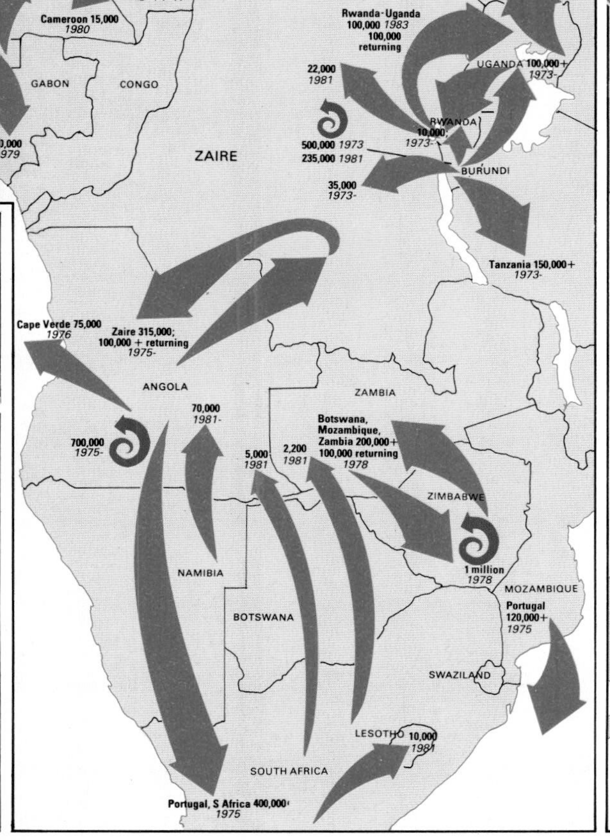

Resettlement of Indo-Chinese Refugees, 1975 July 1980
Argentina 1,281
Australia 39,464
Austria 1,136
Belgium 3,282
Canada 60,625
Denmark 1,570
France 66,245
Hong Kong 9,368
Italy 2,48
Japan 557
Malaysia 2,142
Netherlands 3,022
New Zealand 2,825
Norway 1,931
China 265,554
Spain 508
Sweden 1,727
Switzerland 7,192
United Kingdom 10,721
West Germany 14,297
USA 388,802
other countries 1,798
total: 886,533 of whom 504,493 were 'Boat People'
CHINA
250,000 1979
Bangladesh 200,000 1978; 187,000 returning 1978-81
1.5 million 1979 1980
VIETNAM
BURMA
Thailand 630,000; 540,000 returning 1975-
3.5 million
THAILAND
90,000 1982
LAOS
5,000 1982
100,000 1982
4 million 1980
KAMPUCHEA
350,000 1980
Malaysia, Thailand, Vietnam 300,000+ 1980
MALAYSIA
MALAYSIA
INDONESIA
200,000 1980

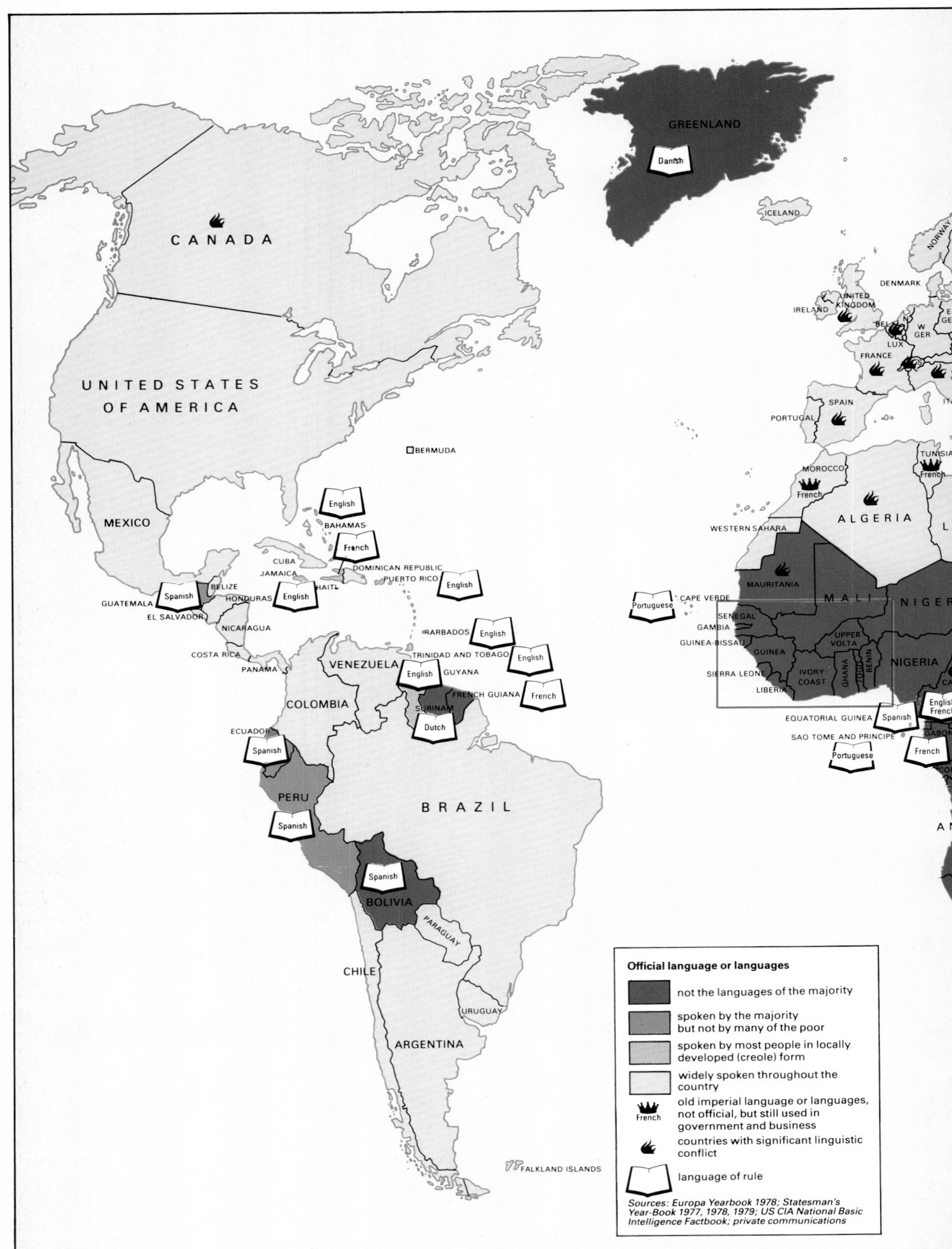

GREENLAND
Danish
ICELAND
CANADA
UNITED STATES OF AMERICA
MEXICO
BERMUDA
English
BAHAMAS
French
CUBA
JAMAICA
DOMINICAN REPUBLIC
PUERTO RICO
English
HAITI
English
BELIZE
Spanish
GUATEMALA
HONDURAS
EL SALVADOR
NICARAGUA
COSTA RICA
PANAMA
BARBADOS
English
TRINIDAD AND TOBAGO
English
VENEZUELA
English
GUYANA
FRENCH GUIANA
French
SURINAM
Dutch
COLOMBIA
ECUADOR
Spanish
PERU
Spanish
BRAZIL
Spanish
BOLIVIA
PARAGUAY
CHILE
URUGUAY
ARGENTINA
FALKLAND ISLANDS
NORWAY
DENMARK
UNITED KINGDOM
IRELAND
W GER
LUX
FRANCE
SPAIN
PORTUGAL
TUNISIA
French
MOROCCO
French
ALGERIA
WESTERN SAHARA
MAURITANIA
MALI
NIGER
Portuguese
CAPE VERDE
SENEGAL
GAMBIA
GUINEA-BISSAU
GUINEA
UPPER VOLTA
SIERRA LEONE
LIBERIA
IVORY COAST
GHANA
TOGO
BENIN
NIGERIA
English
French
EQUATORIAL GUINEA
Spanish
SAO TOME AND PRINCIPE
Portuguese
GABON
French
Official language or languages
not the languages of the majority
spoken by the majority but not by many of the poor
spoken by most people in locally developed (creole) form
widely spoken throughout the country
French
old imperial language or languages, not official, but still used in government and business
countries with significant linguistic conflict
language of rule
Sources: Europa Yearbook 1978; Statesman's Year-Book 1977, 1978, 1979; US CIA National Basic Intelligence Factbook; private communications

27. Languages of Rule

A language of rule is one which is used by the governing classes, and which helps to secure their dominance. It is usually, but not always, designated an official language. And even where different languages spoken in a country are equally official, some are more equal than others.

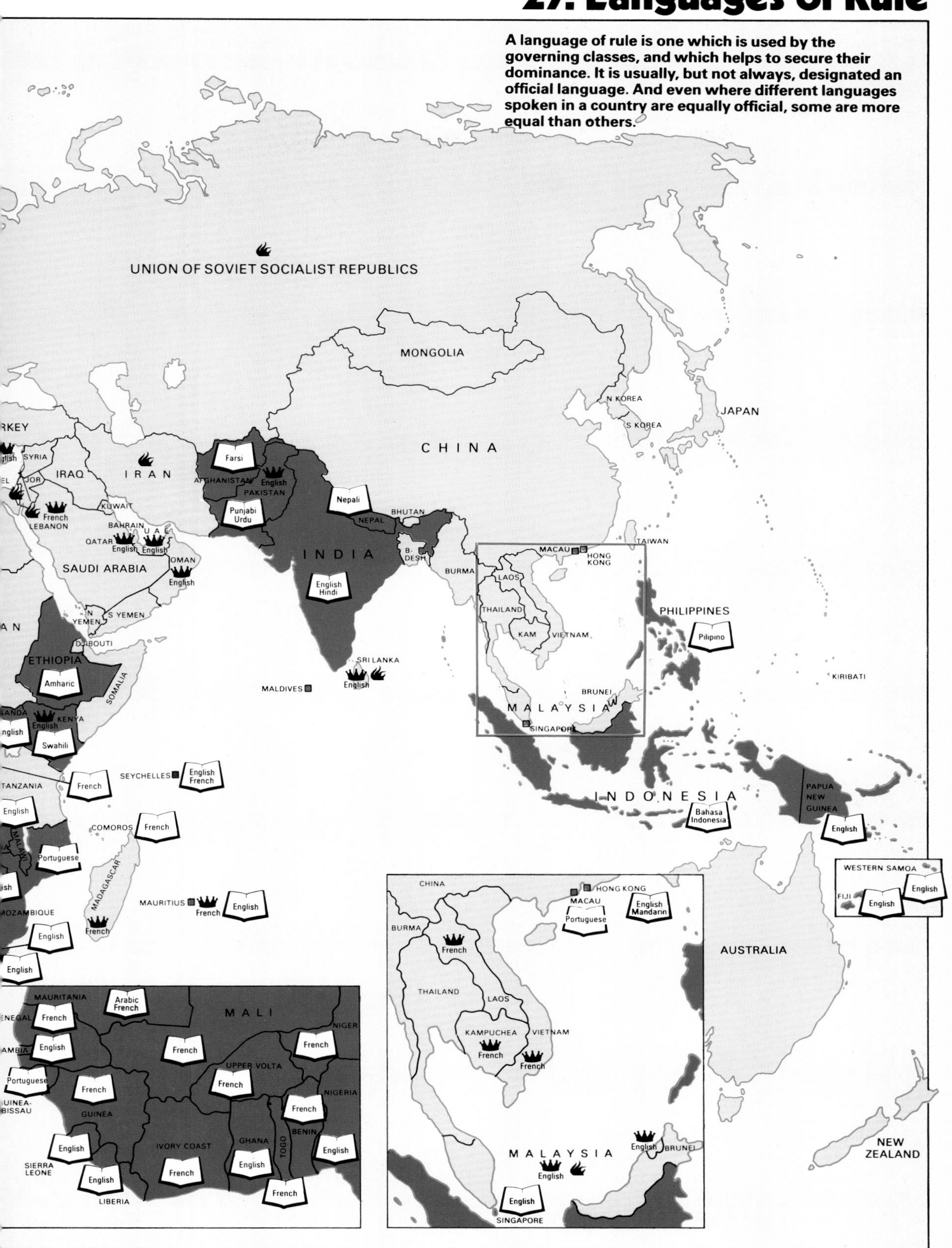

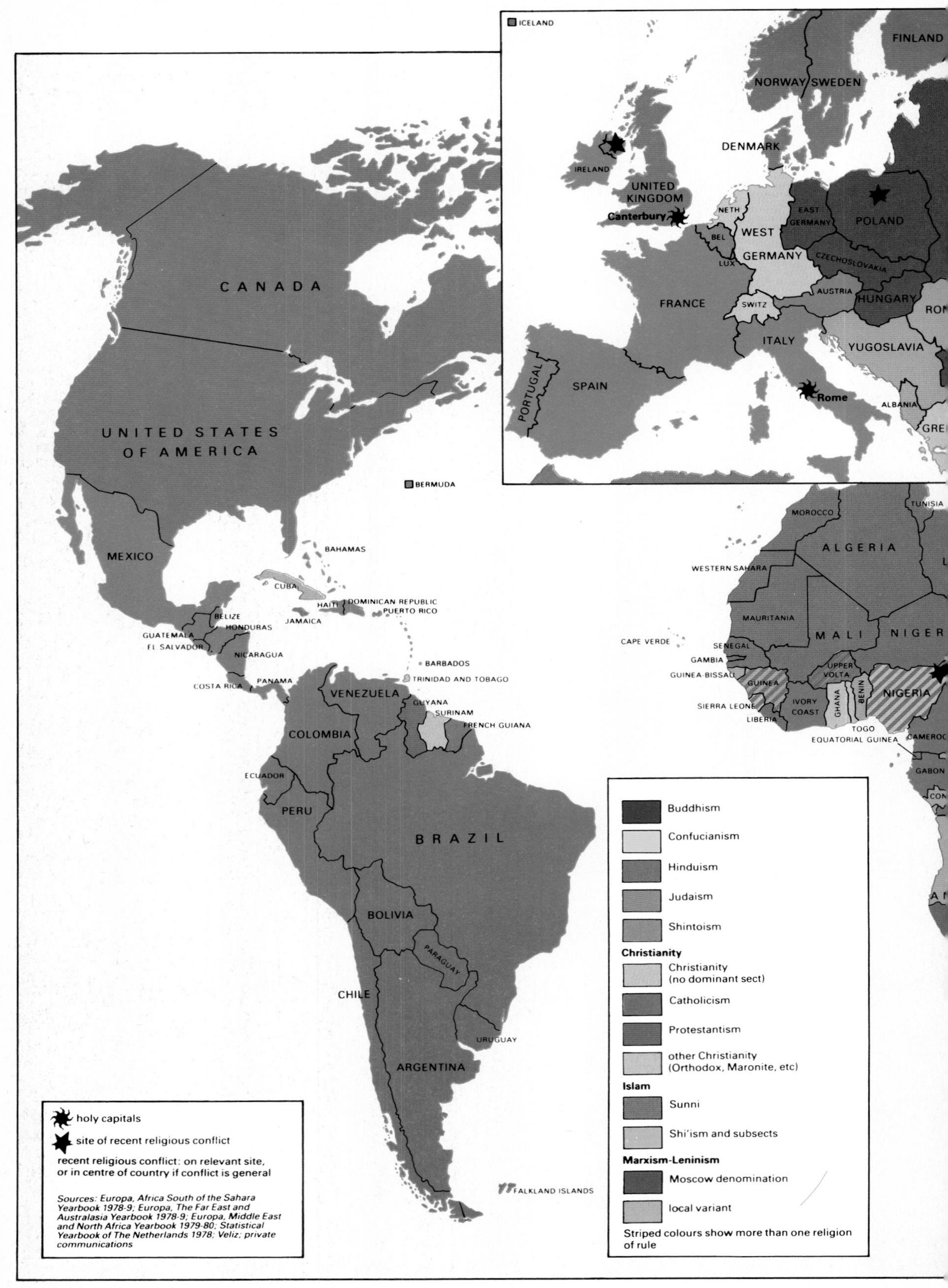
ICELAND
FINLAND
NORWAY
SWEDEN
DENMARK
IRELAND
UNITED KINGDOM
Canterbury
NETH
EAST GERMANY
POLAND
BEL
WEST GERMANY
LUX
CZECHOSLOVAKIA
FRANCE
AUSTRIA
HUNGARY
SWITZ
ITALY
YUGOSLAVIA
PORTUGAL
SPAIN
Rome
ALBANIA
CANADA
UNITED STATES OF AMERICA
BERMUDA
MEXICO
BAHAMAS
CUBA
HAITI
DOMINICAN REPUBLIC
PUERTO RICO
JAMAICA
BELIZE
HONDURAS
GUATEMALA
EL SALVADOR
NICARAGUA
BARBADOS
TRINIDAD AND TOBAGO
COSTA RICA
PANAMA
VENEZUELA
GUYANA
SURINAM
FRENCH GUIANA
COLOMBIA
ECUADOR
PERU
BRAZIL
BOLIVIA
PARAGUAY
CHILE
URUGUAY
ARGENTINA
FALKLAND ISLANDS
TUNISIA
MOROCCO
ALGERIA
WESTERN SAHARA
MAURITANIA
MALI
NIGER
CAPE VERDE
SENEGAL
GAMBIA
GUINEA-BISSAU
GUINEA
UPPER VOLTA
NIGERIA
SIERRA LEONE
LIBERIA
IVORY COAST
GHANA
BENIN
TOGO
EQUATORIAL GUINEA
GABON
Buddhism
Confucianism
Hinduism
Judaism
Shintoism
Christianity
Christianity (no dominant sect)
Catholicism
Protestantism
other Christianity (Orthodox, Maronite, etc)
Islam
Sunni
Shi'ism and subsects
Marxism-Leninism
Moscow denomination
local variant
Striped colours show more than one religion of rule
holy capitals
site of recent religious conflict
recent religious conflict: on relevant site, or in centre of country if conflict is general
Sources: Europa, Africa South of the Sahara Yearbook 1978-9; Europa, The Far East and Australasia Yearbook 1978-9; Europa, Middle East and North Africa Yearbook 1979-80; Statistical Yearbook of The Netherlands 1978; Veliz; private communications

28. Religions of Rule

A religion of rule is one which is professed by the governing classes and which sustains their solidarity. Not surprisingly, religious conflict is intensifying.

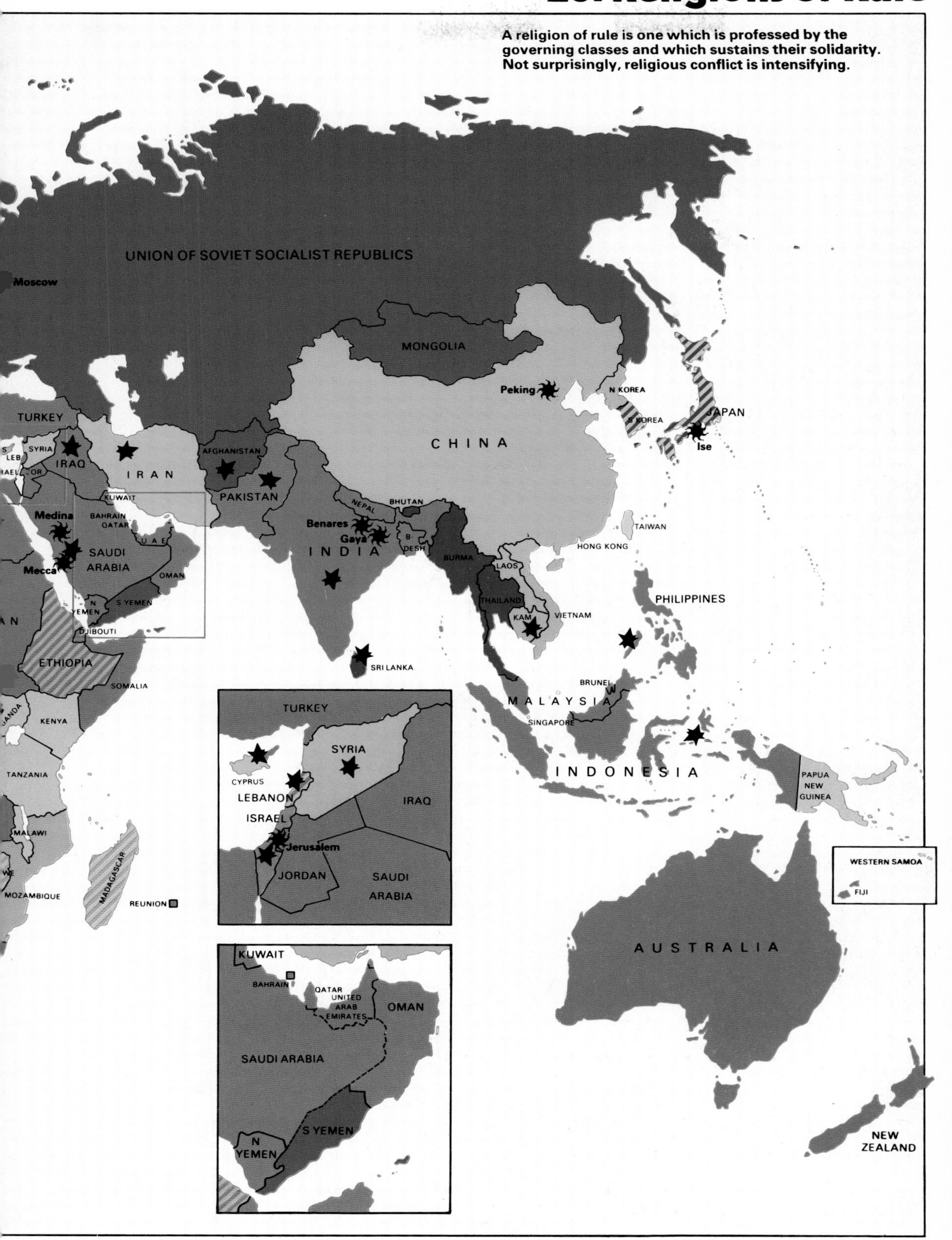

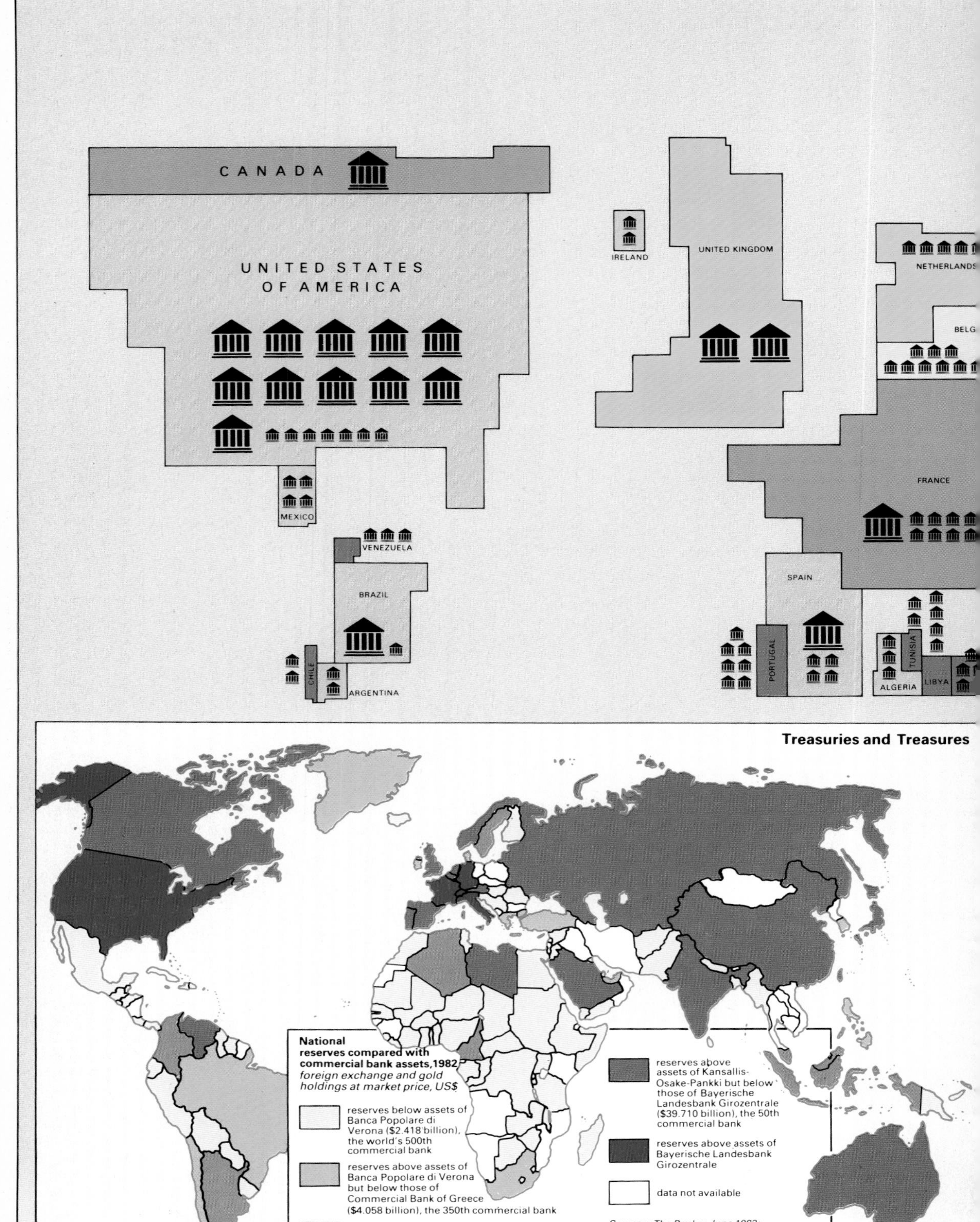

Treasuries and Treasures

National reserves compared with commercial bank assets, 1982
foreign exchange and gold holdings at market price, US$

- reserves below assets of Banca Popolare di Verona ($2.418 billion), the world's 500th commercial bank
- reserves above assets of Banca Popolare di Verona but below those of Commercial Bank of Greece ($4.058 billion), the 350th commercial bank
- reserves above assets of Commercial Bank of Greece but below those of Kansallis-Osake-Pankki ($7.276 billion), the 200th commercial bank
- reserves above assets of Kansallis-Osake-Pankki but below those of Bayerische Landesbank Girozentrale ($39.710 billion), the 50th commercial bank
- reserves above assets of Bayerische Landesbank Girozentrale
- data not available

Sources: *The Banker June 1983; CIA Handbook 1982; IMF International Financial Statistics June 1983; Taiwan Statistical Yearbook 1982*

29. Big Money

The world's big banks are so big that only the USA has reserves of foreign currency and gold worth more than the assets of the top commercial bank, Citicorp of New York, while most countries have reserves worth less than the assets of the world's 500th commercial bank, Banca Popolare di Verona in Italy.

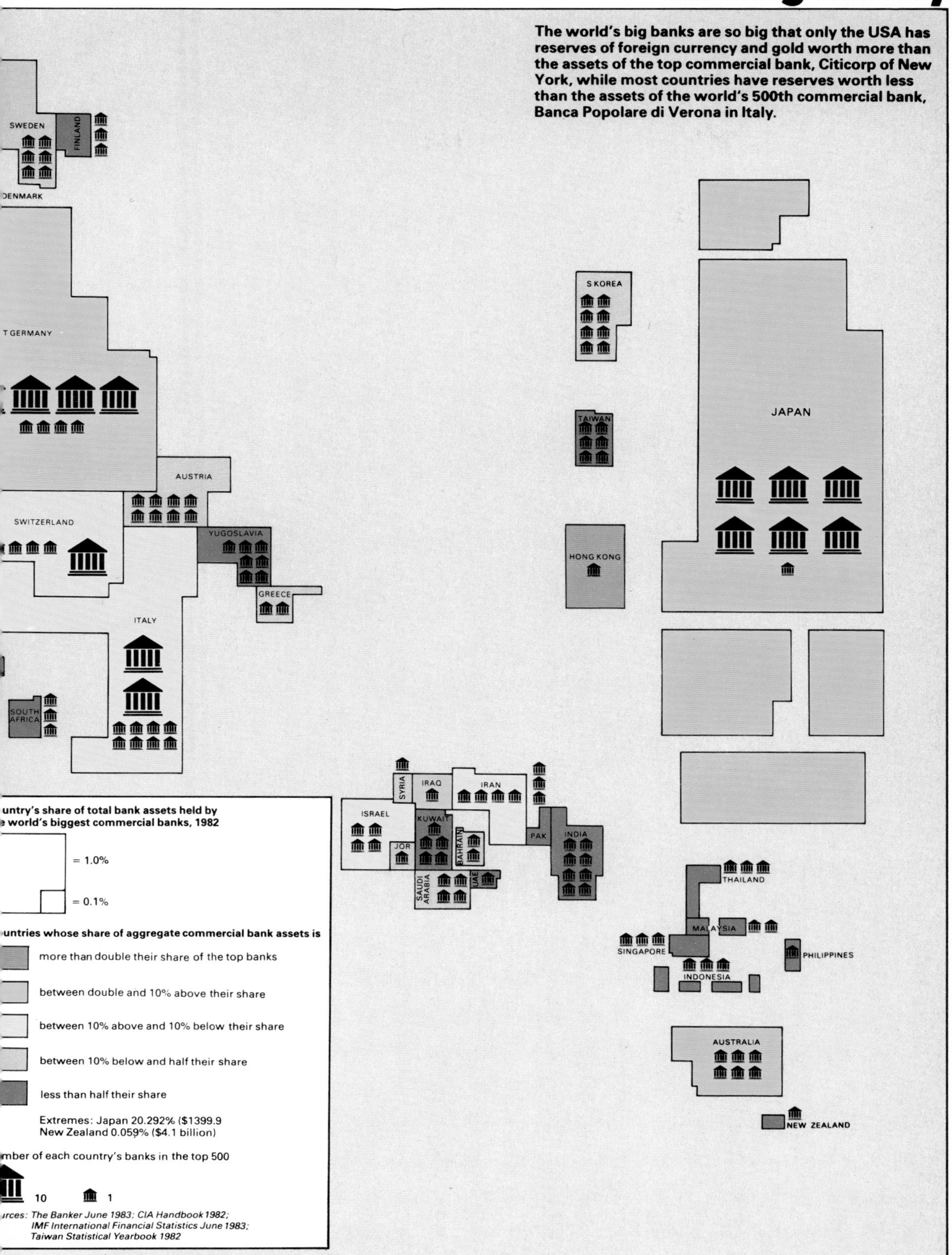

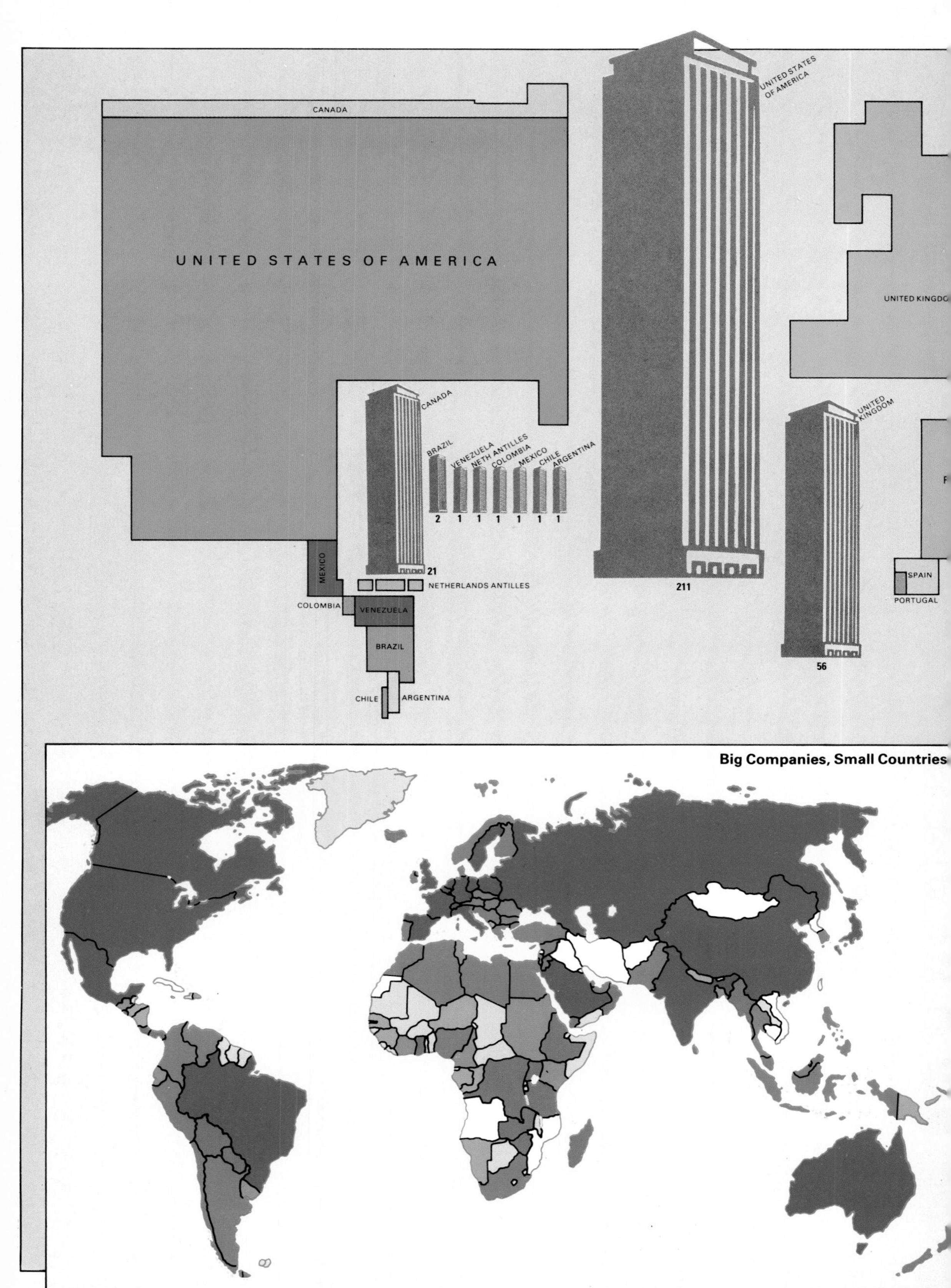

CANADA
UNITED STATES OF AMERICA
MEXICO
COLOMBIA
VENEZUELA
BRAZIL
CHILE
ARGENTINA
NETHERLANDS ANTILLES
CANADA
BRAZIL
VENEZUELA
NETH ANTILLES
COLOMBIA
MEXICO
CHILE
ARGENTINA
2 1 1 1 1 1 1
21
UNITED STATES OF AMERICA
211
UNITED KINGDO
UNITED KINGDOM
56
SPAIN
PORTUGAL
Big Companies, Small Countries

30. Big Business

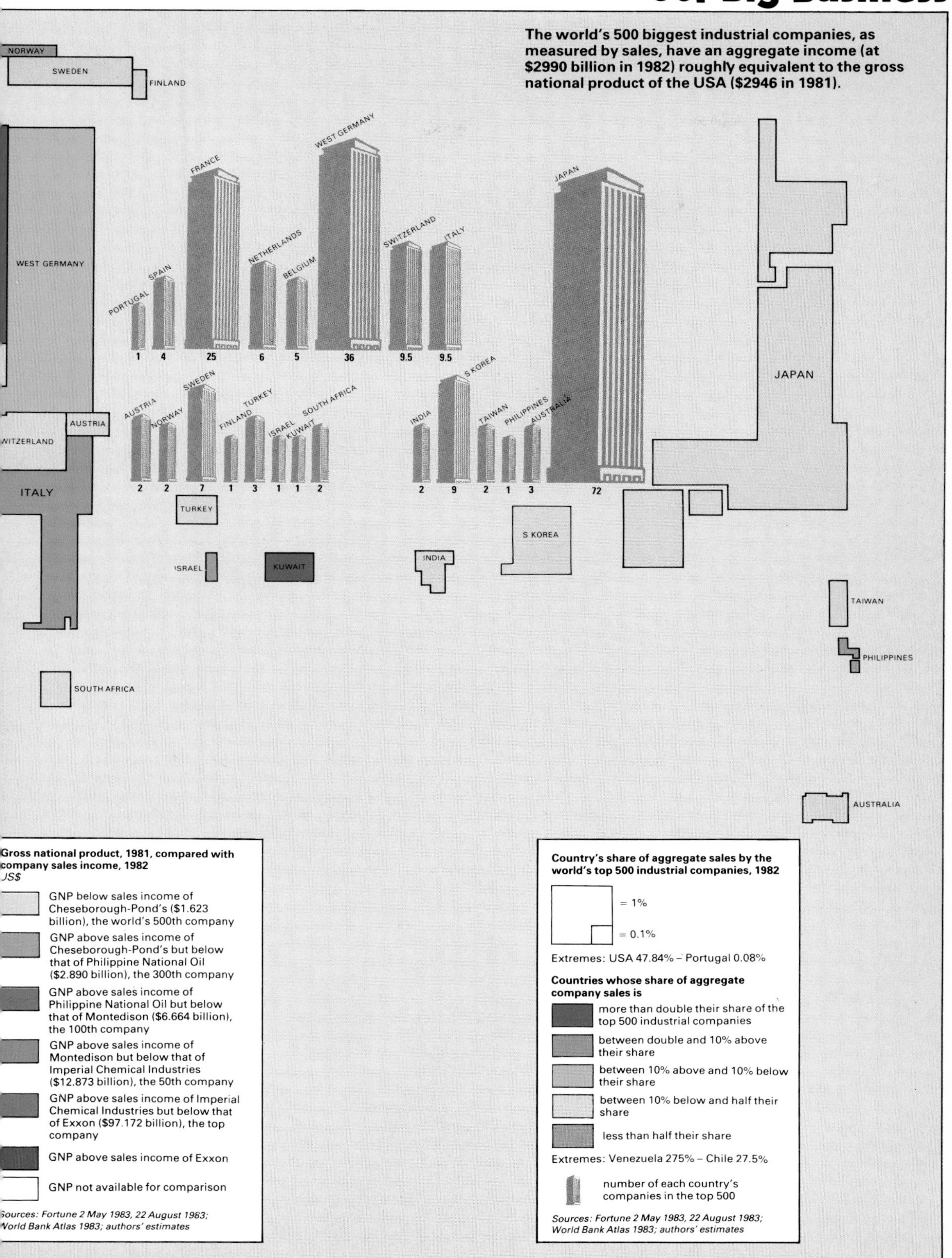

The world's 500 biggest industrial companies, as measured by sales, have an aggregate income (at $2990 billion in 1982) roughly equivalent to the gross national product of the USA ($2946 in 1981).
NORWAY
SWEDEN
FINLAND
WEST GERMANY
AUSTRIA
WITZERLAND
ITALY
TURKEY
ISRAEL
KUWAIT
INDIA
S KOREA
JAPAN
TAIWAN
PHILIPPINES
SOUTH AFRICA
AUSTRALIA
PORTUGAL 1
SPAIN 4
FRANCE 25
NETHERLANDS 6
BELGIUM 5
WEST GERMANY 36
SWITZERLAND 9.5
ITALY 9.5
AUSTRIA 2
NORWAY 2
SWEDEN 7
FINLAND 1
TURKEY 3
ISRAEL 1
KUWAIT 1
SOUTH AFRICA 2
INDIA 2
S KOREA 9
TAIWAN 2
PHILIPPINES 1
AUSTRALIA 3
JAPAN 72
Gross national product, 1981, compared with company sales income, 1982
JS$
GNP below sales income of Cheseborough-Pond's ($1.623 billion), the world's 500th company
GNP above sales income of Cheseborough-Pond's but below that of Philippine National Oil ($2.890 billion), the 300th company
GNP above sales income of Philippine National Oil but below that of Montedison ($6.664 billion), the 100th company
GNP above sales income of Montedison but below that of Imperial Chemical Industries ($12.873 billion), the 50th company
GNP above sales income of Imperial Chemical Industries but below that of Exxon ($97.172 billion), the top company
GNP above sales income of Exxon
GNP not available for comparison
Sources: Fortune 2 May 1983, 22 August 1983; World Bank Atlas 1983; authors' estimates
Country's share of aggregate sales by the world's top 500 industrial companies, 1982
= 1%
= 0.1%
Extremes: USA 47.84% – Portugal 0.08%
Countries whose share of aggregate company sales is
more than double their share of the top 500 industrial companies
between double and 10% above their share
between 10% above and 10% below their share
between 10% below and half their share
less than half their share
Extremes: Venezuela 275% – Chile 27.5%
number of each country's companies in the top 500
Sources: Fortune 2 May 1983, 22 August 1983; World Bank Atlas 1983; authors' estimates

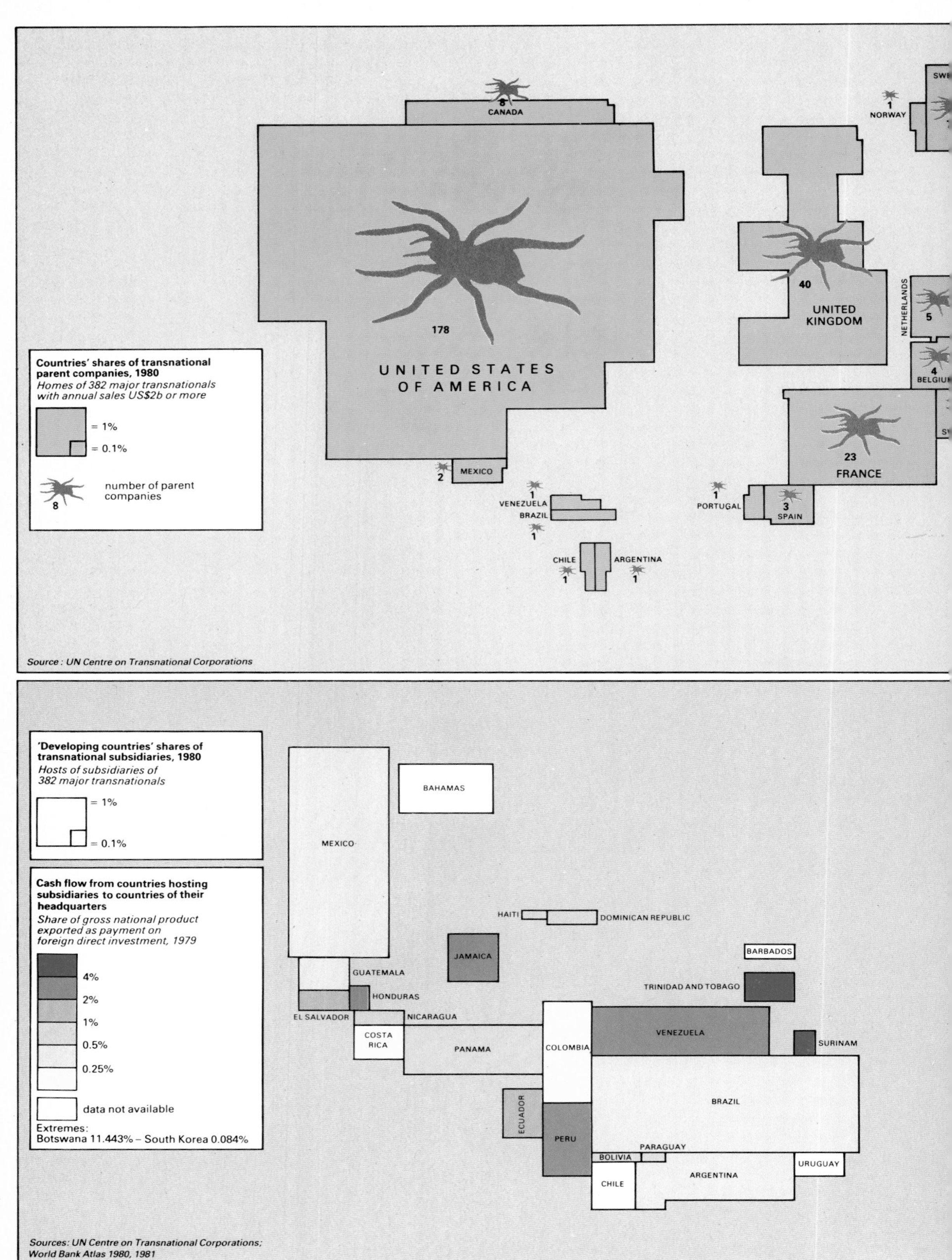

Countries' shares of transnational parent companies, 1980
Homes of 382 major transnationals with annual sales US$2b or more
= 1%
= 0.1%
number of parent companies
8
CANADA
UNITED STATES OF AMERICA
178
MEXICO
2
VENEZUELA
1
BRAZIL
1
CHILE
1
ARGENTINA
1
NORWAY
1
UNITED KINGDOM
40
NETHERLANDS
5
BELGIUM
4
FRANCE
23
PORTUGAL
1
SPAIN
3
Source: UN Centre on Transnational Corporations
'Developing countries' shares of transnational subsidiaries, 1980
Hosts of subsidiaries of 382 major transnationals
= 1%
= 0.1%
Cash flow from countries hosting subsidiaries to countries of their headquarters
Share of gross national product exported as payment on foreign direct investment, 1979
4%
2%
1%
0.5%
0.25%
data not available
Extremes:
Botswana 11.443% – South Korea 0.084%
MEXICO
BAHAMAS
HAITI
DOMINICAN REPUBLIC
JAMAICA
BARBADOS
TRINIDAD AND TOBAGO
GUATEMALA
HONDURAS
EL SALVADOR
NICARAGUA
COSTA RICA
PANAMA
COLOMBIA
VENEZUELA
SURINAM
BRAZIL
ECUADOR
PERU
PARAGUAY
BOLIVIA
URUGUAY
CHILE
ARGENTINA
Sources: UN Centre on Transnational Corporations; World Bank Atlas 1980, 1981

31. Webs and Flows

Well over 90 per cent of major transnationals are sited in rich countries. One quarter of the top transnational companies raise more than half their sales income abroad; 8 per cent raise more than three-quarters of their income abroad; and 4 per cent more than nine-tenths.

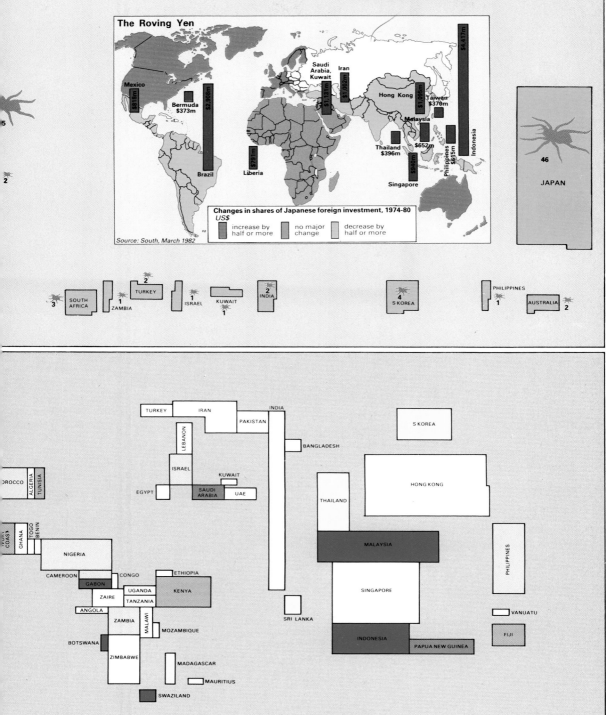

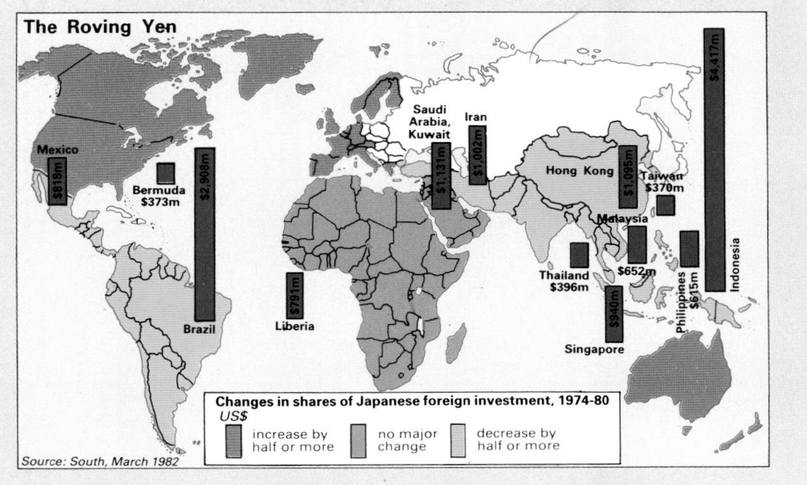

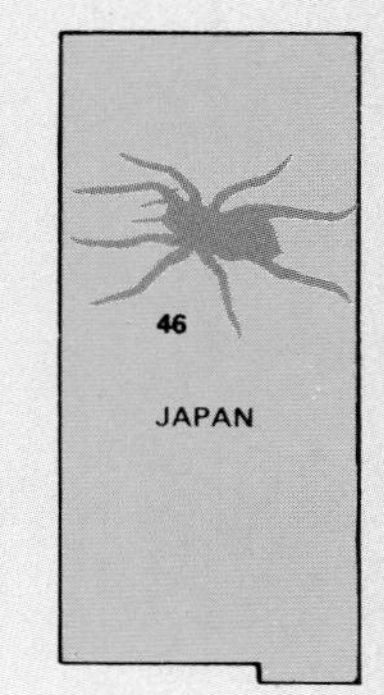

5

2

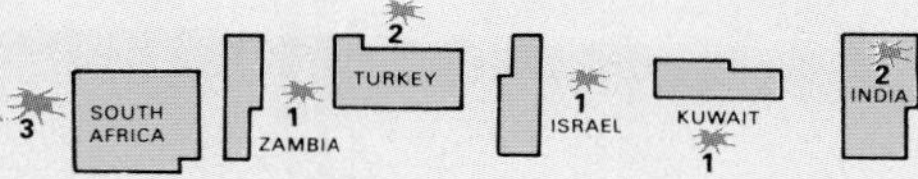

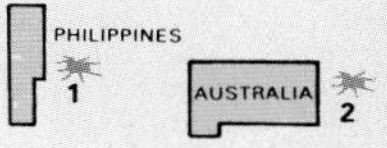

TURKEY
IRAN
INDIA
PAKISTAN
LEBANON
BANGLADESH
ISRAEL
KUWAIT
)ROCCO
ALGERIA
TUNISIA
EGYPT
SAUDI ARABIA
UAE
S KOREA
HONG KONG
THAILAND
COAST
GHANA
TOGO
BENIN
NIGERIA
MALAYSIA
CAMEROON
CONGO
ETHIOPIA
GABON
KENYA
UGANDA
ZAIRE
TANZANIA
SINGAPORE
PHILIPPINES
ANGOLA
ZAMBIA
MALAWI
SRI LANKA
VANUATU
MOZAMBIQUE
BOTSWANA
INDONESIA
PAPUA NEW GUINEA
FIJI
ZIMBABWE
MADAGASCAR
MAURITIUS
SWAZILAND

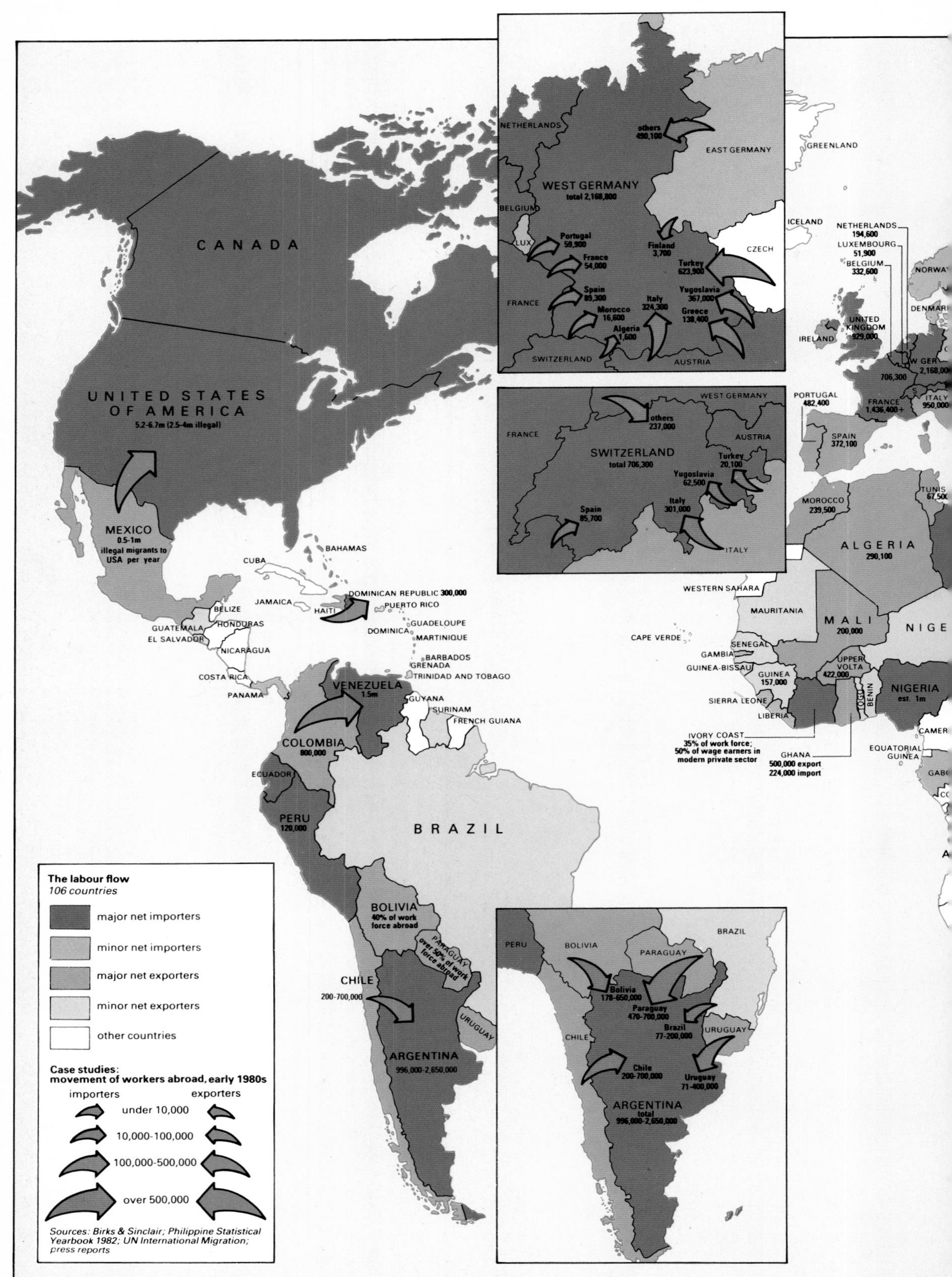

CANADA
UNITED STATES OF AMERICA
5.2-6.7m (2.5-4m illegal)
MEXICO
0.5-1m
illegal migrants to USA per year
BAHAMAS
CUBA
DOMINICAN REPUBLIC 300,000
JAMAICA
HAITI
PUERTO RICO
BELIZE
GUATEMALA
HONDURAS
EL SALVADOR
NICARAGUA
GUADELOUPE
DOMINICA
MARTINIQUE
BARBADOS
GRENADA
TRINIDAD AND TOBAGO
COSTA RICA
PANAMA
VENEZUELA
1.5m
GUYANA
SURINAM
FRENCH GUIANA
COLOMBIA
800,000
ECUADOR
PERU
120,000
BRAZIL
BOLIVIA
40% of work force abroad
PARAGUAY
over 50% of work force abroad
CHILE
200-700,000
URUGUAY
ARGENTINA
996,000-2,650,000
NETHERLANDS
others
490,100
EAST GERMANY
WEST GERMANY
total 2,168,800
BELGIUM
LUX
Portugal
59,900
France
54,000
Finland
3,700
CZECH
Turkey
623,900
Spain
85,300
FRANCE
Morocco
16,600
Italy
324,300
Yugoslavia
367,000
Greece
138,400
Algeria
1,600
SWITZERLAND
AUSTRIA
WEST GERMANY
others
237,000
FRANCE
AUSTRIA
SWITZERLAND
total 706,300
Turkey
20,100
Yugoslavia
62,500
Italy
301,000
Spain
85,700
ITALY
GREENLAND
ICELAND
NETHERLANDS
194,600
LUXEMBOURG
51,900
BELGIUM
332,600
NORWAY
DENMARK
UNITED KINGDOM
929,000
IRELAND
W GER
2,168,000
706,300
PORTUGAL
482,400
FRANCE
1,436,400+
ITALY
950,000
SPAIN
372,100
TUNIS
67,500
MOROCCO
239,500
ALGERIA
290,100
WESTERN SAHARA
MAURITANIA
MALI
200,000
NIGE
CAPE VERDE
SENEGAL
GAMBIA
GUINEA-BISSAU
GUINEA
157,000
UPPER VOLTA
422,000
TOGO
BENIN
NIGERIA
est. 1m
SIERRA LEONE
LIBERIA
IVORY COAST
35% of work force;
50% of wage earners in modern private sector
GHANA
500,000 export
224,000 import
CAMER
EQUATORIAL GUINEA
GABO
PERU
BOLIVIA
BRAZIL
PARAGUAY
Bolivia
178-650,000
Paraguay
470-700,000
Brazil
77-200,000
URUGUAY
CHILE
Chile
200-700,000
Uruguay
71-400,000
ARGENTINA
total
996,000-2,650,000
The labour flow
106 countries
major net importers
minor net importers
major net exporters
minor net exporters
other countries
Case studies:
movement of workers abroad, early 1980s
importers
exporters
under 10,000
10,000-100,000
100,000-500,000
over 500,000
Sources: Birks & Sinclair; Philippine Statistical Yearbook 1982; UN International Migration; press reports

32. In Search of Work

Despite economic recession, the world market in labour is growing. This growth is sometimes in conflict, sometimes in accordance, with government intentions.

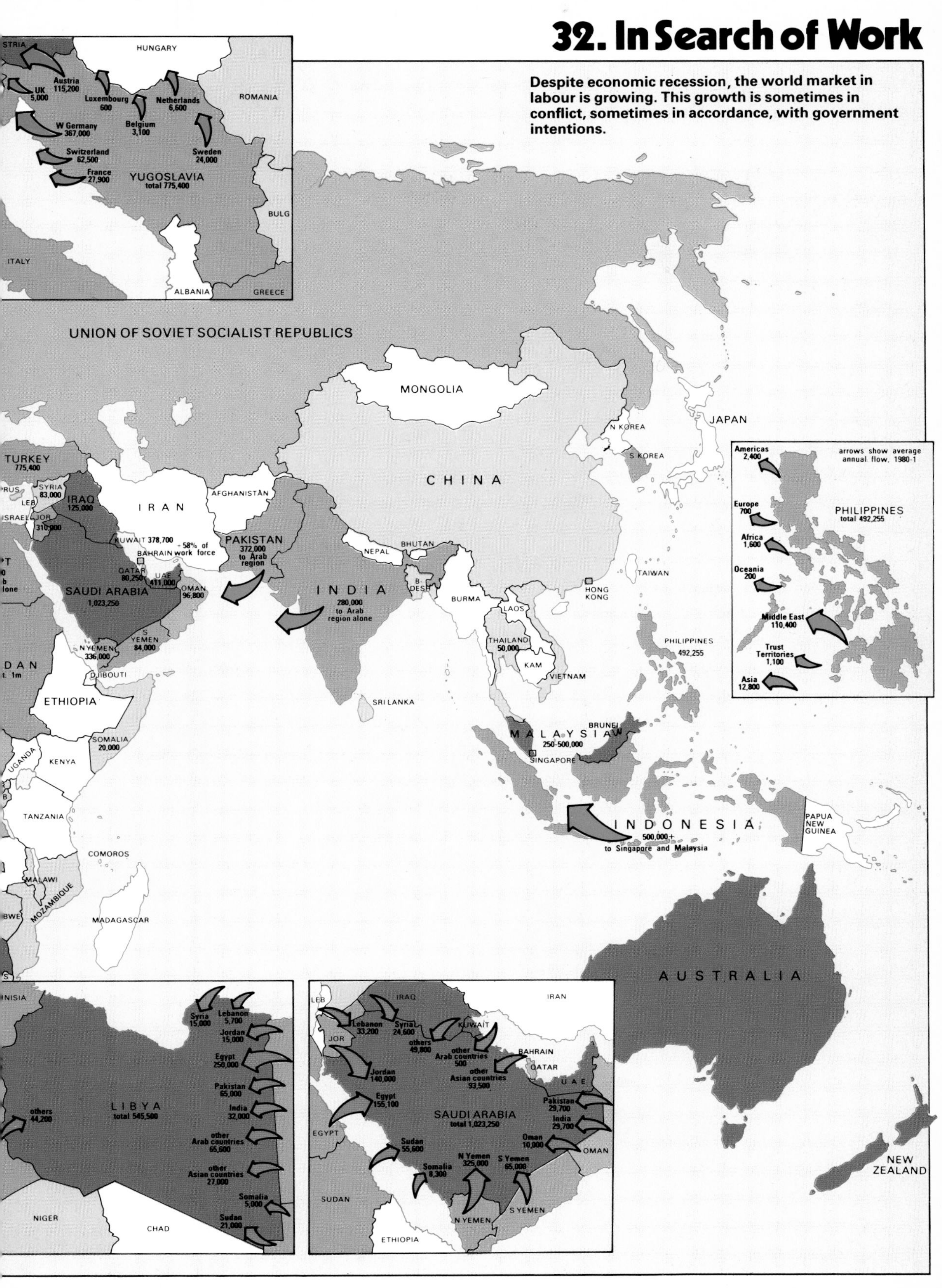

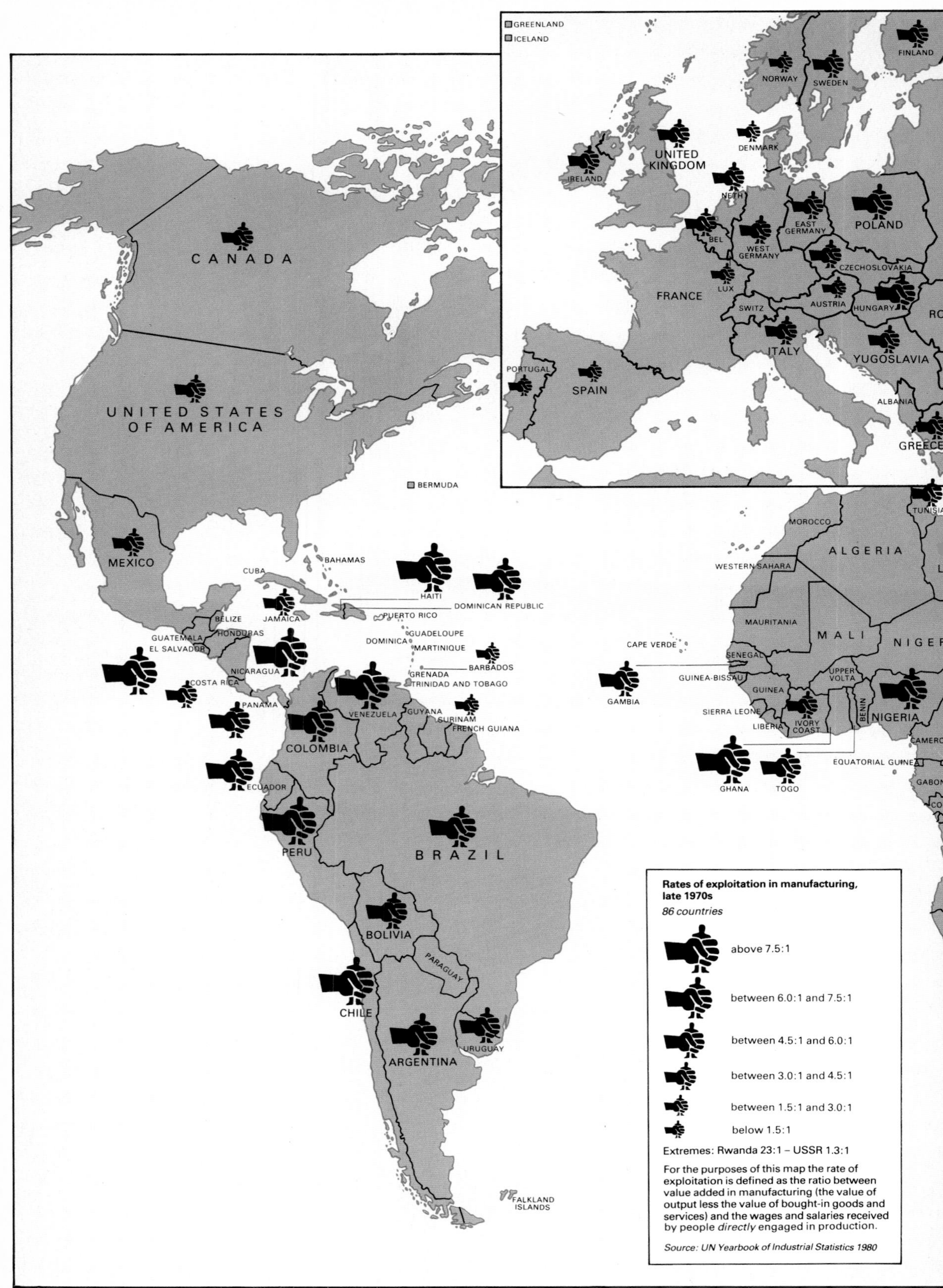
GREENLAND
ICELAND
FINLAND
NORWAY
SWEDEN
UNITED KINGDOM
DENMARK
IRELAND
NETH
BEL
EAST GERMANY
POLAND
WEST GERMANY
CZECHOSLOVAKIA
LUX
FRANCE
AUSTRIA
HUNGARY
SWITZ
ITALY
YUGOSLAVIA
PORTUGAL
SPAIN
ALBANIA
GREECE
CANADA
UNITED STATES OF AMERICA
BERMUDA
TUNISIA
MOROCCO
ALGERIA
WESTERN SAHARA
MEXICO
BAHAMAS
CUBA
HAITI
DOMINICAN REPUBLIC
JAMAICA
PUERTO RICO
BELIZE
GUATEMALA
HONDURAS
EL SALVADOR
GUADELOUPE
DOMINICA
MARTINIQUE
BARBADOS
NICARAGUA
GRENADA
TRINIDAD AND TOBAGO
COSTA RICA
PANAMA
VENEZUELA
GUYANA
SURINAM
FRENCH GUIANA
COLOMBIA
ECUADOR
PERU
BRAZIL
BOLIVIA
PARAGUAY
CHILE
URUGUAY
ARGENTINA
FALKLAND ISLANDS
MAURITANIA
MALI
NIGER
CAPE VERDE
SENEGAL
GAMBIA
GUINEA-BISSAU
UPPER VOLTA
GUINEA
SIERRA LEONE
LIBERIA
IVORY COAST
BENIN
NIGERIA
GHANA
TOGO
CAMERO
EQUATORIAL GUINEA
GABON
Rates of exploitation in manufacturing, late 1970s
86 countries
above 7.5:1
between 6.0:1 and 7.5:1
between 4.5:1 and 6.0:1
between 3.0:1 and 4.5:1
between 1.5:1 and 3.0:1
below 1.5:1
Extremes: Rwanda 23:1 – USSR 1.3:1
For the purposes of this map the rate of exploitation is defined as the ratio between value added in manufacturing (the value of output less the value of bought-in goods and services) and the wages and salaries received by people directly engaged in production.
Source: UN Yearbook of Industrial Statistics 1980

33. Exploitation

Most people produce more than they earn – for the few who get more than they produce. The difference is measured by the rate of exploitation.
Oppression and exploitation are not the same. Some people are socially and politically oppressed more than they are exploited; of others the opposite is true.

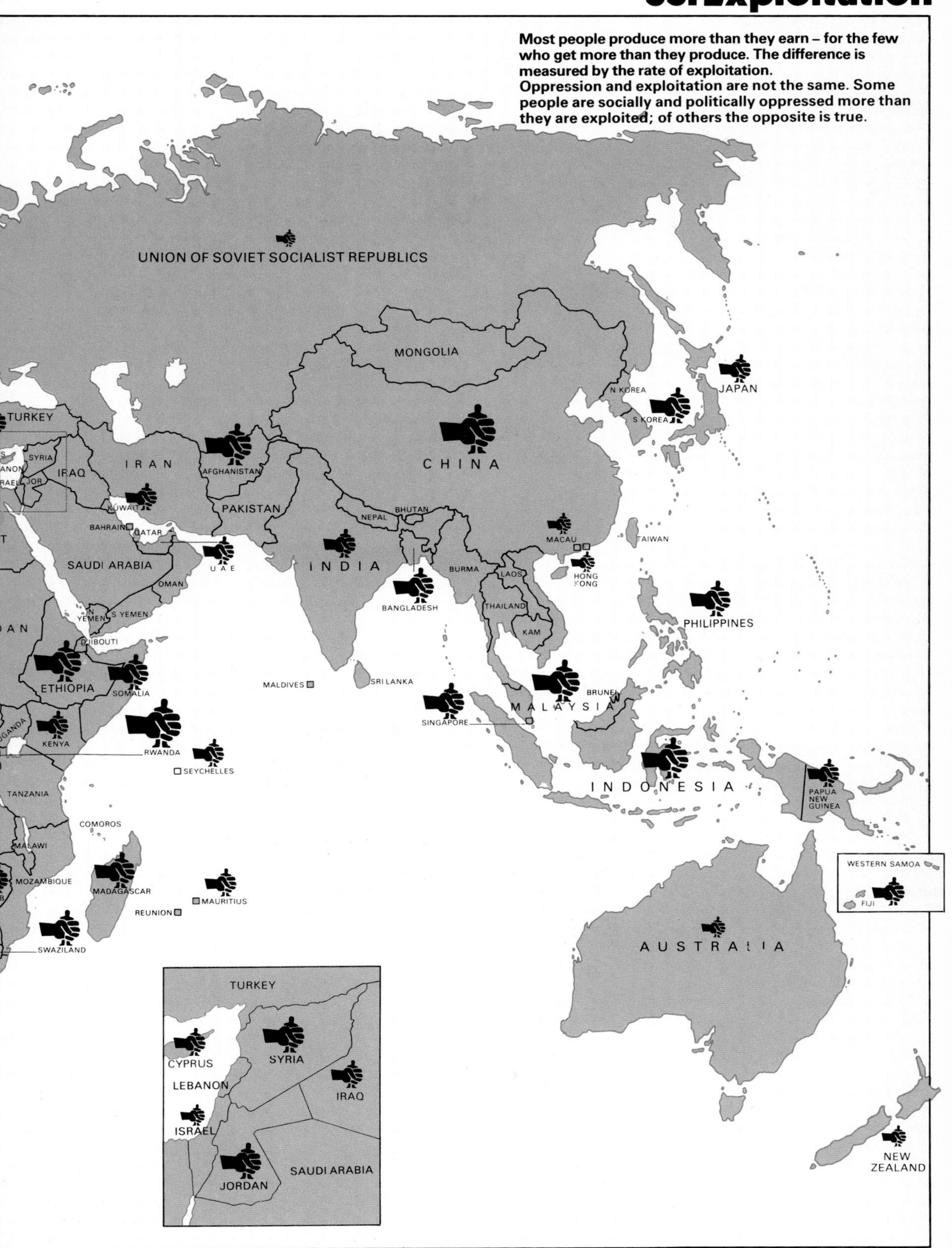

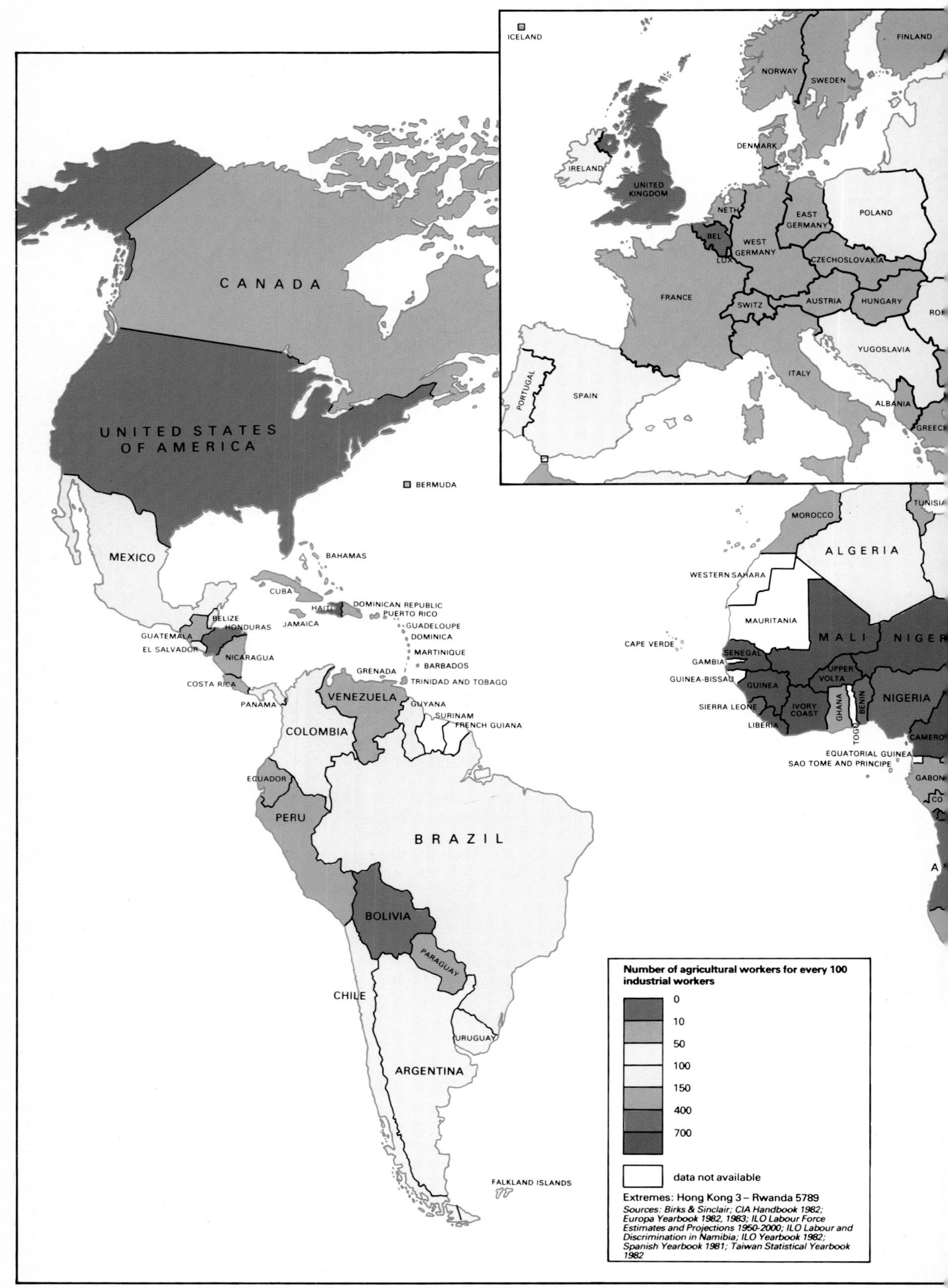
ICELAND
FINLAND
NORWAY
SWEDEN
DENMARK
IRELAND
UNITED KINGDOM
NETH
EAST GERMANY
POLAND
BEL
LUX
WEST GERMANY
CZECHOSLOVAKIA
FRANCE
SWITZ
AUSTRIA
HUNGARY
YUGOSLAVIA
PORTUGAL
SPAIN
ITALY
ALBANIA
CANADA
UNITED STATES OF AMERICA
BERMUDA
MEXICO
BAHAMAS
CUBA
HAITI
DOMINICAN REPUBLIC
PUERTO RICO
JAMAICA
GUADELOUPE
DOMINICA
MARTINIQUE
BARBADOS
GRENADA
TRINIDAD AND TOBAGO
BELIZE
HONDURAS
GUATEMALA
EL SALVADOR
NICARAGUA
COSTA RICA
PANAMA
VENEZUELA
GUYANA
SURINAM
FRENCH GUIANA
COLOMBIA
ECUADOR
PERU
BRAZIL
BOLIVIA
PARAGUAY
CHILE
URUGUAY
ARGENTINA
FALKLAND ISLANDS
MOROCCO
ALGERIA
WESTERN SAHARA
MAURITANIA
CAPE VERDE
MALI
SENEGAL
GAMBIA
GUINEA-BISSAU
GUINEA
UPPER VOLTA
SIERRA LEONE
LIBERIA
IVORY COAST
GHANA
TOGO
BENIN
NIGERIA
EQUATORIAL GUINEA
SAO TOME AND PRINCIPE
Number of agricultural workers for every 100 industrial workers
0
10
50
100
150
400
700
data not available
Extremes: Hong Kong 3 – Rwanda 5789
Sources: Birks & Sinclair; CIA Handbook 1982; Europa Yearbook 1982, 1983; ILO Labour Force Estimates and Projections 1950-2000; ILO Labour and Discrimination in Namibia; ILO Yearbook 1982; Spanish Yearbook 1981; Taiwan Statistical Yearbook 1982

34. The Labour Force

The industrial age is more than two centuries old, but most workers in most countries work on the land.

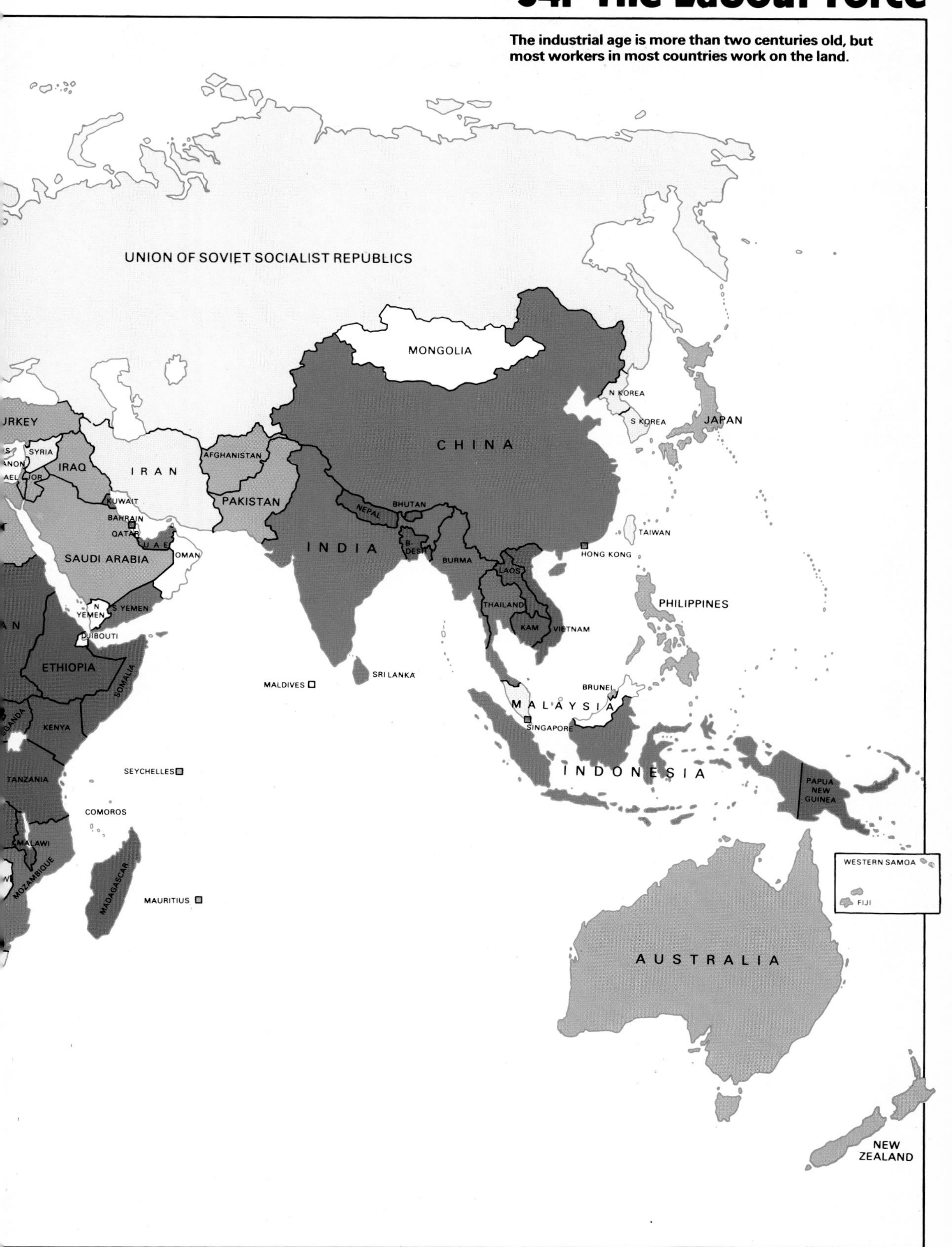

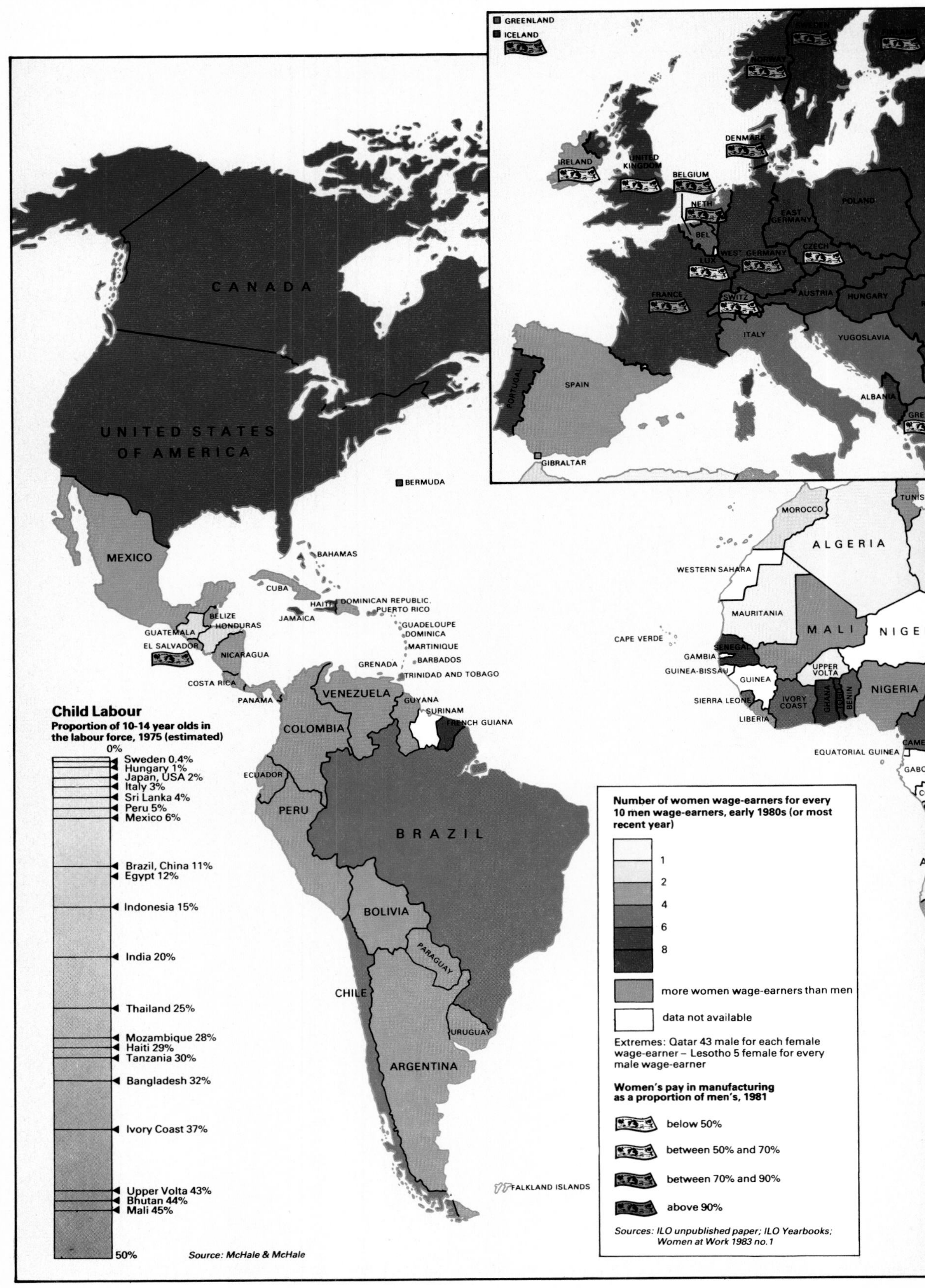

GREENLAND
ICELAND
IRELAND
UNITED KINGDOM
BELGIUM
DENMARK
NETH
BEL
POLAND
EAST GERMANY
WEST GERMANY
CZECH
LUX
FRANCE
SWITZ
AUSTRIA
HUNGARY
ITALY
YUGOSLAVIA
PORTUGAL
SPAIN
ALBANIA
GIBRALTAR
CANADA
UNITED STATES OF AMERICA
BERMUDA
MEXICO
BAHAMAS
CUBA
HAITI
DOMINICAN REPUBLIC
PUERTO RICO
JAMAICA
BELIZE
HONDURAS
GUATEMALA
EL SALVADOR
NICARAGUA
GUADELOUPE
DOMINICA
MARTINIQUE
BARBADOS
GRENADA
TRINIDAD AND TOBAGO
COSTA RICA
PANAMA
VENEZUELA
GUYANA
SURINAM
FRENCH GUIANA
COLOMBIA
ECUADOR
PERU
BRAZIL
BOLIVIA
PARAGUAY
CHILE
URUGUAY
ARGENTINA
FALKLAND ISLANDS
MOROCCO
TUNISIA
ALGERIA
WESTERN SAHARA
MAURITANIA
MALI
NIGER
CAPE VERDE
SENEGAL
GAMBIA
GUINEA-BISSAU
GUINEA
UPPER VOLTA
SIERRA LEONE
LIBERIA
IVORY COAST
GHANA
TOGO
BENIN
NIGERIA
EQUATORIAL GUINEA

Child Labour
Proportion of 10-14 year olds in the labour force, 1975 (estimated)
0%
Sweden 0.4%
Hungary 1%
Japan, USA 2%
Italy 3%
Sri Lanka 4%
Peru 5%
Mexico 6%
Brazil, China 11%
Egypt 12%
Indonesia 15%
India 20%
Thailand 25%
Mozambique 28%
Haiti 29%
Tanzania 30%
Bangladesh 32%
Ivory Coast 37%
Upper Volta 43%
Bhutan 44%
Mali 45%
50%
Source: McHale & McHale

Number of women wage-earners for every 10 men wage-earners, early 1980s (or most recent year)
1
2
4
6
8
more women wage-earners than men
data not available
Extremes: Qatar 43 male for each female wage-earner – Lesotho 5 female for every male wage-earner
Women's pay in manufacturing as a proportion of men's, 1981
below 50%
between 50% and 70%
between 70% and 90%
above 90%
Sources: ILO unpublished paper; ILO Yearbooks; Women at Work 1983 no. 1

35. Women Workers

Men dominate paid labour and the higher rates of pay; women work longer hours and for much of their work are not paid at all.

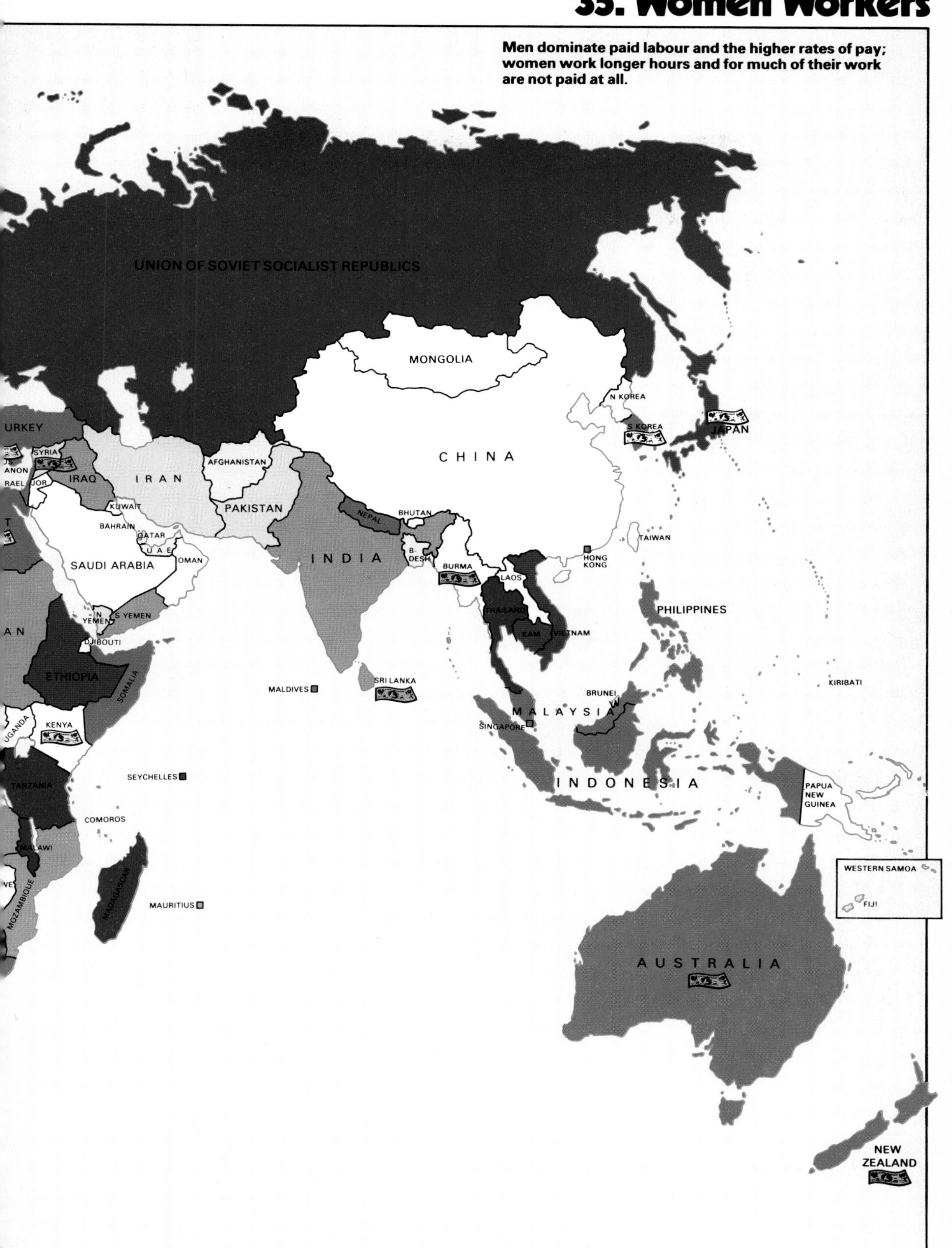

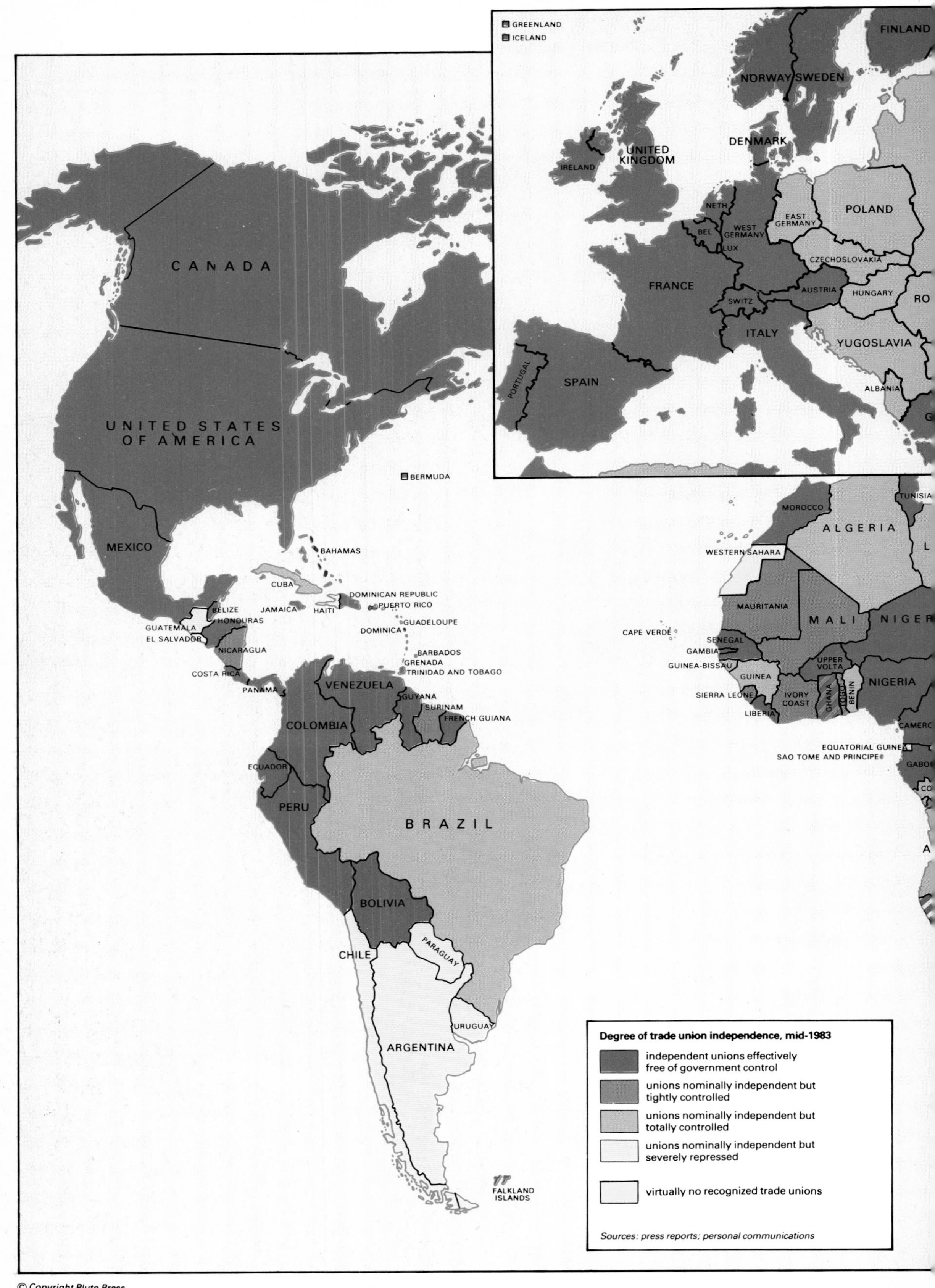
GREENLAND
ICELAND
FINLAND
NORWAY
SWEDEN
DENMARK
IRELAND
UNITED KINGDOM
NETH
BEL
LUX
WEST GERMANY
EAST GERMANY
POLAND
CZECHOSLOVAKIA
FRANCE
SWITZ
AUSTRIA
HUNGARY
RO
ITALY
YUGOSLAVIA
PORTUGAL
SPAIN
ALBANIA
CANADA
UNITED STATES OF AMERICA
BERMUDA
MEXICO
BAHAMAS
CUBA
JAMAICA
HAITI
DOMINICAN REPUBLIC
PUERTO RICO
GUADELOUPE
DOMINICA
BELIZE
HONDURAS
GUATEMALA
EL SALVADOR
NICARAGUA
COSTA RICA
PANAMA
BARBADOS
GRENADA
TRINIDAD AND TOBAGO
VENEZUELA
GUYANA
SURINAM
FRENCH GUIANA
COLOMBIA
ECUADOR
PERU
BRAZIL
BOLIVIA
PARAGUAY
CHILE
URUGUAY
ARGENTINA
FALKLAND ISLANDS
MOROCCO
TUNISIA
ALGERIA
WESTERN SAHARA
MAURITANIA
MALI
NIGER
CAPE VERDE
SENEGAL
GAMBIA
GUINEA-BISSAU
GUINEA
UPPER VOLTA
NIGERIA
SIERRA LEONE
IVORY COAST
GHANA
TOGO
BENIN
LIBERIA
EQUATORIAL GUINEA
SAO TOME AND PRINCIPE
Degree of trade union independence, mid-1983
independent unions effectively free of government control
unions nominally independent but tightly controlled
unions nominally independent but totally controlled
unions nominally independent but severely repressed
virtually no recognized trade unions
Sources: press reports; personal communications

36. The Force of Labour

The essential conflict for authority between the state and its alternatives runs through trade unionism and the trade unions.

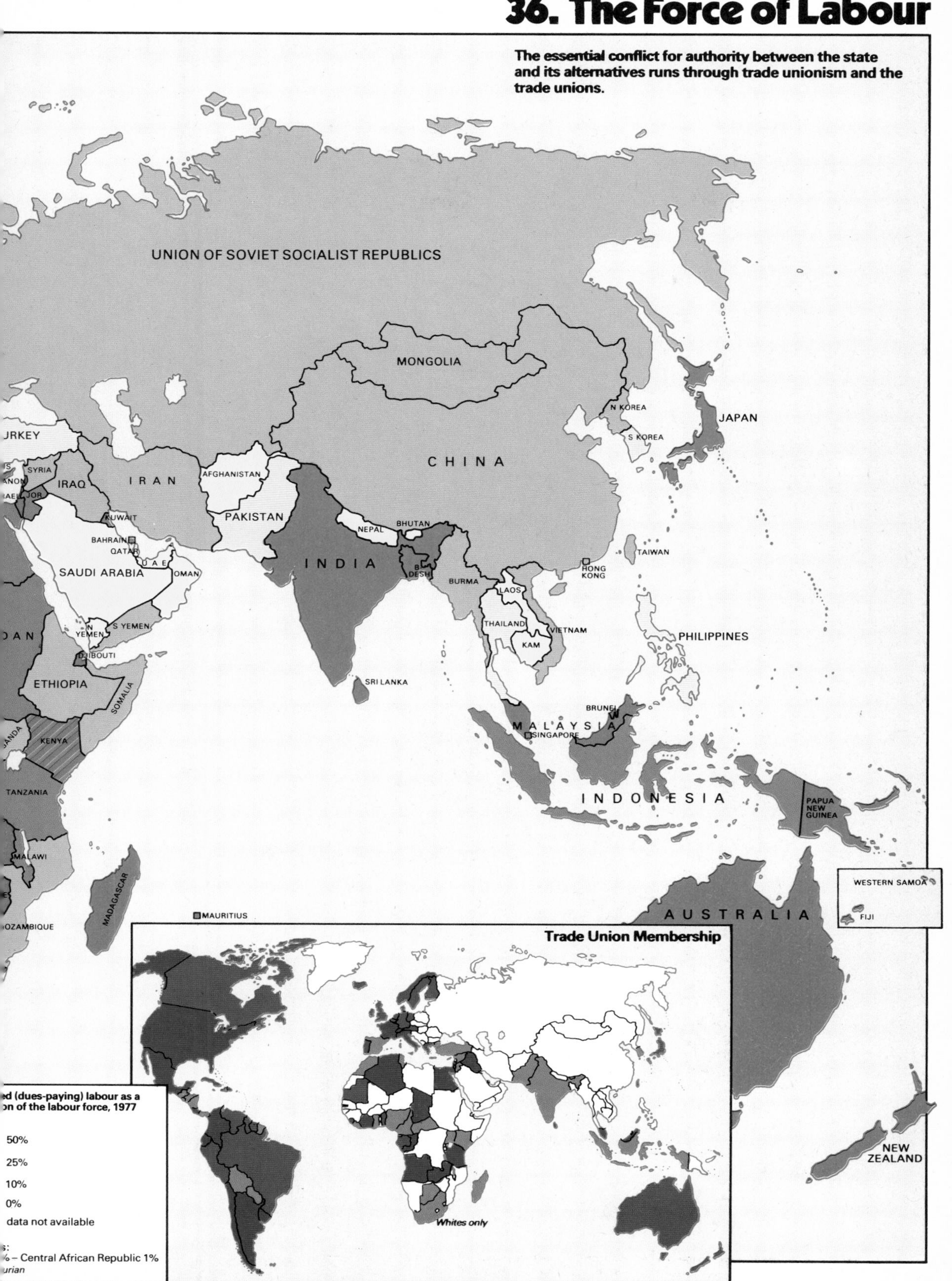

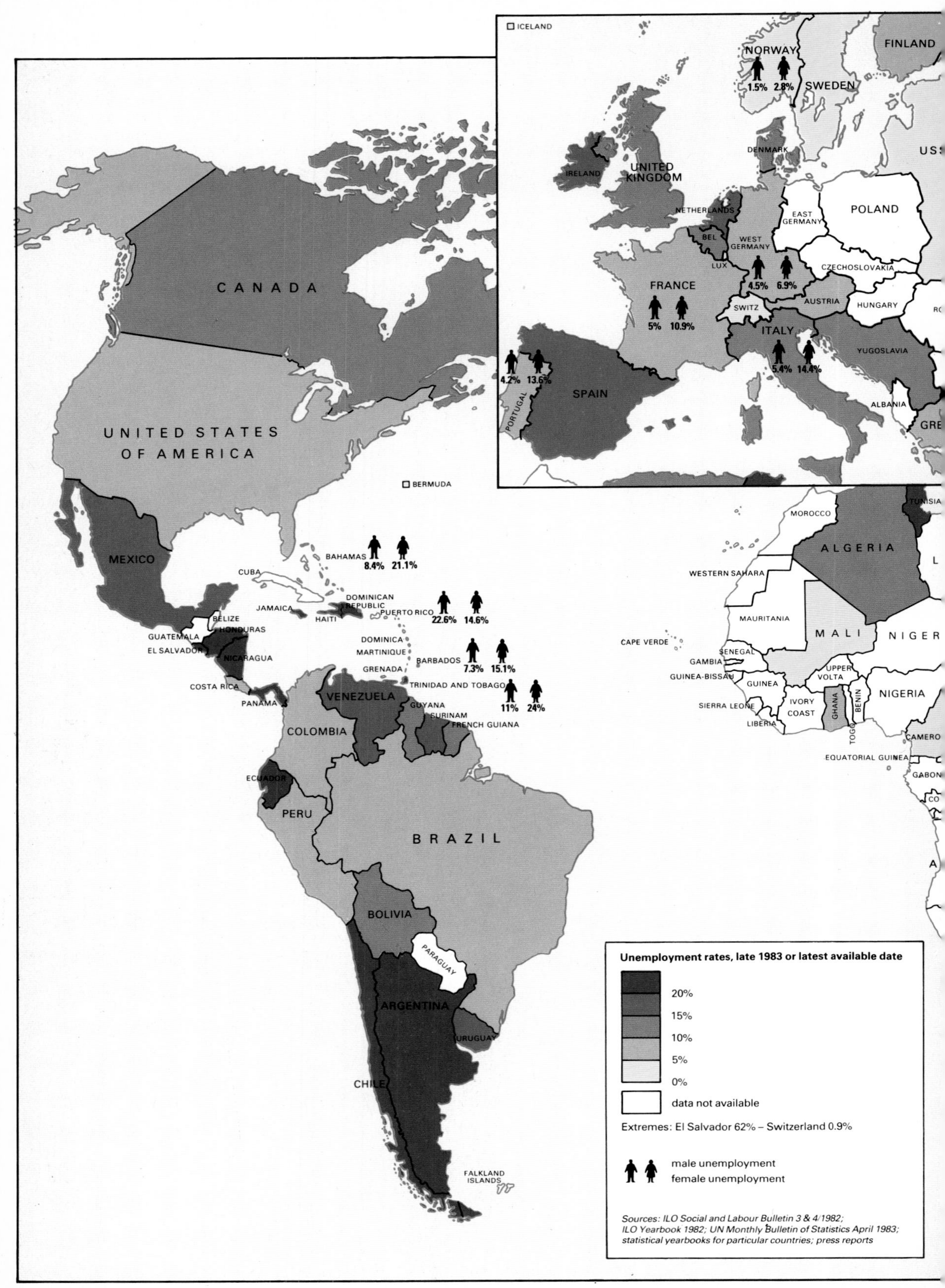
ICELAND
NORWAY
1.5% 2.8%
SWEDEN
FINLAND
DENMARK
IRELAND
UNITED KINGDOM
NETHERLANDS
BEL
LUX
EAST GERMANY
POLAND
WEST GERMANY
4.5% 6.9%
CZECHOSLOVAKIA
FRANCE
5% 10.9%
SWITZ
AUSTRIA
HUNGARY
ITALY
5.4% 14.4%
YUGOSLAVIA
4.2% 13.6%
PORTUGAL
SPAIN
ALBANIA
CANADA
UNITED STATES OF AMERICA
BERMUDA
MEXICO
BAHAMAS
8.4% 21.1%
CUBA
DOMINICAN REPUBLIC
JAMAICA
HAITI
PUERTO RICO
22.6% 14.6%
BELIZE
GUATEMALA
HONDURAS
EL SALVADOR
NICARAGUA
DOMINICA
MARTINIQUE
BARBADOS
7.3% 15.1%
GRENADA
TRINIDAD AND TOBAGO
11% 24%
COSTA RICA
PANAMA
VENEZUELA
GUYANA
SURINAM
FRENCH GUIANA
COLOMBIA
ECUADOR
PERU
BRAZIL
BOLIVIA
PARAGUAY
ARGENTINA
URUGUAY
CHILE
FALKLAND ISLANDS
TUNISIA
MOROCCO
ALGERIA
WESTERN SAHARA
MAURITANIA
MALI
NIGER
CAPE VERDE
SENEGAL
GAMBIA
GUINEA-BISSAU
GUINEA
UPPER VOLTA
SIERRA LEONE
LIBERIA
IVORY COAST
GHANA
TOGO
BENIN
NIGERIA
EQUATORIAL GUINEA
GABON
Unemployment rates, late 1983 or latest available date
20%
15%
10%
5%
0%
data not available
Extremes: El Salvador 62% – Switzerland 0.9%
male unemployment
female unemployment
Sources: ILO Social and Labour Bulletin 3 & 4/1982; ILO Yearbook 1982; UN Monthly Bulletin of Statistics April 1983; statistical yearbooks for particular countries; press reports

37. Unemployment

Unemployment is a matter of political semantics rather than of economic or social statistics. In the Philippines the unemployment figures exclude anyone who has had at least one hour of paid employment in the previous three months. In most countries they have no relevance to most of the population, who live on the land.

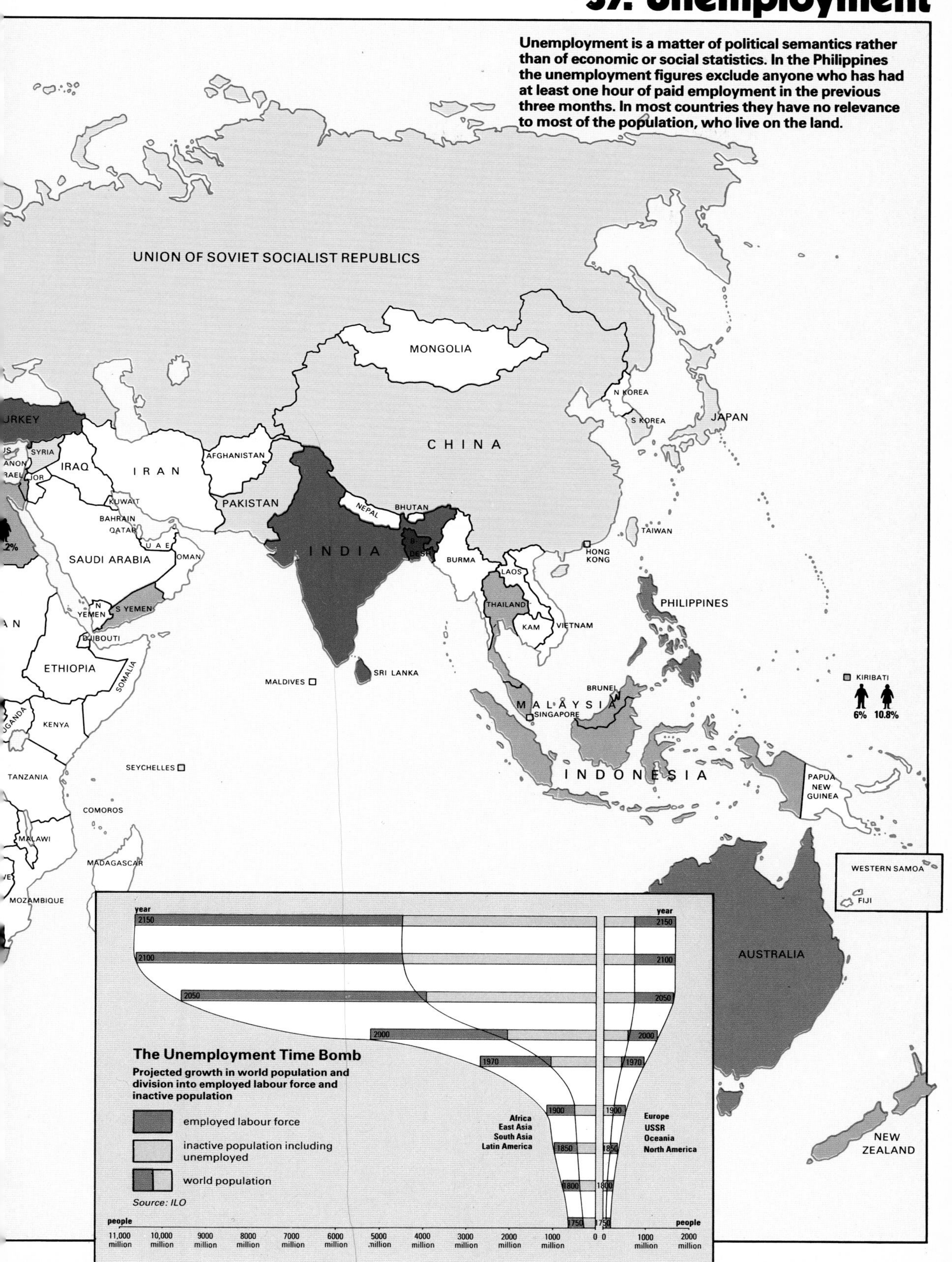

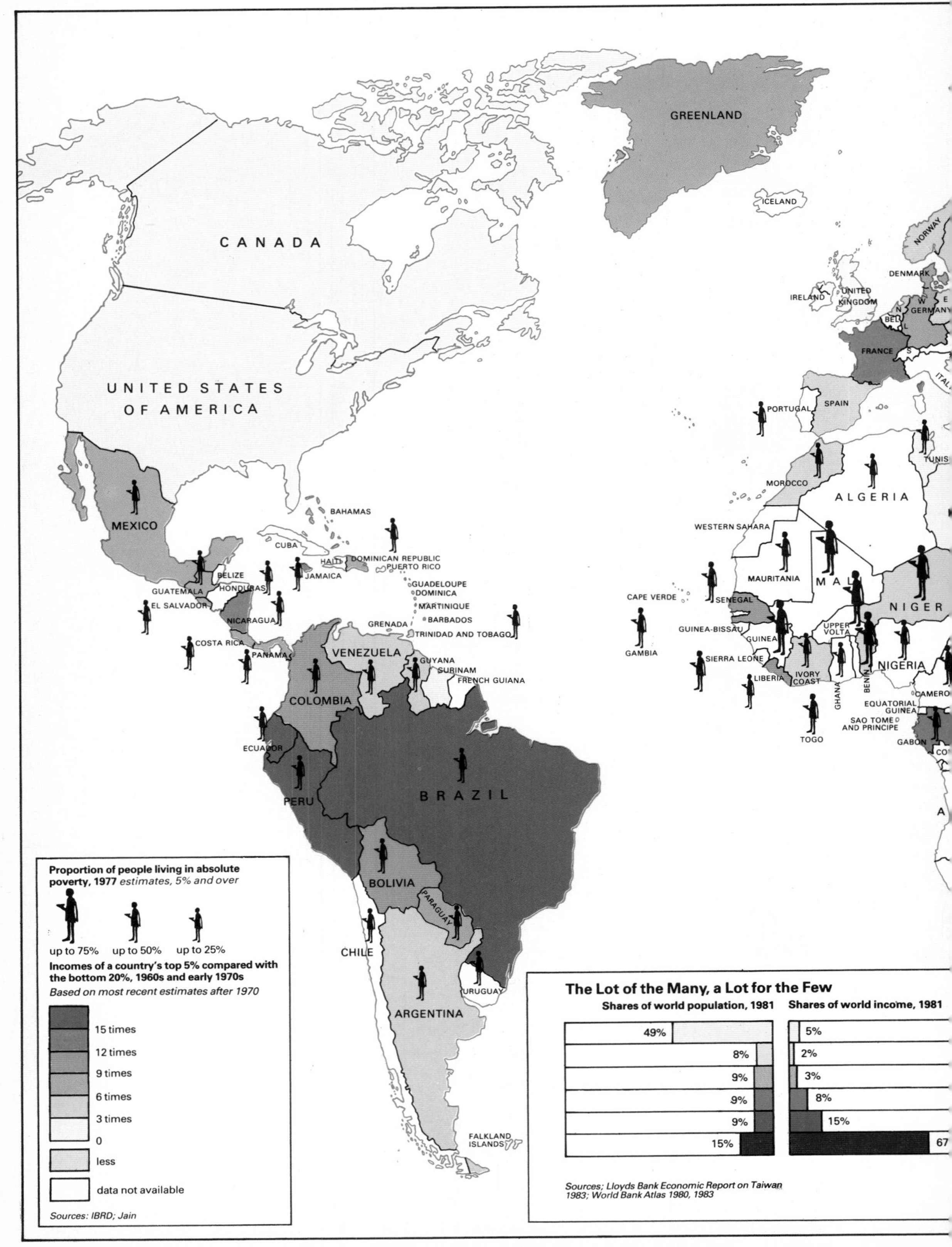
GREENLAND
ICELAND
CANADA
UNITED STATES OF AMERICA
NORWAY
DENMARK
IRELAND
UNITED KINGDOM
W GERMANY
BEL
FRANCE
SPAIN
PORTUGAL
TUNIS
MOROCCO
ALGERIA
WESTERN SAHARA
MAURITANIA
MAL
NIGER
CAPE VERDE
SENEGAL
GAMBIA
GUINEA-BISSAU
GUINEA
SIERRA LEONE
LIBERIA
IVORY COAST
UPPER VOLTA
GHANA
TOGO
BENIN
NIGERIA
CAMERO
EQUATORIAL GUINEA
SAO TOME AND PRINCIPE
GABON
MEXICO
BAHAMAS
CUBA
HAITI
DOMINICAN REPUBLIC
PUERTO RICO
JAMAICA
BELIZE
GUATEMALA
HONDURAS
EL SALVADOR
NICARAGUA
COSTA RICA
PANAMA
GUADELOUPE
DOMINICA
MARTINIQUE
BARBADOS
GRENADA
TRINIDAD AND TOBAGO
VENEZUELA
GUYANA
SURINAM
FRENCH GUIANA
COLOMBIA
ECUADOR
PERU
BRAZIL
BOLIVIA
PARAGUAY
CHILE
URUGUAY
ARGENTINA
FALKLAND ISLANDS
Proportion of people living in absolute poverty, 1977 estimates, 5% and over
up to 75%
up to 50%
up to 25%
Incomes of a country's top 5% compared with the bottom 20%, 1960s and early 1970s
Based on most recent estimates after 1970
15 times
12 times
9 times
6 times
3 times
0
less
data not available
Sources: IBRD; Jain
The Lot of the Many, a Lot for the Few
Shares of world population, 1981
Shares of world income, 1981
49%
8%
9%
9%
9%
15%
5%
2%
3%
8%
15%
67
Sources; Lloyds Bank Economic Report on Taiwan 1983; World Bank Atlas 1980, 1983

38. Rich and Poor People

It is the world order that makes rich and poor states, and rich and poor people within each of them. It is said that the poor will inherit the earth. But meanwhile the rich are in profitable possession.

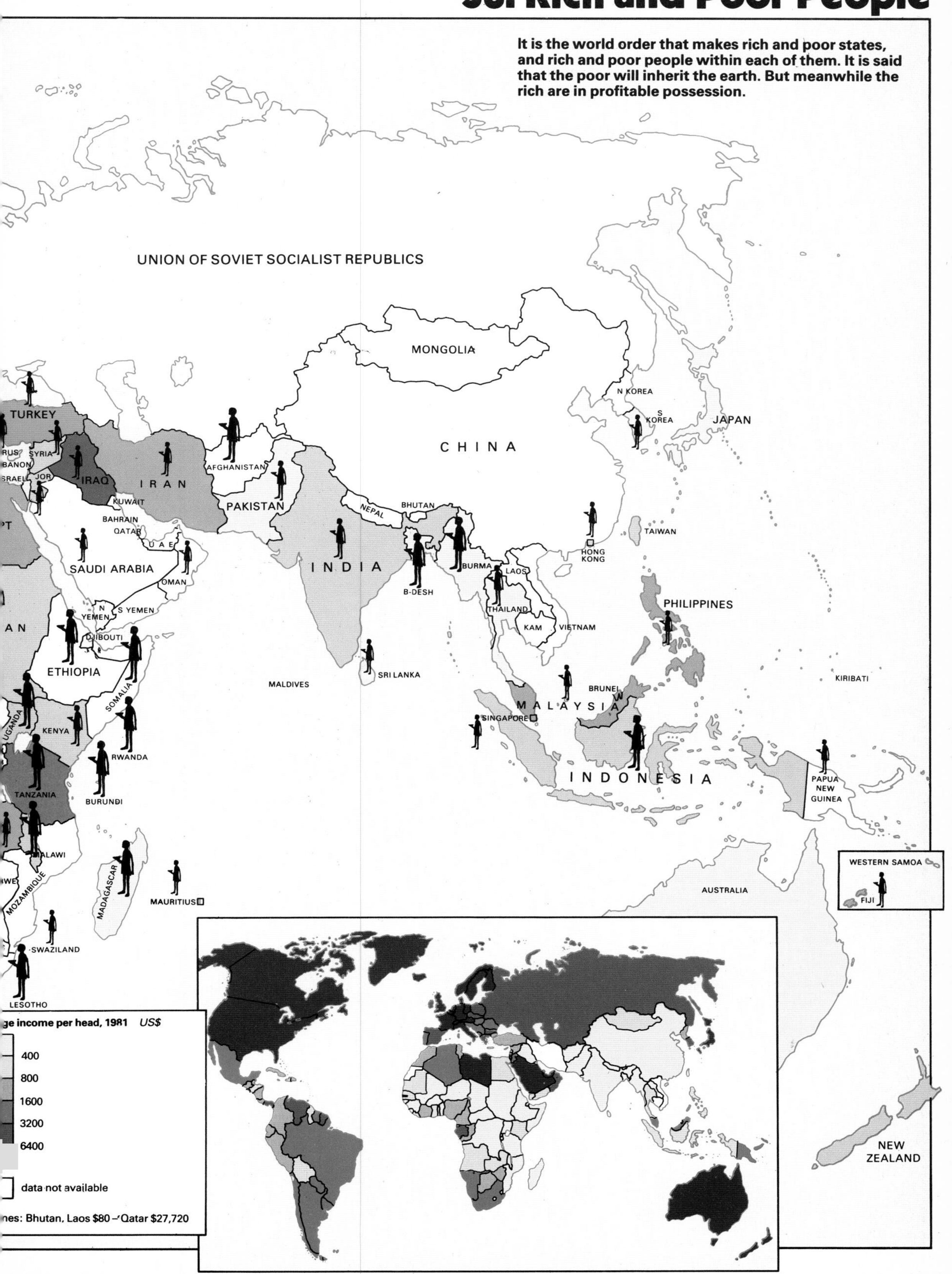

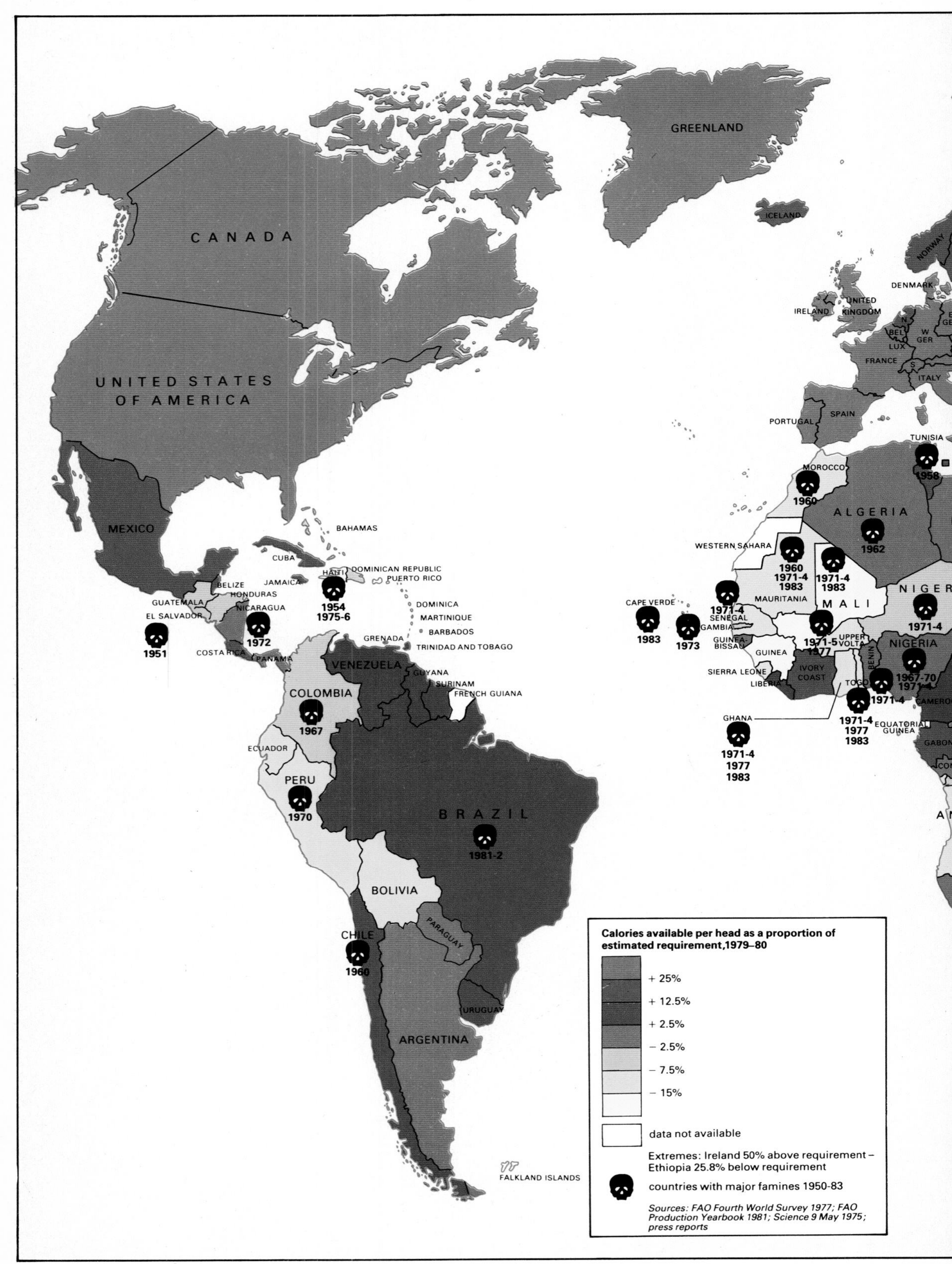

Calories available per head as a proportion of estimated requirement, 1979–80
+ 25%
+ 12.5%
+ 2.5%
– 2.5%
– 7.5%
– 15%
data not available
Extremes: Ireland 50% above requirement – Ethiopia 25.8% below requirement
countries with major famines 1950-83
Sources: FAO Fourth World Survey 1977; FAO Production Yearbook 1981; Science 9 May 1975; press reports
GREENLAND
ICELAND
CANADA
UNITED STATES OF AMERICA
MEXICO
BAHAMAS
CUBA
HAITI
1954
1975-6
DOMINICAN REPUBLIC
PUERTO RICO
JAMAICA
BELIZE
HONDURAS
GUATEMALA
NICARAGUA
1972
EL SALVADOR
1951
COSTA RICA
PANAMA
DOMINICA
MARTINIQUE
BARBADOS
GRENADA
TRINIDAD AND TOBAGO
VENEZUELA
GUYANA
SURINAM
FRENCH GUIANA
COLOMBIA
1967
ECUADOR
PERU
1970
BRAZIL
1981-2
BOLIVIA
PARAGUAY
CHILE
1960
URUGUAY
ARGENTINA
FALKLAND ISLANDS
NORWAY
DENMARK
IRELAND
UNITED KINGDOM
BEL
LUX
W GER
FRANCE
ITALY
SPAIN
PORTUGAL
TUNISIA
1958
MOROCCO
1960
ALGERIA
1962
WESTERN SAHARA
1960
1971-4
1983
MAURITANIA
1971-4
1983
MALI
NIGER
1971-4
CAPE VERDE
1983
SENEGAL
1971-4
GAMBIA
1973
GUINEA-BISSAU
GUINEA
1971-5
1977
UPPER VOLTA
SIERRA LEONE
LIBERIA
IVORY COAST
TOGO
BENIN
1971-4
NIGERIA
1967-70
GHANA
1971-4
1977
1983
1971-4
1977
1983
EQUATORIAL GUINEA
GABON

39. Our Daily Bread

'If the world was a village of 1000 inhabitants, 240 would not have enough to eat.' Victor Michel, in the European Parliament, 1982.

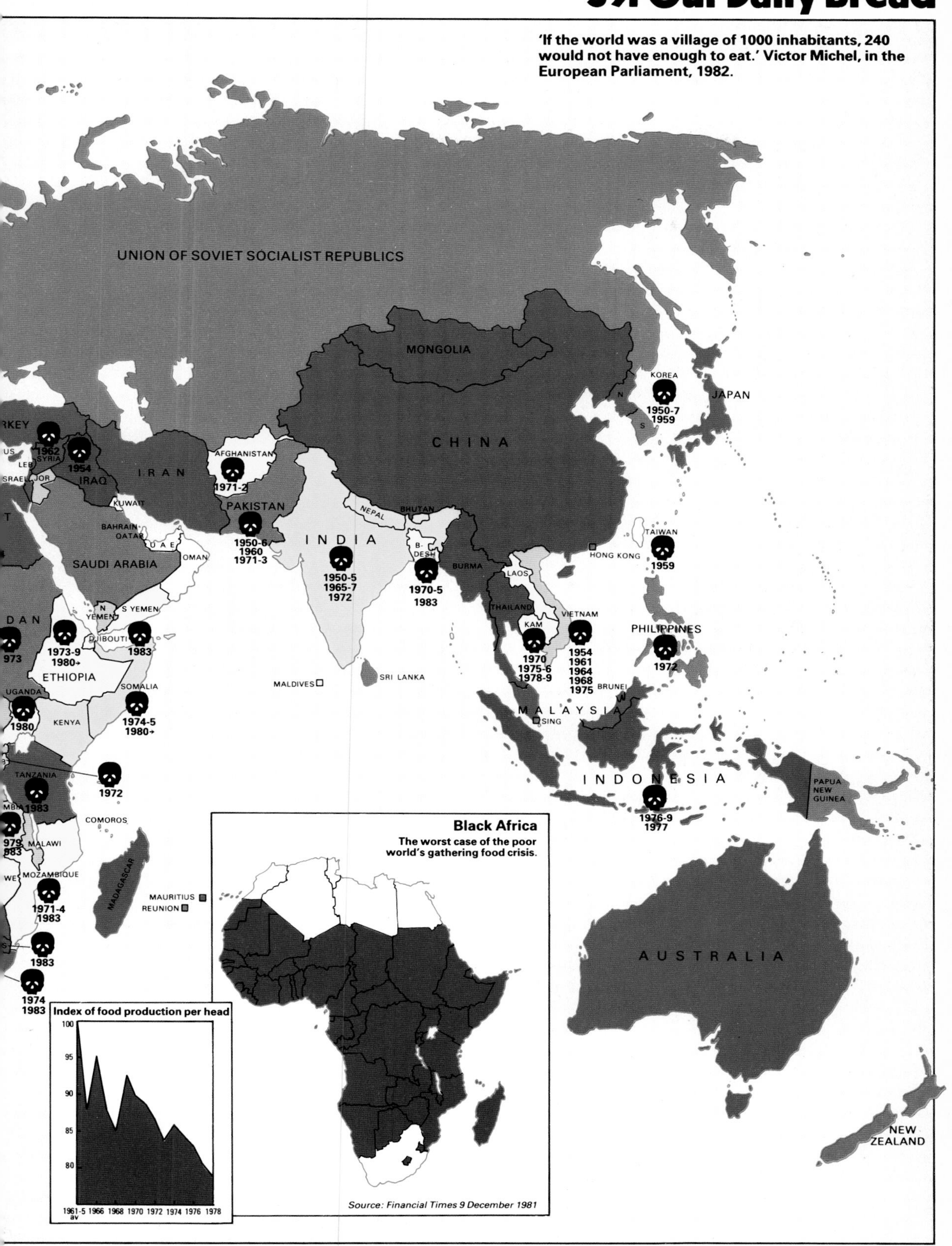

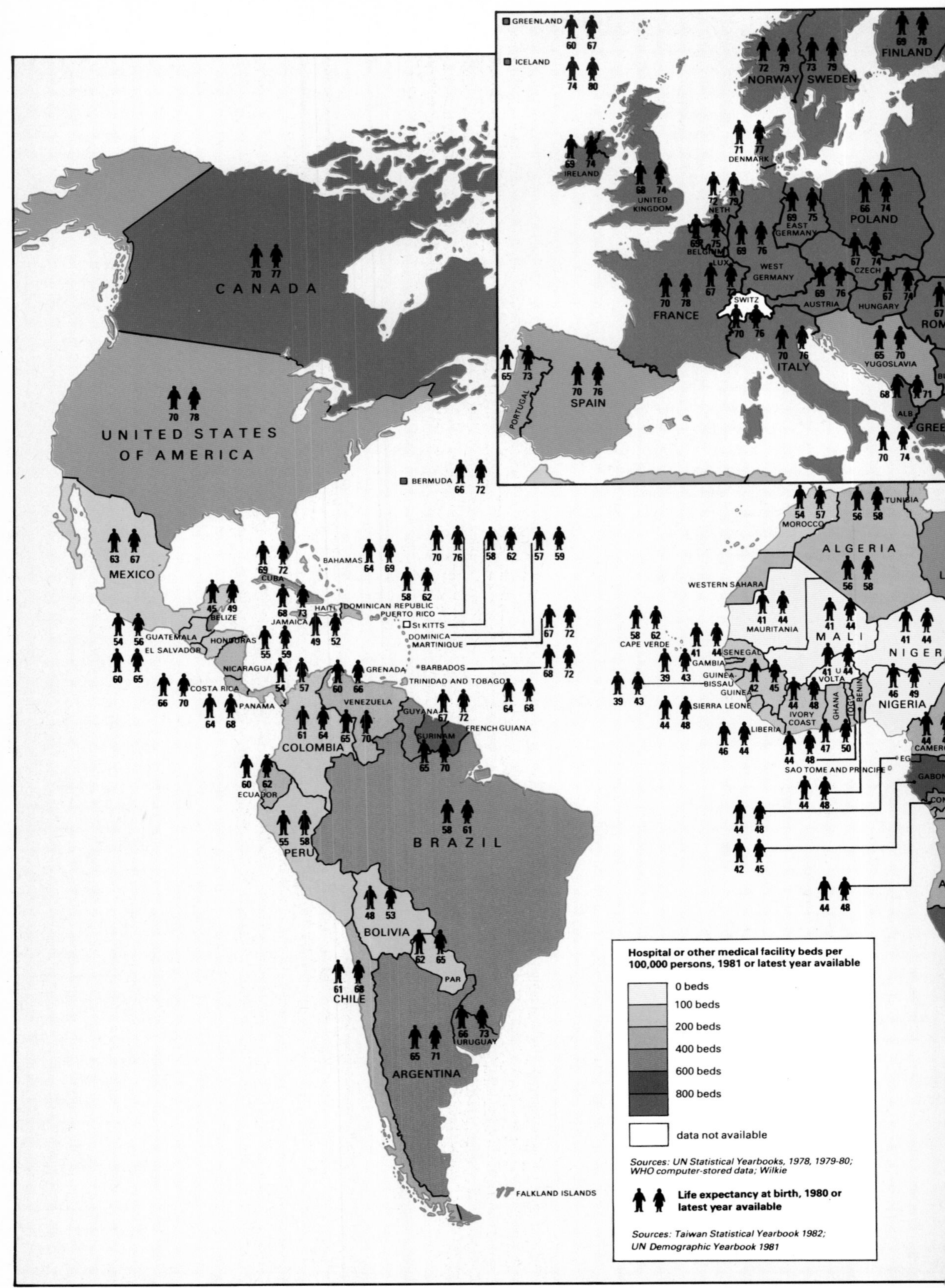

GREENLAND 60 67
ICELAND 74 80
FINLAND 69 78
NORWAY 72 79
SWEDEN 73 79
DENMARK 71 77
IRELAND 69 74
UNITED KINGDOM 68 74
NETH 72 79
BELGIUM 69 75
LUX 67 73
EAST GERMANY 69 75
WEST GERMANY 69 76
POLAND 66 74
CZECH 67 74
AUSTRIA 69 76
HUNGARY 67 74
ROM 67
FRANCE 70 78
SWITZ 70 76
ITALY 70 76
YUGOSLAVIA 65 70
ALB 68 71
GREE 70 74
PORTUGAL 65 73
SPAIN 70 76
CANADA 70 77
UNITED STATES OF AMERICA 70 78
BERMUDA 66 72
MEXICO 63 67
CUBA 69 72
BAHAMAS 64 69
DOMINICAN REPUBLIC 58 62
HAITI 49 52
JAMAICA 68 73
PUERTO RICO 70 76
St KITTS 58 62
DOMINICA 57 59
MARTINIQUE 67 72
BARBADOS 68 72
TRINIDAD AND TOBAGO 64 68
GRENADA
BELIZE 45 49
GUATEMALA 54 56
EL SALVADOR 60 65
HONDURAS 55 59
NICARAGUA 54 57
COSTA RICA 66 70
PANAMA 64 68
VENEZUELA 60 66
COLOMBIA 61 64
GUYANA 67 72
SURINAM 65 70
FRENCH GUIANA
ECUADOR 60 62
PERU 55 58
BRAZIL 58 61
BOLIVIA 48 53
PAR 62 65
CHILE 61 68
URUGUAY 66 73
ARGENTINA 65 71
FALKLAND ISLANDS
MOROCCO 54 57
TUNISIA 56 58
ALGERIA 56 58
WESTERN SAHARA
MAURITANIA 41 44
MALI 41 44
NIGER 41 44
CAPE VERDE 58 62
SENEGAL 41 44
GAMBIA 39 43
GUINEA-BISSAU 39 43
GUINEA 42 45
SIERRA LEONE 44 48
LIBERIA 46 44
IVORY COAST 44 48
U VOLTA 41 44
GHANA 44 48
TOGO 47 50
BENIN
NIGERIA 46 49
CAMER 44
SAO TOME AND PRINCIPE 44 48
EG 44 48
GABON 42 45
CON 44 48
Hospital or other medical facility beds per 100,000 persons, 1981 or latest year available
0 beds
100 beds
200 beds
400 beds
600 beds
800 beds
data not available
Sources: UN Statistical Yearbooks, 1978, 1979-80; WHO computer-stored data; Wilkie
Life expectancy at birth, 1980 or latest year available
Sources: Taiwan Statistical Yearbook 1982; UN Demographic Yearbook 1981

40. Without Due Care and Attention

'The days of our years are three-score years and ten' - if you happen to be European or North American.

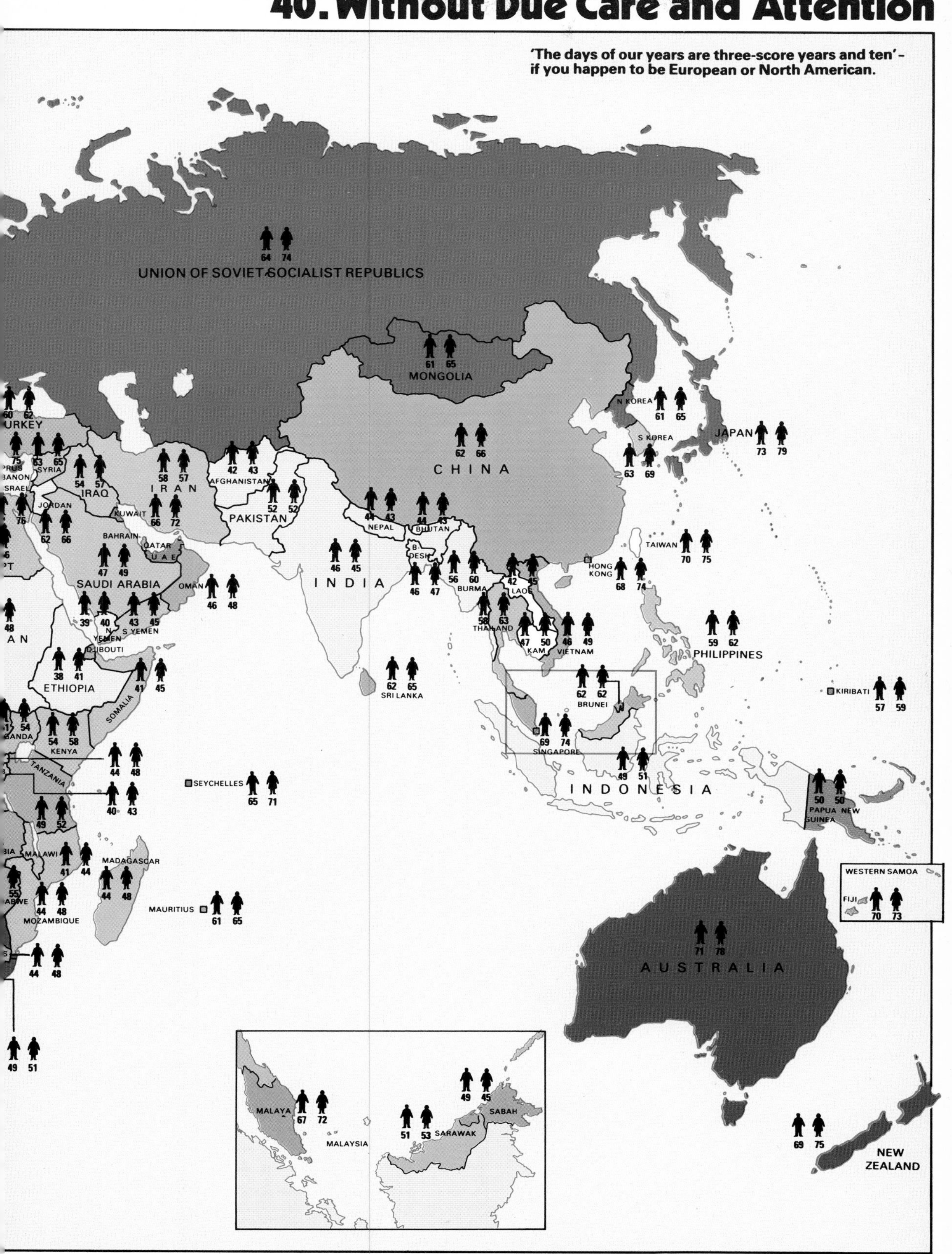

1. No E

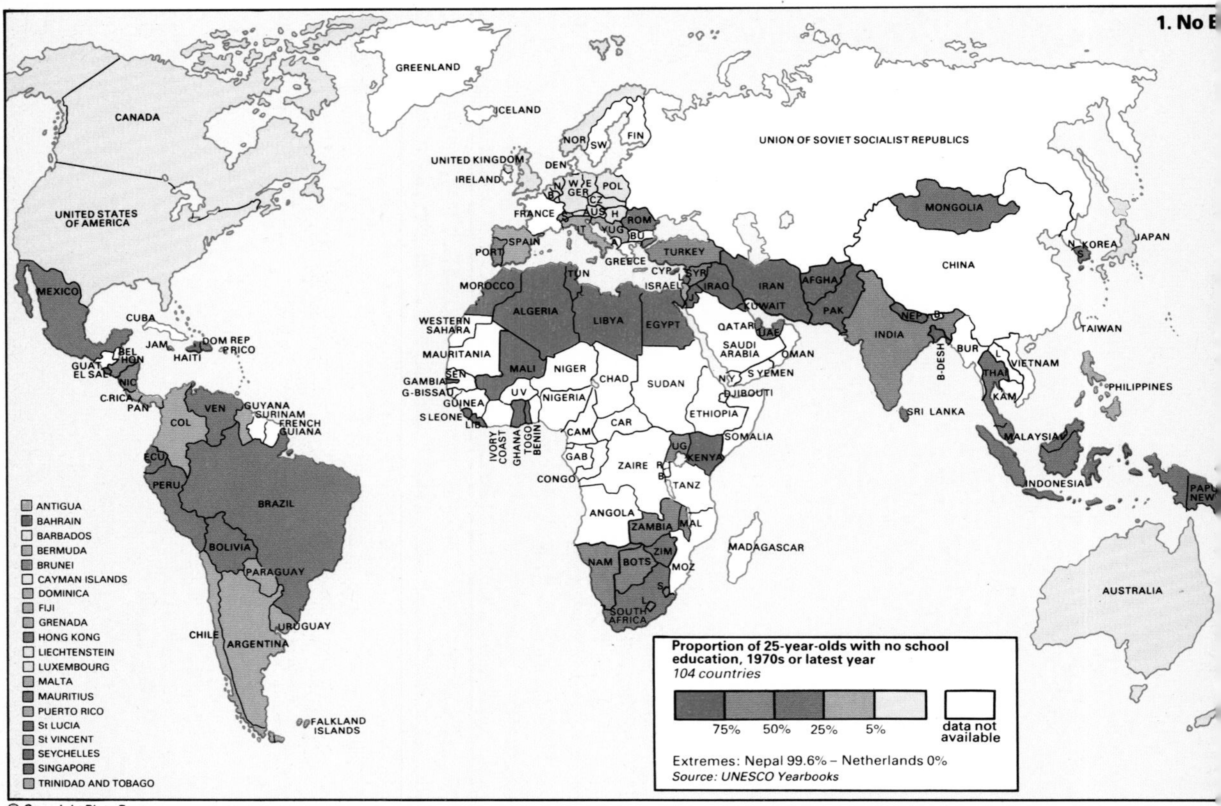

ANTIGUA
BAHRAIN
BARBADOS
BERMUDA
BRUNEI
CAYMAN ISLANDS
DOMINICA
FIJI
GRENADA
HONG KONG
LIECHTENSTEIN
LUXEMBOURG
MALTA
MAURITIUS
PUERTO RICO
St LUCIA
St VINCENT
SEYCHELLES
SINGAPORE
TRINIDAD AND TOBAGO

Proportion of 25-year-olds with no school education, 1970s or latest year
104 countries

75% 50% 25% 5% — data not available

Extremes: Nepal 99.6% – Netherlands 0%
Source: UNESCO Yearbooks

2. Along the

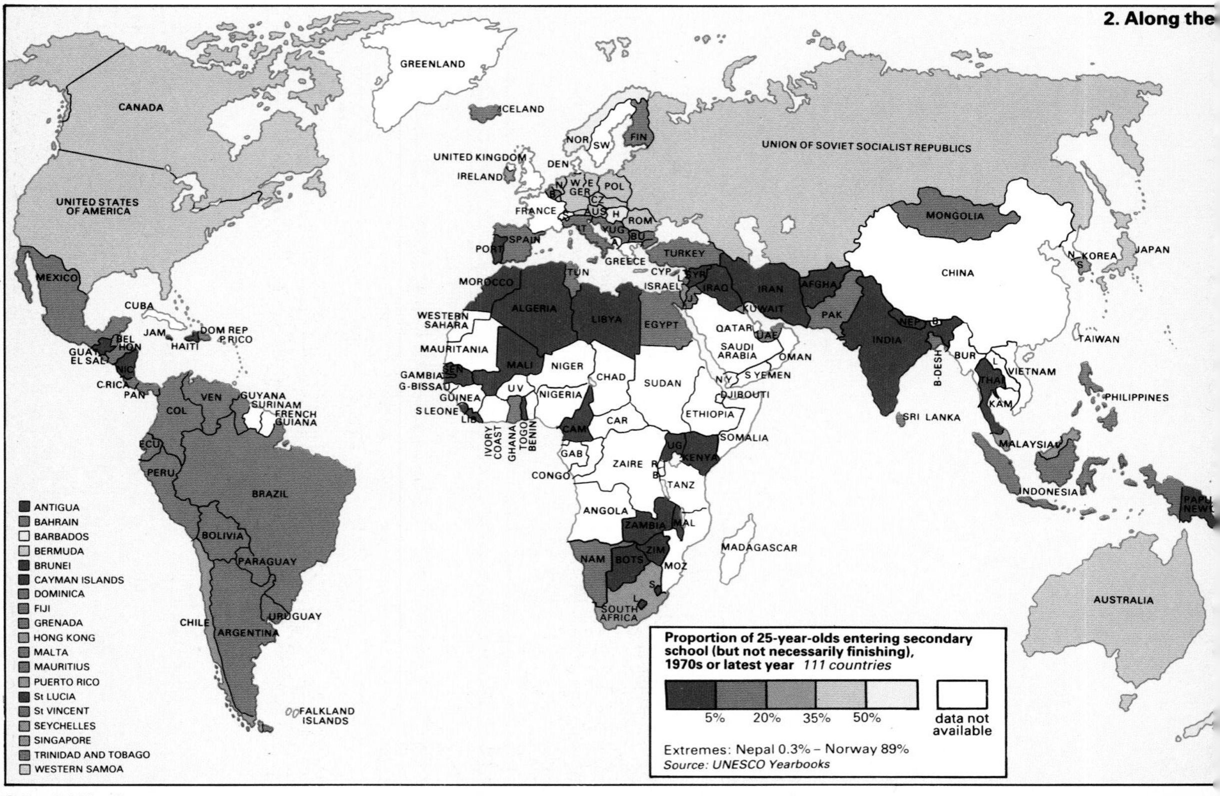

ANTIGUA
BAHRAIN
BARBADOS
BERMUDA
BRUNEI
CAYMAN ISLANDS
DOMINICA
FIJI
GRENADA
HONG KONG
MALTA
MAURITIUS
PUERTO RICO
St LUCIA
St VINCENT
SEYCHELLES
SINGAPORE
TRINIDAD AND TOBAGO
WESTERN SAMOA

Proportion of 25-year-olds entering secondary school (but not necessarily finishing), 1970s or latest year *111 countries*

5% 20% 35% 50% — data not available

Extremes: Nepal 0.3% – Norway 89%
Source: UNESCO Yearbooks

41. The Right to Learn

3. The Lucky Few

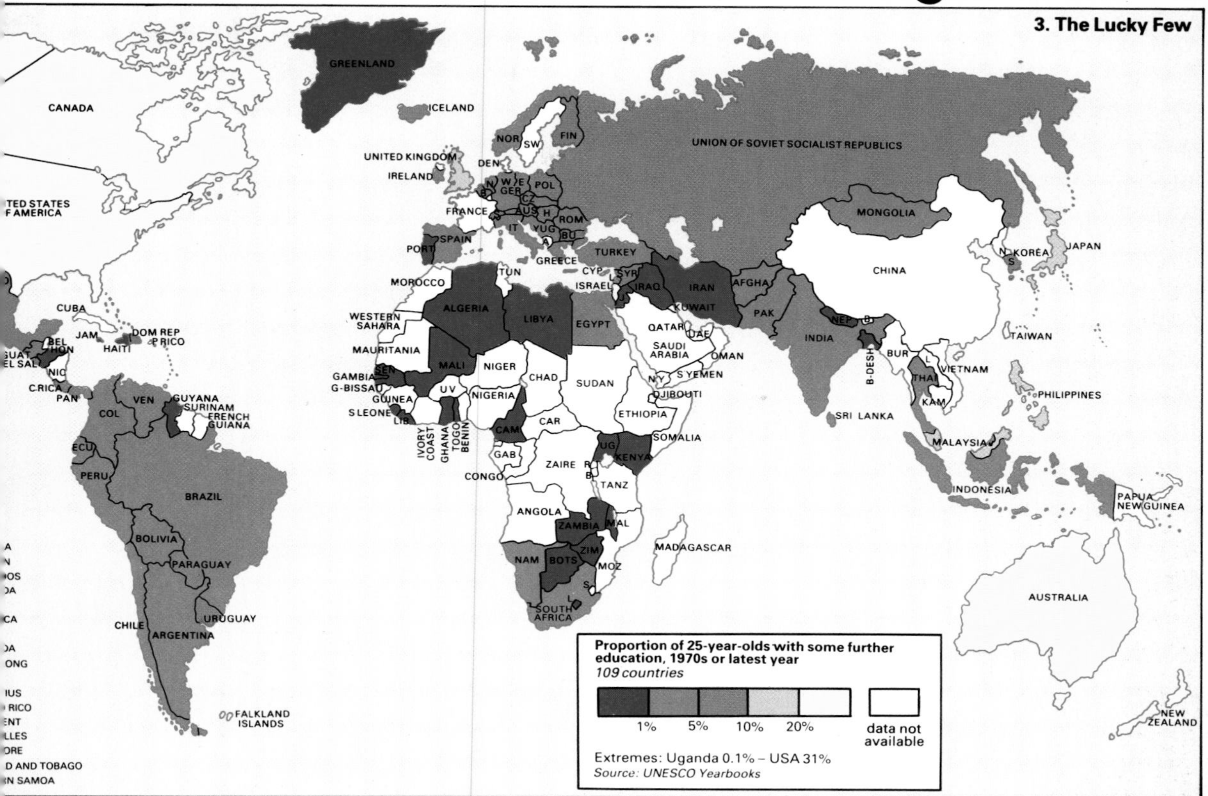

Proportion of 25-year-olds with some further education, 1970s or latest year
109 countries

1% 5% 10% 20%

data not available

Extremes: Uganda 0.1% – USA 31%
Source: UNESCO Yearbooks

Pluto Press

4. Not Even a Beginning

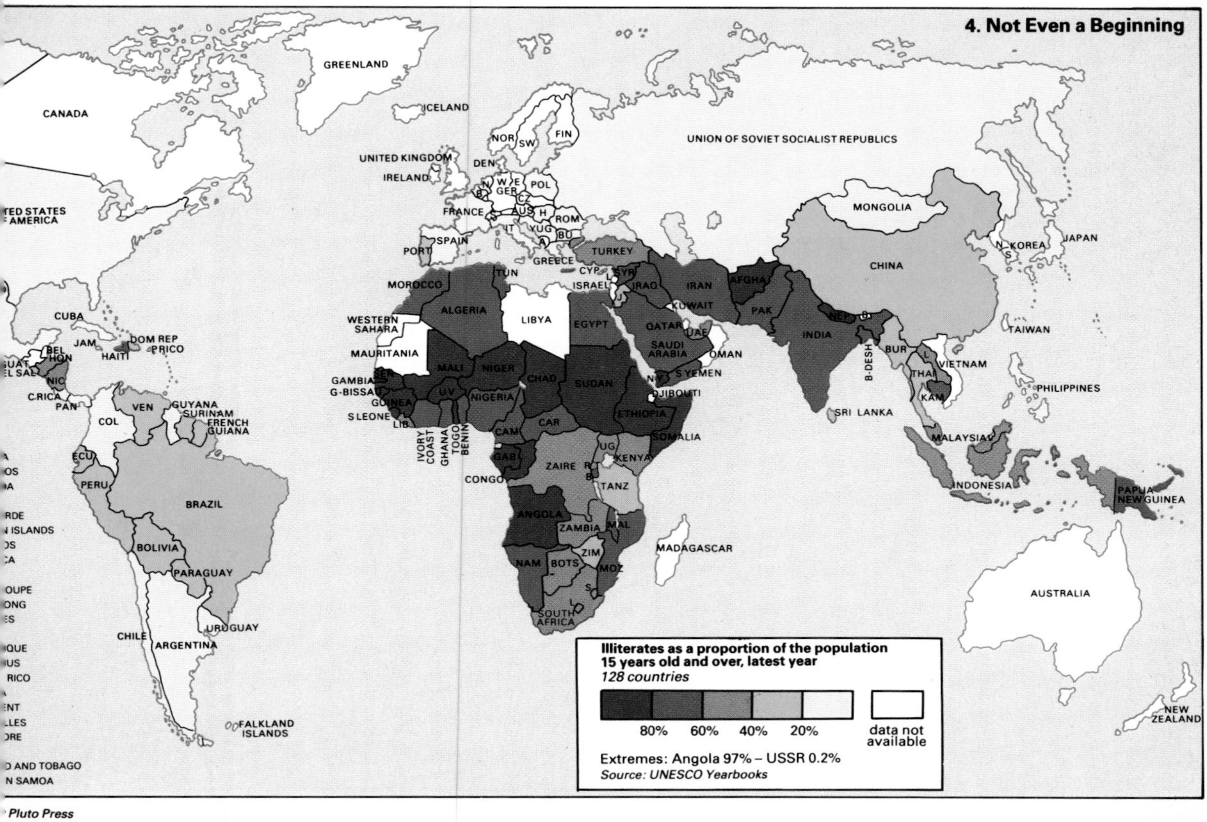

Illiterates as a proportion of the population 15 years old and over, latest year
128 countries

80% 60% 40% 20%

data not available

Extremes: Angola 97% – USSR 0.2%
Source: UNESCO Yearbooks

Pluto Press

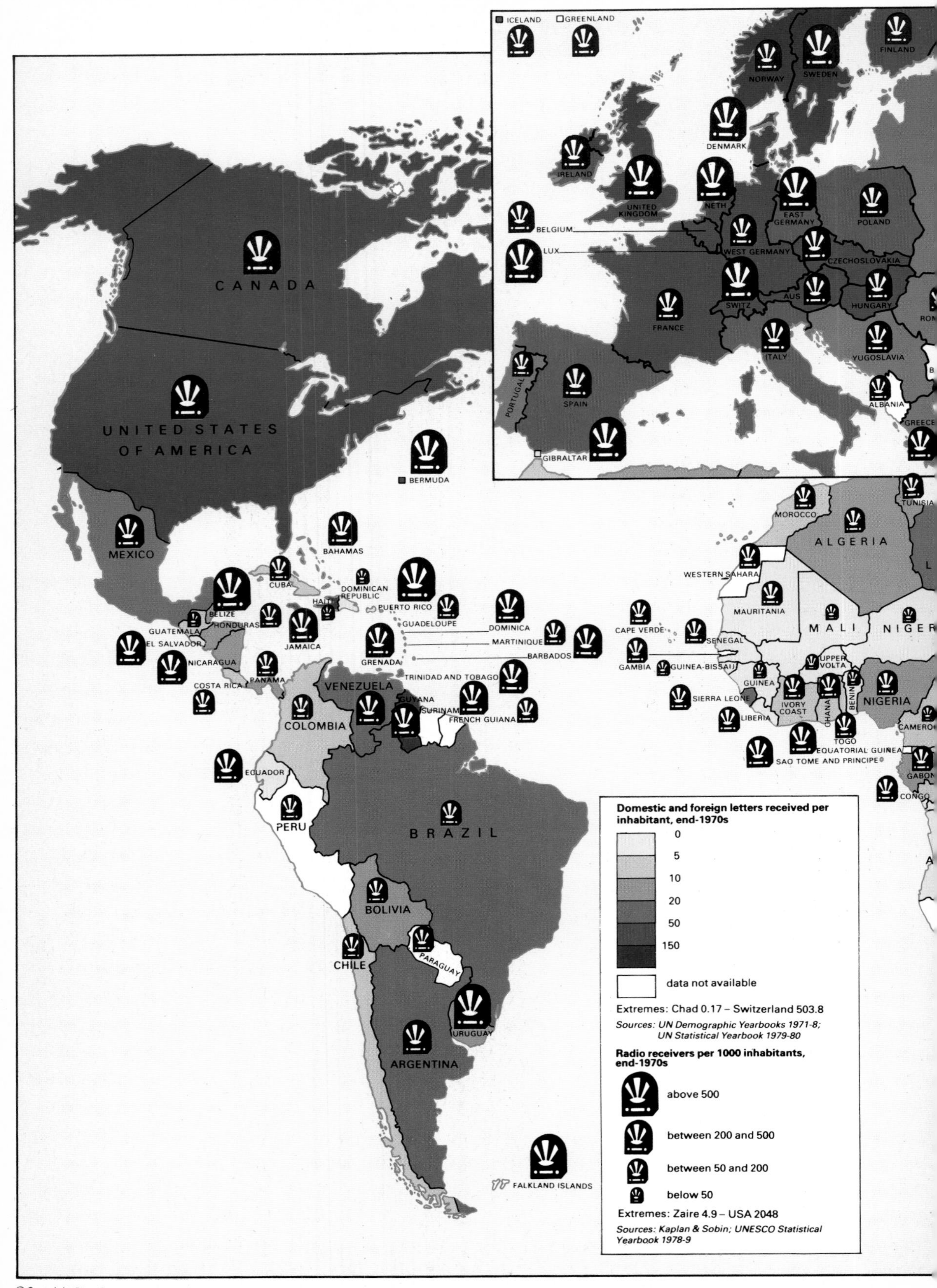
ICELAND
GREENLAND
FINLAND
NORWAY
SWEDEN
DENMARK
IRELAND
UNITED KINGDOM
NETH
EAST GERMANY
POLAND
BELGIUM
LUX
WEST GERMANY
CZECHOSLOVAKIA
AUS
SWITZ
HUNGARY
FRANCE
ITALY
YUGOSLAVIA
PORTUGAL
SPAIN
ALBANIA
GREECE
GIBRALTAR
CANADA
UNITED STATES OF AMERICA
BERMUDA
MEXICO
BAHAMAS
CUBA
DOMINICAN REPUBLIC
HAITI
PUERTO RICO
BELIZE
HONDURAS
GUATEMALA
EL SALVADOR
NICARAGUA
COSTA RICA
PANAMA
JAMAICA
GUADELOUPE
DOMINICA
MARTINIQUE
BARBADOS
GRENADA
TRINIDAD AND TOBAGO
VENEZUELA
GUYANA
SURINAM
FRENCH GUIANA
COLOMBIA
ECUADOR
PERU
BRAZIL
BOLIVIA
CHILE
PARAGUAY
URUGUAY
ARGENTINA
FALKLAND ISLANDS
MOROCCO
TUNISIA
ALGERIA
WESTERN SAHARA
MAURITANIA
MALI
NIGER
CAPE VERDE
SENEGAL
GAMBIA
GUINEA-BISSAU
UPPER VOLTA
GUINEA
SIERRA LEONE
LIBERIA
IVORY COAST
GHANA
BENIN
TOGO
NIGERIA
EQUATORIAL GUINEA
SAO TOME AND PRINCIPE
GABON
CONGO
Domestic and foreign letters received per inhabitant, end-1970s
0
5
10
20
50
150
data not available
Extremes: Chad 0.17 – Switzerland 503.8
Sources: UN Demographic Yearbooks 1971-8; UN Statistical Yearbook 1979-80
Radio receivers per 1000 inhabitants, end-1970s
above 500
between 200 and 500
between 50 and 200
below 50
Extremes: Zaire 4.9 – USA 2048
Sources: Kaplan & Sobin; UNESCO Statistical Yearbook 1978-9

42. The Longer Reach

Often it is poverty that imprisons people in their place; sometimes it is policy.

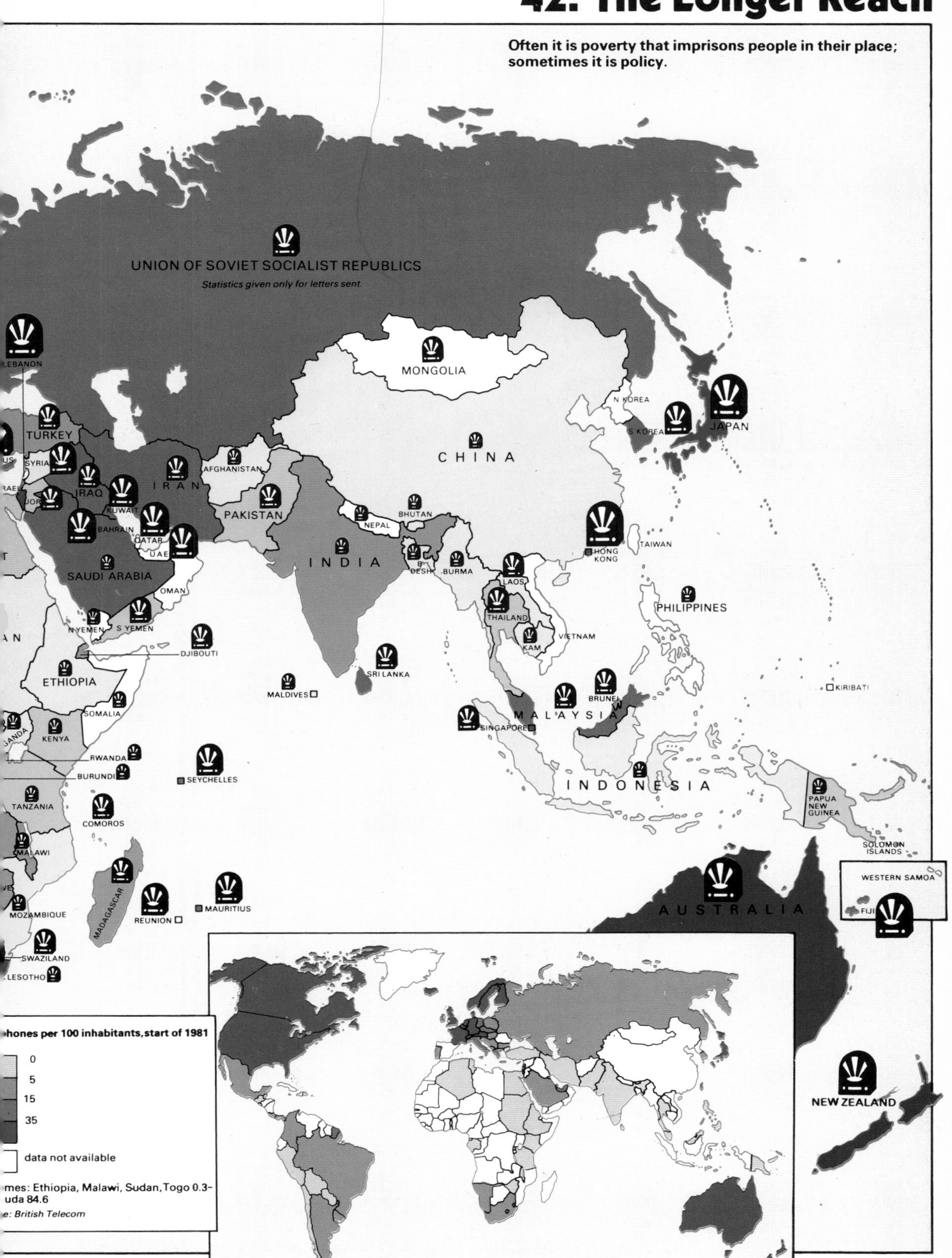

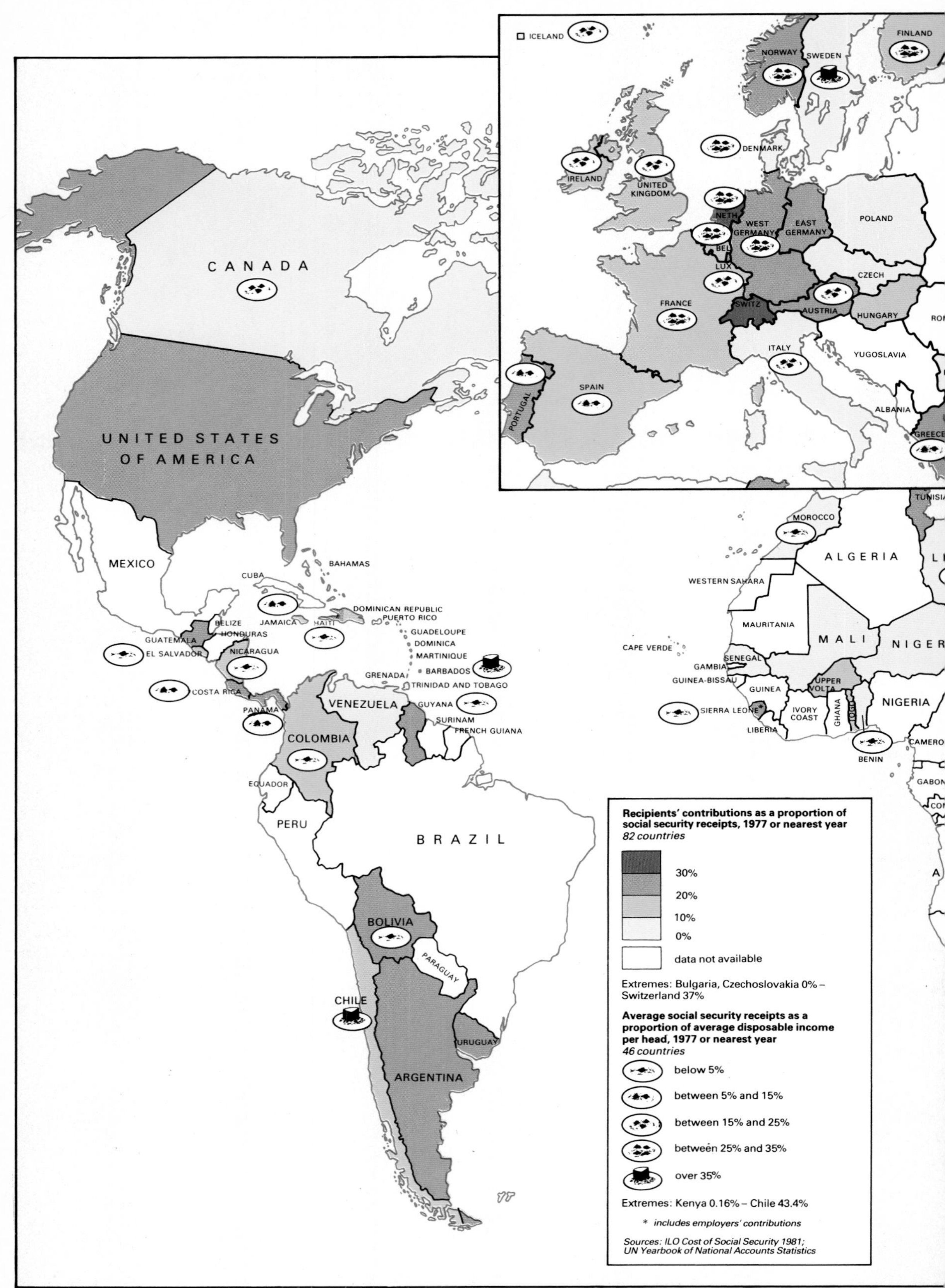
ICELAND
NORWAY
SWEDEN
FINLAND
DENMARK
IRELAND
UNITED KINGDOM
NETH
WEST GERMANY
EAST GERMANY
POLAND
BEL
LUX
CZECH
FRANCE
SWITZ
AUSTRIA
HUNGARY
ITALY
YUGOSLAVIA
PORTUGAL
SPAIN
ALBANIA
GREECE
TUNISIA
MOROCCO
ALGERIA
WESTERN SAHARA
MAURITANIA
MALI
NIGER
CAPE VERDE
SENEGAL
GAMBIA
GUINEA-BISSAU
GUINEA
UPPER VOLTA
SIERRA LEONE*
LIBERIA
IVORY COAST
GHANA
TOGO
NIGERIA
BENIN
GABON
CANADA
UNITED STATES OF AMERICA
MEXICO
BAHAMAS
CUBA
DOMINICAN REPUBLIC
PUERTO RICO
JAMAICA
HAITI
BELIZE
HONDURAS
GUATEMALA
EL SALVADOR
NICARAGUA
GUADELOUPE
DOMINICA
MARTINIQUE
BARBADOS
GRENADA
TRINIDAD AND TOBAGO
COSTA RICA
PANAMA
VENEZUELA
GUYANA
SURINAM
FRENCH GUIANA
COLOMBIA
ECUADOR
PERU
BRAZIL
BOLIVIA
PARAGUAY
CHILE
URUGUAY
ARGENTINA
Recipients' contributions as a proportion of social security receipts, 1977 or nearest year
82 countries
30%
20%
10%
0%
data not available
Extremes: Bulgaria, Czechoslovakia 0% – Switzerland 37%
Average social security receipts as a proportion of average disposable income per head, 1977 or nearest year
46 countries
below 5%
between 5% and 15%
between 15% and 25%
between 25% and 35%
over 35%
Extremes: Kenya 0.16% – Chile 43.4%
* includes employers' contributions
Sources: ILO Cost of Social Security 1981; UN Yearbook of National Accounts Statistics

43. Crumbs from the Cake

In general, the richer the government, the more it intrudes, even with its 'benevolence', in the life of the individual citizen.

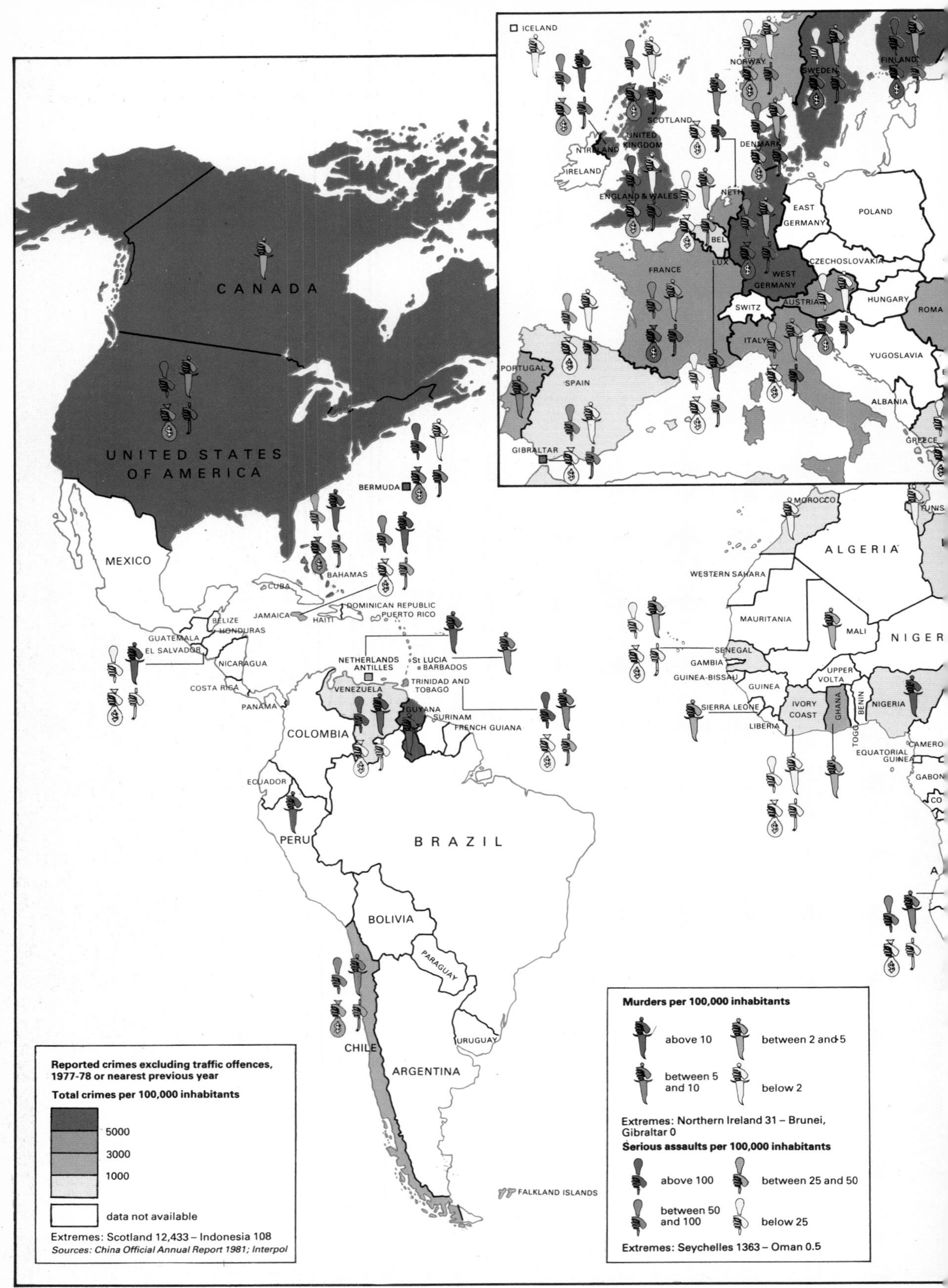

ICELAND
NORWAY
FINLAND
SWEDEN
SCOTLAND
UNITED KINGDOM
N IRELAND
IRELAND
DENMARK
ENGLAND & WALES
NETH
EAST GERMANY
POLAND
BEL
LUX
FRANCE
WEST GERMANY
CZECHOSLOVAKIA
SWITZ
AUSTRIA
HUNGARY
ROMA
ITALY
YUGOSLAVIA
PORTUGAL
SPAIN
ALBANIA
GREECE
GIBRALTAR
CANADA
UNITED STATES OF AMERICA
BERMUDA
MEXICO
BAHAMAS
CUBA
JAMAICA
HAITI
DOMINICAN REPUBLIC
PUERTO RICO
BELIZE
HONDURAS
GUATEMALA
EL SALVADOR
NICARAGUA
COSTA RICA
PANAMA
NETHERLANDS ANTILLES
St LUCIA
BARBADOS
TRINIDAD AND TOBAGO
VENEZUELA
GUYANA
SURINAM
FRENCH GUIANA
COLOMBIA
ECUADOR
PERU
BRAZIL
BOLIVIA
PARAGUAY
CHILE
URUGUAY
ARGENTINA
FALKLAND ISLANDS
MOROCCO
TUNIS
ALGERIA
WESTERN SAHARA
MAURITANIA
MALI
NIGER
SENEGAL
GAMBIA
GUINEA-BISSAU
UPPER VOLTA
GUINEA
SIERRA LEONE
LIBERIA
IVORY COAST
GHANA
TOGO
BENIN
NIGERIA
CAMERO
EQUATORIAL GUINEA
GABON
CO
Reported crimes excluding traffic offences, 1977-78 or nearest previous year
Total crimes per 100,000 inhabitants
5000
3000
1000
data not available
Extremes: Scotland 12,433 – Indonesia 108
Sources: China Official Annual Report 1981; Interpol
Murders per 100,000 inhabitants
above 10
between 2 and 5
between 5 and 10
below 2
Extremes: Northern Ireland 31 – Brunei, Gibraltar 0
Serious assaults per 100,000 inhabitants
above 100
between 25 and 50
between 50 and 100
below 25
Extremes: Seychelles 1363 – Oman 0.5

44. Law and Disorder

Not all crimes are similarly defined; not all similarly defined crimes are reported; not all reported crimes are recorded; and not all recorded crimes are communicated.

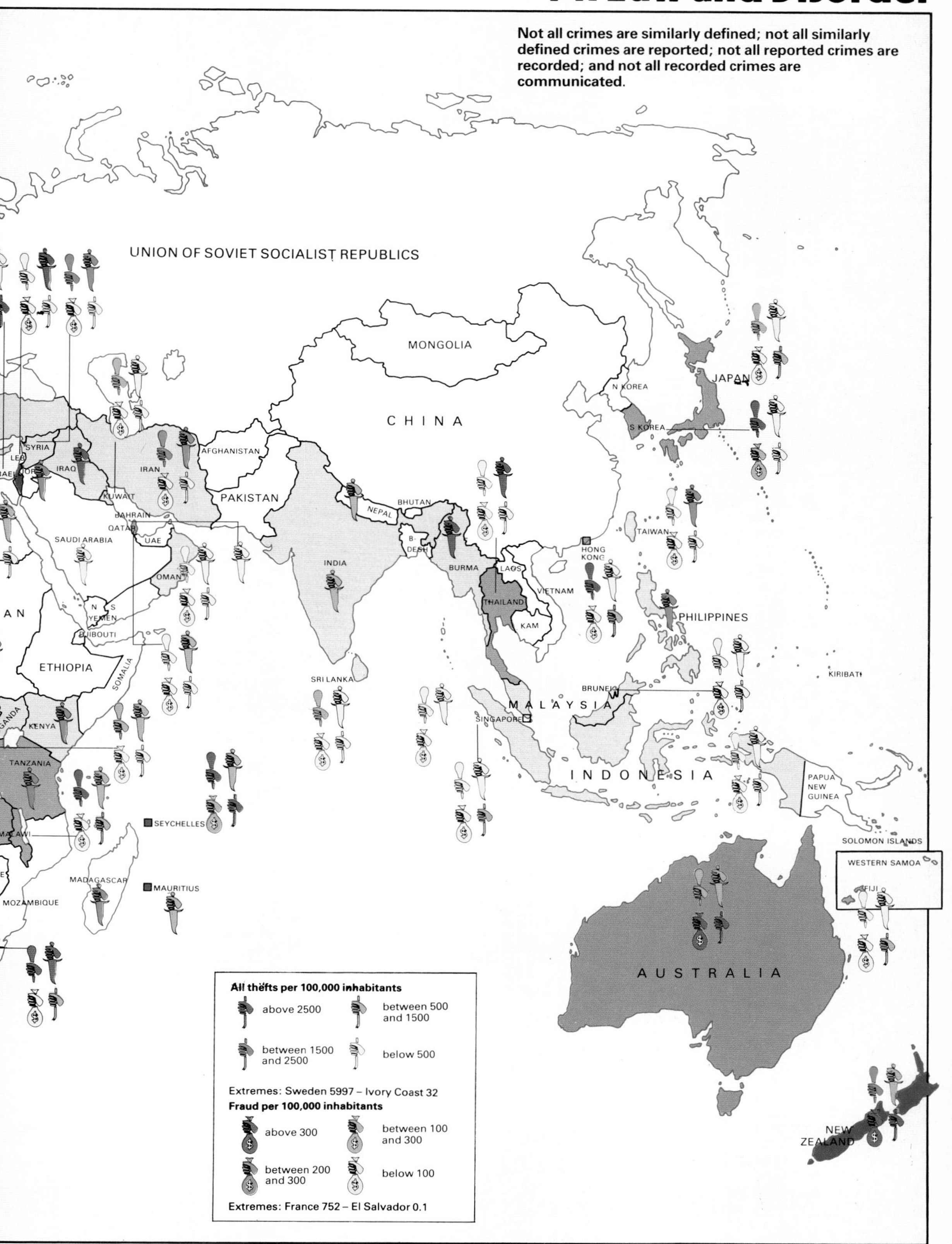

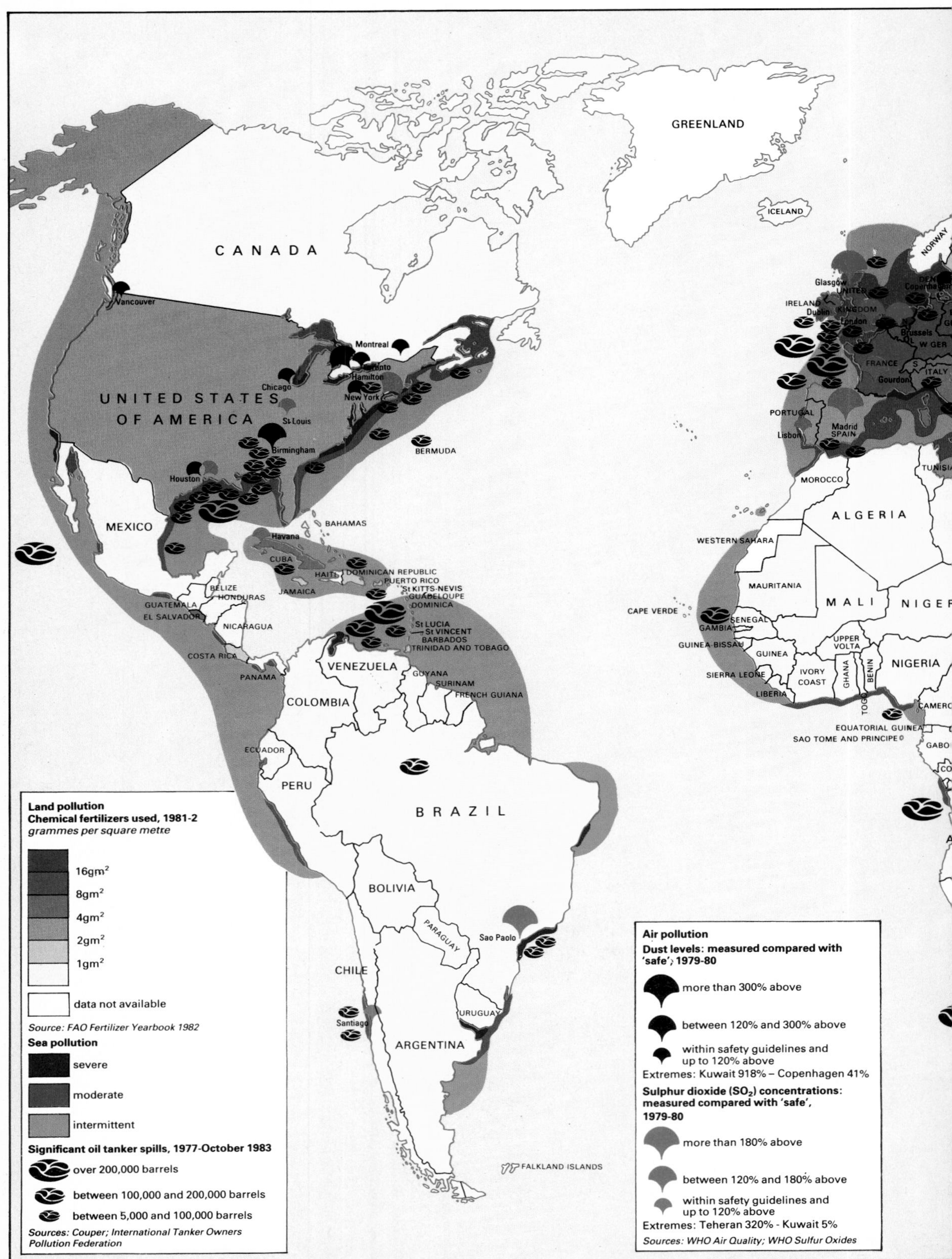
GREENLAND
ICELAND
CANADA
UNITED STATES OF AMERICA
Vancouver
Montreal
Toronto
Hamilton
Chicago
New York
St Louis
Birmingham
Houston
BERMUDA
MEXICO
BAHAMAS
Havana
CUBA
HAITI
DOMINICAN REPUBLIC
PUERTO RICO
St KITTS-NEVIS
GUADELOUPE
DOMINICA
St LUCIA
St VINCENT
BARBADOS
TRINIDAD AND TOBAGO
JAMAICA
BELIZE
HONDURAS
GUATEMALA
EL SALVADOR
NICARAGUA
COSTA RICA
PANAMA
VENEZUELA
GUYANA
SURINAM
FRENCH GUIANA
COLOMBIA
ECUADOR
PERU
BRAZIL
BOLIVIA
PARAGUAY
Sao Paolo
CHILE
Santiago
URUGUAY
ARGENTINA
FALKLAND ISLANDS
NORWAY
Glasgow
UNITED KINGDOM
IRELAND
Dublin
London
Copenhagen
Brussels
W GER
FRANCE
Gourdon
ITALY
PORTUGAL
Lisbon
Madrid
SPAIN
TUNISIA
MOROCCO
ALGERIA
WESTERN SAHARA
MAURITANIA
MALI
NIGER
CAPE VERDE
GAMBIA
SENEGAL
GUINEA-BISSAU
GUINEA
UPPER VOLTA
SIERRA LEONE
IVORY COAST
GHANA
TOGO
BENIN
NIGERIA
LIBERIA
EQUATORIAL GUINEA
SAO TOME AND PRINCIPE
GABON
Land pollution
Chemical fertilizers used, 1981-2
grammes per square metre
16gm²
8gm²
4gm²
2gm²
1gm²
data not available
Source: FAO Fertilizer Yearbook 1982
Sea pollution
severe
moderate
intermittent
Significant oil tanker spills, 1977-October 1983
over 200,000 barrels
between 100,000 and 200,000 barrels
between 5,000 and 100,000 barrels
Sources: Couper; International Tanker Owners Pollution Federation
Air pollution
Dust levels: measured compared with 'safe', 1979-80
more than 300% above
between 120% and 300% above
within safety guidelines and up to 120% above
Extremes: Kuwait 918% – Copenhagen 41%
Sulphur dioxide (SO2) concentrations: measured compared with 'safe', 1979-80
more than 180% above
between 120% and 180% above
within safety guidelines and up to 120% above
Extremes: Teheran 320% - Kuwait 5%
Sources: WHO Air Quality; WHO Sulfur Oxides

45. Fouling the Nest

Pollution is the measure of our failure to organize for a larger human presence in the biosphere.

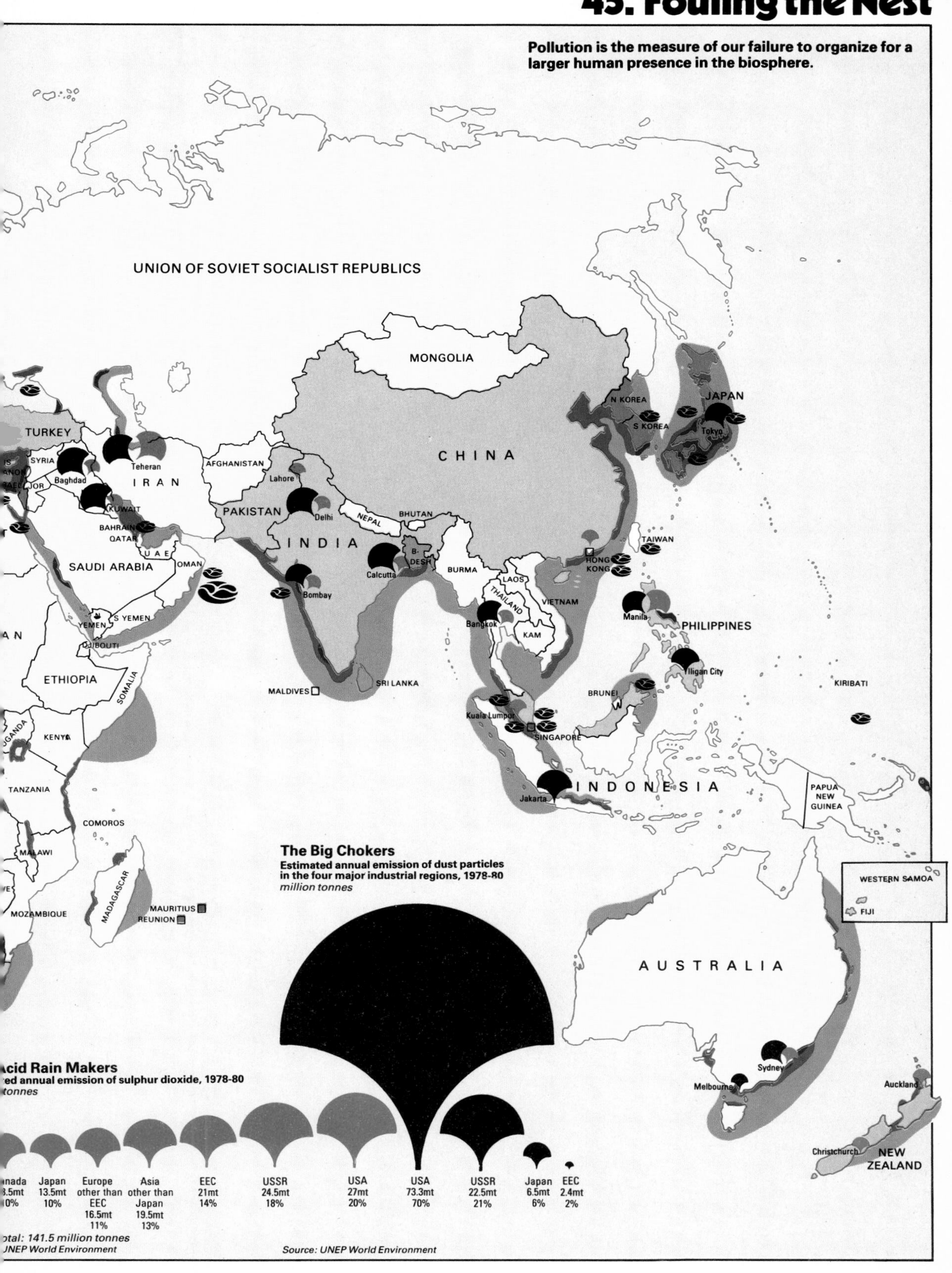

The Big Chokers
Estimated annual emission of dust particles in the four major industrial regions, 1978-80
million tonnes

USA	USSR	Japan	EEC
73.3mt	22.5mt	6.5mt	2.4mt
70%	21%	6%	2%

Source: UNEP World Environment

cid Rain Makers
ed annual emission of sulphur dioxide, 1978-80
tonnes

nada	Japan	Europe other than EEC	Asia other than Japan	EEC	USSR	USA
.5mt	13.5mt	16.5mt	19.5mt	21mt	24.5mt	27mt
0%	10%	11%	13%	14%	18%	20%

otal: 141.5 million tonnes
UNEP World Environment

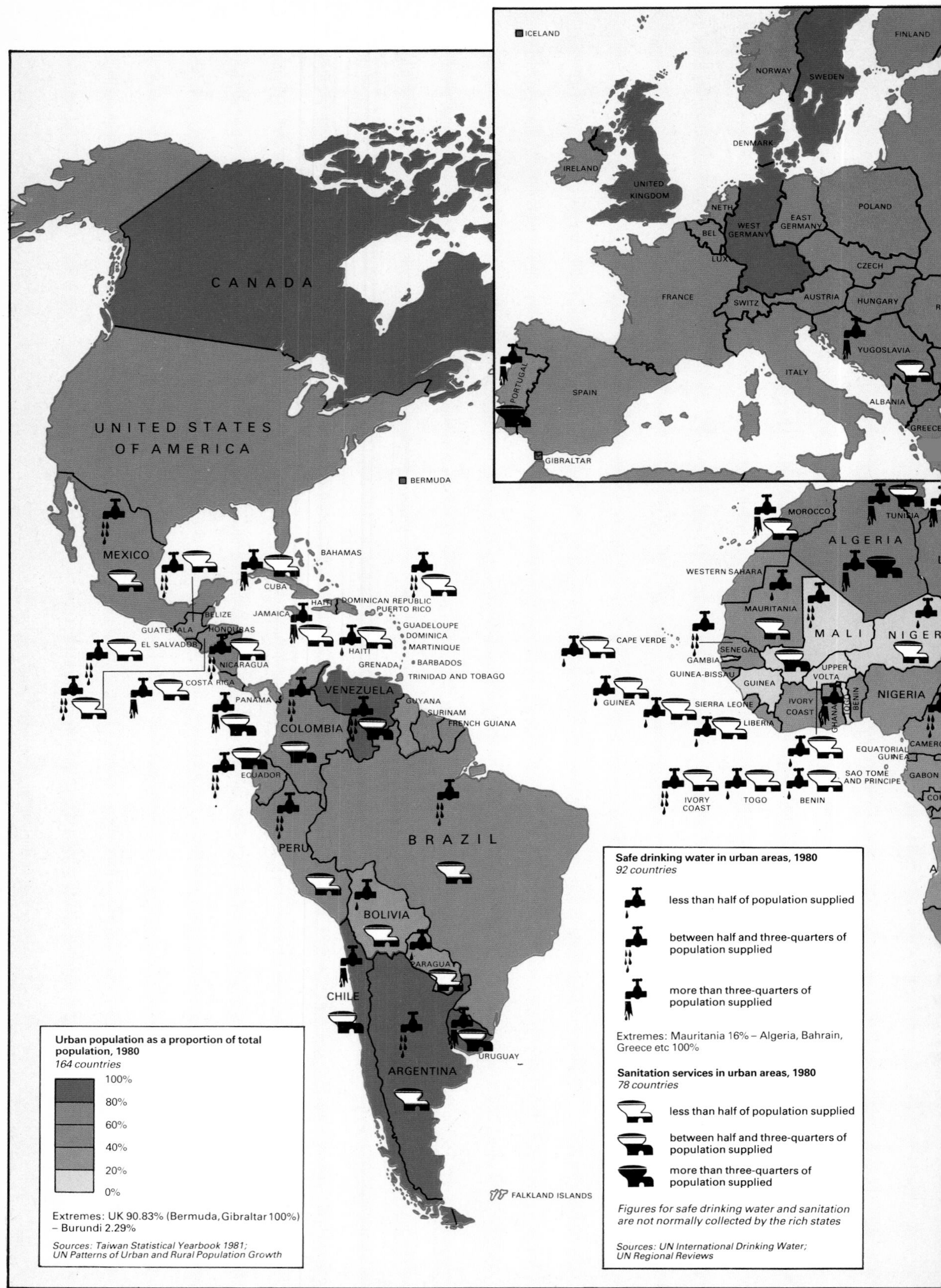
Urban population as a proportion of total population, 1980
164 countries
100%
80%
60%
40%
20%
0%
Extremes: UK 90.83% (Bermuda, Gibraltar 100%) – Burundi 2.29%
Sources: Taiwan Statistical Yearbook 1981; UN Patterns of Urban and Rural Population Growth
Safe drinking water in urban areas, 1980
92 countries
less than half of population supplied
between half and three-quarters of population supplied
more than three-quarters of population supplied
Extremes: Mauritania 16% – Algeria, Bahrain, Greece etc 100%
Sanitation services in urban areas, 1980
78 countries
less than half of population supplied
between half and three-quarters of population supplied
more than three-quarters of population supplied
Figures for safe drinking water and sanitation are not normally collected by the rich states
Sources: UN International Drinking Water; UN Regional Reviews
CANADA
UNITED STATES OF AMERICA
MEXICO
BERMUDA
BAHAMAS
CUBA
HAITI
DOMINICAN REPUBLIC
PUERTO RICO
JAMAICA
BELIZE
GUATEMALA
HONDURAS
EL SALVADOR
NICARAGUA
COSTA RICA
PANAMA
GUADELOUPE
DOMINICA
MARTINIQUE
BARBADOS
GRENADA
TRINIDAD AND TOBAGO
VENEZUELA
GUYANA
SURINAM
FRENCH GUIANA
COLOMBIA
ECUADOR
PERU
BRAZIL
BOLIVIA
PARAGUAY
CHILE
URUGUAY
ARGENTINA
FALKLAND ISLANDS
ICELAND
FINLAND
NORWAY
SWEDEN
DENMARK
IRELAND
UNITED KINGDOM
NETH
BEL
LUX
WEST GERMANY
EAST GERMANY
POLAND
CZECH
FRANCE
SWITZ
AUSTRIA
HUNGARY
YUGOSLAVIA
ITALY
ALBANIA
GREECE
PORTUGAL
SPAIN
GIBRALTAR
MOROCCO
TUNISIA
ALGERIA
WESTERN SAHARA
MAURITANIA
MALI
NIGER
CAPE VERDE
SENEGAL
GAMBIA
GUINEA-BISSAU
GUINEA
UPPER VOLTA
IVORY COAST
SIERRA LEONE
LIBERIA
GHANA
TOGO
BENIN
NIGERIA
EQUATORIAL GUINEA
SAO TOME AND PRINCIPE
GABON
TOGO
BENIN

46. Urban Blight

Two out of every five people live in cities and their number is growing faster, by a quarter, than the total population.

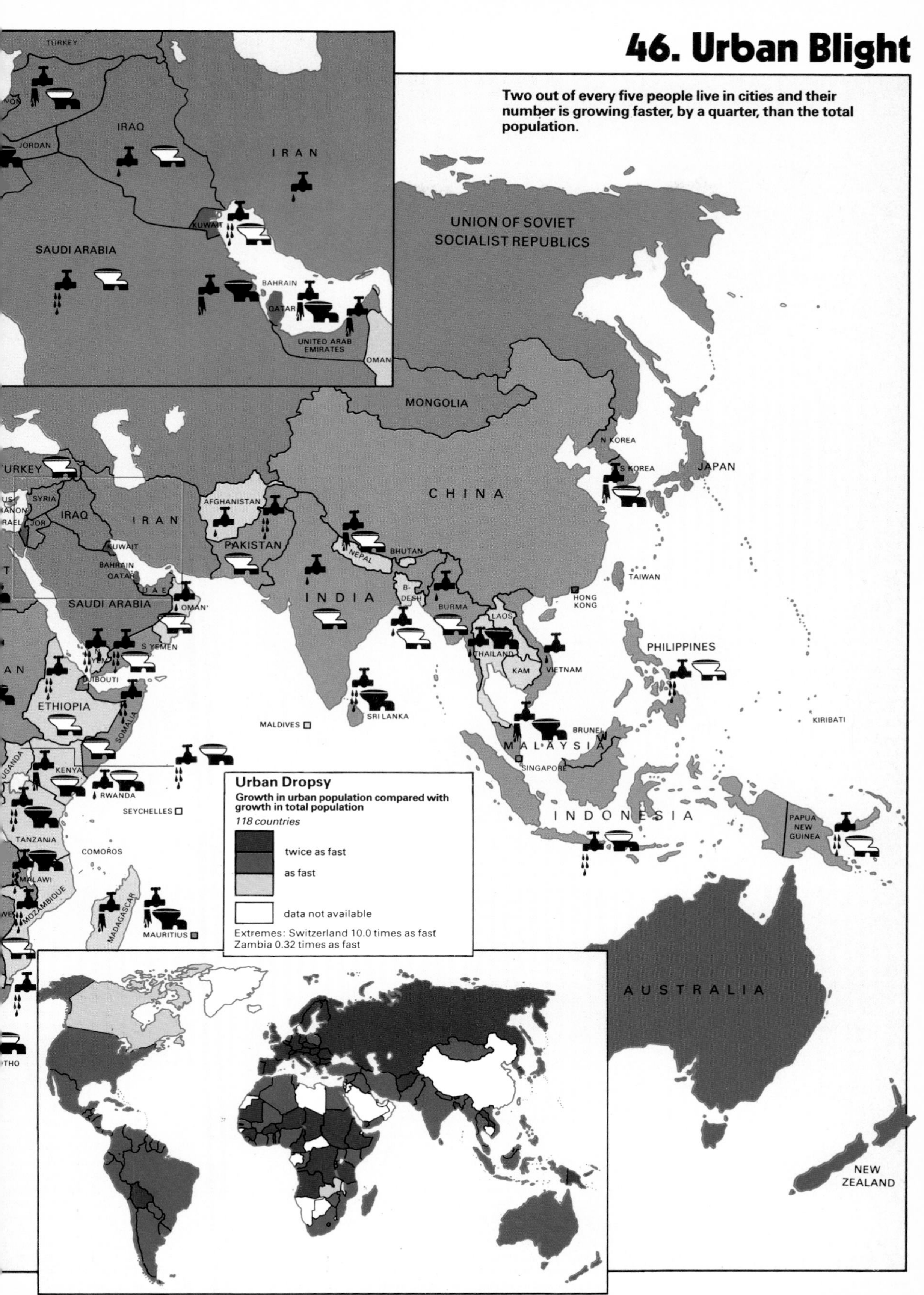

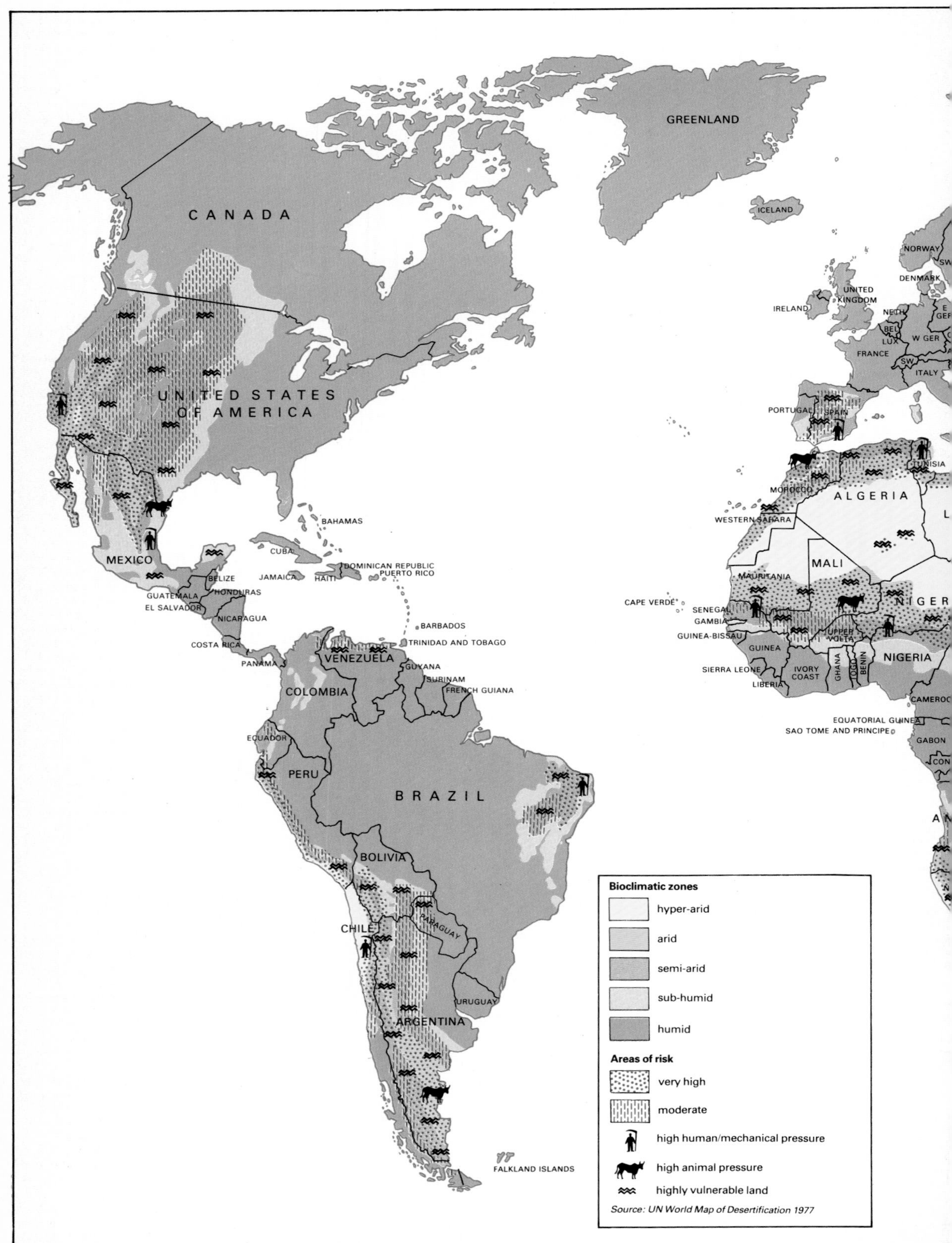

GREENLAND
ICELAND
CANADA
UNITED STATES OF AMERICA
MEXICO
BAHAMAS
CUBA
DOMINICAN REPUBLIC
PUERTO RICO
JAMAICA
HAITI
BELIZE
HONDURAS
GUATEMALA
EL SALVADOR
NICARAGUA
COSTA RICA
PANAMA
BARBADOS
TRINIDAD AND TOBAGO
VENEZUELA
GUYANA
SURINAM
FRENCH GUIANA
COLOMBIA
ECUADOR
PERU
BRAZIL
BOLIVIA
CHILE
PARAGUAY
URUGUAY
ARGENTINA
FALKLAND ISLANDS
NORWAY
DENMARK
UNITED KINGDOM
IRELAND
NETH
BEL
LUX
W GER
FRANCE
SW
ITALY
PORTUGAL
SPAIN
TUNISIA
MOROCCO
ALGERIA
WESTERN SAHARA
MALI
MAURITANIA
CAPE VERDE
SENEGAL
GAMBIA
GUINEA-BISSAU
GUINEA
SIERRA LEONE
LIBERIA
IVORY COAST
GHANA
TOGO
BENIN
UPPER VOLTA
NIGER
NIGERIA
EQUATORIAL GUINEA
SAO TOME AND PRINCIPE
GABON
Bioclimatic zones
hyper-arid
arid
semi-arid
sub-humid
humid
Areas of risk
very high
moderate
high human/mechanical pressure
high animal pressure
highly vulnerable land
Source: UN World Map of Desertification 1977

47. The Dying Earth

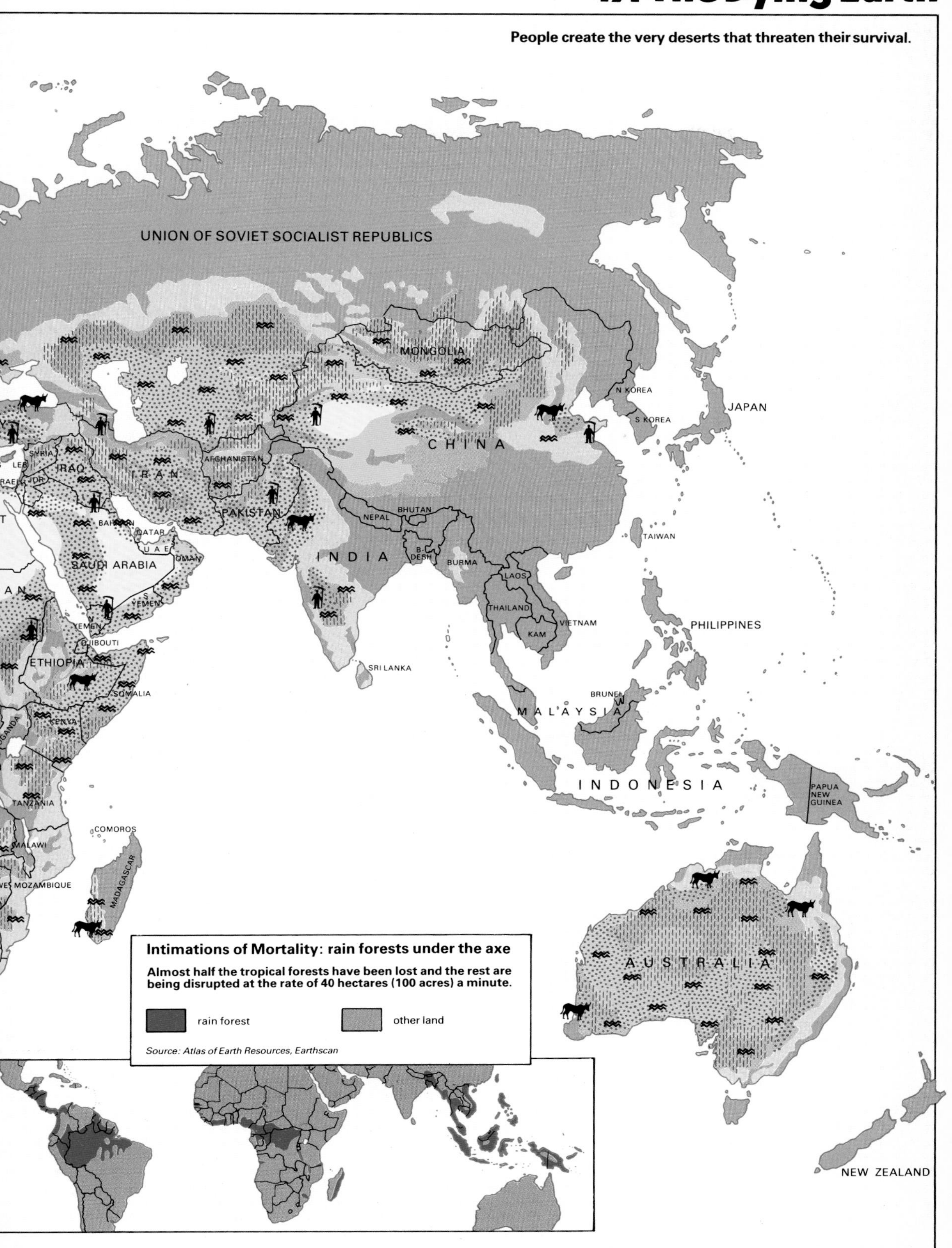
People create the very deserts that threaten their survival.
UNION OF SOVIET SOCIALIST REPUBLICS
MONGOLIA
N KOREA
S KOREA
JAPAN
CHINA
SYRIA
LEB
IRAQ
JOR
IRAN
AFGHANISTAN
PAKISTAN
NEPAL
BHUTAN
INDIA
B-DESH
BURMA
LAOS
THAILAND
KAM
VIETNAM
TAIWAN
PHILIPPINES
QATAR
U A E
OMAN
SAUDI ARABIA
S YEMEN
N YEMEN
DJIBOUTI
ETHIOPIA
SOMALIA
KENYA
UGANDA
TANZANIA
MALAWI
MOZAMBIQUE
COMOROS
MADAGASCAR
SRI LANKA
BRUNEI
MALAYSIA
INDONESIA
PAPUA NEW GUINEA
AUSTRALIA
NEW ZEALAND
Intimations of Mortality: rain forests under the axe
Almost half the tropical forests have been lost and the rest are being disrupted at the rate of 40 hectares (100 acres) a minute.
rain forest
other land
Source: Atlas of Earth Resources, Earthscan

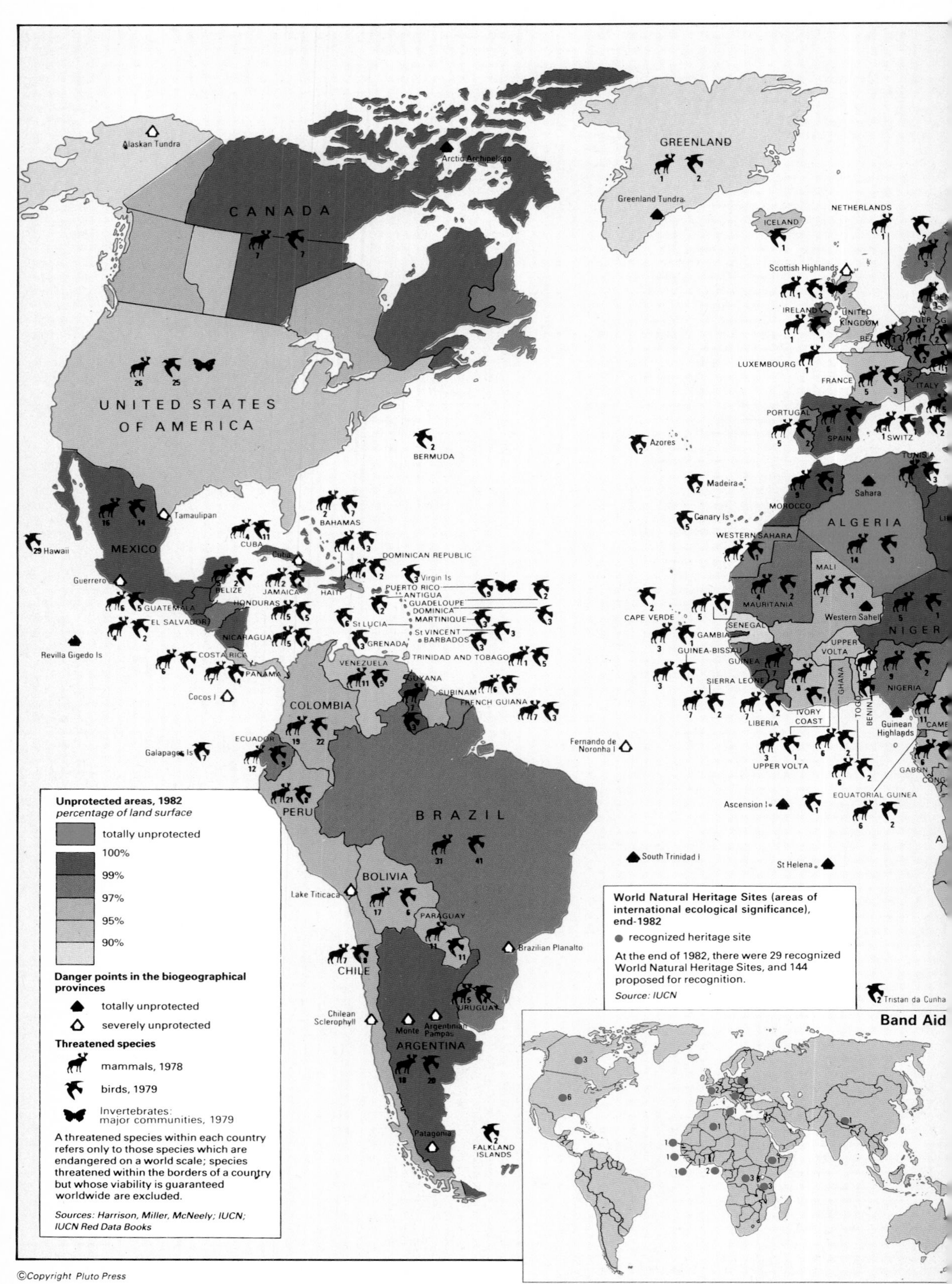

Alaskan Tundra
Arctic Archipelago
GREENLAND
Greenland Tundra
CANADA
ICELAND
NETHERLANDS
Scottish Highlands
IRELAND
UNITED KINGDOM
LUXEMBOURG
FRANCE
ITALY
PORTUGAL
SPAIN
SWITZ
TUNISIA
UNITED STATES OF AMERICA
BERMUDA
Azores
Madeira
Sahara
MOROCCO
Canary Is
ALGERIA
WESTERN SAHARA
MALI
MAURITANIA
Western Sahel
NIGER
CAPE VERDE
SENEGAL
GAMBIA
GUINEA-BISSAU
GUINEA
UPPER VOLTA
SIERRA LEONE
LIBERIA
IVORY COAST
GHANA
TOGO
BENIN
NIGERIA
Guinean Highlands
GABON
EQUATORIAL GUINEA
Ascension I
St Helena
Tristan da Cunha
Tamaulipan
MEXICO
Hawaii
Guerrero
Revilla Gigedo Is
BAHAMAS
CUBA
Cuba
DOMINICAN REPUBLIC
Virgin Is
PUERTO RICO
ANTIGUA
GUADELOUPE
DOMINICA
MARTINIQUE
St VINCENT
BARBADOS
St LUCIA
GRENADA
TRINIDAD AND TOBAGO
BELIZE
JAMAICA
HAITI
GUATEMALA
HONDURAS
EL SALVADOR
NICARAGUA
COSTA RICA
PANAMA
Cocos I
VENEZUELA
GUYANA
SURINAM
FRENCH GUIANA
COLOMBIA
ECUADOR
Galapagos Is
PERU
BRAZIL
Fernando de Noronha I
South Trinidad I
BOLIVIA
Lake Titicaca
PARAGUAY
Brazilian Planalto
CHILE
URUGUAY
Chilean Sclerophyll
Monte
Argentinian Pampas
ARGENTINA
Patagonia
FALKLAND ISLANDS
Unprotected areas, 1982
percentage of land surface
totally unprotected
100%
99%
97%
95%
90%
Danger points in the biogeographical provinces
totally unprotected
severely unprotected
Threatened species
mammals, 1978
birds, 1979
Invertebrates: major communities, 1979
A threatened species within each country refers only to those species which are endangered on a world scale; species threatened within the borders of a country but whose viability is guaranteed worldwide are excluded.
Sources: Harrison, Miller, McNeely; IUCN; IUCN Red Data Books
World Natural Heritage Sites (areas of international ecological significance), end-1982
recognized heritage site
At the end of 1982, there were 29 recognized World Natural Heritage Sites, and 144 proposed for recognition.
Source: IUCN
Band Aid

48. Protection and Extinction

Some 2611 protected areas covering nearly 4 million square kilometres have been established in 124 countries, but a thousand species of mammals and birds are currently in danger of elimination.

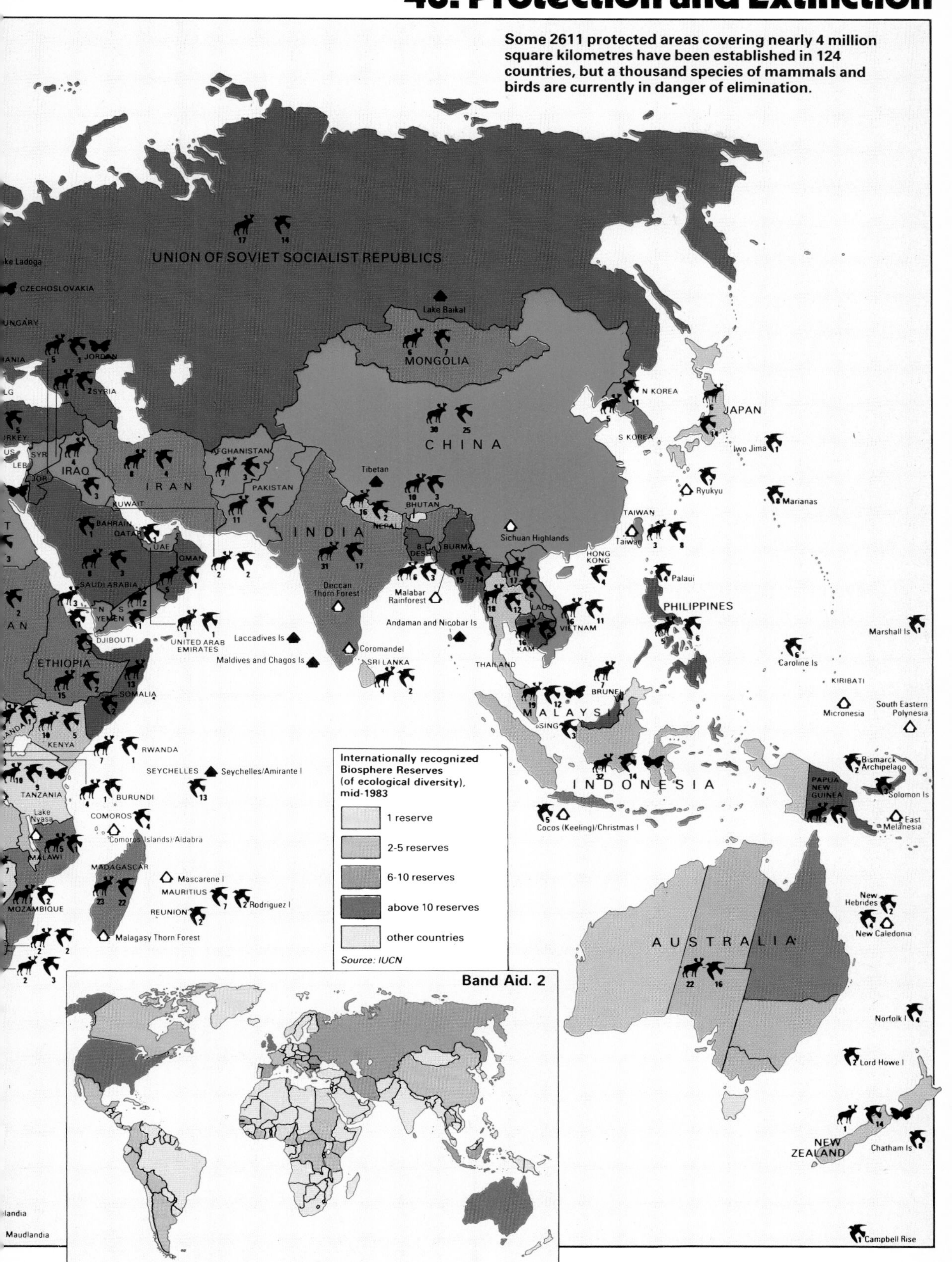

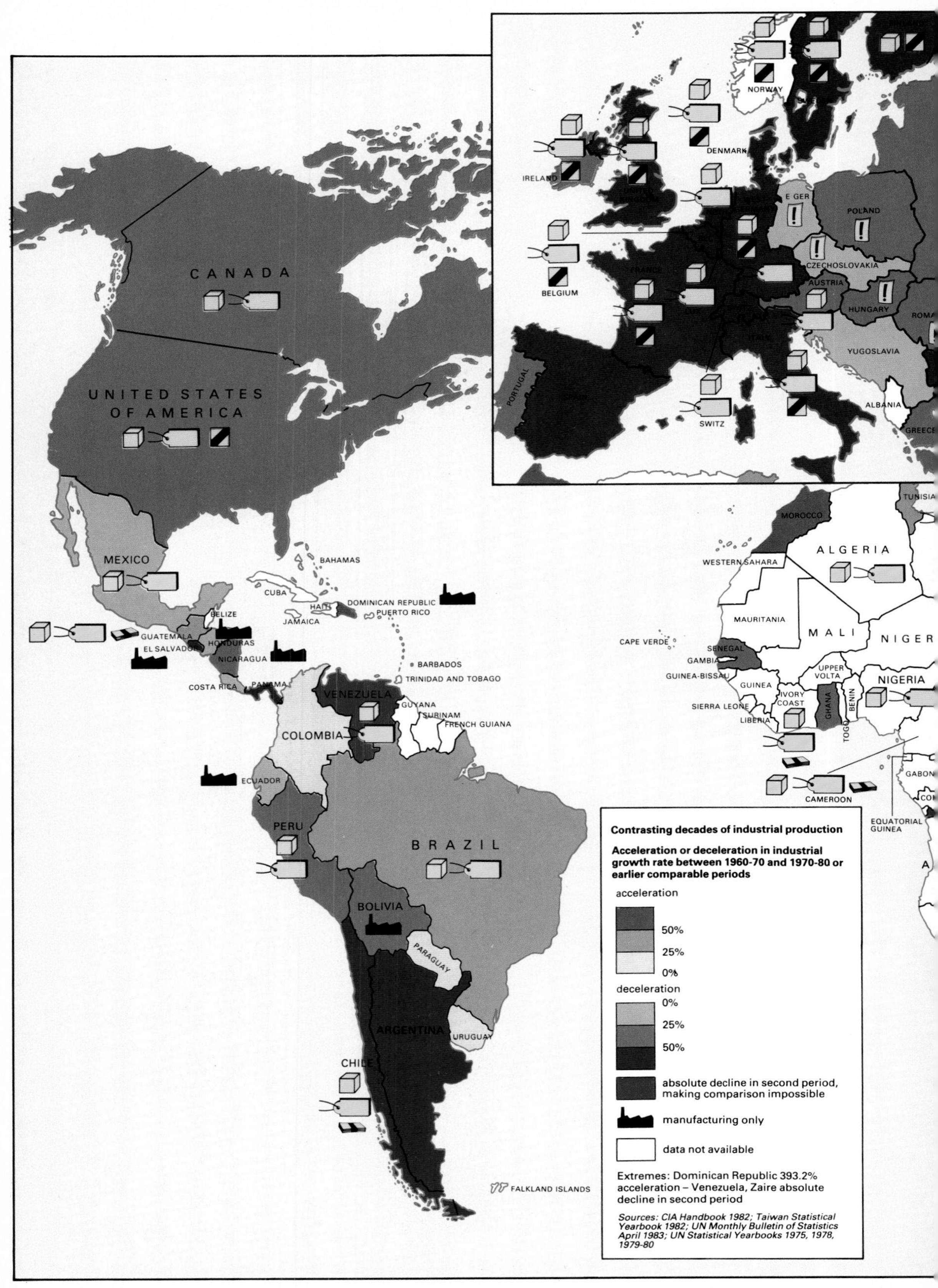

CANADA
UNITED STATES OF AMERICA
MEXICO
BAHAMAS
CUBA
HAITI
DOMINICAN REPUBLIC
PUERTO RICO
JAMAICA
BELIZE
GUATEMALA
HONDURAS
EL SALVADOR
NICARAGUA
COSTA RICA
PANAMA
BARBADOS
TRINIDAD AND TOBAGO
VENEZUELA
GUYANA
SURINAM
FRENCH GUIANA
COLOMBIA
ECUADOR
PERU
BRAZIL
BOLIVIA
PARAGUAY
URUGUAY
ARGENTINA
CHILE
FALKLAND ISLANDS
NORWAY
DENMARK
IRELAND
BELGIUM
FRANCE
E GER
POLAND
CZECHOSLOVAKIA
AUSTRIA
HUNGARY
YUGOSLAVIA
PORTUGAL
SPAIN
SWITZ
ITALY
ALBANIA
MOROCCO
TUNISIA
ALGERIA
WESTERN SAHARA
MAURITANIA
MALI
NIGER
CAPE VERDE
SENEGAL
GAMBIA
GUINEA-BISSAU
GUINEA
SIERRA LEONE
LIBERIA
IVORY COAST
UPPER VOLTA
GHANA
TOGO
BENIN
NIGERIA
CAMEROON
EQUATORIAL GUINEA
GABON
Contrasting decades of industrial production
Acceleration or deceleration in industrial growth rate between 1960-70 and 1970-80 or earlier comparable periods
acceleration
50%
25%
0%
deceleration
0%
25%
50%
absolute decline in second period, making comparison impossible
manufacturing only
data not available
Extremes: Dominican Republic 393.2% acceleration – Venezuela, Zaire absolute decline in second period
Sources: CIA Handbook 1982; Taiwan Statistical Yearbook 1982; UN Monthly Bulletin of Statistics April 1983; UN Statistical Yearbooks 1975, 1978, 1979-80

49. Industrial Droop

Decline in industrial growth has promoted the development of devices to discourage or prevent imports.

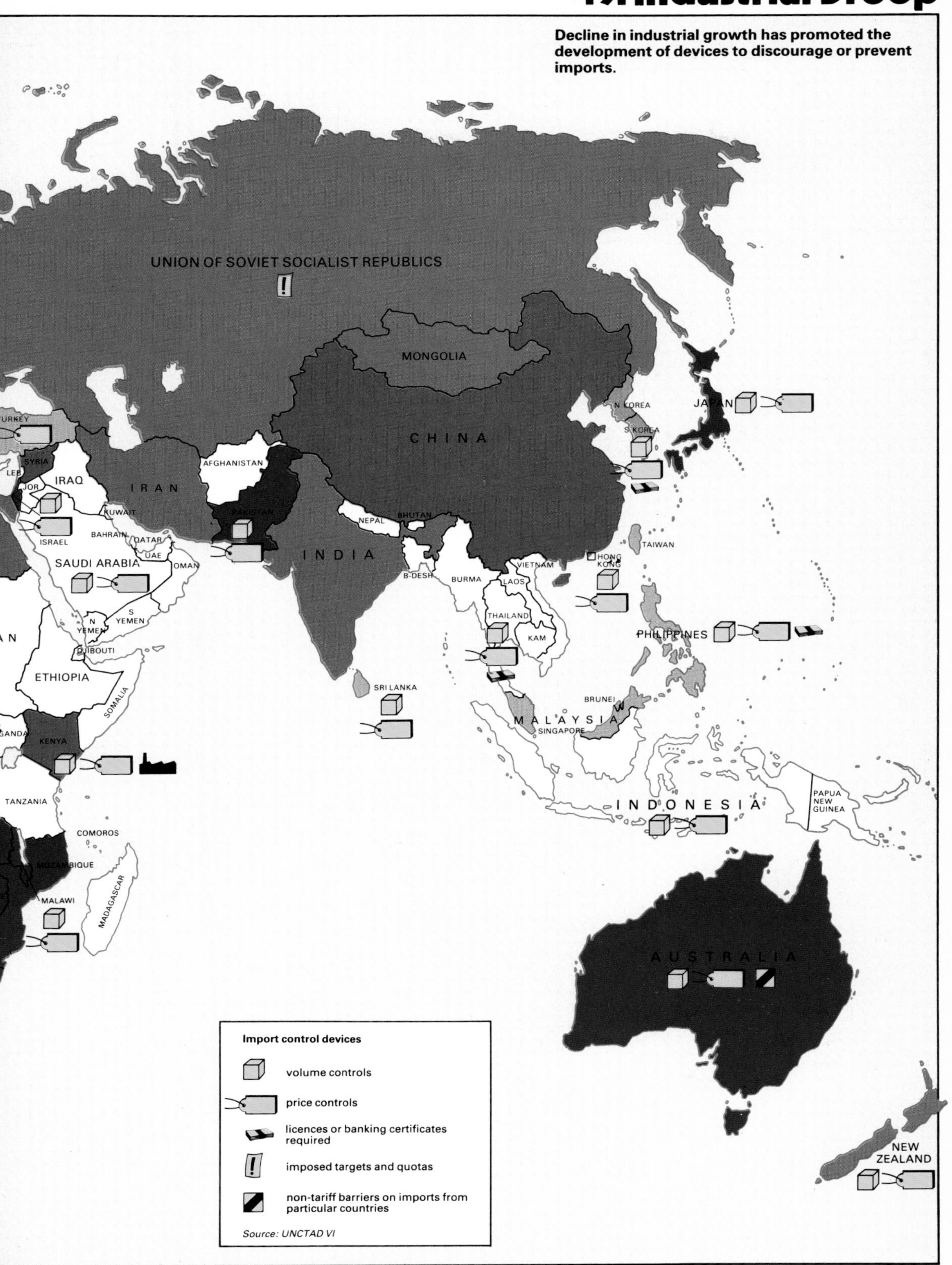

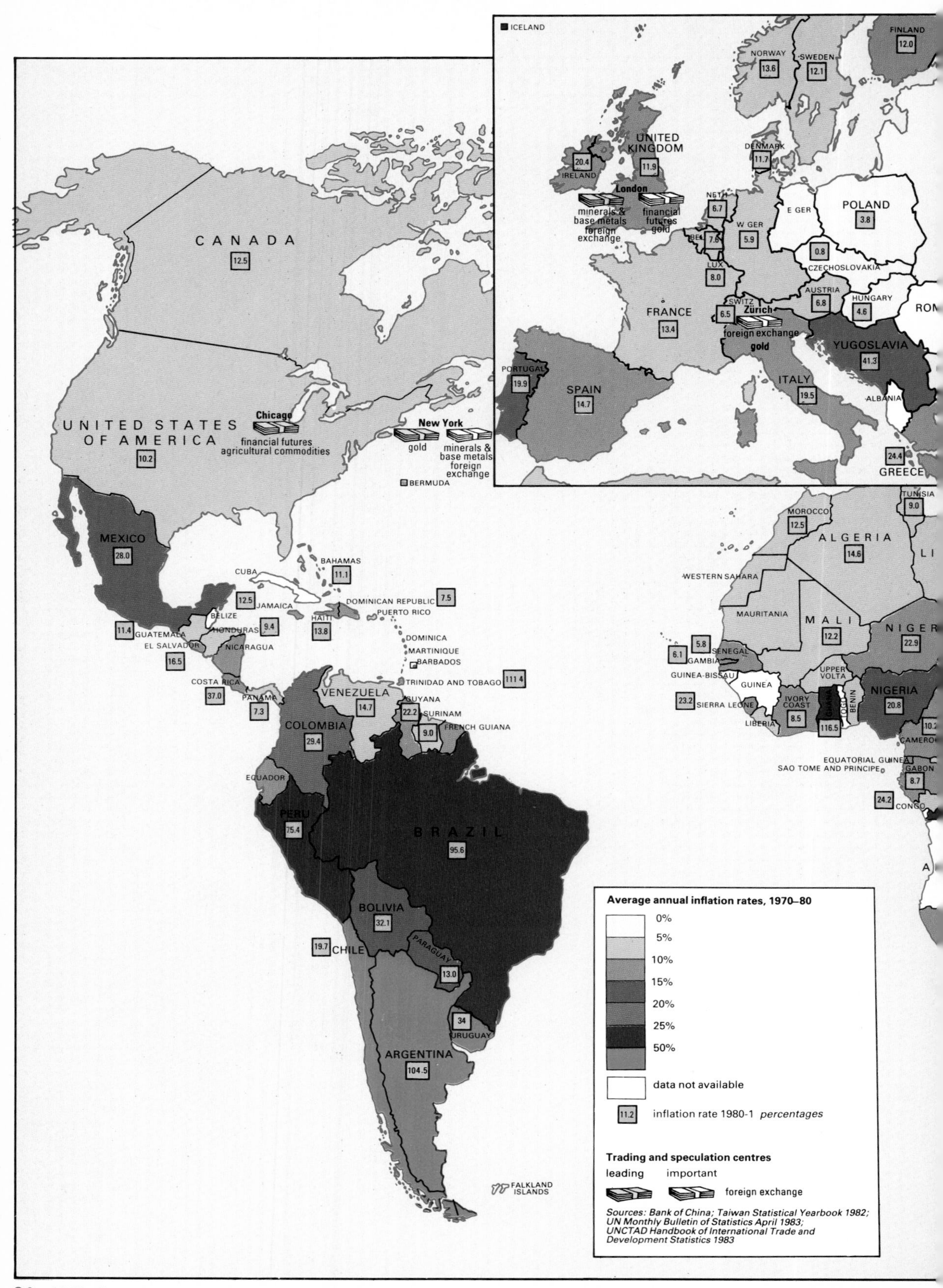
Average annual inflation rates, 1970–80
0%
5%
10%
15%
20%
25%
50%
data not available
11.2 inflation rate 1980-1 *percentages*
Trading and speculation centres
leading important
foreign exchange
Sources: Bank of China; Taiwan Statistical Yearbook 1982; UN Monthly Bulletin of Statistics April 1983; UNCTAD Handbook of International Trade and Development Statistics 1983
CANADA 12.5
UNITED STATES OF AMERICA 10.2
Chicago financial futures agricultural commodities
New York gold minerals & base metals foreign exchange
BERMUDA
MEXICO 28.0
BAHAMAS 11.1
CUBA
12.5 JAMAICA
DOMINICAN REPUBLIC 7.5
PUERTO RICO
HAITI 13.8
BELIZE
11.4 GUATEMALA
HONDURAS 9.4
EL SALVADOR 16.5
NICARAGUA
DOMINICA
MARTINIQUE
BARBADOS
TRINIDAD AND TOBAGO 111 4
COSTA RICA 37.0
PANAMA 7.3
VENEZUELA 14.7
GUYANA 22.2
SURINAM 9.0
FRENCH GUIANA
COLOMBIA 29.4
EQUADOR
PERU 75.4
BRAZIL 95.6
BOLIVIA 32.1
19.7 CHILE
PARAGUAY 13.0
34 URUGUAY
ARGENTINA 104.5
FALKLAND ISLANDS
ICELAND
NORWAY 13.6
SWEDEN 12.1
FINLAND 12.0
UNITED KINGDOM 11.9
20.4 IRELAND
DENMARK 11.7
London minerals & base metals foreign exchange financial futures gold
NETH 6.7
BEL 7.6
LUX 8.0
W GER 5.9
E GER
POLAND 3.8
0.8 CZECHOSLOVAKIA
AUSTRIA 6.8
HUNGARY 4.6
ROM
SWITZ 6.5
Zürich foreign exchange gold
FRANCE 13.4
YUGOSLAVIA 41.3
PORTUGAL 19.9
SPAIN 14.7
ITALY 19.5
ALBANIA
24.4 GREECE
TUNISIA 9.0
MOROCCO 12.5
ALGERIA 14.6
WESTERN SAHARA
MAURITANIA
MALI 12.2
NIGER 22.9
5.8 SENEGAL
6.1 GAMBIA
GUINEA-BISSAU
GUINEA
UPPER VOLTA
23.2 SIERRA LEONE
LIBERIA
IVORY COAST 8.5
GHANA 116.5
TOGO
BENIN
NIGERIA 20.8
CAMEROON 10.2
EQUATORIAL GUINEA
SAO TOME AND PRINCIPE
GABON 8.7
24.2 CONGO

50. The Paper Chase

Governments show themselves increasingly unable to provide what the state needs above all for its survival – a currency of stable value.

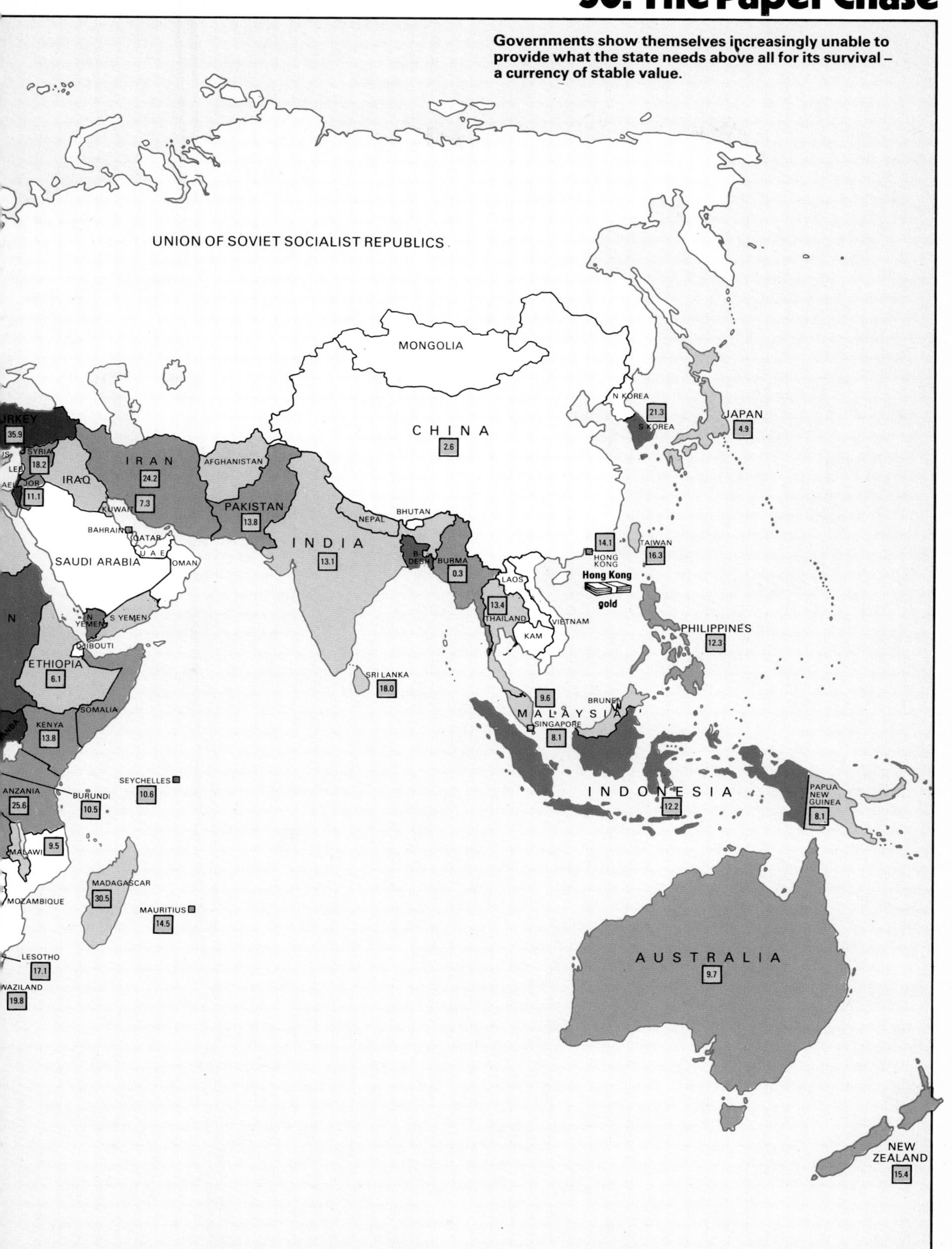

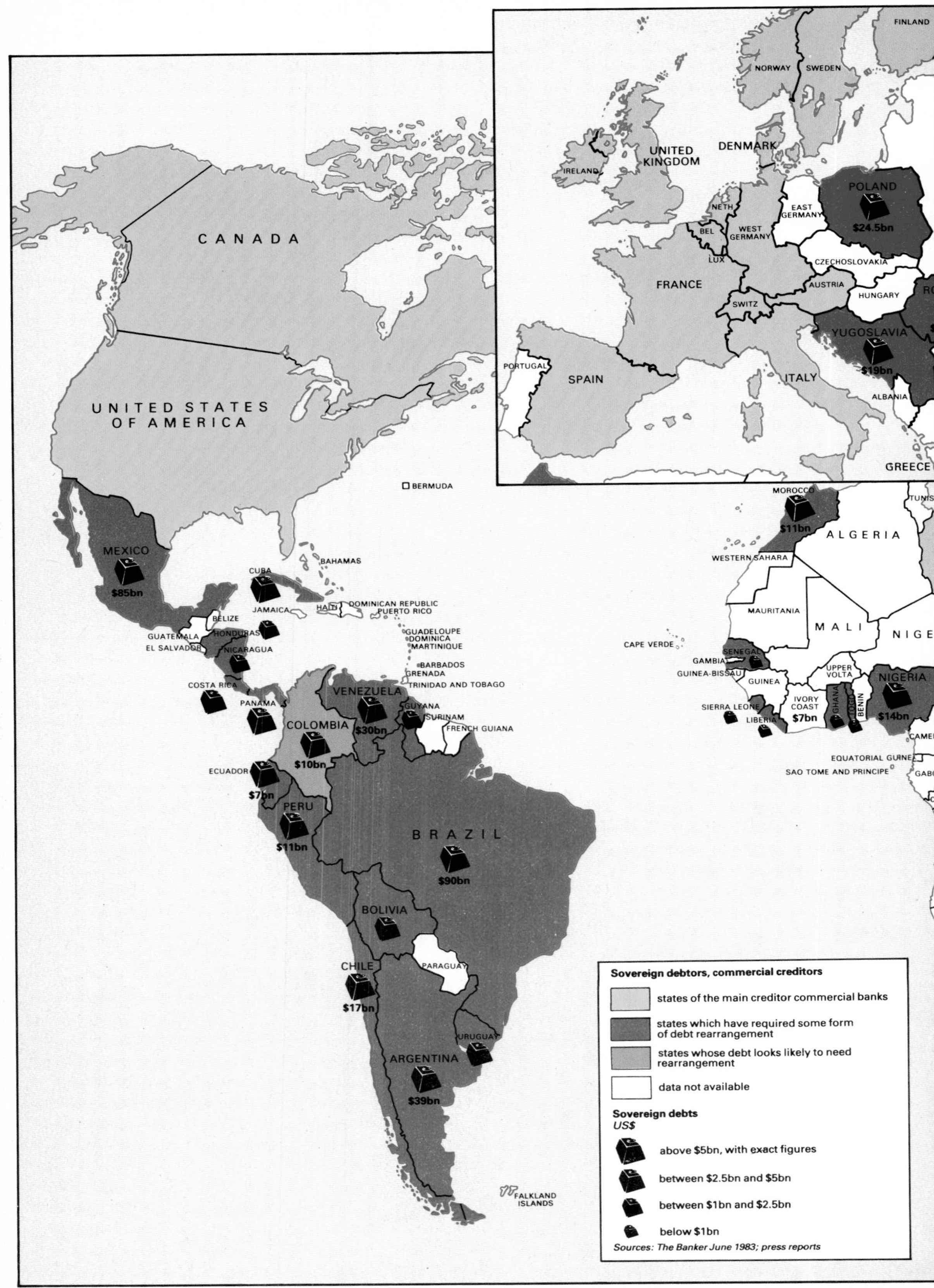

CANADA
UNITED STATES OF AMERICA
BERMUDA
MEXICO
$85bn
CUBA
BAHAMAS
JAMAICA
HAITI
DOMINICAN REPUBLIC
PUERTO RICO
BELIZE
GUATEMALA
HONDURAS
EL SALVADOR
NICARAGUA
GUADELOUPE
DOMINICA
MARTINIQUE
BARBADOS
GRENADA
TRINIDAD AND TOBAGO
COSTA RICA
PANAMA
VENEZUELA
$30bn
GUYANA
SURINAM
FRENCH GUIANA
COLOMBIA
$10bn
ECUADOR
$7bn
PERU
$11bn
BRAZIL
$90bn
BOLIVIA
PARAGUAY
CHILE
$17bn
URUGUAY
ARGENTINA
$39bn
FALKLAND ISLANDS
FINLAND
NORWAY
SWEDEN
DENMARK
UNITED KINGDOM
IRELAND
NETH
BEL
LUX
EAST GERMANY
WEST GERMANY
POLAND
$24.5bn
CZECHOSLOVAKIA
FRANCE
AUSTRIA
HUNGARY
SWITZ
YUGOSLAVIA
$19bn
PORTUGAL
SPAIN
ITALY
ALBANIA
GREECE
MOROCCO
$11bn
ALGERIA
WESTERN SAHARA
MAURITANIA
MALI
CAPE VERDE
SENEGAL
GAMBIA
GUINEA-BISSAU
GUINEA
UPPER VOLTA
NIGERIA
$14bn
SIERRA LEONE
LIBERIA
IVORY COAST
$7bn
GHANA
TOGO
BENIN
EQUATORIAL GUINEA
SAO TOME AND PRINCIPE
Sovereign debtors, commercial creditors
states of the main creditor commercial banks
states which have required some form of debt rearrangement
states whose debt looks likely to need rearrangement
data not available
Sovereign debts
US$
above $5bn, with exact figures
between $2.5bn and $5bn
between $1bn and $2.5bn
below $1bn
Sources: The Banker June 1983; press reports

51. A Question of Terms

States can, and do, go broke. But their insolvency is disguised to avoid, if only by postponement, the problem for their creditor banks.

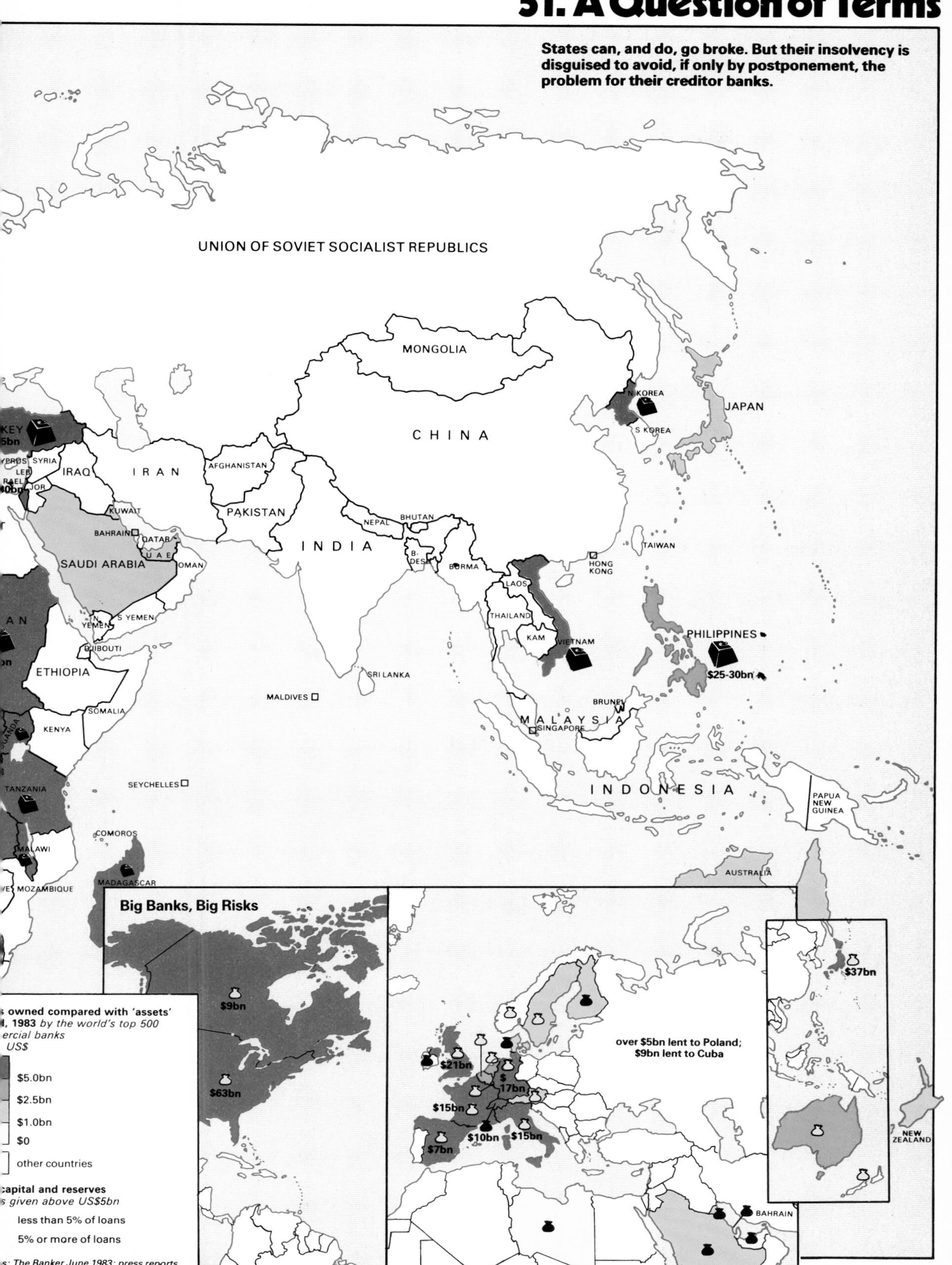

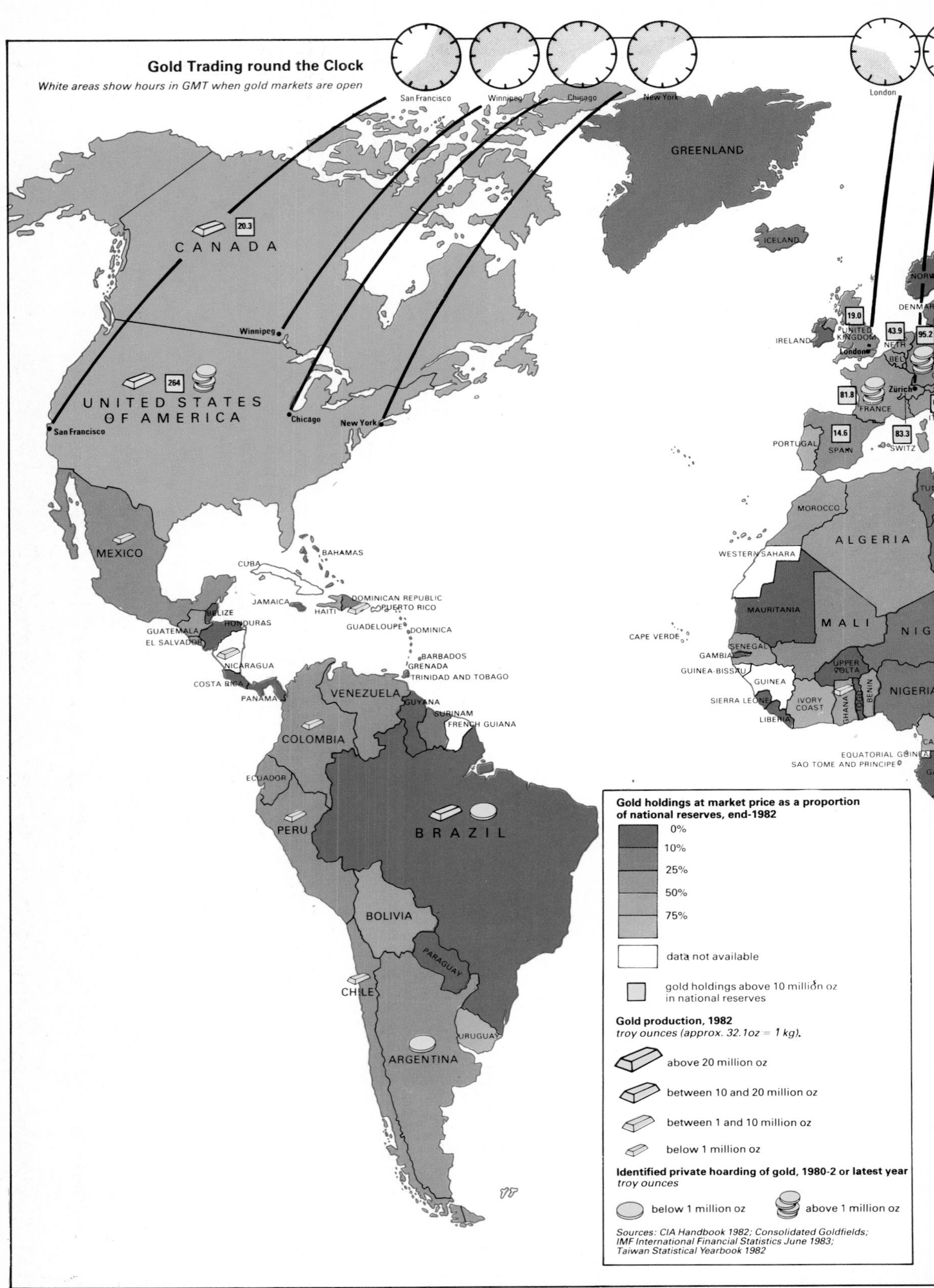

Gold Trading round the Clock
White areas show hours in GMT when gold markets are open
San Francisco
Winnipeg
Chicago
New York
London
GREENLAND
ICELAND
CANADA
20.3
UNITED STATES OF AMERICA
264
Winnipeg
Chicago
New York
San Francisco
NORWAY
DENMARK
19.0
UNITED KINGDOM
London
IRELAND
43.9
NETH
95.2
BEL
81.8
FRANCE
Zürich
66.7
ITALY
14.6
SPAIN
PORTUGAL
83.3
SWITZ
MOROCCO
ALGERIA
WESTERN SAHARA
MAURITANIA
MALI
CAPE VERDE
SENEGAL
GAMBIA
GUINEA-BISSAU
UPPER VOLTA
GUINEA
SIERRA LEONE
LIBERIA
IVORY COAST
GHANA
TOGO
BENIN
NIGERIA
EQUATORIAL GUINEA
SAO TOME AND PRINCIPE
MEXICO
BAHAMAS
CUBA
JAMAICA
HAITI
DOMINICAN REPUBLIC
PUERTO RICO
GUADELOUPE
DOMINICA
BELIZE
HONDURAS
GUATEMALA
EL SALVADOR
NICARAGUA
COSTA RICA
PANAMA
BARBADOS
GRENADA
TRINIDAD AND TOBAGO
VENEZUELA
GUYANA
SURINAM
FRENCH GUIANA
COLOMBIA
ECUADOR
PERU
BRAZIL
BOLIVIA
PARAGUAY
CHILE
URUGUAY
ARGENTINA
Gold holdings at market price as a proportion of national reserves, end-1982
0%
10%
25%
50%
75%
data not available
gold holdings above 10 million oz in national reserves
Gold production, 1982
troy ounces (approx. 32.1oz = 1 kg).
above 20 million oz
between 10 and 20 million oz
between 1 and 10 million oz
below 1 million oz
Identified private hoarding of gold, 1980-2 or latest year
troy ounces
below 1 million oz
above 1 million oz
Sources: CIA Handbook 1982; Consolidated Goldfields; IMF International Financial Statistics June 1983; Taiwan Statistical Yearbook 1982

52. The Gold Rush

Gold is the insurance policy of those states and people who doubt the security of their own system.

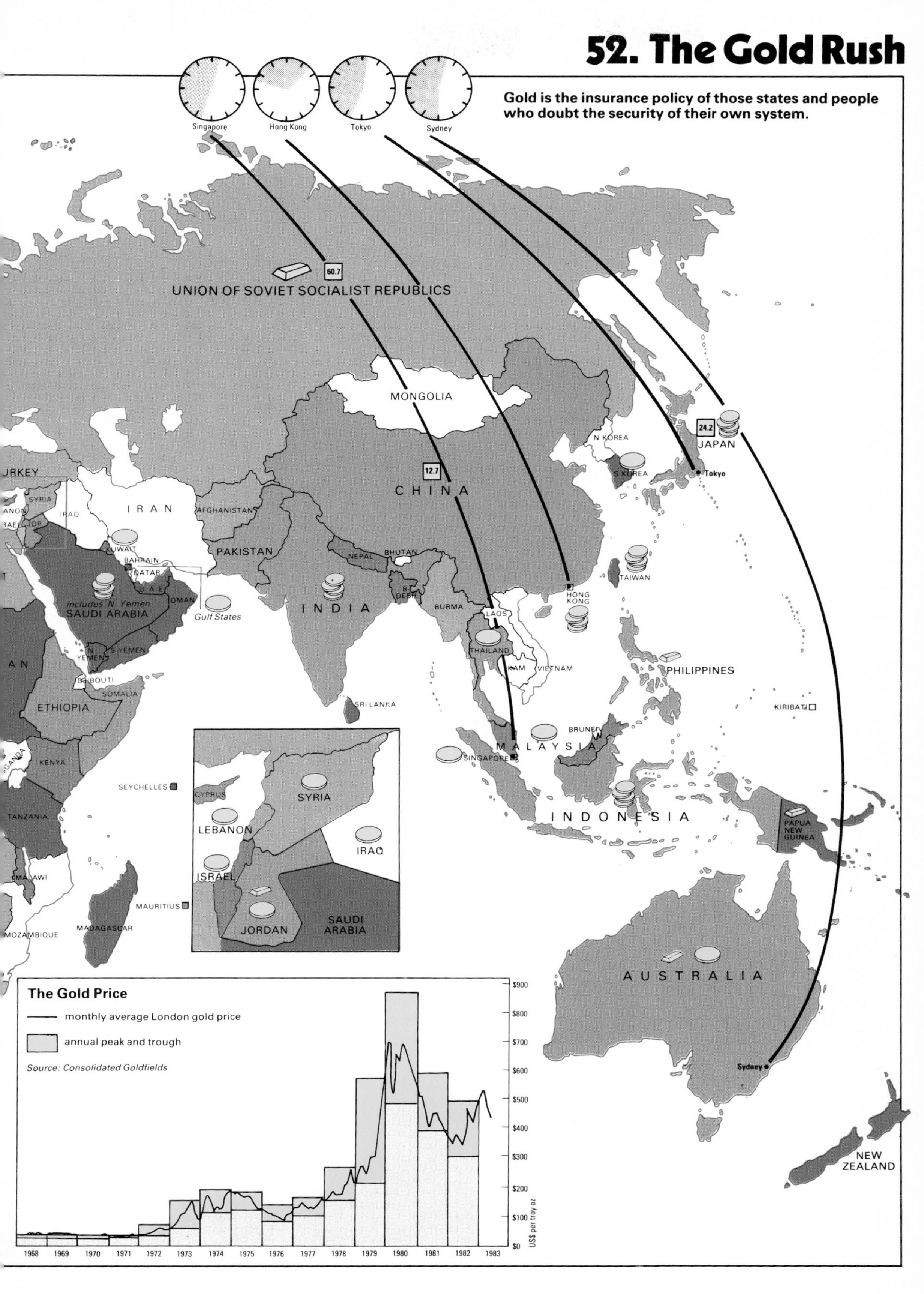

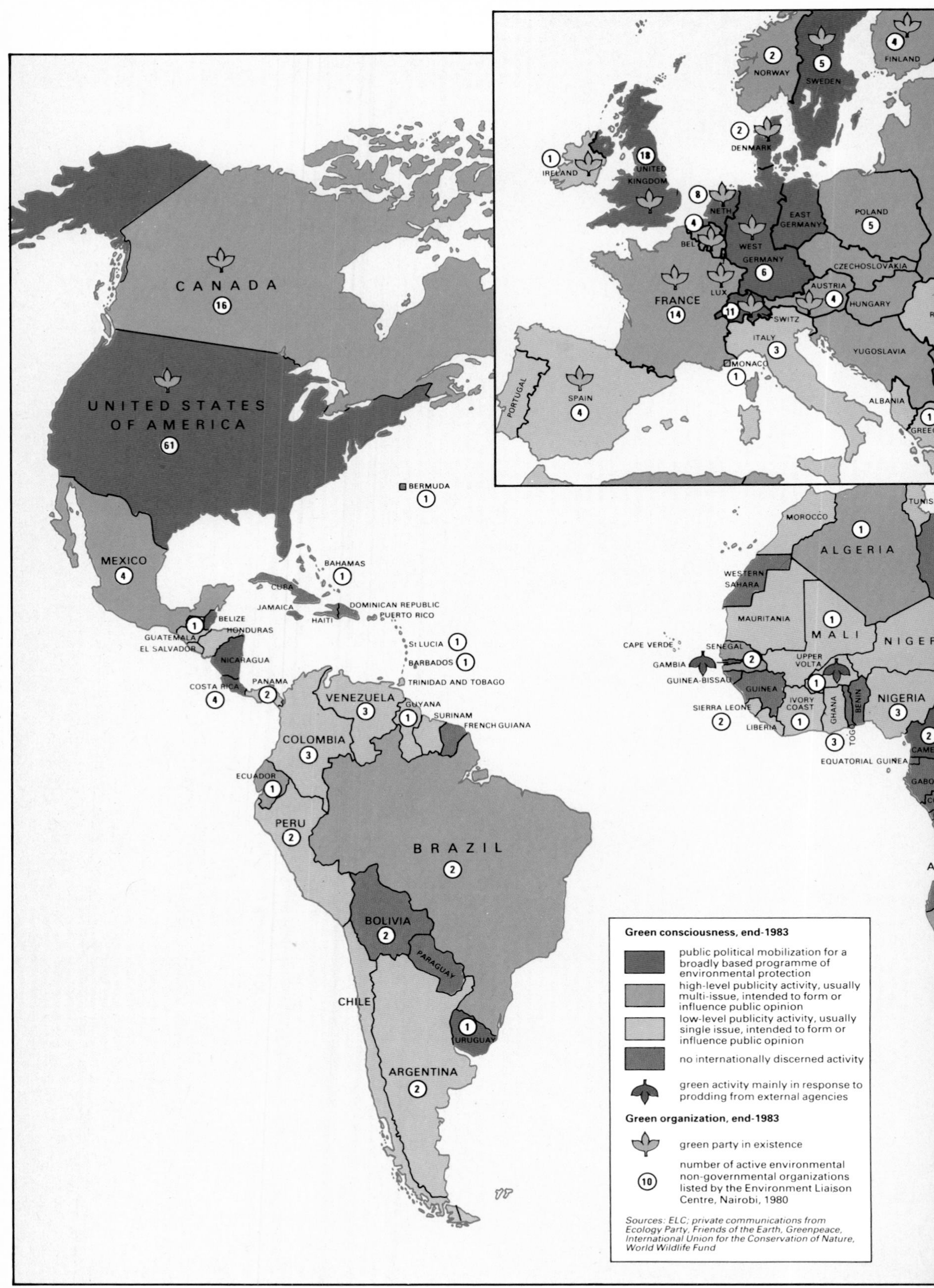
CANADA
16
UNITED STATES OF AMERICA
61
BERMUDA
1
MEXICO
4
BAHAMAS
1
CUBA
JAMAICA
HAITI
DOMINICAN REPUBLIC
PUERTO RICO
BELIZE
GUATEMALA
HONDURAS
EL SALVADOR
NICARAGUA
St LUCIA 1
BARBADOS 1
TRINIDAD AND TOBAGO
COSTA RICA
4
PANAMA
2
VENEZUELA
3
GUYANA
1
SURINAM
FRENCH GUIANA
COLOMBIA
3
ECUADOR
1
PERU
2
BRAZIL
2
BOLIVIA
2
PARAGUAY
CHILE
URUGUAY
1
ARGENTINA
2
NORWAY 2
SWEDEN 5
FINLAND 4
DENMARK 2
IRELAND 1
UNITED KINGDOM 18
NETH 8
BEL 4
LUX
EAST GERMANY
POLAND 5
WEST GERMANY 6
CZECHOSLOVAKIA
FRANCE 14
AUSTRIA 4
HUNGARY
SWITZ 11
ITALY 3
MONACO 1
YUGOSLAVIA
PORTUGAL
SPAIN 4
ALBANIA
MOROCCO
ALGERIA 1
WESTERN SAHARA
MAURITANIA
MALI 1
NIGER
CAPE VERDE
SENEGAL 2
GAMBIA
GUINEA-BISSAU
UPPER VOLTA 1
GUINEA
SIERRA LEONE 2
LIBERIA
IVORY COAST 1
GHANA 3
BENIN
NIGERIA 3
EQUATORIAL GUINEA
Green consciousness, end-1983
public political mobilization for a broadly based programme of environmental protection
high-level publicity activity, usually multi-issue, intended to form or influence public opinion
low-level publicity activity, usually single issue, intended to form or influence public opinion
no internationally discerned activity
green activity mainly in response to prodding from external agencies
Green organization, end-1983
green party in existence
number of active environmental non-governmental organizations listed by the Environment Liaison Centre, Nairobi, 1980
Sources: ELC; private communications from Ecology Party, Friends of the Earth, Greenpeace, International Union for the Conservation of Nature, World Wildlife Fund

53. Green Revolution

Public sensitivity to environmental issues is rising as the green movement divides into two broad streams: separatists who wish to protect nature from humanity, and integrationists who wish politically to promote a benign relationship between the social and natural orders.

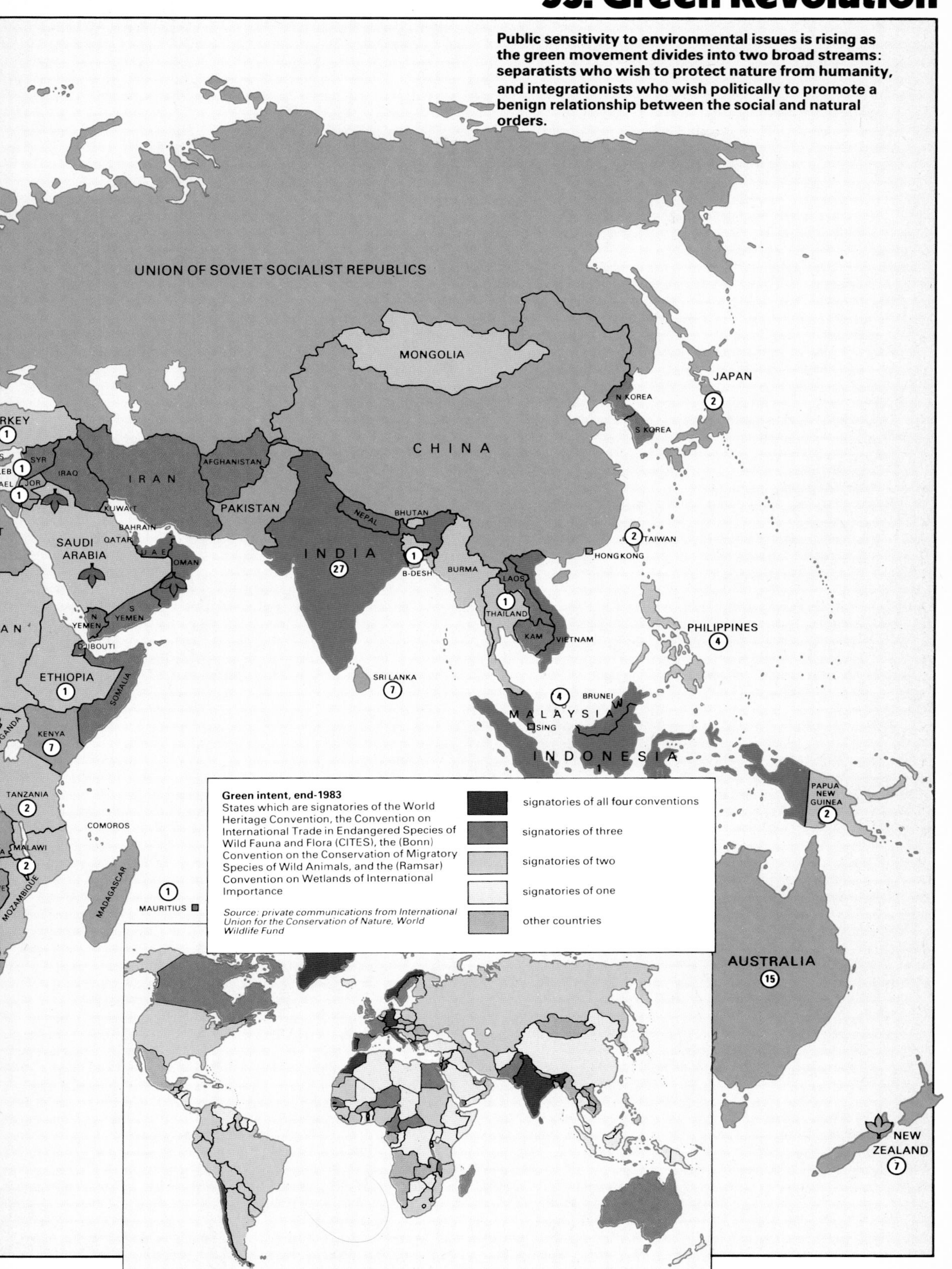

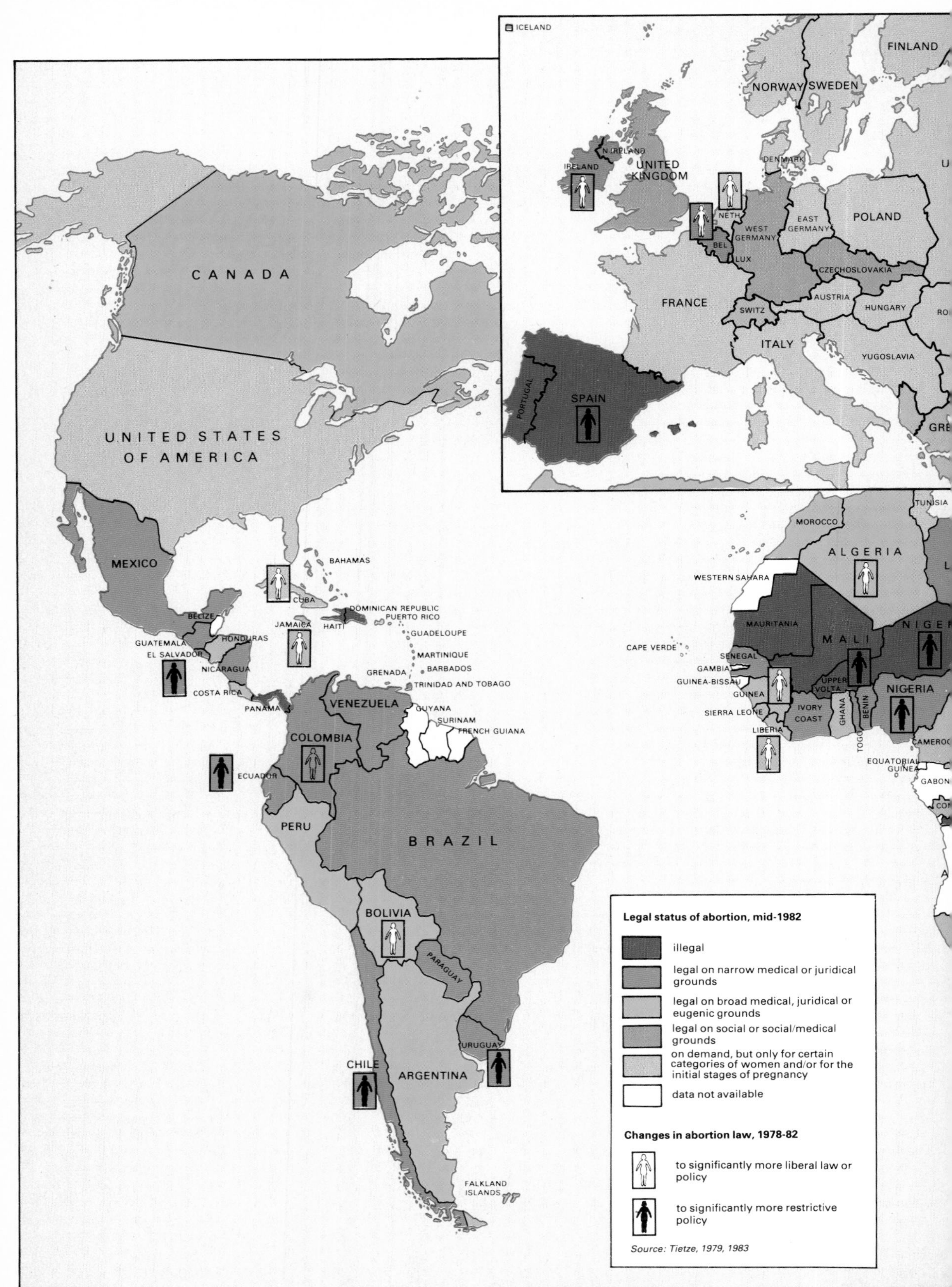
ICELAND
FINLAND
NORWAY
SWEDEN
N IRELAND
IRELAND
UNITED KINGDOM
DENMARK
NETH
BEL
LUX
WEST GERMANY
EAST GERMANY
POLAND
CZECHOSLOVAKIA
AUSTRIA
HUNGARY
SWITZ
FRANCE
ITALY
YUGOSLAVIA
PORTUGAL
SPAIN
CANADA
UNITED STATES OF AMERICA
MEXICO
BAHAMAS
CUBA
DOMINICAN REPUBLIC
PUERTO RICO
BELIZE
JAMAICA
HAITI
GUADELOUPE
GUATEMALA
HONDURAS
EL SALVADOR
MARTINIQUE
BARBADOS
NICARAGUA
GRENADA
TRINIDAD AND TOBAGO
COSTA RICA
PANAMA
VENEZUELA
GUYANA
SURINAM
FRENCH GUIANA
COLOMBIA
ECUADOR
PERU
BRAZIL
BOLIVIA
PARAGUAY
URUGUAY
CHILE
ARGENTINA
FALKLAND ISLANDS
TUNISIA
MOROCCO
ALGERIA
WESTERN SAHARA
MAURITANIA
MALI
CAPE VERDE
SENEGAL
GAMBIA
GUINEA-BISSAU
GUINEA
UPPER VOLTA
SIERRA LEONE
IVORY COAST
GHANA
TOGO
BENIN
NIGERIA
LIBERIA
EQUATORIAL GUINEA
GABON
Legal status of abortion, mid-1982
illegal
legal on narrow medical or juridical grounds
legal on broad medical, juridical or eugenic grounds
legal on social or social/medical grounds
on demand, but only for certain categories of women and/or for the initial stages of pregnancy
data not available
Changes in abortion law, 1978-82
to significantly more liberal law or policy
to significantly more restrictive policy
Source: Tietze, 1979, 1983

54. Women's Rights

Nowhere are women fully equal to men. What little progress has been made is under constant threat in a male-dominated world. Women's control over reproduction is a case in point.

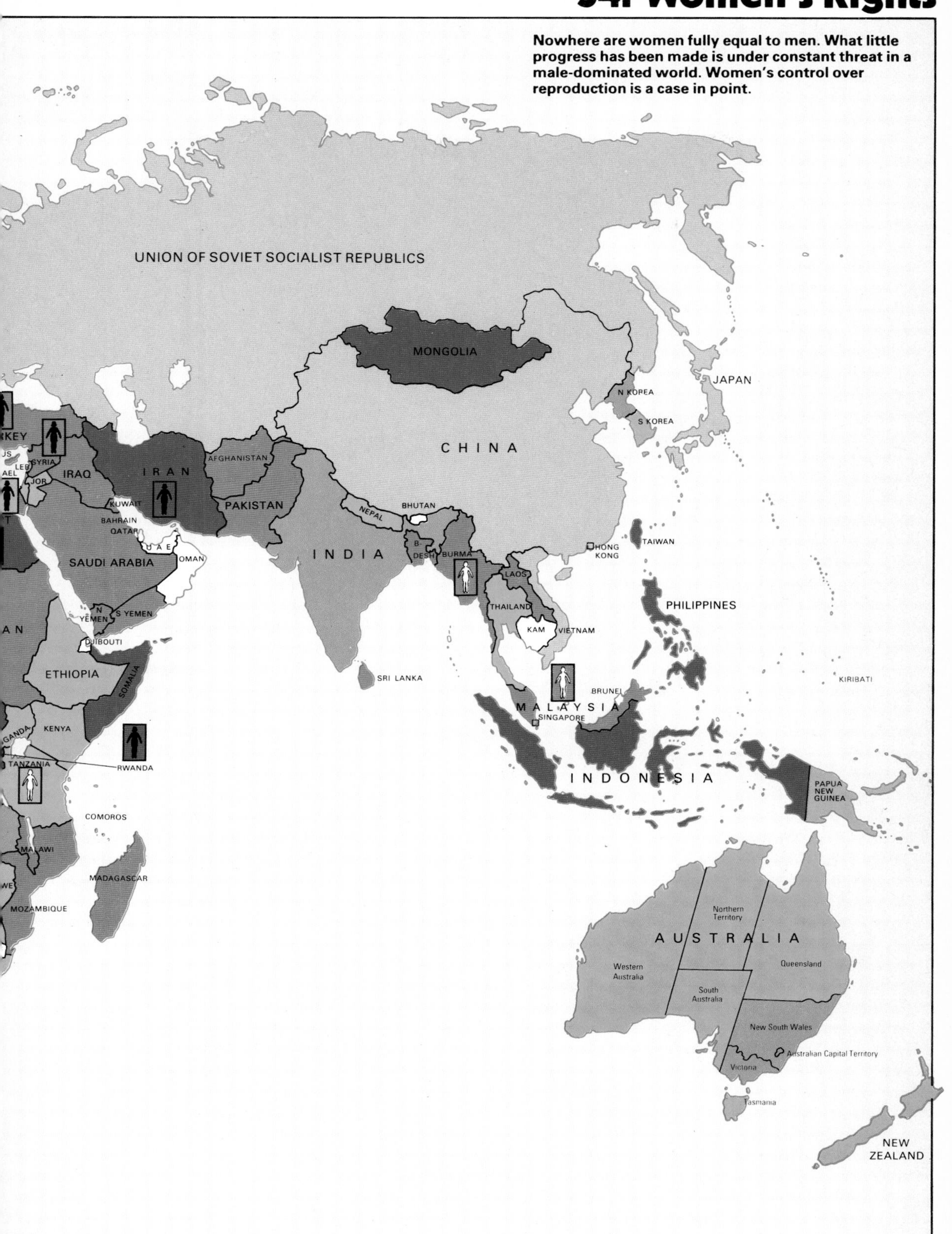

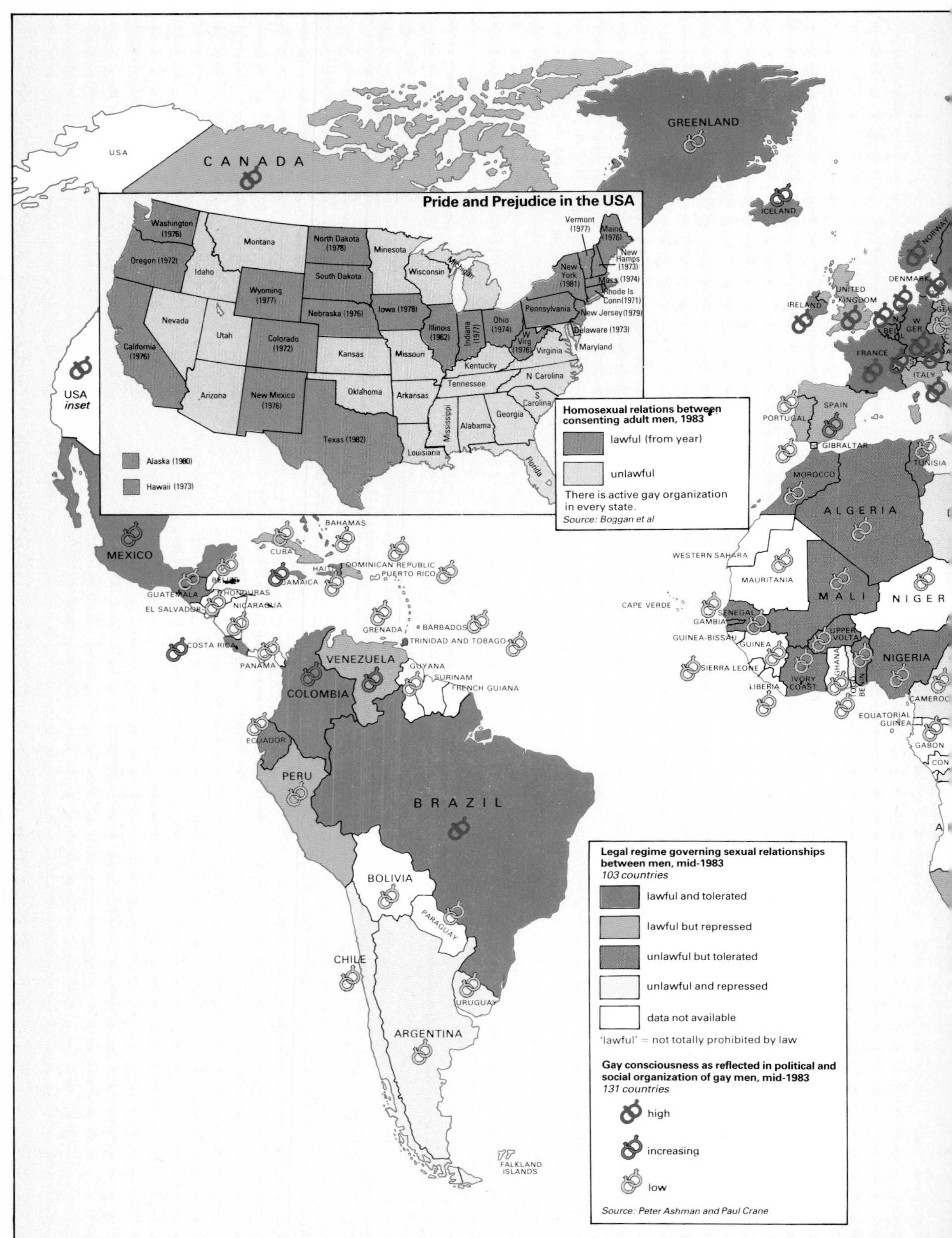

Pride and Prejudice in the USA
Washington (1976)
Oregon (1972)
California (1976)
Idaho
Nevada
Montana
Wyoming (1977)
Utah
Colorado (1972)
Arizona
New Mexico (1976)
North Dakota (1978)
South Dakota
Nebraska (1976)
Kansas
Oklahoma
Texas (1982)
Minesota
Iowa (1978)
Missouri
Arkansas
Louisiana
Wisconsin
Michigan
Illinois (1962)
Indiana (1977)
Ohio (1974)
Kentucky
Tennessee
Mississippi
Alabama
Georgia
Florida
S Carolina
N Carolina
Virginia
W Virg (1976)
Pennsylvania
New York (1981)
Vermont (1977)
Maine (1976)
New Hamps (1973)
Mass (1974)
Rhode Is
Conn (1971)
New Jersey (1979)
Delaware (1973)
Maryland
Alaska (1980)
Hawaii (1973)
Homosexual relations between consenting adult men, 1983
lawful (from year)
unlawful
There is active gay organization in every state.
Source: Boggan et al
USA
CANADA
GREENLAND
ICELAND
USA inset
NORWAY
DENMARK
IRELAND
UNITED KINGDOM
W GER
FRANCE
ITALY
PORTUGAL
SPAIN
GIBRALTAR
TUNISIA
MOROCCO
ALGERIA
WESTERN SAHARA
MAURITANIA
MALI
NIGER
CAPE VERDE
SENEGAL
GAMBIA
GUINEA-BISSAU
GUINEA
SIERRA LEONE
LIBERIA
IVORY COAST
UPPER VOLTA
GHANA
BENIN
NIGERIA
EQUATORIAL GUINEA
GABON
MEXICO
BAHAMAS
CUBA
HAITI
DOMINICAN REPUBLIC
PUERTO RICO
JAMAICA
BELIZE
GUATEMALA
HONDURAS
EL SALVADOR
NICARAGUA
COSTA RICA
PANAMA
BARBADOS
GRENADA
TRINIDAD AND TOBAGO
VENEZUELA
GUYANA
SURINAM
FRENCH GUIANA
COLOMBIA
ECUADOR
PERU
BRAZIL
BOLIVIA
PARAGUAY
CHILE
URUGUAY
ARGENTINA
FALKLAND ISLANDS
Legal regime governing sexual relationships between men, mid-1983
103 countries
lawful and tolerated
lawful but repressed
unlawful but tolerated
unlawful and repressed
data not available
'lawful' = not totally prohibited by law
Gay consciousness as reflected in political and social organization of gay men, mid-1983
131 countries
high
increasing
low
Source: Peter Ashman and Paul Crane

55. Gay Survival, Gay Assertion

Entrenched public attitudes, whether enshrined in the law or not, make it physically perilous to be gay in most states, and socially precarious in almost all.

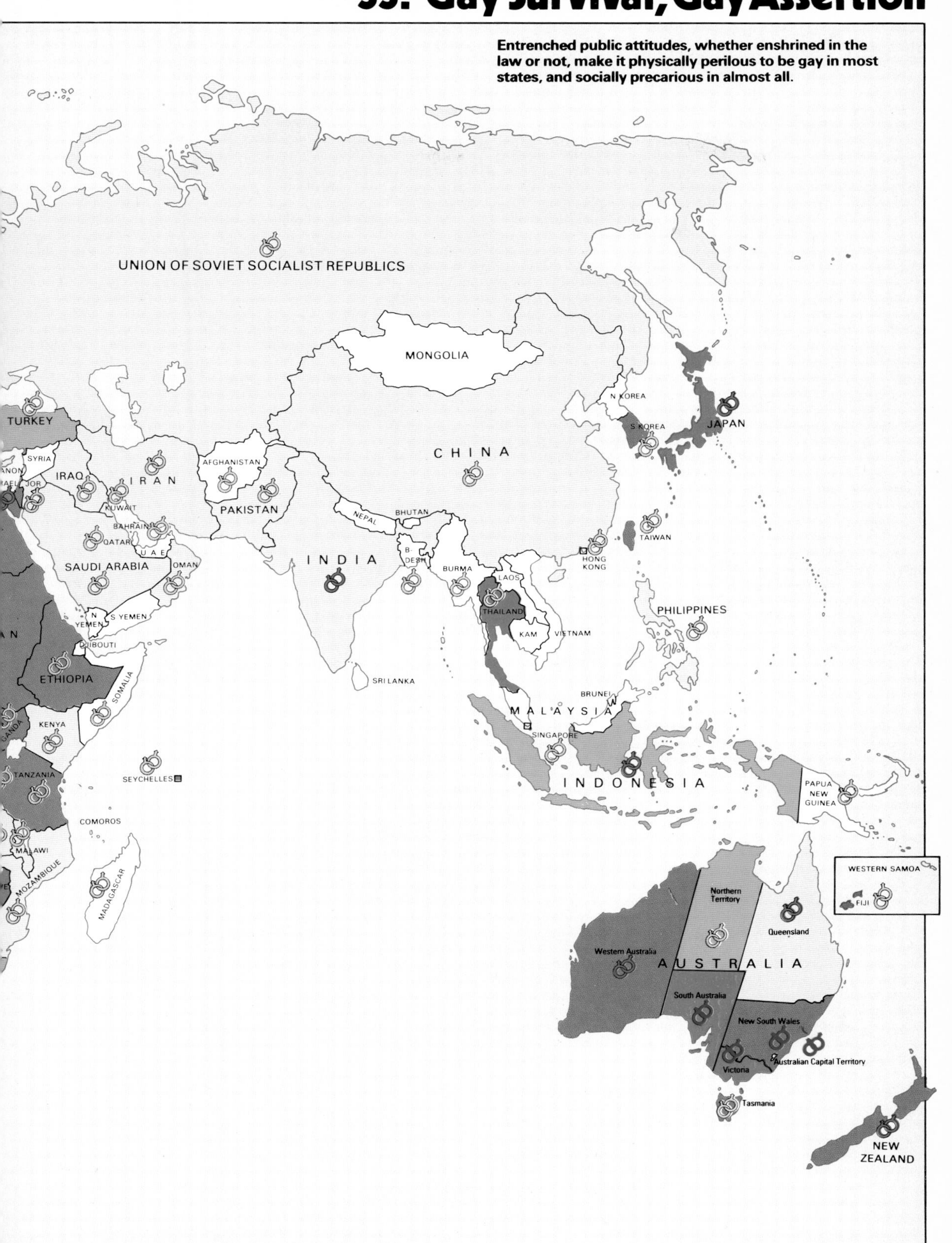

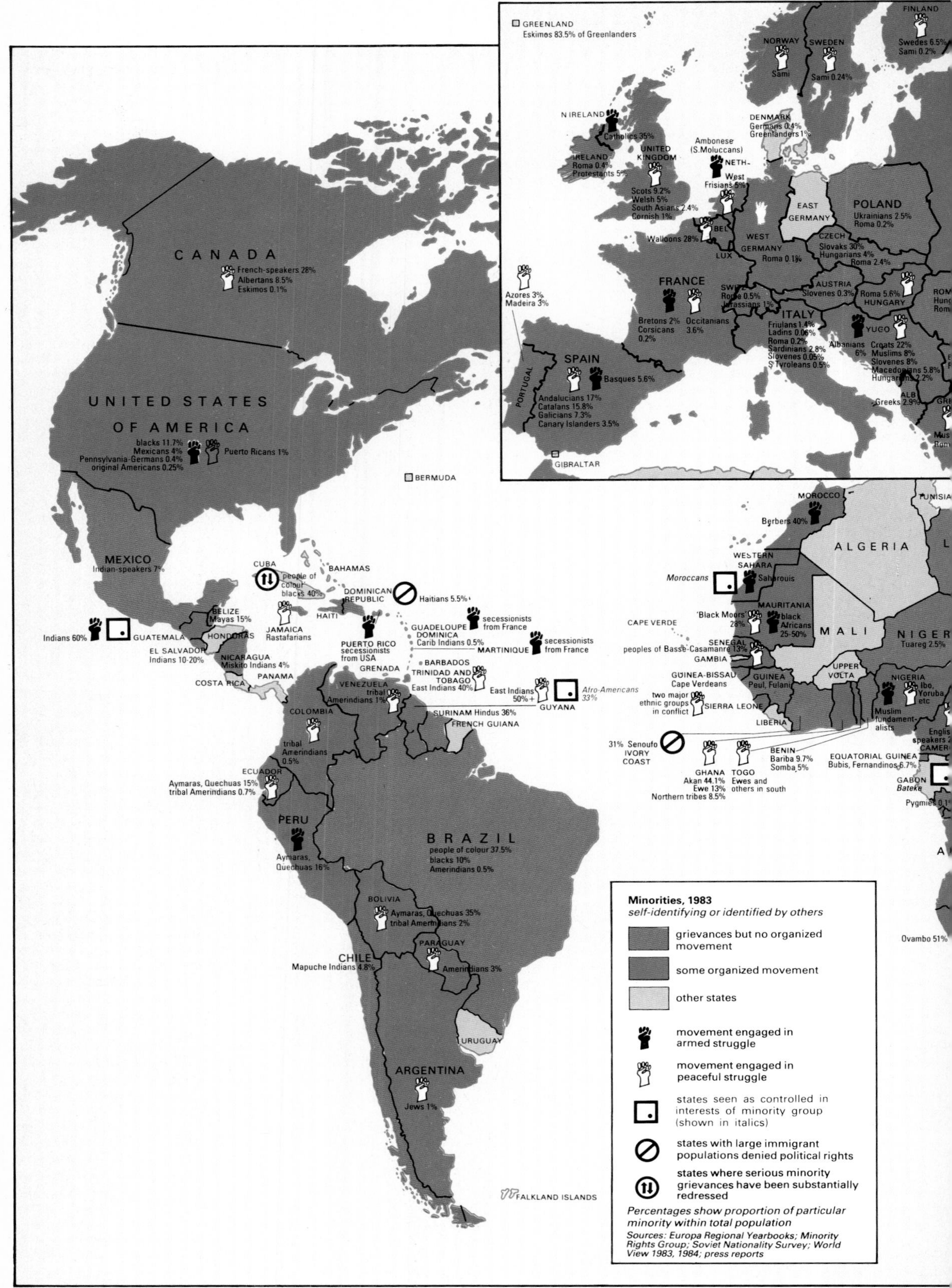

GREENLAND
Eskimos 83.5% of Greenlanders
NORWAY
Sami
SWEDEN
Sami 0.24%
FINLAND
Swedes 6.5%
Sami 0.2%
N IRELAND
Catholics 35%
DENMARK
Germans 0.4%
Greenlanders 1%
Ambonese
(S.Moluccans)
NETH-
West
Frisians 5%
IRELAND
Roma 0.4%
Protestants 5%
UNITED
KINGDOM
Scots 9.2%
Welsh 5%
South Asians 2.4%
Cornish 1%
EAST
GERMANY
POLAND
Ukrainians 2.5%
Roma 0.2%
Walloons 28%
BEL
LUX
WEST
GERMANY
Roma 0.1%
CZECH
Slovaks 30%
Hungarians 4%
Roma 2.4%
FRANCE
Bretons 2%
Corsicans
0.2%
Occitanians
3.6%
Azores 3%
Madeira 3%
SWITZ
Roma 0.5%
Jurassians 1%
AUSTRIA
Slovenes 0.3%
Roma 5.6%
HUNGARY
ITALY
Friulans 1.4%
Ladins 0.06%
Roma 0.2%
Sardinians 2.8%
Slovenes 0.05%
S Tyroleans 0.5%
YUGO
Albanians
6%
Croats 22%
Muslims 8%
Slovenes 8%
Macedonians 5.8%
Hungarians 2.2%
ALB
Greeks 2.9%
SPAIN
Basques 5.6%
Andalucians 17%
Catalans 15.8%
Galicians 7.3%
Canary Islanders 3.5%
PORTUGAL
GIBRALTAR
CANADA
French-speakers 28%
Albertans 8.5%
Eskimos 0.1%
UNITED STATES
OF AMERICA
blacks 11.7%
Mexicans 4%
Pennsylvania-Germans 0.4%
original Americans 0.25%
Puerto Ricans 1%
BERMUDA
MEXICO
Indian-speakers 7%
CUBA
people of
colour
blacks 40%
BAHAMAS
DOMINICAN
REPUBLIC
Haitians 5.5%
HAITI
JAMAICA
Rastafarians
PUERTO RICO
secessionists
from USA
GUADELOUPE
secessionists
from France
DOMINICA
Carib Indians 0.5%
MARTINIQUE
secessionists
from France
BARBADOS
GRENADA
TRINIDAD AND
TOBAGO
East Indians 40%
BELIZE
Mayas 15%
Indians 60%
GUATEMALA
HONDURAS
EL SALVADOR
Indians 10-20%
NICARAGUA
Miskito Indians 4%
PANAMA
COSTA RICA
VENEZUELA
tribal
Amerindians 1%
East Indians
50%+
Afro-Americans
33%
GUYANA
SURINAM Hindus 36%
FRENCH GUIANA
COLOMBIA
tribal
Amerindians
0.5%
ECUADOR
Aymaras, Quechuas 15%
tribal Amerindians 0.7%
PERU
Aymaras,
Quechuas 16%
BRAZIL
people of colour 37.5%
blacks 10%
Amerindians 0.5%
BOLIVIA
Aymaras, Quechuas 35%
tribal Amerindians 2%
PARAGUAY
Amerindians 3%
CHILE
Mapuche Indians 4.8%
URUGUAY
ARGENTINA
Jews 1%
FALKLAND ISLANDS
MOROCCO
Berbers 40%
ALGERIA
WESTERN
SAHARA
Moroccans
Saharouis
MAURITANIA
'Black Moors'
28%
black
Africans
25-50%
MALI
NIGER
Tuareg 2.5%
CAPE VERDE
peoples of Basse-Casamanre 13%
SENEGAL
GAMBIA
GUINEA-BISSAU
Cape Verdeans
GUINEA
Peul, Fulani
UPPER
VOLTA
NIGERIA
Ibo,
Yoruba
etc
Muslim
fundament-
alists
two major
ethnic groups
in conflict
SIERRA LEONE
LIBERIA
31% Senoufo
IVORY
COAST
GHANA
Akan 44.1%
Ewe 13%
Northern tribes 8.5%
TOGO
Ewes and
others in south
BENIN
Bariba 9.7%
Somba 5%
EQUATORIAL GUINEA
Bubis, Fernandinos 6.7%
GABON
Bateke
Pygmies
Ovambo 51%
Minorities, 1983
self-identifying or identified by others
grievances but no organized movement
some organized movement
other states
movement engaged in armed struggle
movement engaged in peaceful struggle
states seen as controlled in interests of minority group (shown in italics)
states with large immigrant populations denied political rights
states where serious minority grievances have been substantially redressed
Percentages show proportion of particular minority within total population
Sources: Europa Regional Yearbooks; Minority Rights Group; Soviet Nationality Survey; World View 1983, 1984; press reports

56. Minority Views

'Civilization is to be judged by its treatment of minorities.' Mahatma Gandhi.

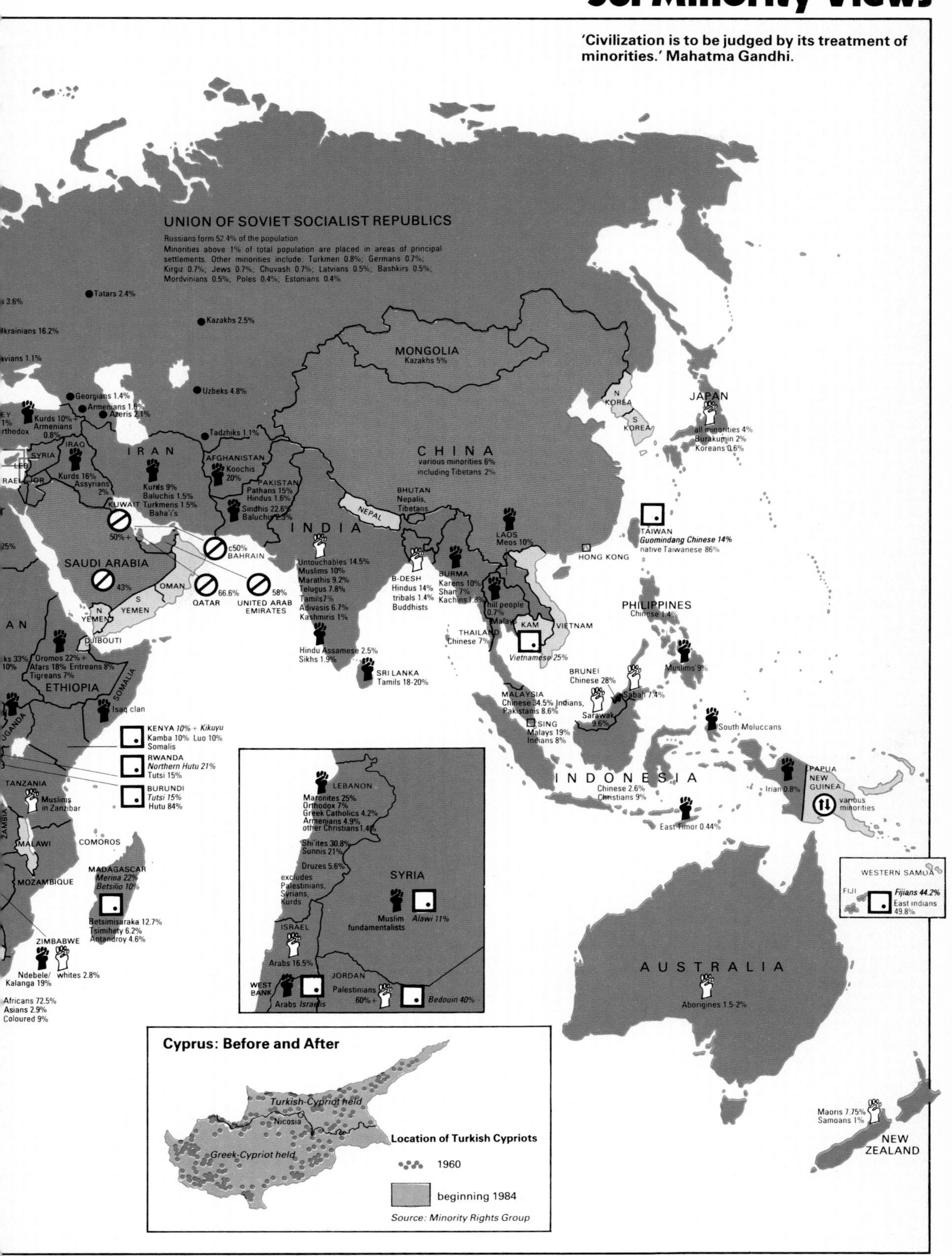

UNION OF SOVIET SOCIALIST REPUBLICS
Russians form 52.4% of the population
Minorities above 1% of total population are placed in areas of principal settlements. Other minorities include: Turkmen 0.8%; Germans 0.7%; Kirgiz 0.7%; Jews 0.7%; Chuvash 0.7%; Latvians 0.5%; Bashkirs 0.5%; Mordvinians 0.5%; Poles 0.4%; Estonians 0.4%
Tatars 2.4%
Kazakhs 2.5%
Uzbeks 4.8%
Georgians 1.4%
Armenians 1.6%
Azeris 2.1%
Tadzhiks 1.1%
MONGOLIA
Kazakhs 5%
Kurds 10% + Armenians 0.8%
IRAQ
Kurds 16%
Assyrians 2%
SYRIA
IRAN
Kurds 9%
Baluchis 1.5%
Turkmens 1.5%
Baha'is
AFGHANISTAN
Koochis 20%
PAKISTAN
Pathans 15%
Hindus 1.6%
Sindhis 22.6%
Baluchis 2.3%
KUWAIT
50% +
BAHRAIN
c50%
SAUDI ARABIA
43%
OMAN
QATAR
66.6%
UNITED ARAB EMIRATES
58%
N YEMEN
S YEMEN
DJIBOUTI
Oromos 22% +
Afars 18%
Eritreans 8%
Tigreans 7%
ETHIOPIA
SOMALIA
Isaq clan
KENYA 10% + Kikuyu
Kamba 10% Luo 10%
Somalis
RWANDA
Northern Hutu 21%
Tutsi 15%
BURUNDI
Tutsi 15%
Hutu 84%
TANZANIA
Muslims in Zanzibar
MALAWI
COMOROS
MOZAMBIQUE
MADAGASCAR
Merina 22%
Betsilio 10%
Betsimisaraka 12.7%
Tsimihety 6.2%
Antandroy 4.6%
ZIMBABWE
Ndebele/Kalanga 19%
whites 2.8%
Africans 72.5%
Asians 2.9%
Coloured 9%
CHINA
various minorities 6%
including Tibetans 2%
NEPAL
BHUTAN
Nepalis, Tibetans
INDIA
Untouchables 14.5%
Muslims 10%
Marathis 9.2%
Telugus 7.8%
Tamils 7%
Adivasis 6.7%
Kashmiris 1%
Hindu Assamese 2.5%
Sikhs 1.9%
SRI LANKA
Tamils 18-20%
B-DESH
Hindus 14%
tribals 1.4%
Buddhists
BURMA
Karens 10%
Shan 7%
Kachins 1.8%
LAOS
Meos 10%
hill people 0.7%
Malays
THAILAND
Chinese 7%
KAM
Vietnamese 25%
VIETNAM
HONG KONG
N KOREA
S KOREA
JAPAN
all minorities 4%
Burakumin 2%
Koreans 0.6%
TAIWAN
Guomindang Chinese 14%
native Taiwanese 86%
PHILIPPINES
Chinese 1.4%
Muslims 9%
BRUNEI
Chinese 28%
Sabah 7.4%
Sarawak 9.6%
MALAYSIA
Chinese 34.5% Indians, Pakistanis 8.6%
SING
Malays 19%
Indians 8%
South Moluccans
INDONESIA
Chinese 2.6%
Christians 9%
East Timor 0.44%
Irian 0.8%
PAPUA NEW GUINEA
various minorities
WESTERN SAMOA
FIJI
Fijians 44.2%
East Indians 49.8%
AUSTRALIA
Aborigines 1.5-2%
Maoris 7.75%
Samoans 1%
NEW ZEALAND
LEBANON
Maronites 25%
Orthodox 7%
Greek Catholics 4.2%
Armenians 4.9%
other Christians 1.4%
Shi'ites 30.8%
Sunnis 21%
Druzes 5.6%
excludes Palestinians, Syrians, Kurds
SYRIA
Muslim fundamentalists
Alawi 11%
ISRAEL
Arabs 16.5%
WEST BANK
Arabs
Israelis
JORDAN
Palestinians 60% +
Bedouin 40%
Cyprus: Before and After
Turkish-Cypriot held
Nicosia
Greek-Cypriot held
Location of Turkish Cypriots
1960
beginning 1984
Source: Minority Rights Group

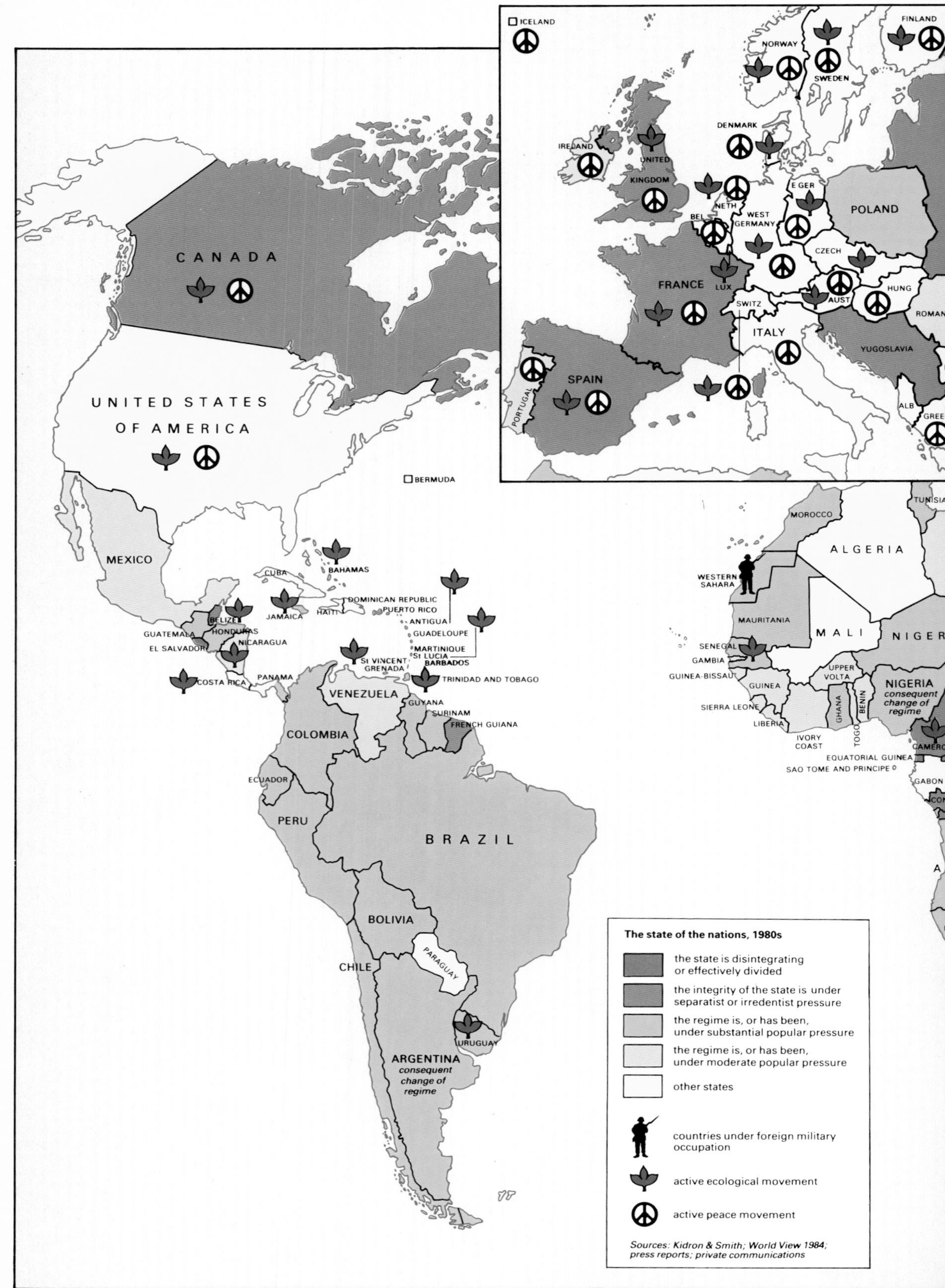
ICELAND
FINLAND
NORWAY
SWEDEN
DENMARK
IRELAND
UNITED
KINGDOM
NETH
BEL
E GER
WEST
GERMANY
POLAND
CZECH
LUX
FRANCE
AUST
HUNG
SWITZ
ITALY
YUGOSLAVIA
SPAIN
PORTUGAL
ALB
CANADA
UNITED STATES
OF AMERICA
BERMUDA
MEXICO
CUBA
BAHAMAS
DOMINICAN REPUBLIC
PUERTO RICO
ANTIGUA
GUADELOUPE
MARTINIQUE
St LUCIA
BARBADOS
JAMAICA
HAITI
BELIZE
GUATEMALA
HONDURAS
EL SALVADOR
NICARAGUA
COSTA RICA
PANAMA
St VINCENT
GRENADA
TRINIDAD AND TOBAGO
VENEZUELA
GUYANA
SURINAM
FRENCH GUIANA
COLOMBIA
ECUADOR
PERU
BRAZIL
BOLIVIA
PARAGUAY
CHILE
URUGUAY
ARGENTINA
consequent
change of
regime
TUNISIA
MOROCCO
ALGERIA
WESTERN
SAHARA
MAURITANIA
MALI
NIGER
SENEGAL
GAMBIA
GUINEA-BISSAU
GUINEA
SIERRA LEONE
LIBERIA
IVORY
COAST
UPPER
VOLTA
GHANA
TOGO
BENIN
NIGERIA
consequent
change of
regime
EQUATORIAL GUINEA
SAO TOME AND PRINCIPE
GABON
The state of the nations, 1980s
the state is disintegrating or effectively divided
the integrity of the state is under separatist or irredentist pressure
the regime is, or has been, under substantial popular pressure
the regime is, or has been, under moderate popular pressure
other states
countries under foreign military occupation
active ecological movement
active peace movement
Sources: Kidron & Smith; World View 1984; press reports; private communications

57. The State Under Pressure

The state has in its time been an instrument for the extension of personal liberty and for much material progress. It has also been an instrument of personal oppression, collective violence and economic waste. These destructive aspects of the state, which have come crucially to exceed the constructive ones, are inciting popular revulsion and some opposition.

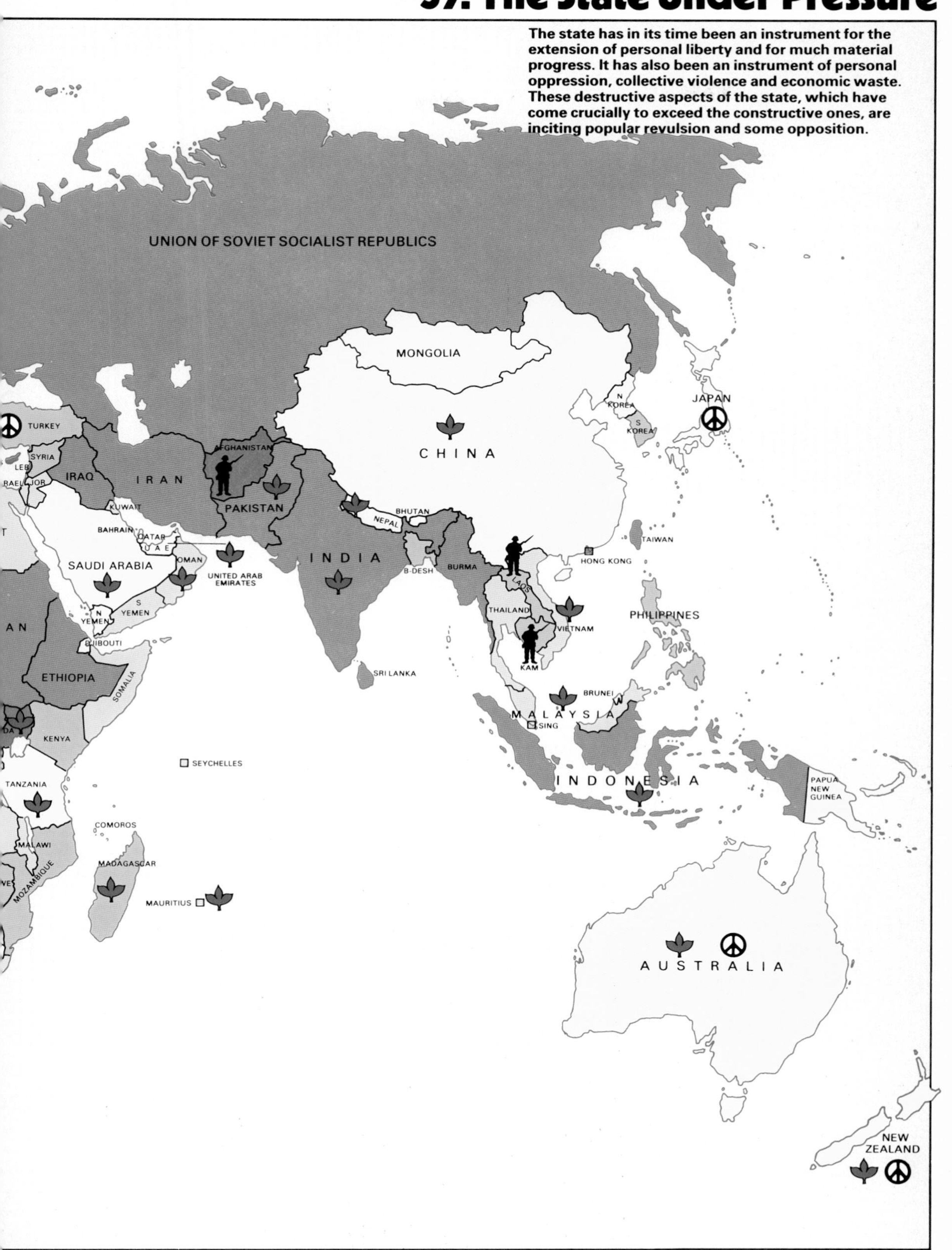

The States of the World

	capital	population mid-1981 *millions*	area *000km²*
Afghanistan	Kabul	16.3	648
Albania	Tirana	2.8	29
Algeria	Algiers	19.6	2382
Andorra	Andorra-la-Vieja	0.04	0.5
Angola	Luanda	7.8	1247
Antigua and Barbuda	St John's	0.08	0.4
Argentina	Buenos Aires	28.2	2767
Australia	Canberra	14.9	7687
Austria	Vienna	7.5	84
Bahamas	Nassau	0.2	14
Bahrain	Manama	0.4	0.6
Bangladesh	Dhaka (Dacca)	90.7	144
Barbados	Bridgetown	0.3	0.4
Belgium	Brussels	9.9	31
Belize	Belmopan	0.1	23
Benin	Porto Novo	3.6	113
Bermuda*	Hamilton	0.06	0.05
Bhutan	Thimphu	1.3	47
Bolivia	La Paz	5.7	1099
Botswana	Gaborone	0.9	600
Brazil	Brasilia	120.5	8512
Brunei	Bandar Seri Begawan	0.2	6
Bulgaria	Sofia	8.9	111
Burma	Rangoon	34.1	677
Burundi	Bujumbura	4.2	28
Cambodia *see* **Kampuchea**			
Cameroon	Yaoundé	8.7	475
Canada	Ottawa	24.2	9976
Cape Verde	Praia	0.3	4

	capital	population mid-1981 *millions*	area *000km²*
Cayman Islands*	Georgetown	0.02	0.3
Central African Republic	Bangui	2.4	623
Chad	N'djamena	4.5	1284
Chile	Santiago	11.3	757
China	Beijing (Peking)	991.3	9597
Colombia	Bogotá	26.4	1139
Comoros	Moroni	0.4	2
Congo	Brazzaville	1.7	342
Costa Rica	San José	2.3	51
Cuba	Havana	9.7	115
Cyprus	Nicosia	0.6	9
Czechoslovakia	Prague	15.3	128
Denmark	Copenhagen	5.1	43
Djibouti	Djibouti	0.4	22
Dominica	Roseau	0.07	0.4
Dominican Republic	Santo Domingo	5.6	49
Ecuador	Quito	8.6	284
Egypt	Cairo	43.3	1001
El Salvador	San Salvador	4.7	21
Equatorial Guinea	Malabo	0.3	28
Ethiopia	Addis Ababa	31.8	1222
Falkland Islands*	Stanley	0.002	12
Fiji	Suva	0.6	18
Finland	Helsinki	4.8	337
France	Paris	54.0	547
French Guiana*	Cayenne	0.06	91
Gabon	Libreville	0.7	268
Gambia	Banjul	0.6	11
Germany, East	Berlin	16.7	108
Germany, West	Bonn	61.7	249
Ghana	Accra	11.8	239
Greece	Athens	9.7	132
Greenland*	Godthaab	0.05	2186
Grenada	St George's	0.1	0.8
Guadeloupe*	Basse-Terre	7.5	2
Guatemala	Guatemala City	7.5	109

	capital	population mid-1981 *millions*	area *000km²*
Guinea	Conakry	5.6	246
Guinea-Bissau	Bissau	0.8	36
Guyana	Georgetown	0.8	215
Haiti	Port-au-Prince	5.1	28
Honduras	Tegucigalpa	3.8	112
Hong Kong*	Hong Kong	5.2	1
Hungary	Budapest	10.7	93
Iceland	Reykjavík	0.2	103
India	New Delhi	690.2	3288
Indonesia	Jakarta	149.5	1904
Iran	Tehrán	40.0	1648
Iraq	Baghdad	13.5	435
Ireland	Dublin	3.4	70
Israel	Jerusalem	4.0	21
Italy	Rome	56.2	301
Ivory Coast	Yamoussoukro	8.5	322
Jamaica	Kingston	2.2	11
Japan	Tokyo	117.6	372
Jordan	Amman	3.4	98
Kampuchea (Cambodia)	Phnom Penh	7.1	181
Kenya	Nairobi	17.4	583
Kiribati	Tarawa	0.06	0.9
Korea, North	Pyongyang	18.7	121
Korea, South	Seoul	38.9	98
Kuwait	Kuwait	1.5	18
Laos	Vientiane	3.5	237
Lebanon	Beirut	2.7	10
Lesotho	Maseru	1.4	30
Liberia	Monrovia	1.9	111
Libya	Tripoli	3.1	1760
Liechtenstein	Vaduz	0.03	0.2
Luxembourg	Luxembourg	0.4	3
Madagascar	Antananarivo	9.0	587
Malawi	Lilongwe	6.2	118
Malaysia	Kuala Lumpur	14.2	330
Maldives	Malé	0.2	0.3

	capital	population mid-1981 *millions*	area *000km²*
Mali	Bamako	6.9	1240
Malta	Valletta	0.4	0.3
Martinique*	Fort-de-France	0.3	1
Mauritania	Nouakchott	1.6	1031
Mauritius	Port Louis	1.0	2
Mexico	Mexico City	71.2	1973
Monaco	Monaco	0.03	0.002
Mongolia	Ulaanbaatar (Ulan Bator)	1.7	1567
Morocco	Rabat	20.9	447
Mozambique	Maputo	12.5	783
Namibia†	Windhoek	1.0	824
Nauru		0.007	0.02
Nepal	Katmandu	15.0	141
Netherlands	Amsterdam	14.2	37
New Zealand	Wellington	3.3	269
Nicaragua	Managua	2.8	130
Niger	Niamey	5.7	1267
Nigeria	Lagos	87.6	925
Norway	Oslo	4.1	324
Oman	Muscat	0.9	212
Pakistan	Islamabad	84.5	804
Panama	Panama City	1.9	77
Papua New Guinea	Port Moresby	3.1	462
Paraguay	Asunción	3.1	407
Peru	Lima	17.0	1285
Philippines	Manila	49.6	300
Poland	Warsaw	35.9	313
Portugal	Lisbon	9.8	92
Puerto Rico*	San Juan	3.7	9
Qatar	Doha	0.2	11
Réunion*	Saint-Denis	0.5	3
Romania	Bucharest	22.5	238
Rwanda	Kigali	5.3	26
St Christopher (St Kitts) - Nevis	Basseterre	0.05	0.3
St Lucia	Castries	0.1	0.6
St Vincent	Kingstown	0.1	0.3

	capital	population mid-1981 *millions*	area *000km²*
San Marino	San Marino	0.02	0.06
São Tomé and Principe	São Tomé	0.1	1
Saudi Arabia	Riyadh	9.3	2150
Senegal	Dakar	5.9	196
Seychelles	Victoria	0.06	0.3
Sierra Leone	Freetown	3.6	72
Singapore	Singapore	2.4	0.6
Solomon Islands	Honiara	0.2	28
Somalia	Mogadishu	4.4	638
South Africa	Pretoria	29.5	1221
Spain	Madrid	38.0	505
Sri Lanka	Colombo	15.0	66
Sudan	Khartoum	19.2	2506
Surinam	Paramaribo	0.4	163
Swaziland	Mbabane	0.6	17
Sweden	Stockholm	8.3	450
Switzerland	Berne	6.5	41
Syria	Damascus	9.3	185
Taiwan	Taipei	18.3	36
Tanzania	Dodoma	19.1	945
Thailand	Bangkok	48.0	514
Togo	Lomé	2.7	56
Tonga	Nuku'alofa	0.1	0.8
Trinidad and Tobago	Port-of-Spain	1.2	5
Tunisia	Tunis	6.5	164
Turkey	Ankara	45.5	781
Tuvalu	Funafuti	0.008	0.02
Uganda	Kampala	13.0	236
Union of Soviet Socialist Republics (USSR)	Moscow	268.0	22402
United Arab Emirates	Abu Dhabi	1.1	87
United Kingdom	London	56.0	244
United States of America (USA)	Washington DC	229.8	9363
Upper Volta	Ouagadougou	6.3	274
Uruguay	Montevideo	2.9	176
Vanuatu	Vila	0.1	15
Vatican City		0.001	0.4

	capital	population mid-1981 *millions*	area *000km²*
Venezuela	Caracas	15.4	912
Vietnam	Hanoi	55.7	330
Virgin Islands, British	Road Town	0.01	0.1
Western Sahara†	El Aaiún	n.a.	267.8
Western Samoa	Apia	0.2	3
Yemen, North	San'a	7.3	195
Yemen, South	Aden	2.0	333
Yugoslavia	Belgrade	22.3	256
Zaire	Kinshasa	29.8	2345
Zambia	Lusaka	5.8	753
Zimbabwe	Harare	7.2	391

* Colonies, 'overseas departments', 'commonwealth' and other anomalies
† States generally recognized as independent but under the rule of neighbouring state
Sources: Statesman's Year-Book 1983-4; US Department of State; World Bank Atlas 1983; World View 1984

Notes to the Maps

1. The World of States

We identify as states those territories which are recognized as such by most governments and inter-governmental agencies, although not always by some or even most of their inhabitants.

Taiwan is included as a sovereign state, although both its own government and that of mainland China insist that it is an integral part of a single Chinese state. Similarly, the South African 'Bantu homelands' and the Ukraine and Byelorussia are excluded; the first is recognized by South Africa alone and the second two, while represented at the United Nations, are not deemed sovereign by any member state. Namibia and Western Sahara are designated as states, although occupied by other countries, because their independent existence is widely accepted within the community of states. Greenland is not an independent state, although its measure of autonomy is such that it is in the process of withdrawing from the European Economic Community (EEC), while its metropolitan country, Denmark, remains a member. Several states, such as Martinique, Guadeloupe and French Guiana, are legally Overseas Provinces of France, with representation in the metropolitan political institutions. Puerto Rico is a so-called 'free state' but with the United States continuing to control its defence policy and foreign affairs. Puerto Ricans are held to be US citizens and so able to emigrate freely to the USA, but they have no representation in the US Congress. An elected governor is the primary political authority, though with various restrictions on his power.

The two Germanies are shown as new states, since neither existed in its present form before 1945; even though we recognize that historical continuity runs essentially through West Germany.

2. The State by Population

The world would look very different if the sizes of states corresponded to their populations. It would also change shape continuously as populations in the rich states shrink relatively to populations in the poor ones.

Counting people is not an exact science. In some states, important sections of the community do their utmost to avoid being noticed. Obvious examples are the illegal immigrant populations in the USA and Venezuela. In others, political arrangements are so closely involved with the results of the population census that the census itself becomes the product of politics and not only its determinant. In Nigeria, for instance, it has long been believed in the south that the census is so organized as to inflate the population figures in the north. In the Lebanon, a census of the different religious communities has long been avoided, since that country's distinctive political arrangements were based on a communal ratio that is increasingly historical. In many states, there are simply no provisions made for a separate census administration; population figures are supplied by officials who are engaged in other, seemingly more pressing business, and who have not necessarily been appointed for their numeracy.

In consequence of the local poverty in statistical services, many of the figures used in the cartogram are estimates from the Population Division of the United Nations Secretariat. Externally-generated figures promote international comparisons. These increase the political importance of national statistics, which, in turn, provoke political interference in their collection or manufacture. The result is even greater reliance on the services and authority of the international agencies.

Forty-eight territories with populations below one million each are excluded from the cartogram. They are: Andorra; Bahamas; Bahrain; Barbados; Belize; Bermuda; Botswana; Brunei; Cape Verde; Comoros; Cyprus; Dominica; Equatorial Guinea; Fiji; French Guiana; Gabon; Gambia; Gibraltar; Greenland; Grenada; Guinea-Bissau; Guyana; Guadeloupe; Guam; Iceland; Kiribati; Liechtenstein; Luxembourg; Macau; Maldives; Malta; Mauritius; Martinique; Monaco; Oman; Qatar; Reunion; St Lucia; St Vincent and the Grenadines; San Marino; Sao Tome & Principe; Seychelles; Solomon Islands; Surinam; Swaziland; United Arab Emirates; Vanuatu; Vatican City.

Four states actually lost population in the five year period with which the map deals. In Kampuchea (−2.7%) and the Lebanon (−2.5%) conflict and disorder were primary causes. East Germany (−0.3%) has a low birth rate. The population decrease in the UK was so small (−0.1%) that it would be misleading to make much of it.

3. The State Invades Antarctica

Antarctica is rich in resources. It is already a major source of protein in the form of fish, whalemeat, and increasingly krill (the many species of oceanic shrimp, which constitute the basic food of whales). It promises to be a major source of many minerals already mined in Southern Africa, Australia, and South America, with which Antarctica shares a common geological past. It is thought to be rich in mineral oil and gas deposits. It also harbours 70 per cent of the world's fresh water, in the form of ice.

The Antarctic Treaty was signed in 1959. Its fourteen consultative parties are Argentina, Australia, Belgium, Chile, France, West Germany, Japan, Poland, New Zealand, Norway, South Africa, USSR, UK and USA. States that subsequently acceded to the treaty are Brazil, Bulgaria, China (in June 1983), Czechoslovakia, Denmark, East Germany, Italy, Netherlands, Peru, Papua New Guinea, Romania, Spain and Uruguay.

The purpose of the treaty is to ensure the peaceful administration of the southern polar region. But history suggests that there is nothing quite so pregnant with the possibilities of conflict as the treaty arrangements made by states for professedly pacific purposes. And already there are moves to transfer the administration of Antarctica from the haphazard collection of treaty states to an international body such as the United Nations.

4. The State Invades the Sea

Although not yet ratified, the 1982 Convention on the Law of the Sea is shaping an inter-state oceanic regime. Littoral states are claiming Exclusive Economic Zones (EEZs) extending 200 nautical miles off-shore or 350 miles and more into the continental shelf. It is obvious that in the process of establishing and extending EEZs, even the smallest of island territories has enormous value. One third of the seas (which themselves cover 70 per cent of the world's surface, all of its off-shore oil and mineral resources, and most of its seawater fish) is being attached in this way.

The many areas where EEZs overlap are areas of potential conflict. Some of these have caused, or exacerbated, existing disputes, the most important of which are shown on the map.

The general acceptance of EEZs and the more narrowly conceived but similar Exclusive Fishing Zones has restrained the rush to extend territorial waters, which are the recognized preserve of state law. The normal limit for territorial waters now appears to be settling at twelve nautical miles. This is substantially more than the traditional three miles still asserted by the old maritime powers (UK, USA and others) but far less than the claims of some Latin American and African countries which extend to the limit of their EEZs.

Unhappily for the claimants to Exclusive Fishing Zones, fish have no passports. 'British fishermen say 60 per cent of Common Market fish swim in British waters, but a lot of them were born in Danish waters and came here only when they grew up. So are they British or Danish fish?' So ran a British press report at the height of the Danish-EEC fishing dispute in 1982.

5. Space Invaders

Most satellites are designed and dispatched for purely military purposes: early warning, communications, navigation, surveillance and, increasingly, the midflight guidance of ballistic missiles. But it is unwise, if not impossible , to distinguish at all precisely between military and commercial satellites, since some of each also perform functions associated with the other. The furthest that one authority will go is to estimate that around 40 per cent of total launchings by mid-September 1983 (2,486) had been primarily commercial.

The commercialization of space was inaugurated in 1962, when the US Congress established the Communications Satellite Corporation (Comsat) as a private company to be the country's basic 'common carrier' for satellite communications. A decade later, the US Federal Communications Commission declared that the US industry should develop further in a 'free enterprise mode'. US business was not slow to explore the new possibilities.

Commercial satellites are used for the transmission of telephone, telex and data services. They are used for the internal communications of corporations; for facsimile transmission of newspapers and documents; for entertainment. Six years after Home Box Office, the US cable TV company, transmitted its first program by satellite, 12 million homes in the US alone were paying $1 billion a year for cable television.

The USA was the first country to use space for commercial purposes. There are now others. In one area alone, the arcane art of remote sensing for earth mapping, France is preparing to launch two satellites, the first in 1985; Japan is planning one for 1986; and eleven West European states grouped in the European Space Agency are also in the running. In other fields – TV, data transmission, telephone services – private and public business satellites are becoming, if not commonplace, fairly unremarkable.

6. Big Brother

Military bases are 'foreign' in one of two respects: they are either in the territory of another sovereign state, or in that of a dependency or near-dependency. A French base in Guadeloupe (effectively a French dependency) or the British base on Ascension Island (a British dependency) are as 'foreign' in this sense as are US and USSR bases in the sovereign states of West and East Germany respectively; or the US base on Diego Garcia (a British dependency).

These bases are protected by a secrecy far more effective than their perimeter fences. Even where the presence of the bases is publicly recorded, as in Britain, Norway and Sweden, peace researchers have been arrested and tried, essentially for drawing attention to this. For that reason, our map is not as comprehensive as we would like it to be. Furthermore, the symbols on each country distinguish only particular kinds of base belonging to a foreign state, where several or even many such bases may exist. We show, for instance, only one set of symbols for US bases in the UK, although more than a hundred such bases are located there.

The presence of military advisers and trainees indicates a relationship between states that goes far beyond mere technical training. It embraces trade ties, the convergence of attitudes, political lobbying and influence, along with many other aspects of inter-state relations in the increasingly militarized international order.

It is obvious that the presence of foreign military bases and advisers for the proclaimed purpose of defence against a common external enemy can easily become intervention to sustain an unpopular and threatened regime. Examples are abundant. Among the more important current ones are the Russians in Afghanistan; the Americans in El Salvador; Cubans in Ethiopia; Belgians, French and others in Zaire.

The pattern of military bases and alignments is far from fixed. Even as this map was being prepared, intervention by the USA in Grenada disposed of the Cuban and East European presence there, for the arrival of another, Western in alignment.

We define a major air base as one which normally contains more than two squadrons of combat aircraft or more than one hundred personnel; a major naval base as one which is regularly used by major warships; a major army base as one with more than 10,000 soldiers.

7. Military Spending

Military spending is a term beset by problems of definition, verification, and comparison between states and between periods. The problems are greatest with the two giant spenders, the USA and USSR, each of them responsible for approximately one quarter of the world's estimated total military expenditure. We have used the latest figures supplied by the Stockholm International Peace Research Institute (SIPRI), updated, where necessary, from other sources. SIPRI itself is the most authoritative non-government source for such information.

The inset map on the military share of central government expenditure is based on official US estimates, themselves ultimately derived from the Central Intelligence Agency (CIA). Not surprisingly, these tend to exaggerate the military bias of the Soviet budget. They are, however, the most comprehensive available.

This map does not deal with the arms trade, about which SIPRI says: 'There is no exact, reliable or even reasonable information' on its real value. But the trade is undeniably huge and is important not only for its economic dimensions but for its social and political effects. It diverts scarce resources from productive use. It invests the military with economic and social privileges which they are uniquely placed to defend and promote. Not least, it is an abundant source of corruption both in importing and exporting countries.

Italy provides a notable instance. With restraints less precise or effectual than apply in Britain and West Germany, for instance, Italy constitutes a channel for some British and West German arms exports. In this way, arms otherwise embargoed reach countries at war with each other. An article in the *Financial Times* (11 November 1983) reports: 'Part of Italy's success in defence sales is due to the skill of its salesmen. "They know exactly who to pay the commission to, and how much to give them, and they cover everyone," said one businessman in the defence sales business.'

In the league of arms sales, the USSR comes top, with 36.5% of the world market in major weapons; the USA second, with 33.6%; France, third, with 9.7%; Italy, fourth, with 4.3%; Britain, fifth, with 3.6%; and West Germany, sixth, with 3%. (Figures for international arms sales, 1979-81). Together these six countries account for over 90% of international arms sales.

8. Shares in the Apocalypse

Since the bombs dropped on Japan in 1945, no nuclear weapon has been exploded, outside of test programmes. But this has been as much a matter of luck as of anything else. It is known that the US strategic early warning system produced more than eight false alarms monthly on average in a year and a half from around the beginning of 1980.

A 'known nuclear weapons state' is one which has manufactured and detonated a nuclear weapon or other nuclear explosive device. A 'suspected nuclear weapons state' is one which is widely reputed to have constructed, or be able to construct within a very short time, some nuclear weapons. A 'near nuclear weapons state' is one which could develop this capability by the year 2000. An important component of this capability is the use of a nuclear reactor for either research or electricity production.

There are many more missiles than missile launchers. In NATO, for example, the ratio for short-range missiles is six or seven to one. Similarly, there are more nuclear bombs than nuclear bombers and more nuclear shells than nuclear cannon. We have adopted the convention of counting missile launchers while designating them as missiles. It is misleading, but our sources leave us with no choice.

We have sited nuclear weapons in the states of their deployment, not in the states that own or control them. In Europe, only France and the UK independently possess such weapons. The USA or the USSR control all other nuclear weapons, including every type of cruise missile.

The approach of the apocalypse is as much a matter for those countries that do not yet have nuclear weapons as for those who keep on adding to the stockpiles they already possess. The diffusion of the technology has made it increasingly cheap and easy for states to join the nuclear club without an invitation from its existing members to do so.

9. Conventional Killing

While the threat of nuclear war commands the headlines, the many thousands killed and maimed in battle every year are victims of a more accepted but increasingly horrible conventional weaponry.

The arsenal is the state's assertion of statehood. But the profusion of armaments is not necessarily the measure of effectual military power. Some weapons are more sophisticated and accordingly more destructive than others; or more sophisticated than the capacity of the society to service them and so keep them operational. Some military forces are more impressive for their equipment than for their loyalty or morale. Some weapons, expensively accumulated in enormous quantities, have the drawback of rapidly becoming obsolete. Nonetheless, alongside these reservations, the relative strength in major weapons is an indication of relative military power: always excepting the new dimensions produced by the possession of nuclear weapons.

In the first edition of this atlas we employed air power as a measure of conventional military strength. In this edition we use land power for the same purpose. The picture that emerges is much the same, since the hierarchies of land and, to a lesser extent, sea power are similar to those of their air equivalent.

This map does not allow for the increasingly refined distinctions between one method of killing and another, any more than it allows for a measure of the waste, in human intelligence and resources, that is involved in their design and production.

10. War in Our Time

This map seeks to identify the wars fought during the past decade or so: the different kinds of war; and the potential occasions or pretexts for future wars, in active or dormant border disputes.

War itself we define as a series of connected armed clashes in which at least one of the contenders employs regular, uniformed forces.

A border war we distinguish as one which normally – though not necessarily – involves a conflicting claim to territory and which is limited to fighting along the border. It does not include simple boundary demarcation disputes. A general war between neighbouring states is one which may well begin as a border war but which spreads so as to involve virtually the total armed forces of the belligerents and, if only through air attacks, territory far from the border. It is easy to cite instances where a war may appear to be neither of these but contains elements of both, and we have used our own judgement to determine which term most usefully to apply.

A state in general war with a non-neighbouring state and a state with major military engagement in a foreign conflict constitute separate categories that allow even more room for confusion. And again, of course, determination is a matter of judgement. It seems to us clear that, in the late 1960s and early 1970s, the United States was waging in Vietnam and Kampuchea, by the sheer scale of its military operations within those countries, a general war, while its military operations in Laos were closer to a massive military engagement. This definition of general war accordingly applies to a belligerent state even when, as with the United States, its own territory remains untouched.

The difference between a major and a minor military engagement in foreign conflict is, obviously, arguable. In our view, it depends on the scale and/or implications of the engagement. Clearly, French and Libyan engagements in the Chad civil war are major more for their implications than for their scale, while the Cuban engagement in Angola is major both by scale and implication. The Russian engagement in Afghanistan presents a particular problem, since in scale it amounts to a general war. We have classified it as a major military engagement only because, strictly, the war in Afghanistan is not one between states but a civil war. It is not, therefore, the same as the US involvement in Vietnam and Kampuchea, where the war was an interstate one as well as a civil war.

Not least, the definition of civil war bristles with difficulties. It is general, in our view, when its operations or contending forces involve, actively or passively, by impetus or design, the issue of sovereignty throughout the state; regional when a particular area, usually though not always for separatist objectives, is alone involved, even if operations spill over into other areas. Thus, South Africa has general civil war, even though the scale of operations is not yet remotely comparable with that in El Salvador, for instance; while in Spain we have used the designation of regional civil war, even though Basque separatism is partly manifested by armed acts in the country's capital.

General civil war is shown in Poland, on the basis that there has been widespread conflict between a large sector of the population and the armed forces of the government.

The distinction between interstate and civil wars is frequently blurred. We have excluded as interstate wars, wars in which foreign intervention is of a disguised or 'technical' kind (as is the USA's in El Salvador); but have included wars in which foreign troops have been committed against the existing authority (e.g. Turkey in Cyprus).

We have distinguished anti-colonial wars, since the description of such conflict as civil war misleads more than it illuminates.

Active border disputes are those in which a government maintains an overt claim to all or part of a neighbouring territory. A dormant dispute may be very unlikely to become an active one but remains a dispute while there are those – as in West Germany over the very division of Germany – active in promoting the issue. The border between Poland and East Germany is designated as the subject of a dormant border dispute because its settlement relates to the division of Germany, and the symbol could scarcely have been placed on a border between West Germany and Poland.

States are depicted as they were at the end of 1983; they may not have existed, or existed in their current form, at the time of some of the conflicts shown. For example, most of the interstate clashes associated with Zimbabwe on the map predate the transition, in 1980, from white minority Rhodesia to the present regime.

11. Mineral Power

Power does not necessarily result from the substantial production of a particular mineral. Some minerals may be in general over-supply; allowing consumers to determine the price or play off one supplier against another. Some are marketable only or chiefly in a processed form, which may invest the processors themselves with more power than the producers can exercise. In all such cases, it is often the transnational corporation, with interests in both mining and processing, and with operations in numerous countries, that is effectively more powerful than the governments to which it pays formal obeisance. To illustrate this, we have included in the map processing centres; identifying states where the processing of particular metals and minerals or their ores substantially exceeds existing, if any, production from mining. A few states – notably the USA and USSR – are both major processors and major producers. They are identified as processors only for those metals which they produce in significantly lower quantities than they process.

Power attaches as well to the marketing of minerals and the manipulation of their price. The map accordingly shows the centres of trading and speculation for particular metals and minerals.

Nonetheless, the possession of minerals can and does confer power; when cyclical conditions produce the reality or appearance of scarcity; where, as with platinum and chrome, there are very few producers; or where particular countries are so rich in different minerals that their dependence on any one market or corporation is correspondingly reduced. In this last regard, the map distinguishes the five mineral powers, each of which produces significant proportions of more than five major minerals.

The relative importance of producers changes as new sources of supply are discovered. Australia, for instance, is set to become an important source of industrial diamonds.

On a technical note: bauxite ore is reduced to alumina powder which is refined to aluminium, in the ratio of 4:2:1 by weight.

Gold and oil are excluded from this map, since each is considered elsewhere (*Map 13: Oil Power* and *Map 52: The Gold Rush*).

12. Energy Power

This map is mainly concerned with commercial energy: energy produced for sale rather than for direct use. Such energy accounts for some 85 per cent of all human energy use.

Most of the commercial energy produced is from non-renewable sources; and most of the renewable energy sources, notably wood and charcoal, are used directly by the producers – poor rural populations in the poor states.

An increasing interest in renewable energy sources – in principle limited only by the all but limitless power of the sun – has resulted from two main factors: the growing scarcity of the traditional, easily accessible non-renewable fossil fuels (whatever the temporary surpluses of supply) and the growing public awareness of the dangers in nuclear power (heightened in particular by the frightening accident at the Three Mile Island nuclear power plant in the eastern United States in March 1979). It is for this reason that we have included renewable sources in this edition.

But commercial energy remains the core of energy use for the time being. Indeed, it constitutes the single biggest item in international trade. The top 15 energy surplus countries, ranked by size of surplus in the early 1980s, were: Saudi Arabia, which exported nearly three quarters of a billion metric tons of coal equivalent, in the form of oil; USSR; Venezuela; Iraq; Nigeria; United Arab Emirates; Libya; Kuwait; Indonesia; Mexico; Iran; Algeria; Norway; Qatar; and Australia, with some 28 million metric tons of coal equivalent. All but Australia were oil exporters.

Comparison between coal and other sources of energy is based on calorific value. One metric ton of coal is equivalent to 1.47 metric tons of crude petroleum or 1.67 metric tons of natural gas liquid.

The still relatively high price of oil, with the possibility of steep price rises in the event of sustained industrial recovery, has excited renewed interest in the world's coal resources. Coal can be used as a substitute fuel for power stations and is itself a source of oil. As the inset map demonstrates, there is a large international trade in coal.

13. Oil Power

Oil has become the dominant indicator of industrial and hence general economic activity.

The information on the map relates to the early 1980s, which were affected by world recession; a corresponding drop in the demand for oil, with its impact on the prevailing price; an agreed attempt by OPEC members to support prices by limiting production; and some infringements of the agreement through price discounting and concealed increases in production.

The apparent decline in the power of the OPEC cartel, however, was due not only to the recession but to the erosion in the cartel's share of world exports, with the entry of important new producers, notably Mexico, Britain and Norway. Delighted to take advantage of the minimum prices set by OPEC, such countries have shown some reluctance to join OPEC members in even the pretence of deliberately limiting production. Indeed, the drop in oil prices might well have been more drastic in consequence, had it not been for the long war between Iran and Iraq, which has seriously affected the oil production and export facilities of both countries, especially Iraq.

Oil is important not only for those countries usually classified as oil exporters. The note to *Map 19: Dependence and Diversity* indicates its importance for export revenue even where it is not the sole or even major export.

Despite the much proclaimed measures adopted in the industrial West to reduce the wasteful use of energy, it is probable that any sustained economic recovery would soon be reflected in a renewed preoccupation with the scarcity of oil and a return to the scramble for supplies. The problems of the USA, as a huge oil producer but yet one still dependent upon massive imports, may well in that event become more pressing than they were before the recession. Meanwhile, the USSR remains at least as wasteful in its use of energy, with a rate of depletion in reserves that must make a recourse to oil imports a matter of only a few years. The economic and political consequences of competition between the two superpowers for scarce and costly supplies are unlikely to be comfortable.

14. Food Power

The equivalent map in the first edition of this atlas dealt with all designated foods, including such non-nutritional 'beverages' as coffee, cocoa and tea. We pointed out in the notes that this produced an essentially distorted view of the subject: with Africa, a region of widespread undernourishment and even starvation, emerging as possessed of an overall surplus in the food trade, through massive exports of beverage crops and tropical fruits. In this edition, we have rejected the general food category altogether and employ instead the category of cereals, the paramount source of nourishment for the vast majority of people.

The following tables illustrate the dominance of the export trade by the USA and the failure of the USSR, across a decade, to secure a substantial increase in its production of wheat. As is also shown, the dominance of the USA and dependence of the USSR extend to the trade in coarse grains.

Production of Wheat
thousands of metric tons

	world	*USSR*	*USA*	*Canada*	*Australia*	*Argentina*
1971-2	322,562	98,760	44,029	14,412	8,651	5,680
1981-8	452,300	88,000	76.025	24,500	16,400	7,800
change (%)	*+40.22%*	*−10.89%*	*+72.67%*	*+69.99%*	*+89.57%*	*+37.82%*

Imports and Exports of Wheat and Wheat Flour, 1980-1
thousands of metric tons

Imports	*Exports*
USSR 16,000	USA 41,900
Eastern Europe 5,800	Canada 17,000
	Australia 10,400

Imports and Exports of Coarse Grains, 1980-1
thousands of metric tons

Imports	*Exports*
USSR 18,000	USA 72,400
Eastern Europe 11,000	Argentina 9,800
	Western Europe 7,300

Source: Commodity Research Bureau Inc

Six years after Earl Butz's celebrated remark that we have used as a caption on the map, the USA embargoed all sales of domestic grain, not already pledged by contract, to the USSR. But the very abundance of US harvests, with the plight of US farmers in a period of low commodity prices and high interest rates, led the US government to retreat from this position and assure the USSR of dependable supplies.

The absurd cruelty remains: of a world order by which many hundreds of millions are permanently undernourished or die of starvation, while the European Economic Community heaps up stocks of grain, and farmers in the USA are paid to stop growing grain at all.

15. Industrial Power

Industrial power is the paramount source of much other power, from military to financial, that the state possesses. It is also the measure which most dramatically demonstrates the economic disproportion between one state and another.

There is no rigid correspondence between industrial performance and investment, as is all too apparent from the record of the USSR. But in general, states with a consistently high level of investment make progress as industrial powers, to catch up with or leave behind those with a consistently lower level. We have combined, therefore, two measures – relative current output and relative rates of investment in manufacturing – so as to indicate the likely pecking order of states as industrial powers in the future as well as their present relative positions.

We have chosen to present this comparison by relation to the performance of a single state. And what better state may be employed as a benchmark than the United Kingdom. It deserves recognition as historically the first industrial state. It is, among the industrially developed, a small enough power to constitute a suitable target for industrial aspirants to reach, while recording a low enough level of investment to excite confidence that this aspiration will not be disappointed.

As so often in such exercises, there is the problem of converting an immense variety of products, measured physically in different ways for different purposes by different authorities, into a single measure of value. The conversion of this measure, from the national to an international currency – the United States dollar – provides further room for fallibility: even where there is something resembling free trade, if only for a small proportion of total output. Where trade is restricted in price and quantity, as between East and West, conversion often borders on an act of faith.

Nonetheless, we have undertaken the exercise. Most national currencies have been given dollar values at the average annual rates provided by the IMF. Where these are not provided, we have chosen end-of-year rates for the years in question.

For countries not members of the IMF, notably most of those in COMECON, conversion has been made at 'effective' exchange rates (generally at mid-year, for the years employed) as given in Pick's *Currency Yearbook.*

The graphic on advertising is included here because advertising is so closely connected with the distribution and sale of goods in industrial society. We have used the UK as a benchmark for much the same reason as before.

Figures for advertising expenditure cover different types of advertising in different countries. In many, the cost of cinema advertisements, direct advertising, exhibitions and demonstrations, of display material and sales promotion and reference publications, is excluded. We have not been able to allow for such variations.

16. Nuclear Power

The enthusiasm demonstrated by states for the development of nuclear power depends on the interplay of several factors: the price and security of conventional energy sources, especially oil; the pressure from the military for research and production facilities that might be used for the development of nuclear weapons; the projection of electricity needs and the extent of facilities for the expansion of conventional electricity production; the issue of safety and the related intensity of public protest. Since the first edition of this atlas, this interplay has resulted in a marked cooling of the commitment to the development of nuclear power; to such an extent, indeed, that current plans for nuclear power production by the year 2000 are still well short of earlier projections for the year 1985.

The issue of safety has become increasingly acknowledged. The US Nuclear Regulatory Commission released its own study of the subject in 1982. Having considered 19,400 accidents in nuclear power plants between 1969 and 1979, it selected 169 for detailed review. It found 52 of these to have been significant; that is, potentially contributing to a melt-down of the nuclear core in the plant. The study concluded that the likelihood of a major accident was around one in every ten or twenty years. Following the Three Mile Island accident in March 1979, changes made in nuclear reactor operating procedures are claimed to have reduced the chances of serious accident but not, it should be stressed, to have eliminated them.

The possibility of accidents is far from being the only source of public concern. In Britain, for example, there is spreading disquiet at evidence that the operations of nuclear power plants might be responsible for abnormally high rates of cancer in nearby populations. The disposal of nuclear waste, active for thousands of years, has stirred considerable controversy over the use of the high seas, let alone mines and quarries in and near inhabited areas, as burial grounds.

The cartogram here provides background information, showing shares of world electricity production; while colour is used to indicate shares of installed nuclear capacity.

In general the biggest producers of electricity are also the biggest investors in nuclear power. But the present degree of correlation may not persist. While the drive to develop nuclear power has significantly slowed down in the West, it proceeds heedlessly apace in the USSR and elsewhere.

17. Financial Power

The International Monetary Fund (IMF), with its headquarters in Washington DC, is indisputably the world's largest and arguably its most important interstate financial organization. The Bank for International Settlements, with headquarters at Basle in Switzerland, is a closed club of certain central banks from rich Western countries and plays a more reticent – if certainly influential – role in interstate financial decisions, including whether or not and in what measure to provide support for states in economic difficulties. But the IMF remains the paramount immediate source of loans and lines of credit, as well as being the only interstate financial authority that issues what may be termed supranational money in its Special Drawing Rights (or SDRs; each valued, in April 1983, at US $1.075). Moreover, though a few states, notably Switzerland and the USSR, are not members, the extent of its importance may be gauged from the membership of both Hungary and Romania, two close economic associates of the USSR, and from the application of Poland, another such associate, to join.

The IMF acquires much the most of its resources from the subscriptions of its members. These subscriptions are equivalent to what are termed 'quotas'. And the size of a member's quota determines that member's voting power, the extent of its potential access to fund resources, and its share in allocations of SDRs.

In March 1983, the IMF's Board of Governors decided to increase the total value of quotas by 47.5 per cent, from SDR 61,060 million to SDR 90,035 million. In the process, the relative shares of member states were readjusted, so as to reflect, if still only in part, changes in relative economic strength.

Two particular features of the readjustment should be noted. The share of the USA (down from 20.64% to 19.902%) still leaves it with a blocking vote, since a minimum of 85% is required for all essential decisions. And largely for historical reasons – a proportion of any quota increase is related to existing shares – the United Kingdom and some other 'old' members emerged from the readjustment with quotas and so voting power still disproportionate to their relative economic strength. Thus the UK, with 6.88%, will continue to have more weight than West Germany, with 6.002%, and Japan, with 4.691%. Canada, with 3.267%, emerges as holding almost 70% the voting power of Japan.

The decision of the IMF's Board of Governors required ratification from member governments, and this did not have an easy ride. Crucially, the US Congress contained a considerable body of opposition, much of it suspicious of a measure that seemed directed in the main at rescuing the world's big commercial banks from the consequences of imprudent lending to states now unable to repay their debts. After months of pressure from the US Administration and dire warnings of a world-wide collapse of credit if the IMF were denied augmented resources, Congress ratified the changes; and such other governments as had waited for this decision soon followed suit.

Not all the hostility shown to the IMF was due to an alleged subservience to the interests of the banks. There has been increasing criticism, not least in poor countries, of the Fund's loan criteria, which have more to do with policies of economic restraint than with considerations of social development. But then the IMF represents the prevailing financial order and is, naturally, more preoccupied by the need to sustain that order than to undermine it.

18. Trade Power

The dominance of world trade by the member countries of the European Economic Community (EEC) is in part due to their considerable trade with one another. And it is arguable that such trade is more internal than international. But the EEC is still no more than a qualified economic association, and it is accordingly reasonable to accept the conventional classification of its internal trade as international, or different in kind from the trade, for instance, among the constituent states of the USA.

Certainly, there is a remarkable disproportion between the importance of these individual EEC countries as trade and as economic powers. But then such a remarkable disproportion is far from uncommon. The USA, with around a quarter of the world's aggregate of gross national products, accounts for less than 14 per cent of world trade. Even more striking, the USSR has a share of world trade that is about the same as Switzerland's, with a gross national product that is around ten times as large.

Yet this does not deny the meaning or relevance of trade power, which is a measure of the relative part played by a state in the world economy and which derives from such factors as industrial specialization and sophistication, the command of particular commodities, and the development of competitively priced products.

As the map demonstrates, there have been substantial changes in the relative shares of world trade enjoyed by particular countries. Many individual increases may be ascribed to the enormous rise in the price of oil over the period. Some others have been due to the rapid development of such so-called new industrial states as Singapore, South Korea and Taiwan. Corresponding declines have been due to steep falls in certain commodity prices, for countries such as Zambia; or, as in the case of Kampuchea and Uganda, to protracted civil disorder and war.

The inset map on export income per head of population is included for the staggering contrasts it reveals. It is necessary, however, to point out that countries with tiny populations but thriving tourist and financial sectors may have an export revenue per head that is out of all proportion to their relative trading power.

19. Dependence and Diversity

This map demonstrates how many states are dependent, for the bulk of their export income, on the sale of either one product or a very few products. The extreme case is Libya, where the total export income comes from oil.

The economic weakness of a state dependent upon a single major export is evident: especially when the state is poor, in competition with other poor states and even with rich ones, and when the product is an agricultural commodity. Not only is there the persistent threat of bad or too bountiful harvests, there is also the danger that access to major traditional markets may, for one reason or another, be denied. In particular, when major customers are also themselves producers – as with sugar, for instance – they may proceed to protect their own production at the expense of traditional suppliers.

Some poor countries seem to have a stronger, more diversified economic base than really exists, since their principal export takes more than one form. Bangladesh provides a striking example: 25% of its export income comes from 'raw jute'; another 25% comes from 'textile products' that are made mainly from jute; and a further 33% comes from 'woven non-cotton textiles' which are also made mainly from jute. A rare example among rich states is New Zealand, fully two thirds of whose exports are animal products.

Finally, it must be stressed that oil constitutes an important export even where it does not account for the bulk of export income. In three countries – Tunisia (49.7%), Cameroon (30.6%) and the USSR (22%) – it is the largest single export. In six others – Norway (31%), Panama (23%), Peru (17%), Senegal (19%), Sri Lanka (15%) and Togo (26%) – it is clearly a substantial one.

20. Science Power

We have used an unusual measure to depict science power; one which is based on the number and citations of articles published in science journals, classified by the country in which the author lives (or the first author, when there is more than one). It is far from satisfactory, for it seriously understates the concentration of science power. We have chosen this measure because the relevant information is by far the best that is generally available.

Only some 35 per cent of the articles by Third World authors are published in Third World journals. The great majority are published in the West, particularly in the USA and Britain. Indeed, the USA ranks as the largest single publisher of Third World science articles. India is second and Britain is third.

This map is a telling example of the phenomenon highlighted in *Map 27: Languages of Rule*. About 88% of all science articles published are in English, as are no less than 92% of all science articles in the Third World.

Not all science journals are equal. One fifth of all science articles in the world are published in 60 journals, which constitute a mere 0.12% of the total; while 400 journals, still a mere 0.8% of the total, account for half of all such articles.

Added to this, the impact of articles published in the West is far greater than that of articles published elsewhere. In the mid-1970s, science articles published in the Netherlands were cited on average 3.9 times; in the USA, 3.6 times; in Britain, 3.3; Denmark, 2.8; Switzerland, 2.7; West Germany, 2.3: in contrast with 1.2 for articles published in Costa Rica; 1.1 in India; 0.2 in Brazil and 0.1 in Venezuela.

India is an anomaly in the science world. It is a considerable science power; accounting for half of all science articles published in poor countries and for 60 per cent of all poor country science publishing. Its scientific research reaches beyond the clinical and biomedical fields on which science in the poor countries concentrates, to biochemistry, physics, chemistry, and – especially – chemical physics. Yet its impact is relatively small.

21. National Income

The information available on gross national products must be treated with a great deal of caution. The value of subsistence production is inadequately measured. The value of unpaid domestic labour is wholly ignored. Variously thriving so-called black economies, where goods and especially services are sold or exchanged privately in order to escape taxes, are excluded.

The measure of value is the US dollar, and movements in exchange rates for the dollar have a corresponding impact on the figures for other countries. In an era of exceptional monetary excitement, amounting at times to hysteria, such movements can have a grotesque effect. It is manifestly absurd that a country's income should be considered to have shrunk by one per cent in a few days or even hours because its currency has, under the influence of rising interest rates in the USA, fallen by that proportion against the dollar.

Not least, the methods by which the gross national product is calculated differ so markedly in certain states from those commonly employed that comparison of any real precision becomes impossible. The World Bank, which constitutes the main source of such statistics, did not supply relevant information on 17 countries in its latest (1983) *Atlas*. For a few of these, such as Iran, Iraq, Kampuchea and Lebanon, war and social upheaval made the collection of adequate statistics for the given year impossible. For other countries, generally those with centralized economies, the World Bank declared that it would cease to publish estimates, 'until a broadly acceptable methodology is developed'.

Our own map on national income is concerned with such broad bands of comparison as to permit, in our view, a productive use of all available information this side of fantasy. For Angola, Mozambique, Afghanistan, Iraq and Mongolia, we have used the 1979 statistics published in the World Bank's *Atlas 1980*. For the centralized economies of the USSR and Eastern Europe (excluding Yugoslavia), we have used the estimates of the CIA. The Agency has its own in-built bias, which is scarcely a secret; but its calculations have some basis.

In a few cases, we have been unable to find acceptable information. The map bears no data for Iran, Kampuchea, Lebanon, Western Samoa and Vietnam.

22. The First Slice of the Cake

All governments take slices of national income for themselves. Some take larger slices than others do. This map depicts broad bands of difference in government appetite, along with relative shares of states in the aggregate government income of the world. Further comparisons are evident from viewing this map alongside *Map 21: National Income*. There are some remarkable discrepancies. Italy, with a gross national product (GNP) some 19 times the size of Israel's, has a government income that is actually smaller. The USA, with a GNP more than two and a half times that of the USSR, has a government income of around four fifths the size.

As so often, there are reservations to be recorded. The most recent year for which figures are available is not the same for every state. And the conversion of national currencies into the US dollar, as the common measure of value, gives rise to such distortions as have been mentioned in previous notes. Relative shares of aggregate government income in the world are accordingly very approximate; especially since some states have been excluded because no relevant information is available.

Figures for Eastern European countries were derived from: the CIA, for estimates of GNP (on the basis of standard Western national income accounting concepts); national statistical yearbooks or their equivalents; and the conversion of currencies at 'effective' exchange rates for the period, as provided by Pick's *Currency Yearbook*.

23. Complexions of Government

The authors do not pretend to be providing a definitive differentiation of governments throughout the world. We offer only a rough guide to various broad categories of distinction.

It may be argued that all parliamentary regimes are more or less restricted. The designation 'restricted parliamentary' is here applied to the considerable variety of governments whose parliamentary institutions are patently qualified by controls or limitations of one sort or another. In Bangladesh, for instance, the military do not rule directly but in practice choose which candidates for office should be selected or excluded. In Singapore, there is a parliamentary opposition, but one circumscribed by difficulties and tolerated only for as long as it has only a token presence. In South Africa, conventional parliamentary government is effectively restricted to the minority white population.

The designation 'despotic' is applied to a government where a single personal authority is in such overriding control that any other institutionalized form of power, whether restricted parliamentary, one-party bureaucratic or military, is essentially a mere instrument of the despotism. It is on this basis that we have designated Paraguay and Libya as having despotic rather than military regimes, and Albania, North Korea and Romania as despotic rather than being one-party states. Some despotisms are, of course, a great deal worse than others. The despotism in Guinea, for instance, is much more oppressive than the despotism in Kuwait. Such distinctions are not the subject of the map.

For some countries, Afghanistan, Chad, El Salvador, Equatorial Guinea, Lebanon and Uganda, we have been forced to find a special category, for a society so riven by conflict and a formal sovereign authority so widely challenged that it is a distortion to apply any of the other designations employed.

For those who question the implicit judgements of our categories, we offer the words of Rosa Luxemburg, writing in some alarm at the course of the revolutionary government in Russia:

'Freedom for supporters of the government only, for the members of one party only – no matter how big its membership may be – is no freedom at all. Freedom is always freedom for the person who thinks differently. This contention does not spring from a fanatical love of abstract "justice", but from the fact that everything which is enlightening, healthy and purifying in political freedom derives from its independent character, and from the fact that freedom loses all its virtues when it becomes a privilege ... Without general elections, freedom of the press, freedom of assembly, and freedom of speech, life in every public institution slows down, becomes a caricature of itself, and bureaucracy rises as the only deciding factor.' *The Russian Revolution*

24. Harmworkers and Healthworkers

The morally repulsive priorities of the state can be illustrated in many ways; but perhaps nowhere more eloquently than in the comparison between expenditure on preparations to promote injury or death and expenditure to heal and sustain life. Most states spend more on their armed forces than on their medical services. The states that deploy fewer military than medical personnel are outnumbered more than eight to one by those that prefer the bullet to the bandage.

Military expenditure is virtually everywhere and always a monopoly of the state. Medical expenditure is, in many countries and often, also part of the private sector. Comparing public outlays on the two pursuits is accordingly less an exercise in the measurement of relative expenditure than a pointer to where the state's own priorities lie.

The same holds true for the deployment of personnel. There are usually more doctors, dentists and nurses at work in a society than are employed in its public sector. Moreover, there are peculiarities in the published statistics that tend to understate the number of public service personnel in some countries. Thailand and the Philippines, for example, report the numbers of doctors but not those of dentists. Some military establishments are also understated by the exclusion of paramilitary forces; though the exclusions constitute a far smaller proportion of the total in the military than in the medical category.

Overall, however, and with all reservations duly cited, the contrasts evident from the figures are generally valid.

25. Scourges of the State

Torture in some form, applied by agents of the state to those regarded as its enemies, is widely used as an instrument of policy. But in general, wherever it is used, its use is denied, and not only by the authorities directly responsible for it. Many other people, from sheer incredulity or misguided patriotism, will leap to the defence of their own state against such charges.

It is, accordingly, not surprising that the version of this map that appeared in the first edition of this atlas attracted criticism and hostile comment: sometimes official; sometimes public, sometimes private.

As a result we have refined our categories for this edition. We distinguish between states in which torture has been both widely used and officially condoned, such as Chile and Argentina, and states where though officially condoned, it has not been widely used, such as the United Kingdom and West Germany. It is also important to point out the bias in the accumulation of evidence against the rich Western states, where allegations of torture are both more likely to be made and easier to verify than elsewhere.

But our essential position remains unaltered. Amnesty International, the major source for the map on both occasions, propounds a fundamental principle to which we subscribe: 'that if one prisoner of conscience is held, if one single detainee faces torture or execution, this is a violation of human rights that must be confronted.'

Some states, notably the USSR and Romania, use psychiatric hospitals as political prisons, and psychotropic drugs as instruments for the ill-treatment of prisoners.

Self-defence takes precedence over any other value professed by the state, as is demonstrated by the results of a survey submitted to the UN Congress on the Prevention of Crime and Treatment of Offenders in 1980. Out of the 125 states for which information was available, 'in 99 ... homicide is subject to capital punishment, but offences against the state are punishable by death even more frequently – in 113 countries.'

26. A Sort of Survival

Our world is an increasingly violent one. There are more refugees in the 1970s than there were in the 1960s, and likely to be more again in the present decade. Some eventually return to their countries, if not their homes; others settle, with more or less difficulty, as citizens or tolerated aliens, in the societies of other countries; many remain for years in special camps or villages, often in appalling conditions, with their lives in a seemingly endless state of suspense.

The very definition of a refugee is the subject of much dispute. The United Nations High Commission for Refugees, the principal interstate agency for refugee relief, deals essentially with those who have fled across state borders. But multitudes of people are displaced, by war or persecution or the fear of either, from one part of their country to another. Furthermore, individual governments, reluctant to provide sanctuary but concerned to protect their humanitarian pretensions, are sometimes peculiarly, sometimes capriciously, exacting in their own definitions of what constitutes a refugee. The US authorities, for instance, have tended to consider Haitians, fleeing an oppressive government and conditions of intolerable poverty, 'economic refugees' and have accorded them a correspondingly cold reception. They have generally been far more liberal in accepting for settlement similarly motivated refugees from Vietnam.

There is much dispute as well over numbers. Some host governments, with an eye to financial assistance from the UN High Commission and other relief agencies, are tempted to exaggerate the numbers in their care. On the other hand, there are many refugees who slip across state borders and, uncertain of their reception, assiduously seek to escape official scrutiny.

In short, it is extremely difficult to determine the numbers of refugees according to the broadly compassionate criteria that we wish to apply. We have included as refugees those displaced within their own state boundaries. We have not attempted to sort out the so-called 'economic' from the so-called 'political' refugees, so as to exclude the former. But we have excluded those who may reasonably be considered migrant workers, themselves the subject of *Map 32: In Search of Work*.

27. Languages of Rule

In 1492 Don Elio Antonio de Nebrija dedicated his Castilian grammar – the first grammar produced for a modern European language – to Queen Isabella la Catolica. His declared object was to 'turn the Castilian language from a loose possession of the people into an artifact so that whatever shall henceforth be said or written in this language shall be of standard coinage, of a coinage that can outlast the times.' For Nebrija, this structured language 'has forever been the mate of empire and always shall remain its comrade.'

The future course of Castilian, or Spanish, as of other imperial languages, was to prove him right. And if the great European empires came in time to disintegrate, the imperial languages generally remained, as instruments of rule.

We define a language of rule as one which is used by a political and/or economic elite to sustain its cohesion and control. It effectively excludes from any real participation in power those who do not speak or read it. It promotes, most notably in Africa, a closer association among the elites of individual states than between such elites and the populace of their own societies. The contemporary record shows how widespread such languages of rule still are. The map shows too, the sites of significant linguistic conflict, or those states where the issue of language has manifested itself in serious protest, usually involving some resort to violence. In many – perhaps all – instances, of course, such conflict is essentially an expression of a deeper and often wider social conflict.

In certain states, mainly of the Caribbean, a local or so-called Creole version of the imperial language is widely used. We have identified such cases where we have been advised that it is necessary to do so.

The map is a contemporary rather than historical record. Portuguese, for instance, was brought by conquest to what is now known as Brazil. It then so far displaced the indigenous languages as to constitute no longer a language of rule.

28. Religions of Rule

The belief in future fulfilment, peace and happiness; the representation of that belief in ritual; its justification through reference to some holy writ, interpreted by a special category of people; and its involvement with state-associated or -supported institutions: such are the hallmarks of many religions. In this sense, official Marxism-Leninism is such a religion: with its concentration on the benefits of the future through present sacrifice; its ritual parades and ceremonies; its revealed truths, whose texts are to be interpreted acceptably only by those appointed to do so; and its association with the power of the state. Furthermore, like some other religions, it has its own schismatic orthodoxies: mainly the Moscow denomination, but with local variants, primarily the Chinese; and it has its popular low church heterodoxy (Titoism in Yugoslavia), anathematized heresy (Trotskyism), and fundamentalist sects (revolutionary Marxism).

We define a religion of rule as one which is professed by those in power and which sustains their solidarity. Poland provides a celebrated example, with official Marxism-Leninism, of the Moscow denomination, ruling over a population almost entirely Catholic in allegiance. Britain provides another, much more muted, manifestation. There the majority of the population is either secular in persuasion or holds a variety of 'unestablished' religious beliefs. But the Church of England is the 'established' Church or state religion, with the monarch at its head and with its bishops or 'lords spiritual' members of the upper house in parliament.

In dealing with Christianity, we have distinguished between Catholicism and Protestantism only where one of these is clearly dominant, and no distinction is made between different versions of Protestantism. For Islam, the only distinction drawn is between Sunni and Shi'ite.

Sites of current or recent religious conflict are shown on the map only where violence, due wholly or in considerable part to religious differences, has been involved. The incidence of such conflict has markedly increased since the first edition of this atlas. This has partly been due to an upsurge in militant Islamic fundamentalism and to the particular intervention or influence of the Shi'ite regime in Iran. But the resurgent, increasingly violent Sikh separatist movement in India and violent clashes between Tamil and Singhalese in Sri Lanka suggest that the increase is far from being an Islamic phenomenon.

29. Big Money

The size of a commercial bank is conventionally measured by its assets, although these are not, as may be mistakenly supposed, mainly such property, direct investments and cash that it holds, but, overwhelmingly, the loans it has given. By this measure, the world's 500 biggest commercial banks are very big indeed.

The sums involved are all the more extraordinary because these are not central banks, the state institutions that are in general custodians of national reserves and issuers of the national currency. And only a few commercial banks, notably the major French ones, are owned by the state. The vast majority of the world's biggest 500 banks are so-called public companies, owned by individual shareholders.

It is scarcely strange that the world's leading economic power, the USA, should possess, by a considerable margin, more of the world's top 500 banks than any other country. What may be surprising is that Japan, with little more than half the USA's number, should have a larger share of aggregate assets. But in general, Japan's big banks are bigger than those of the USA. Of the world's top 50 commercial banks, for instance, 15 are Japanese and only 7 are American.

It is this ratio (each country's share of total assets, compared to its share of the total number of the top 500 banks) that is demonstrated by the use of colour in the cartogram. Yet the extent of the disproportion is even greater than the method allows. Hong Kong is perhaps the extreme case, explained by the possession of a single very big bank, the Hong Kong and Shanghai Banking Corporation, ranked 24th in the world. Among less eccentric instances, Canada's banks have a share of assets exactly double, and the Netherlands' banks almost double, their shares of the number of banks. This is why many of the countries with banks among the top 500 emerge with relatively low asset shares.

The national reserves, on which the comparisons in the inset map are based, include gold holdings valued at the prevailing free market price. They would, for many countries, be much smaller, if some artificial fixed price for gold, such as that employed by the United States authorities, were used instead. The comparison between national reserves and commercial banks assets is, to be sure, not a conventional one. But it is serviceable as a guide to the enormous financial power possessed and wielded by what are, in the overwhelming main, essentially private institutions.

30. Big Business

The world's largest industrial companies are conventionally ranked by annual sales income. This income is, for such purposes of comparison, measured in US dollars, and exchange rate movements accordingly have a commensurate impact on both the ranking and the number of US or other companies in any composite list. 1982, the latest year for which information is available, was one in which the US dollar rose in value against almost all other currencies; in many cases, quite substantially. This propelled a number of US corporations into, and a number of companies from other countries out of, a composite list of the top 500, as well as affecting particular rankings. But this factor, however material, affected the extent rather than the fact of a US dominance in big business that is distinctly disproportionate to the relative size of the US economy.

Less than a handful of companies – though amongst them, the two giants, Royal Dutch/Shell and Unilever – belong not to one state but to two. In such cases, each of the two states concerned is credited with half the company, along with half the associated sales income. This accounts for the curious figure of 9.5 companies credited to both Italy and Switzerland, which share Pirelli but have no other company in common.

A state's numerical representation among the top 500 companies may be much smaller than is its proportion of total sales income if the companies are relatively large ones. Among the advanced industrial states, the Netherlands, for instance, has only 1.2% of the total number of companies, but a sales income share of 2.87%. The USA itself has only 42.2% of the companies but 47.8% of total sales.

The colour used in the cartogram demonstrates this disproportion. We have calculated the share of sales as a percentage of the share of the total number of companies, and presented the result in relation to the average. Venezuela's extreme standing here, with a share of sales no less than two and three quarters its share of the total number of companies, is due to the possession of a single company (Petróleos de Venezuela), large enough to rank as 11th in the top 500.

The gross national product figures used for the comparisons in the inset map are generally those given in the World Bank *Atlas 1983*. Figures for a number of centralized economies are not given by the World Bank, and we have used here – in the absence of any more reliable measure – estimates published by the CIA.

31. Webs and Flows

Up-to-date, serviceable information on the spread and operations of the world's major transnational companies is deplorably elusive. The most systematic and significant study so far was prepared by the UN Centre on Transnational Corporations, published in 1983. It is a study that deals with 382 such transnationals among the thousands that exist. And despite the large resources available to the centre, much of the information provided is incomplete.

The distribution of subsidiaries applies to the year 1980, as does the distribution of domiciles. The outflow of payments applies to 1979.

The proportions of gross national product represented by payments on foreign direct investment may seem so small as to be meaningless in many instances. They are not. For a poor country in need of capital to develop its economy, the export of any hard currency at all represents a serious loss. For one, such as Honduras, to be exporting more than $2 out of every $100 generated by all economic activity in a year – let alone a Botswana which exports more than $11 of every $100 – is a recipe for increasing dependence and deprivation.

Furthermore, such payments are concerned only with 'foreign direct investment'. They exclude the enormous drain in interest charges and capital repayments for foreign commercial bank and government loans. They take no account of the incalculable economic loss caused by the recruitment for export of trained people, an activity in which the transnationals are greatly involved.

The United Nations study of transnationals indicates the degree to which the once virtual monopoly of such enterprise by the advanced industrial states of the West has been eroded. Japanese representation among the 382 transnationals examined is exactly twice the French and not far from twice the West German. South Korean representation is exactly the same as the Belgian and some four fifths that of the Netherlands. The operations of these Eastern transnationals are not, of course, limited to the poor countries of the so-called Third World. Their subsidiaries are planted in the heartlands of the system, Western Europe and North America.

The immense economic power wielded internationally by a relatively few companies must be considered alongside their general hierarchical structure. In effect, a few thousand executives, nearly all of them men, are responsible for decisions that have a considerable impact on the lives of countless millions.

32. In Search of Work

Labour is essentially a commodity, bought and sold, in the international marketplace. It is true that many states take measures to impede the trade in labour. But then, similarly, they take measures to impede the trade in other commodities. What distinguishes labour is that it is not inanimate. People can move to jobs across state frontiers, regardless of measures to prevent them; and if some are discovered and expelled, others successfully evade the interventions of authority or are discovered but nonetheless allowed to remain because their labour is more useful than the law. Contributory crucial factors in the flow are the increasing lack of employment opportunities for much of the population in most countries, together with the availability of low paid or disagreeable jobs in others.

Figures for labour migrations are notoriously difficult to determine. The line between migrant labourers and refugees from oppression is frequently blurred. Estimates for that large component of migrant labour which is illegal can be no more than educated guesses.

We have drawn on such information and informed opinion as we encountered. The numbers given on the map apply to the workers themselves and not to the family members that accompany or follow them.

The term 'major', for exporting and importing states alike, is used only where at least 1 per cent of the country's work force and at least 100,000 workers are involved. Some countries designated as exporters are also considerable importers. Italy, for instance, is estimated to have around 500,000 foreign workers, legal and illegal: from Algeria, Egypt, Ethiopia, Libya, Portugal, Somalia, Spain, Tunisia, Turkey, Yugoslavia and other countries. In all cases, the designation of importer or exporter applies to the net flow.

The dynamic of migrant labour is most tellingly illustrated by the attraction of the USA for multitudes of Mexicans. The estimated real wage differential between the USA and Mexico averages around 7 to 1 for unskilled labour, and around 13 to 1 for such labour in agriculture. Above all, there are jobs in the USA and many people without the prospect of a job in Mexico. The huge flow of illegal migrants across the border is easy enough to explain. The official list of Mexican nationals applying for US visas to migrate legally contains about one million names, and it takes an average of seven years for someone on the list to obtain a visa.

Despite the effects of economic recession since the late seventies, and despite the related domestic antagonism to immigrant communities that is encouraged and exploited by reactionaries of almost every political persuasion, few importing countries have reduced the foreign component in their work forces. In Western Europe, Austria, West Germany and Switzerland have engineered some decline; but the foreign component has remained stable in Belgium and France, and increased in the Netherlands and Sweden. World-wide, the evidence suggests that labour migration is a growing phenomenon.

Indeed, economic difficulties are apparently promoting official involvement in the flow. Some Asian governments, for instance – notably those of India, Pakistan, the Philippines and South Korea – encourage and even assist in organizing the migration abroad of their citizens, to reduce the pressures of unemployment at home and increase foreign earnings through remittances from their migrants. In the Philippines, these remittances provide an estimated $1 billion a year, or the biggest single source of foreign exchange.

Conditions for many such recruited workers are extremely harsh. In most Middle Eastern countries, the workers are housed in special camps and forbidden to belong to a trade union or to strike. In theory, controls exist; with model contracts that set out minimum standards of decent treatment. In practice, according to the ILO, the system is 'rife with abuses'.

'Hopeful migrants arrive to find the promised jobs never existed, or that they have been smuggled in on visitors' visas. Some non-licensed agents even use forged documents. Passports are whipped out of the workers' hands on arrival, their contracts are changed, and the fear of being "discovered" and sent home terrorizes them into working impossible hours in conditions near to slave labour.' *Sunday Times*, London, 19 June 1983.

33. Exploitation

Ideally a measure of exploitation would compare the output of all productive workers – those workers whose labour provides essential ingredients for further production – with their disposable income. Such a measure does not exist and cannot be created from the information available. Productive and unproductive workers are not differentiated, analytically or statistically. Inessential is not differentiated from essential output. Statistics do not cover all relevant activity; are not everywhere reliable or even pertinent; and vary in scope from state to state.

We cannot accordingly use the formula we would have wished: value added in productive activity divided by wages in cash and kind for productive activity. We have had to settle instead for: value added in manufacturing (the value of output less the value of bought-in goods and services) divided by the wages and salaries of the people directly engaged in its production.

The data present certain problems. Some states report estimates for value added, some do not: and comparable estimates have had to be derived by using a different coefficient for rich (OECD) countries, middle-income (Comecon) countries and poor countries, from figures for gross output in manufacturing. Similarly, some states report estimates for operatives' pay; some do not, and the figures have had to be derived from those for employees' emoluments. Sometimes statistics for manufacturing cover only a particular range of industries; sometimes they are stretched to include the output of utilities and services. In most cases, a five year average (1976–80) has been used; sometimes a four or three year average; sometimes three or four non-consecutive years have been used to establish an average; and sometimes whatever year or years were available.

The results reflect the inadequacy of the data. In particular, the association of high exploitation rates with poor states is valid only because productivity in manufacturing is partly insulated from, and does not fully reflect, the general level of productivity there.

The range, given on the key to the map – from Rwanda, where the rate of exploitation is seemingly the highest recorded, to the USSR, where it is seemingly the lowest – should alert readers to the complexities of the issue and the difficulties of interpretation. The two states ought not to be seen as exemplars of hell or heaven for workers. In the first case, manufacturing scarcely exists, and the result is due to a statistical quirk. In the second, it results from institutional structures and official dispositions which make the wastage of human resources a most attractive option in many cases.

34. The Labour Force

The economically active population is conventionally defined as that sector which receives wages or salaries in cash or kind. It accordingly excludes most women in most states; and, by definition, those in the unrecorded 'black economy'. It includes, if somewhat erratically, the unemployed, or at least those regarded as such, on the basis that they are no more than temporarily inactive. It is this economically active labour force from which we calculate the ratio between those engaged in agriculture and in industry.

Except in a few instances, figures for industrial employment include workers in transport and mining but not those in construction. Most figures are for 1979, 1980, 1981 or 1982. Some are, unfortunately, available only for earlier years. In all cases, we have used the latest year for which figures are available.

In some poor states, a surprisingly small proportion of the population seems to be employed in agriculture, together with an unsurprisingly small proportion working in industry. This is because in such states, much of what is termed the 'economically active population' is actually unemployed or is engaged on the fringes of the economy in a multitude of elusive 'service' capacities.

A high ratio of industrial to agricultural workers is not always a corresponding index of industrial advancement and power. Britain, as the map demonstrates, has a higher ratio than Japan. Japanese industry is in general more advanced and efficient than British industry; while British agriculture is more mechanized and large-scale in its operations than is Japanese.

35. Women Workers

Women workers are peculiarly invisible to official enumerators, whose scrutiny ignores the world of domestic labour. When noted at all, even women agricultural workers in poor countries or women working at home in the production of marketable goods are likely to be described as 'not economically active' or 'unpaid family workers'. Only when active in the male-defined world of paid jobs do women have a chance of being recognized statistically.

Our map is, of course, as much a geography of ideology as of women's work. And this explains some of the wide regional differences in the ratio of women to men workers: the generally low ratio in Islamic countries; the generally high one in Eastern Europe, where far more women have jobs outside the home.

We have introduced in this edition of the atlas a small study of child labour: small not because the subject is so, in incidence or importance, but because there is so little statistical information. We include it here, in what seemed to us the most suitable conjunction, since like so many unpaid working mothers, some four fifths of recorded working children are unpaid family workers. The data available have forced us to acccept the conventional narrow definition of child labour, which excludes the millions of regular workers below the age of 10.

36. The Force of Labour

Modern trade unions were generally formed to secure independent sources of social power. A few trade unions in a few states are still essentially dedicated to that purpose (with yet fewer dedicated to an internationalist perspective). Many are committed to it formally, but in practice are concerned with making the best available material deal for their immediate members. And many, perhaps most, have no commitment at all, beyond serving their requirement to function as creatures of the state or its governing party.

The map deals, of necessity, with existing, recognized trade union bodies. It can neither capture nor communicate the authentic libertarian spirit of trade unionism: the spirit that breaks out of these bodies or bypasses them, as in Brazil during the summer of 1983; or that sometimes heaves into existence a whole new trade union landscape, as with Solidarity in Poland.

The categories and definitions were determined on the advice of leading international trade union officials. Trade unions that are totally controlled, as in the USSR, Eastern Europe, and parts of Africa and Asia, are essentially organs of government, with no independence of decision. Trade unions that are tightly controlled have independence of decision in form, but are in fact permitted such independence only when it involves no conflict with major government policies. There is, very occasionally, a twilight zone where this category merges into that of indepedent unions free of government control. Given the unstable relations between state power and union independence in Kenya and Ghana, we have placed the trade union movement of these countries in both categories.

37. Unemployment

We are, in this edition of the atlas, including a map on unemployment. We have used the latest official figures or estimates wherever they appear to bear, with all their faults, some relation to reality; and where figures were not available or were manifestly absurd, we have used estimates contained in more or less independent reports from political correspondents and other commentators. We are still convinced that the results beg as many questions as they answer and mask as much as they reveal.

Unemployment is essentially a product and feature of industrial and urbanized society. It should reflect the proportion of those who are capable of economic activity but who are, for one reason or another, excluded from it. In such societies, where there are relatively refined procedures of research and analysis, it might be supposed that official figures for unemployment would be reliable. It is not a supposition that bears serious scrutiny. Apart from political engineering through special training schemes or even military service to deflate the figures, Western authorities define unemployment in various ways which all tend to understate the real extent of the problem. In a number of countries, those people who have searched for work, failed to find it and as a result stop trying, are no longer included in the figures. In all such countries, the figures take no account of many adults, generally women, who would prefer to be employed for a wage or salary but who never are; sometimes because they accept a role which excludes such activity, sometimes because they simply despair of finding acceptable employment.

In the centralized economies of the USSR and Eastern Europe, the distortion is a different one. The political dedication to full employment is reflected in the absence of any unemployment figures. The USSR, for instance, concedes only the existence of 'free hands'. Work is provided without corresponding production, in a form that crowds factory floors.

In other, less 'developed' countries, conventionally defined unemployment is a phenomenon of the urban sector. But the urban sector contains a minority of the total population. In Brazil, for instance, there is – or at least was, at the last available estimate – an unemployment rate of just under 10 per cent for six urban centres. But it has been estimated that there is in the countryside a rate of what is described as 'underemployment' upwards of 25 per cent.

Underemployment itself is a complex and disputed concept. There is no serviceable purpose in making it mean merely the measure of some timing device, so that only people who work for less than an arbitrarily defined number of hours must be considered underemployed. It should reflect the extent of the shortfall between the labour required to produce a decent standard of living and the actual payment given for labour of all kinds. By this definition, which provides a virtual poverty index, studies by the International Labour Organization suggest a rate of underemployment in the so-called developing world of from just under 32% to 42%, and an underemployed population of almost 500 millions (all estimates excluding China).

	Underemployed, 1982 *millions*	**Proportion of labour force, 1982**
Latin America (middle income)	22.6	32.3%
Latin America (low income)	11.2	31.8%
Middle East & Africa (oil)	17.2	35.0%
Asia (excluding China)	293.9	39.0%
Africa (arid)	27.0	42.0%
Africa (tropical)	76.2	38.0%
total	448.1	

Latin America and Caribbean middle-income countries comprise Argentina, Brazil, Chile, Colombia, Costa Rica, Cuba, Ecuador, Guatemala, Jamaica, Mexico, Panama, Paraguay, Trinidad and Tobago, Uruguay, Venezuela.
Latin America and Caribbean low-income countries comprise Bolivia, Dominican Republic, El Salvador, Haiti, Honduras, Nicaragua, Peru.
Source: Hopkins

38. Rich and Poor People

Measuring disparities in income between rich and poor members of the same society is an exercise usually limited to a few Western states. Measures or at least estimates of such disparities within other states are generally irregular and infrequent. A co-ordinated world-wide survey of such disparities is rare indeed. The figures we use are old ones. And they are old because no one with the requisite resources seems interested any longer in undertaking the exercise. We owe what we have to a brief period when the World Bank, under the direction of Robert McNamara, was concerned about investment in social infrastructure such as education and funded some research into this and related subjects of social development.

But wherever and whenever any measuring exercise is undertaken, the disparities that emerge are almost certainly less wide than they really are. For the rich have ways of obscuring their incomes. In the West, they use company-owned apartments and transport, company-subsidized medical care and company-subsidized education for their children, company-paid entertainment and leisure activities, to redefine personal income as business expenses. Furthermore, they (or their accountants) arrange their affairs so as to translate what is essentially earned income into capital gains – the acquisition of stock options is a common device – with the object of reducing their tax liabilities. In the East, they carve private domains out of public provisions: apartments, transport, medical care, education, entertainment, leisure. In the South, they surround themselves with a privacy that is normally impenetrable by officials, including statisticians. In all parts of the world, much of what is earned is simply not reported.

The disparity in income between rich and poor states is measured frequently. But the results are not to be regarded as reliable. Faulted by arbitrary definitions of income; by the exchange rate vagaries of the currency (the US dollar) that is used as the international measure of value; by the lack of rudimentary information for a number of important states, the results are indicative rather than conclusive.

All the same, it is alarming to consider the likelihood that half the world's population has to struggle over a mere 5% of the world's income, while 15% contend for 67% of such income.

In October 1983, *Forbes*, the US business magazine, reported that the 400 richest citizens of the USA had a combined wealth of $118 billion. Gordon Peter Getty, the richest of all, was estimated to have a net worth of at least $2.2 billion. The poorest on the list was worth a mere $125 million.

One member, a retailer, saw his family fortune *increase*, through the rise in the value of his holdings, by $1 billion over the year. This increase would be equivalent to the average annual income of 78,000 Americans; some 450,000 Brazilians; some 3,850,000 Indians; and some 9 million Chadians, or twice the actual population of that country.

39. Our Daily Bread

An adequate intake of calories is the most common and the most important measure of adequate nourishment. The minimum calorie intake regarded as adequate by the World Health Organization differs from state to state; taking into account climatic conditions, patterns of work, the average weight of inhabitants, and other relevant factors.

Figures for deficit countries inevitably understate the nutritional deficiency suffered by many inhabitants, as figures for surplus countries mask altogether the existence of any such deficiency. For the figures apply to average calorie intake, and average intake can obscure extremes of self-indulgence and deprivation. There are inhabitants of surplus states who do not have enough to eat, and inhabitants of deficit states who eat as abundantly as do the rich and powerful elsewhere.

The siting of famines in a number of African countries for 1983 is based on a statement from the Director of the Food and Agricultural Organization's Washington office on the effect of drought over much of the continent. Reports, he declared, made it clear that 'we are coming into something far worse than what we had in 1972–73', when between 200,000 and 300,000 people starved to death in the sub-Saharan region of West Africa (*International Herald Tribune*, 8 June 1983).

There are, we suspect, far more famines than those of which we have certain knowledge. China, during the years of the Great Leap Forward and the Cultural Revolution, Laos during and after the 'Vietnam' war, Guinea and others are strong candidates for inclusion by a less haphazard reporting system.

But if the vagaries of the weather contribute to visitations of famine, they are far from accounting for nutritional deficiencies over much of the world. As the graph on black Africa demonstrates, food production per head in that continent has fallen by more than a fifth since the early sixties. The pressures of population growth might have been reduced or even eliminated by appropriate social policies and economic development. Instead, there has been a rapid rate of urbanization, which has drained human and material resources from the countryside. The new urban elites have acquired a taste for foods, such as wheat and rice, which are not traditional crops and have had to be imported in increasing volume at increasing cost. Shortages of foreign exchange, resulting not only from the rising price of oil but from the cost of providing the elites with the foreign consumer goods they demand, have promoted government concentration on non-nutritional cash crops that can be sold abroad. And the decline of the countryside as a provider of food has been further promoted by policies to keep food cheap for the urban populace; with the result that farmers are deprived of adequate material incentives, and the drain of population from the countryside continues apace.

But the mounting plight of Africa is only an extreme example of preoccupations and policies so distorted and distorting across the world of states that many hundreds of millions are permanently undernourished, while certain governments are agitated by the problem of what to do with their accumulated surplus stocks of food. There seems little doubt that the world is perfectly capable of feeding decently all its inhabitants. That it is so conspicuously not doing so at present is the product not of human necessity but of choice.

40. Without Due Care and Attention

The incidence of hospital beds is generally related to the facilities provided for conventional Western medical treatment. It is not exclusively so. In China or Sri Lanka, for instance, a substantial hospital provision exists for medical treatment by traditional methods. But the common use of hospital bed provision as a measure of comparative commitment to medical care in different states essentially reflects the international dominance of conventional Western medicine. In employing this measure ourselves, we are directed by the course of available statistics. We do not imply any belittlement of the unconventional Western or traditional non-Western treatments that avoid hospitals. We simply have no means of determining any comparative social commitment to such treatment.

Figures for life expectancy are, in a number of instances. evidently vague estimates. The coincidence of identical figures – such as 44.4 years for males and 47.6 years for females in well over a handful of African states – must excite a certain doubt.

Equatorial Guinea provides a more than usually vivid case of statistical unreliability. With a reported life expectancy of 44.4 years for males and 47.6 years for females, it has no fewer than 1,111 hospital beds per 100,000 inhabitants, or a ratio well above that in Belgium, Denmark, the UK or USA. Either there is no credible connection between life expectancy and the provision of hospital beds or the statistic in one of the categories is even more suspect than the statistic in the other. Common sense would suggest that the figure for hospital beds owes less to reality than to public relations.

41. The Right To Learn

Most of the world is poorly furnished with facilities for formal education. And in general, the poorer the state, the smaller are the resources devoted to such facilities. Even then, much home produced training and talent is ultimately diverted to the rich states, in what is now known as the brain-drain (the migration abroad, or recruitment by foreign business, of those with the most valuable skills and exploitable experience). The educational system in poor states is often largely irrelevant to their own needs; being too closely modelled on imported curricula which reflect other demands and priorities. The consequences are socially wasteful and explosive.

Facilities for primary education are much the cheapest and easiest to develop; but pressure for places in primary schools and economic or other pressures outside them mean that not all who enter stay the course. For the multitudes who do, finding a place in the much smaller sector of secondary education can be very difficult. And to get into the tiny sector of further education, needs quite exceptional ability or influence. At every stage, many are forced to leave with their expectations frustrated.

Some states, it must be stressed, score badly because their educational reporting has not kept pace with their educational activity.

Our study implies that any formal education, however bad, is better than no education at all. It is not appropriate here to do more than record that this should be a question and to admit that we have necessarily begged it.

42. The Longer Reach

There are few ways in which the individual citizen can reach out to give and receive news, ideas and opinions, in exchanges which so many governments see as a source of mischief and even danger. In this edition of the atlas, we have chosen the incidence of letters and radios as our measure, while providing an inset map with updated statistics on access to telephones.

In many states, it is poverty that above all accounts for the low levels of access. In some others, notably the USSR, it is government policy rather than economic backwardness that seems to be largely responsible.

Access is, of course, no guarantee of free communication. Telephone calls can be tapped and interrupted. Letters can be opened and 'lost'. Radio receivers can provide only limited reception, and foreign broadcasts can be jammed. The very fear of discovery may inhibit the enjoyment of access. But surveillance is not infallible. Even in the most closely policed societies, human ingenuity can find ways to give and receive news, ideas and opinions, by telephone, radio and mail.

The statistics for the distribution of telephones are woefully incomplete. Many reporting authorities simply do not know how many telephones there are in their own countries.

In a few cases, the figures for mail exclude one or more of the three categories: 'small packets', 'postcards' and 'printed matter'. A few countries – Brazil, China, Czechoslovakia, Fiji, Liechtenstein – provide figures not for foreign letters received but only for those sent. The USSR is alone in treating domestic mail in the same way.

Some countries provide figures not for radio receivers but only for licences issued. In those few cases where the figures for both are given, the number of radio receivers is usually around double the number of licences. Where only the number of licences is available, we have accordingly doubled it to reach an estimate for the number of receivers.

43. Crumbs from the Cake

In the first edition of this atlas, we pointed out that assistance received from the state by those of its citizens officially recognized as being in need had, in the early 1970s, declined as a proportion of total state outlays in the whole of Africa, all of Asia except Japan, and all of South America apart from oil-rich Venezuela. Since then, the old principle – from those who do not have, it shall be taken – has gained impetus and excuse from world-wide economic recession.

This recession has dragged more people and larger proportions of the population into poverty traps of one sort or another, while governments, attempting to restrain public expenditure, have in general sought to reduce the real value of individual welfare payments. Nearly all the exceptions of the early 1970s have, in the early 1980s, joined the rule.

The cruel truth remains that, for many countries, welfare payments exist, if at all, for very few of the needy.

If few countries on the map carry information, it is because the best measure we have found – average welfare receipts as a proportion of average disposable income – is one for which few states provide figures. The fact that only one in four states responds to the International Labour Office's requests for information on such issues is a telling comment on the value accorded them by officialdom in general.

44. Law and Disorder

Interpol warns against the use of its crime statistics for purposes of comparison, even though these are the least incomplete generally available. The statistics are supplied by the countries themselves and accordingly represent what the various authorities in such countries are able to identify, competent to compile, or willing to admit.

The Interpol statistics, indeed, invite suspicion. It seems improbable that El Salvador should have virtually no incidence of fraud; unless the activities of government officials and members of the business community are generically excluded. It seems curious that Turkey, with a reputation for considerable violence, should report one of the lowest rates for murder and for serious assault.

The particular crimes of murder and serious assault present, of course, some difficulties of definition for the authorities in various states. It is unlikely, for instance, that the figures for the Lebanon, high as they are, fully reflect the incidence of deaths directly due to the protracted civil conflict in that country. It is absurd to believe that the moderate figures for Chile reflect the deaths and serious assaults directly due to those serving the security of the military regime.

Even among the advanced industrial states, whose statistics are widely regarded as less than usually unreliable, it is difficult to understand how France should have by far the highest rate of fraud (at some 750 cases per 100,000 inhabitants) and neighbouring Belgium, with a society so similar in so many respects, one of the lowest (at 10.5).

45. Fouling the Nest

The subject of pollution is an immensely complex one. And, moreover, authority has almost everywhere shown itself unwilling to recognize the importance of the problem. There are, accordingly, no surveys of land, water and air pollution world-wide in scope, and very few national ones. Nor, indeed, are there any agreed criteria for measurement. Ironically, a number of such criteria were suggested to us by officers of institutions much better equipped to make productive use of them. We have had, therefore, to rely on the scant material available, with all its manifold defects.

The criterion chosen for measuring land pollution – chemical fertilizers applied – is crude but serviceable enough. It does not, however, take into account those few areas of modern agriculture which conform to the best practices of humus renewal even while using chemical products.

The criteria for measuring air pollution are unsatisfactory on two counts: by substance (they do not cover lead, the most pervasive and among the most dangerous of pollutants); and by geography (they are confined to selected urban areas only). The World Health Organization very cautiously suggests, as guidelines for 'exposure limits consistent with the protection of human health', 40–60 micrograms per cubic metre on average per year in the case of sulphur dioxide (SO_2, the main suspected source of 'acid rain'), and 60–80 micrograms per cubic metre for dust ('suspended particulate matter'). We have taken the mid-point in each range to illustrate these two aspects of urban air pollution.

We have had to make some crude assumptions about the relative values produced by the two major testing methods for sulphur dioxide and about the relative importance of the sites chosen. In general, we have opted for City Centre Commercial sites, when available; otherwise, for City Centre Residential; and thirdly for Industrial; before using suburban sites.

Oil spills are reported primarily on a voluntary basis, although Lloyds of London supplements the reports with their own. Predictably, more information is available for the rich Western states than for the rest of the world. The map includes oil spills on inland waterways.

46. Urban Blight

In September 1980, within two weeks of reporting that only 30% of city-dwellers in Bolivia were served with water and only 31% covered by sanitation services, the United Nations Secretary-General published a second report which revealed that the fortunate Bolivian city-dwellers were covered to the extent of 100% in both respects. The two reports (A/35/341 of 5 September and A/35/367 of 18 September) gave the coverage of urban sanitation in Brazil as 65% and 35% respectively; in Chile, as 50% and 66%; in Cuba as 46% and 97%; in El Salvador, as 34% and 79%; in Ethiopia, as 'low' and 'not available'; in Haiti, as 0% (sic) and 67%; in Jamaica, as 33% and 95%; in Mozambique, as 'low' and 60%; in Nicaragua, as 38% and 92%; in Uruguay, as 54% and 94%; and in Zaire, as 8% and 80%.

We do not for a moment suppose that the Secretary-General's Office was doctoring the evidence. We cite such figures merely to demonstrate that available evidence, even in respect of such public, measurable properties as safe water and sanitation pipes, is highly suspect. In cases where two different figures are provided, we have adopted the lower one as generally the more probable.

With the world's urban population growing, both absolutely and as a proportion of the total, and with this population crowding into ever more gargantuan centres, the pressure on services to provide even the rudiments of a safe and sane environment will grow well beyond what is currently planned, let alone likely to be implemented. An urban crisis on a tremendous scale is manifestly in the making.

47. The Dying Earth

It has taken thousands of years for large tracts of desert and semi-desert land to develop out of what were once fertile regions; years in which haphazard human encroachment has often been responsible for upsetting the delicate balance on which ecological renewal depends.

Recently, this encroachment has become more rapid and violent. In many parts of the world, population pressure, patterns of landownership, government economic policies, war – or some combination of these – have destroyed or blighted huge areas of land, to produce, particularly in much of Africa, expanses of endemic famine.

A report of the UN Conference on Desertification (1977) concluded that although more than one third of the earth's land is already arid, this is very far from the full extent of the problem. Declining land fertility, caused by current pressures, will in due course affect the livelihood of well over 600 million people, most of whom live in poor states.

Tropical moist forests cover only 6% of the world's land area but have a special significance in the world's ecological balance. They harbour as much as half of the world's animal and plant species, along with the people who know best about such species, their behaviour and possible uses; they are essential for the world's oxygen supply; and they are of immeasurable climatic importance. Yet they are being felled – to make way for farmland, roadbuilding, cattle ranching, mining, and to support the appetite of the timber industry – at the rate of 40 hectares or 100 acres every minute. By the mid-1970s, they had been cleared from some 40% of their natural habitat. And little was, or is, being done to repair the damage. Successfully established tree plantations represent a mere 2.5% of the annual loss.

With the trees, go the inhabitants. Brazil, with one third of the world's total tropical forest area, had a forest population of some 6–9 million people three centuries ago. Its present estimated forest population is 200,000 people. In some cases, such declines have resulted from ruthless methods of elimination or displacement. In Brazil, the Indians have been bombed, poisoned, and deliberately infected with tuberculosis, influenza and smallpox. In Bolivia, they have been forced into debt bondage. In Paraguay, they have been the target of military manhunts and imprisoned in reserves. In the Philippines, they have been swept off the land and into armed rebellion.

48. Protection and Extinction

According to the International Union for the Conservation of Nature and Natural Resources, about a thousand species of mammals and birds are currently threatened with elimination; as are many more, one in ten, species of flowering plants. The number of entire species under threat of extinction may seem relatively small. But the extinction of any must represent an irreparable loss and one, moreover, which may have damaging consequences for those that are left. Besides, the number of provenances (sub-populations) of species that are threatened with severe genetic depletion or extinction is large. These endangered provenances are often at the limits of their particular specie range and have developed, through natural selection, corresponding characteristics – such as tolerance to drought or cold or other adverse environmental conditions – that are of immense potential value to humanity.

We have used data for 1978 and 1979 in preference to those for later years because the coverage by our main source, the IUCN's Red Data Books, is greater for the earlier period. But even that coverage is far from evenly distributed around the world. North America and Northern Europe feature disproportionately, not because they are exceptionally lethal environments for living species but because they are monitored more closely and cited more systematically than are other regions.

The 214 Biosphere Reserves in 58 countries are representative habitat types, established to protect genetic and ecological diversity for research, monitoring, education and training. The World Natural Heritage Sites are areas of international significance. They were selected because they represent a major stage in evolution; an important continuing geological process, biological evolution or social/natural interaction; contain unique, rare or superlative natural phenomena, formations or features, or areas of exceptional beauty; or contain habitats for populations of rare or endangered plant and animal species.

49. Industrial Droop

The decline in the rate of industrial growth from the decade of the 1960s to that of the 1970s – there has even been, in a few instances, an actual contraction during the second period – is a major source and symptom of the gathering economic crisis in the world. As the map demonstrates, the decline involves the USSR and its associates in Eastern Europe as well as the advanced industrial states of the West and, inevitably, the poor countries.

The CIA disputes the official figures for industrial production in the USSR and certain countries of Eastern Europe. It offers instead its own estimates, allegedly to conform with Western measures of industrial output. The authors accept the criticism that holds both the official figures and the CIA estimates to be, in their different ways, distortions. For the purpose of this map, we have decided to take figures midway between the official ones and the CIA calculations; on the principle that it is better to be half wrong than to risk being wholly so.

For those who wish to make up their own minds, we provide the conflicting figures:

	growth, 1960s	*growth, 1970s*	*rate of decline*
Bulgaria	194.1%(Off.)	107%(Off.)	−44.9%
	194.1%(CIA)	58%(CIA)	−70.1%
Czechoslovakia	81.8%(Off.)	74%(Off.)	− 9.5%
	56.25%(CIA)	38%(CIA)	−32.4%
East Germany	81.8%(Off.)	72%(Off.)	−12%
	53.8%(CIA)	37%(CIA)	−31.2%
Hungary	92.3%(Off.)	72%(Off.)	−22%
	78.6%(CIA)	28%(CIA)	−64.4%
Poland	122.2%(Off.)	100%(Off.)	−18.2%
	96.1%(CIA)	49%(CIA)	−49%

Romania	233.3%(Off.)	190%(Off.)	−18.6%
	185.7%(CIA)	93%(CIA)	−49.9%
USSR	127.3%(Off.)	78%(Off.)	−38.7%
	85.2%(CIA)	58%(CIA)	−31.9%

We have considerably simplified the protectionist devices reported in the 1983 UNCTAD survey. Targets and quotas are of four main kinds: for all commodities in foreign prices (Bulgaria, Czechoslovakia, East Germany, Romania); for selected commodities in quantities (Bulgaria, Czechoslovakia, East Germany, Romania); for all commodities, in foreign prices and in quantities (USSR); and with many exceptions (Hungary, Poland).

Non-tariff barriers involve measures affecting price; measures restraining volume; and measures requiring specific authorization for particular imports. As examples: Australia imposes the first; Sweden, the second and third; the United States, the first and second; while member countries of the European Economic Community (EEC) impose all three kinds.

Information on duties, a major form of protectionism, is too vague for useful inclusion.

The 1983 UNCTAD survey furnished examples and not a complete study of protectionist devices around the world. There are countries with which the survey did not deal and which may be assumed to have devices of various kinds as well.

All the evidence demonstrates that far from promoting free trade to encourage economic growth, the world of states is reacting to its gathering economic problems by rearming for a trade war.

50. The Paper Chase

The phenomenon of inflation reflects both the power and the vulnerability of the state: its power to extract resources, by providing a means of payment which is worth less than the value assigned to it; its vulnerability to public protest which rejects the deception by assigning its own value to the means of payment. In the process, there is usually a substantial and socially disruptive redistribution of wealth, from the poor and weak, who are helpless victims of the process, to the rich and strong, who manipulate it to their own benefit.

This map gives the average annual rate of inflation for the 1970s and demonstrates that levels which would have been regarded during the fifties and sixties as intolerable, if not incredible, were a widespread feature of the decade that followed. Figures for 1980–1, the latest year for which information on enough countries was available, suggest that economic recession was slow in making a serious impact on high rates of inflation in all but a few countries, and that in a number of cases the rate in the first year of the new decade was above that prevailing in the years of the previous one. More recent figures point to an upturn in inflation for some of the rich states; and new inflationary peaks for several states, notably Israel.

We have decided to include information on a few speculation and trading centres, whose importance has grown alongside the depreciation of paper money and the increase of public distrust in such money as a safeguard of wealth. We have identified only those whose operations and influence are world-wide. Financial futures, themselves products of an anxious age, are instruments by which speculators or traders may purchase 'positions' in anything from the trend of interest rates to the changes in exchange rates between specified currencies.

51. A Question of Terms

Twenty-one developing countries had, by mid-1983, accumulated some $525 billion of debt. And of this enormous sum, more than $400 billion, or close to four-fifths, had been, was being, or manifestly needed to be, 'rescheduled' (i.e. rearranged so that due payments of capital and even interest might be effectively postponed). Of this last amount, well over $200 billion had been lent by the commercial banks.

Precise information on the extent of such 'problem loans', as the commercial banks euphemistically term them, is not generally available. But already by the middle of June 1982, the chairman of the US Federal Reserve referred to an overall exposure of some $100 billion by US commercial banks alone.

The assets, by which the wealth of a commercial bank is commonly measured, are overwhelmingly composed of the loans that the bank has made. And as such, they are as good or as bad as the ability of the debtors to repay them. Commercial banks have capital and reserves to back their business and, when necessary, cope with the professional hazard of bad debts. In 1960, such capital and reserves represented some 8.1% of the assets held by US commercial banks, or what may rather be termed their loan exposure. But this ratio was allowed to fall, as the pursuit of rapid growth and high profits took precedence over conventional prudence. By 1982, the 117 US banks among the world's biggest 500 had an average 4.87% ratio of capital and reserves to assets. And the ratio was even smaller on average for the commercial banks from other major countries in the top 500 list: 4.79% for the 20 British banks; 3.93% for the 28 Italian ones; 2.65% for the 61 Japanese; 2.56% for the 44 West German; and 2.45% for the 18 French.

The 5 per cent benchmark used in the map is based on a decision by the US banking authorities in the summer of 1983 to make this a minimum requirement for US commercial banks. But it is reasonable to wonder whether any such ratio corresponds to the scale of the problem. The top 10 US commercial banks, for instance, have a total of $43.8 billion in loans to only six of the countries in difficulties – Argentina, Brazil, Chile, Mexico, Venezuela, Yugoslavia – and this, on its own, represents no less than 169 per cent of their capital.

Moreover while this map deals with the particular problem of sovereign debt, this is far from being the sole source of 'problem loans': 'Bank exposure to the weaker parts of the international corporate sector, such as the oil services industry, farming equipment and shipping, probably stands at well over $100,000 million, to say nothing of the banks' domestic exposure to problem corporate clients.' *Financial Times*, 21 December 1982

52. The Gold Rush

The world market in gold is veined with apparent contradictions. Some countries – notably, the richest of all, the USA – value the gold holdings in their reserves at a fixed price that is a tiny fraction of the free market value. But they will sell none of their gold at such a price and indeed, when they do sell, sell it at the prevailing price on the free market. The USA has long been in the forefront of a campaign to reduce the importance of gold as a monetary instrument – has even sold gold from its official stocks to counteract the gold rush – yet continues to possess by far the largest single holding in the world and to be one of the very few states with more than three quarters of its reserves, by value, in gold.

Unlike such alternative, supposedly 'safe' investments as bank deposits and government or top quality corporate bonds, gold earns no income and even costs money, in insurance and other security charges.

In fact, given the high prevailing rates of interest during the last ten years, an investment in gold rather than in such other instruments has cost both states and individual citizens a substantial measure of lost income each year. Yet states have been generally reluctant to sell their gold holdings even at high free market prices and have preferred, when in need, to dispose rather of interest-bearing investments in foreign currency; while private citizens have, if erratically, persisted in purchasing gold, and on a massive scale overall.

The key to the contradiction lies in the gathering distrust, among both states and private citizens, of the world's monetary system, with inflation continually – and at times dramatically – eroding the purchasing power of paper currencies. The attraction of gold as a store of value increases alongside the failure of paper currency to perform this essential function of money. In short, investors in gold have more or less contentedly foregone an increase in income from alternative investments in the hope of maintaining the real value of their savings.

Such was the rush into gold during the high inflation years of the 1970s that the free market price rose from $35 an ounce in the early months of 1970 to peak at over $800 an ounce in March 1980. What followed was, perhaps, even more surprising. Given that so enormous a rise in price had been fuelled by fears of a total collapse in the monetary system and a hysterical degree of speculation on some such prospect, the deepening of economic recession and the sharp drop in rates of inflation across most of the advanced industrial world might have been expected to end in a return of the gold price to somewhere near the level of the old days. But after a brief dip below $300 an ounce, the price recovered to hover around $375 in late December 1983. Demonstrably, fears of revived inflation had been far from excised, while the difficulties of the commercial banking system, with the effective bankruptcy of large sovereign borrowers, had added a new element of instability to the financial system.

But if the gold rush is primarily promoted by such considerations, there are other factors. Gold is an alluringly anonymous form of wealth for those who are concerned to keep their financial dispositions secret, especially from tax or other officials. It is supremely negotiable, and without risk of any capital loss, across state frontiers, in a way that very few paper currencies are. And at times of social upheaval – as people seeking to escape from Vietnam knew or were to discover – it may be the only acceptable medium of exchange. In summary, the rush into gold is a measure not only of financial instability but of the wider political instability in the world of states.

Gold trading has developed to the point where there is now a gold market operating sometime, somewhere, 24 hours a day. And there has been a gargantuan growth in what is termed trading in futures, by which investors, speculators and traders – the distinctions are often blurred – may buy or sell contracts, covering a determined weight of gold at a determined price per ounce, for settlement on some determined date in the future. Since such contracts generally involve a down payment that is a small proportion – perhaps 10 per cent – of the face value represented by the contract, a little money can go a long way, and a lot of money can support a scarcely credible edifice of commitment. The total value of contracts traded in only one market, albeit the biggest one – COMEX in New York – during 1982 involved a value (given an average gold price of $400 an ounce) of some $491 billion.

53. Green Revolution

For some people, the way humanity relates to the rest of nature is the most important and pervasive issue of our time, since on it hinges our judgement of all social and political arrangements. For others, the defence of a village green, a threatened tree or a stray animal has no wider implication; however passionately the particular cause is felt or fought.

This map attempts to represent green consciousness in all its forms – the broad and the narrow, the official and the unofficial – at least for as far as our informants could take us.

Its central conclusions were reached through a version of the so-called Delphi method, whereby a number of people actively engaged in the study of a subject are asked to evaluate relevant phenomena according to commonly agreed criteria. This approach has its dangers, in proportion to the homogeneity of background and of view among the participating experts. We make no pretence of having cast the net very wide, geographically or philosophically. Where our informants disagreed with one another, we have adopted the view with the largest measure of support. Where disagreement was balanced, we have in general opted for the more generous judgement.

The existence of a 'green' party is not necessarily an indication of substantial public sensitivity to environmental issues. Nor, equally, should its absence be taken to indicate public insensitivity. Green parties do not exist in one-party states or in many other states with a high degree of political intolerance. Where a Green party does exist, this may reflect the closed minds of the traditional parties rather than an acute public awareness of the issues involved. But political success for such a party can itself create a space for environmental concern within the existing political structures; as has been evidenced in West Germany, with the election to the Bundestag of Green deputies.

In many states, especially the poorer ones and those with highly centralized economies, green consciousness is more likely to course through university departments, scientific institutions and particular government ministries than through the offices of pressure groups. In such countries, action is more likely to follow pressure from international bodies, such as the World Bank or the IUCN, than to result from spontaneous indigenous pressure. For this reason we have included *all* organizations listed in the Environment Liaison Centre's Directory. This has resulted in a massive underrecording of the numbers in some countries, notably the USA.

Official endorsement of green policies, as indicated by a state's adherence to international conventions on environmental protection (our inset map), may mean very little in practice. Of the 37 states that had, by September 1983, considered the IUCN's World Conservation Strategy since its publication three and a half years earlier, only three had established a special task force to implement some of the strategy's provisions.

54. Women's Rights

The right of women to control their pregnancy is variously abridged by male-dominated law. The particular laws on abortion indicate, albeit imperfectly, one aspect of this abridgement, and restrictive changes in such laws show how tenuous is the hold of women on such limited rights as they have won.

The map demonstrates widespread differences in legal provision on abortion. In most states some right to abortion is recognized, but on more or less restricted criteria, and always by leave of a predominantly male authority. In no state does a woman have an unrestricted right to abortion. Even in the Netherlands, perhaps the most liberal in practice, abortion on demand is available only in a few private, 'non-profit' clinics, and then with *formal* legal sanction only on narrow medical grounds. In Cuba, another liberal state in this respect, abortion on demand is available in government hospitals, but only for certain categories of women and/or for the initial stages of pregnancy.

Where abortion is available on demand for certain groups of women only, the criteria differ widely. They include age (usually women over forty); the number of living children (the number varies); and even, in Hungary, whether the woman has a home of her own. Where abortion is permitted only within a specified time, the limit is usually the first ten to twelve weeks of pregnancy, as in most East European states, but can be as little as eight weeks (Sweden) or as much as twenty-four weeks (Singapore).

Very often, legal provision and social practice are far apart. France, for instance, while fairly liberal in theory, is restrictive in practice; the Philippines, while restrictive in theory, is fairly liberal in practice.

The definitions employed need explanation. 'Social or social-medical grounds' cover the well-being of the woman and her existing family; 'juridical grounds' cover rape and incest; 'broad medical and eugenic grounds' grant abortion to safeguard a women's physical health or to prevent the transmission of incurable hereditary diseases; 'narrow medical grounds' cover only cases where a woman's life is at stake. We have taken 'social or social-medical grounds' to be a broader category than 'juridical' or 'medical and eugenic grounds'.

In some states with a federal system of government, national legal provisions are moderated by state law and range from extreme liberality (California in the USA, Slovenia in Yugoslavia, and South Australia) to extreme restrictiveness (Louisiana in the USA, Queensland in Australia).

We add below a table recording the dates on which women first achieved equal status as voters. When denied, equality of franchise presents a challenge to the strength and purpose of women. Once attained, it constitutes perhaps the first milestone in the journey towards a society of equals.

Equal voting rights for women
(sometimes restricted franchise; but equality within the inequality)

1893 New Zealand
1894 Australia
1913 Norway
1915 Denmark
Iceland
1917 Finland
USSR
1918 Austria
Canada
Luxembourg
Poland
1919 Czechoslovakia
Germany
Netherlands
Sweden
1920 Hungary
USA
1922 Ireland
1924 Mongolia
1928 UK
1929 Romania
1930 South Africa
1931 Spain
1932 Brazil
Thailand
Uruguay
1934 Cuba
Turkey
1935 Burma
1937 Philippines
1942 Dominican Republic
1944 Albania
France
Jamaica
1945 Indonesia
Mali
Monaco
Portugal
1946 Benin
CAR
Cameroon
Congo
Ivory Coast
Gabon

1946 Guinea
Italy
Liberia
Madagascar
Mauritania
Panama
Niger
Senegal
Trinidad and Tobago
Upper Volta
1947 Bulgaria
China
Malta
1948 Belgium
Israel
Korea
Sri Lanka
1949 Costa Rica
Chile
India
Syria
1950 El Salvador
Ghana
Haiti
Japan
1951 Nepal
1952 Bolivia
Greece
1953 Lebanon
Mexico
1954 Colombia
Nigeria
1955 Ethiopia
Honduras
Nicaragua
1955 Peru
1956 Kampuchea
Laos
Pakistan
Vietnam
1957 Malaysia
1958 Algeria
Somalia
1959 Cyprus
Morocco
Tunisia
1961 Burundi
Gambia
Paraguay
Sierra Leone
1962 Kuwait
Rwanda
Samoa
Uganda
1963 Kenya
Libya
1964 Afghanistan
Iran
Iraq
Malawi
Zambia
1965 Guatemala
Singapore
Sudan
1966 Barbados
Botswana
Guyana
Lesotho
1967 Ecuador
1971 Switzerland

55. Gay Survival, Gay Assertion

In the 19th century, the word 'gay' was used to describe 'loose women' and prostitutes. By the 1920s, the word was coming to be used as a term of self-identification within the homosexual sub-culture. In 1968, when the word was officially adopted by the Conference of Homophile Organizations in the United States, 'gay' was already so widely used in the homosexual sub-culture as to be an obvious choice.

In the male-dominated culture of the advanced industrial 'Western' states, or what is sometimes termed the First World, attitudes to homosexuality long reflected the generally restrictive attitudes to sexuality in conventional morality and in religion. Homosexual behaviour was commonly illegal and when discovered, prosecuted. The liberalizing and secularizing of attitudes to sexuality in the 1960s promoted changes, too, in attitudes to homosexuality, which began to be freed from legal restrictions, although not from social pressures and condemnation.

In the USSR, Eastern Europe, and the rest of the 'communist' world, homosexuality has tended to be treated as a product of Western capitalism, incompatible with socialist morality. The control of homosexuality is regarded by many of these states as an expression of their own progress. Where there is a more enlightened view, homosexuality is nevertheless presented as a sickness or congenital defect, rather than as an expression of human nature.

Across the mass of states in the Third World, the legal regulation of homosexuality is often the historical product of colonialism and its attendant religious educational system. But if the law has survived its originators, its prosecution has not. In many cases, while homosexuality remains illegal, homosexual behaviour is socially tolerated; often because it is simply not perceived as 'homosexual' or unusual. Progress has been made in many states. In much of Latin America, for instance, the spread of gay liberation ideas has promoted the self-awareness of homosexuals, but the price of this has been to alienate them from the mainstream, 'macho' culture.

Lesbianism is seldom mentioned in the law, because women are not expected to have an independent sexual identity. And indeed, in a male-dominated world, relatively little is publicly known about lesbianism. The gay movement itself is male-orientated and finds it difficult to get lesbians to participate. Even the feminist movement, which has played so crucial a part in promoting the emancipation of women, has tended to avoid any identification with lesbianism; so that many lesbians have felt themselves under pressure to deny their sexuality for the cause of emancipation. Nonetheless, and partly under the influence of the growth in homosexual consciousness and assertion, the 1970s saw the growth of a lesbian consciousness and a lesbian liberation movement.

The special category in our map, 'lawful but repressed', suggests some of the difficulties still confronting gay self-identification. In some states, for instance, gay sex in private between consenting adult men is not illegal; but homosexual organizations and information in favour of homosexuality are banned.

And the law can indirectly remain a threat to self-expression. In most states the social system is based on the conventional family, and the legal system is biased towards it.

But whatever the differences from state to state in legal sanctions, gay experience is much the same everywhere, with the assertion of consciousness encountering social discrimination, risk to employment and a sense of alienation. This explains the world-wide phenomenon of gay organizations, events, newspapers that transcend cultural, racial and political differences.

More than any other organization, the International Gay Association based in Amsterdam – a loose federation of gay groups – plays a vital role in promoting gay consciousness across state frontiers.

56. Minority Views

Virtually every state in the world has within it a minority or minorities: racial, religious, linguistic, cultural, or some combination of these. This sort of social minority is not the same as a political one though the two may often be effectively the same.

This map does not deal with all such social minorities, but in general only with those that are known to be suffering discrimination of some kind. Our information is very far from adequate. Despite the research undertaken by various concerned organizations, most notably the Minority Rights Group in London, much remains to be found out and made known about social conflict and, in particular, discrimination against minorities around the world. This is not surprising. Too many governments patrol their internal affairs to prevent the escape of embarrassing information.

The nature and even existence of an organized movement within minorities that suffer discrimination is often largely a matter of inference and judgement. We have followed – and are grateful for – the advice afforded us by those with specialist knowledge. But in the end we have sometimes had to draw conclusions of our own, from such scraps of information or reports of relevant events as have come our way.

In some states, the regime itself is based on some social minority, and it is the majority that suffers discrimination. We have considered it appropriate to provide such information on the map.

In some states too, there are substantial minorities – in a few cases, even majorities – that are regarded as more or less temporary, since they consist in large measure of immigrant labour and refugees (see *Map 32: In Search of Work* and *Map 26: A Sort of Survival*). Here we have provided only a few extreme examples, where large immigrant populations are denied political rights.

Where a significant armed movement exists, we have given it priority over any peaceful one, on the principle that the organized resort to violence indicates a further stage of discontent or despair. The siting of an armed movement in a particular state must not, accordingly, be taken to mean the absence of an organized peaceful one. Indeed, the peaceful movement of protest may be – and usually is – the larger of the two.

57. The State Under Pressure

Identifying the existence of significant pressure on the state is a difficult exercise. The category of 'other states' is a catch-all, both for those (such as the Western parliamentary democracies) where opposition is directed at a particular government rather than the regime, and those where we have had to accept that our information could not sustain any sort of sensible judgement.

In determining 'moderate pressure', we have been guided by evidence of strike or other protest action aimed essentially at the nature of the regime. The line between 'moderate' and 'substantial pressure' is inevitably a blurred one. We have employed the category of 'substantial pressure' where we have adjudged that it is of a kind to put in some doubt the survival of the regime. In two notable instances, those of Argentina and Nigeria, such pressure led to the fall of the regime in late 1983. In Argentina, a military regime gave place to a parliamentary democracy; in Nigeria, a more or less democratic regime was displaced by a military one. In both states, the record suggests that the change may not be a final one; but it is too early to identify pressure against either of the new regimes.

This category of 'substantial pressure' requires an important caveat. In several instances, the pressure comes significantly from the hand of a foreign government, provoking or promoting domestic discontent. Angola and Mozambique provide notable examples. With the resources of the South African government behind them, guerrilla movements in both states pose increasingly serious challenges.

The state is under more fundamental pressure from organized movements of separatism or irredentism. And where we have judged that this category should apply, it has, accordingly, taken precedence over the preceding ones. This category involves a wide range of intensity, from France to Zaire. We see no way of measuring such differences in degree.

In a few cases – Afghanistan, Chad, Cyprus, El Salvador, Equatorial Guinea, Lebanon and Uganda – the authority of the state is too far disputed for the concept of sovereignty to mean very much. This category, of course, takes precedence over all others.

Foreign military occupation refers to the existence of a foreign military presence so vital to the survival of the regime that the sovereignty of the state is itself in question. Afghanistan and Namibia are celebrated examples. We have placed on particular countries symbols for ecology and peace movements where these are driven, by the very logic of their commitments, to question the relevance of the sovereign state. We make no judgement on the political importance of these, apart from identifying where they are significant in affecting public opinion. Absence of any ascription for a particular state should not imply absence of pressure but merely absence of information. Finally, we would have liked to identify an internationalist movement with a significant popular following, if only in a very few countries. We have not, in all honesty, found adequate evidence to do so.

Sources for the Maps

Ambio: a Journal of the Human Environment, Stockholm, bi-monthly

American Bureau of Metal Statistics, *Non-Ferrous Metal Data 1981*, New York: American Bureau of Metal Statistics, 1982

Amnesty International, London, *Newsletter*, monthly

—, *Report*, annual

Anuarul Statistic al Republicii Socialiste România 1981, Bucharest: Directia Centrala de Statistica Romania, 1981

Ashman, Peter, and Paul Crane, private communications

Ashworth, Georgina (ed), *World Minorities*, Sunbury, Middx: Quartermaine House; vol. 1, 1977; vol. 2, 1978

—, *World Minorities in the Eighties*, Sunbury, Middx: Quartermaine House, 1980

Atlas of Earth Resources, London: Mitchell Beazley, 1979

Bank of China, private communications

The Banker, London, monthly

Birks, J.S, and C.A. Sinclair, *International Migration and Development in the Arab Region*, Geneva: ILO, 1980

—, *The Kingdom of Saudi Arabia and the Libyan Arab Jamahiriya*, Geneva: ILO, 1979

BIS [Bank for International Settlement], *53rd Annual Report*, Basle: BIS, June 1983

Boggan, E.C, *et al*, *The Rights of Gay People*, New York: Bantam Books, 1983

BP [British Petroleum], *BP Statistical Review of World Energy 1982*, London: BP, n.d.

Bridgman, James C, 'Who gets what resources in the EEZ: the top twenty-five', in John J. Logue (ed), *Villanova Colloquium on Peace, Justice and the Law of the Sea*, photocopy supplied

British Telecom, private communications

Buzan, Barry, *A Sea of Troubles? Sources of Dispute in the New Ocean Regime*, Adelphi Papers 143, London: International Institute for Strategic Studies, 1978

China Official Annual Report, Hong Kong: Kingsway International Publications, annual

CIA [United States Central Intelligence Agency], *Handbook of Economic Statistics 1982*, Washington DC: CIA, 1982

—, *Soviet GNP in Current Prices*, SOV 83-10037, Washington DC: CIA, August 1979

—, *The World Oil Market in the Years Ahead*, ER 79-10327U, Washington DC: CIA, August 1979

Commodity Research Bureau, *Commodity Yearbook 1982*, New York: Commodity Research Bureau, 1982

Consolidated Goldfields, *Gold 1983*, London: Consolidated Goldfields, 1983

—, private communications

Council of Europe, Parliamentary Assembly, Strasbourg, 29 September-7 October 1982

Couper, Alistair (ed), *The Times Atlas of the Oceans*, London: Times Books, 1983

Deutsches Institut für Wirtschaftsforschung, *Handbook of the Economy of the German Democratic Republic*, Farnborough, Hants: Saxon House, 1979

Earthscan, London, 'Press Briefings', occasional; see also: Mitchell

—, *Tropical Moist Forests*, Press Briefing Document no. 32 by Catherine Caufield, April 1982

ELC [Environmental Liaison Centre], *Environmental Activities of Non-Governmental Organizations (NGOs) related to UNEP Programmes: Report and Directory*, prepared for the Eighth Governing Council of the United Nations Environment Programme, Nairobi: ELC, April 1980

Europa Publications, *Africa South of the Sahara Yearbook*, London: Europa Publications, annual

—, *Europa Yearbook*, London: Europa Publications, annual

—, *Far East and Australasia Yearbook*, London: Europa Publications, annual

—, *Middle East and North Africa Yearbook*, London: Europa Publications, annual

FAO [United Nations Food and Agricultural Organization], *Fertilizer Yearbook*, Rome: FAO, annual
—, *Fourth World Food Survey*, Rome: FAO, 1977
—, *Production Yearbook*, Rome: FAO, annual
—, *Trade Yearbook*, Rome: FAO, annual
Financial Times, London, daily
Fortune, New York, fortnightly

Garfield, Eugene, 'Mapping Science in the Third World', *Science and Public Policy*, vol. 10, no. 3, June 1983
Guide to World Commodity Markets, 3rd edn, London: Kogan Page, 1982

Harrison, Jeremy, Kenton Miller and Jeffrey McNeely, 'The world coverage of protected areas: development goals and environmental needs', *Ambio*, vol. 11, no. 5, 1982
Hopkins, Michael, 'Employment trends in developing countries: 1960 and beyond', *International Labour Review*, vol. 122, no. 4, July-August 1983

IAEA [International Atomic Energy Agency], *Research Reactors in Member States*, Vienna: IAEA, 1980
IBRD [International Bank for Reconstruction and Development], *World Tables*, 2nd edn, Washington DC: IBRD, 1980
IEA [International Energy Agency], *World Energy Outlook*, Paris: Organization for Economic Cooperation and Development, 1982
IISS [International Institute for Strategic Studies], *The Military Balance*, London: IISS, annual
ILO [International Labour Office], *The Cost of Social Security*, Geneva: ILO, 1981
—, *Labour and Discrimination in Namibia*, Geneva: ILO, 1977
—, *Labour Force Estimates and Projections 1950-2000*, Geneva: ILO, 1977
—, *ILO Social and Labour Bulletin*, 3 & 4/1982, Geneva: ILO, 1983
—, *Yearbook of Labour Statistics*, Geneva: ILO, annual
IMF [International Monetary Fund], *Direction of Trade Annual*, Washington DC: IMF, annual
—, *Direction of Trade Statistics Yearbook*, Washington DC: IMF, annual
—, *International Financial Statistics*, Washington DC: IMF, monthly
—, *International Financial Statistics Yearbook*, Washington DC: IMF, annual
International Tanker Owners Pollution Federation, private communications
Interpol [International Criminal Police Commission], *International Crime Statistics 1977-8*, Paris: Interpol, 1981
IUCN [International Union for Conservation of Nature and Natural Resources], *The IUCN Invertebrate Red Data Book*, Gland: IUCN, 1983
—, *The IUCN Mammal Red Data Book*, part 1, Gland: IUCN, 1982
—, *Red Data Book*, vols. 1-4, Morges: IUCN, 1972-9
—, *World Conservation Strategy: Living Resource Conservation for Sustainable Development*, prepared by the IUCN with the cooperation of UNEP and WWF, and in collaboration with FAO and UNESCO, 1980

Jain, Shail, *Size Distribution of Income: a Compilation of Data*, Washington DC: IBRD, 1975

Kaplan, Frederic M, and Julian M. Sobin (eds), *Encyclopaedia of China Today*, 3rd edn, London: Macmillan, 1982
Kidron, Michael, and Dan Smith, *The War Atlas: Armed Conflict, Armed Peace*, London: Pan Books and Heinemann Educational Books, 1983; New York: Simon & Schuster, 1983
Kurian, George Thomas, *The Book of World Rankings*, London: Macmillan Press, 1979
— (ed), *World Press Encyclopedia*, London: Mansell, 1982

Lloyds Bank, *Economic Report on Taiwan*, London: Lloyds Bank, 1983

McHale, M.C, and J. McHale, *Children in the World*, Washington DC: Population Reference Bureau, 1979
Minority Rights Group, London, occasional publications; see also: Ashworth
Mitchell, Barbara, and Jon Tinker, *Antarctica and its Resources*, London: Earthscan, 1980

Newland, Kathleen, *Refugees*, Worldwatch Paper 43, Washington DC: Worldwatch Institute, March 1981

Philippine Statistical Yearbook 1982, Manila: National Economic and Development Authority, 1982
Pick, Franz, *Pick's Currency Yearbook 1977-9*, New York: Pick Publishing Corporation, 1981

Rocnik Statystyczny 1981, Warsaw: Gatowny Urzad Statystyczny, 1982

Royal Aircraft Establishment, Farnborough, Hants, private communications

SCAR [Scientific Committee on Antarctic Research], *Bulletin,* Cambridge (UK): Scott Polar Research Institute, 3 times a year

Scherer, John L, *China Facts and Figures Annual*, vol. 5, Gulf Breeze, Fla: Academic International Press, 1982

—, *USSR Facts and Figures Annual*, vol. 7, Gulf Breeze, Fla: Academic International Press, 1983

Science, Washington DC, weekly

Singh, Jyoti Shankar (ed), *World Population Policies*, New York: Praeger, 1979

SIPRI [Stockholm International Peace Research Institute], *Yearbook*, London: Taylor & Francis, annual

Sivard, Ruth Leger, *World Military and Social Expenditures*, Leesburg, Va: World Priorities, annual

South, London, monthly

Soviet National Survey, vol. 1, no. 1, London: Suchasnist Publishers, January 1984

Spanish Yearbook, Madrid: Instituto Nacional de Estadistica, Anuario Estadistica de España, annual

Starch INRA Hooper, *World Advertising Expenditures*, 17th edn, New York: Starch INRA Group of Companies and International Advertising Association, 1983

Statesman's Year-Book, London: Macmillan, annual

Statistical Yearbook of the Czechoslovak Socialist Republic 1982, Prague: Federal Statistical Office, 1982

Statistical Yearbook of the Netherlands 1978, The Hague: Central Bureau of Statistics, 1978

Statistički Godišnjak Jugoslavije 1982, Belgrade: Savezni Zavod za Statistiku, 1982

Statisztikai Évkönyv 1981, Budapest: Központi Statisztikai Hivatal, 1982

[Taiwan] Statistical Yearbook, Republic of China [Taiwan]: Directorate-General of Budget, Accounting and Finance, Executive Yuan, annual

Terre des Femmes, Paris: Maspero, 1983

Tietze, Christopher, *Induced Abortion: a World Review*, 5th edn, New York: The Population Council, 1983

UK CEGB [United Kingdom Central Electricity Generating Board], *World Energy Background to 2030*, Sizewell document CEGB/S/331, 1983

UN [United Nations], *Demographic Yearbook*, New York: UN, annual

—, *Energy Resources Development Series*, no. 25, ST/ESCAP/219, New York: UN, 1982

—, *International Drinking Water Supply and Sanitation Decade: Present Situation and Prospects*, Report of the Secretary-General, A/35/367, Geneva: UN, 18 September 1980

—, *International Migration Policies and Programmes: a World Survey*, New York: UN, 1982

—, *Monthly Bulletin of Statistics*, New York: UN, monthly

—, *Patterns of Urban and Rural Population Growth*, New York: UN, 1979

—, *Regional Reviews of Activities Pertaining to the International Water Supply and Sanitation Decade*, Report of the Secretary-General, A/35/341, Geneva: UN, 5 September 1980

—, *Statistical Yearbook*, New York: UN, annual

—, *World Map of Desertification*, 1977

—, *Yearbook of Industrial Statistics*, New York: UN, annual

—, *Yearbook of National Accounts Statistics*, New York: UN, annual

—, *Yearbook of World Energy Statistics*, New York: UN, annual

UN Centre on Transnational Corporations, *Transnational Corporations in World Development: Third Survey*, New York: UN, 1983

UNCTAD [United Nations Conference on Trade and Development], *Handbook of International Trade and Development Statistics*, New York: UN, annual

UNCTAD VI, *Protectionism, Trade Relations and Structural Adjustment*, policy paper, Belgrade, June 1983

UNEP [United Nations Environment Programme], *The World Environment 1972-1982*, Dublin: Tycooly International Publishing, for UNEP, 1982

UNESCO [United Nations Educational, Scientific, and Cultural Organization], *Yearbook*, Paris: UNESCO, annual

UN High Commissioner for Refugees, *Report of the UNHCR to the General Assembly, 37th Session*, New York: UN, 1982

USACDA [US Arms Control and Disarmament Agency], *World Military Expenditures and Arms Transfers 1971-1980*, Washington DC: USACDA, 1983

US Bureau of Mines, *Minerals Yearbook 1981*, Washington DC: US Bureau of Mines, 1982

US Congress, *World Refugee Crisis: the International Community's Response*, Report to US Senate Committee on the Judiciary, Washington DC: USGPO, 1979

US Department of State, Bureau of Intelligence and Research, *Status of the World's Nations*, Washington DC: USGPO, June 1983

Veliz, C. (ed), *Latin America and the Caribbean: a Handbook*, London: Blond, 1968

WHO [World Health Organization], *Air Quality in Selected Urban Areas 1979-1980*, Geneva: WHO, 1983

—, *Sulfur Oxides and Suspended Particulate Matter: Executive Summary*, Environmental Health Criteria 8, Geneva: WHO in conjunction with UNEP, [1981]

—, computer-stored data, 1983

Wilkie, James W. (ed), *Statistical Abstract of Latin America*, vol. 20, Los Angeles: University of California Press, 1980

Wint, Guy (ed), *Asia Handbook*, Harmondsworth, Middx: Penguin Books, 1969

Women at Work, ILO unpublished paper, 1983 no. 1, Geneva: ILO

World Bank Atlas, Washington DC: IBRD, annual

World View, London: Pluto Press, annual

Acknowledgements

We would like to record some of the many people and institutions to whom we are beholden for information and guidance who are not recognized elsewhere in these pages. They are (in London unless otherwise stated):

ASH Films; Janet Barber, World Wildlife Fund, Godalming; Mr Barnett, Department of Transport; Kate Bateman, US Embassy; P.A. Bliss-Guest, UN Environment Programme, Geneva; Roger Böhning, International Labour Office, Geneva; Susan Boxall, Marine Biological Association of the UK, Plymouth; Penny Brooks, Great Britain-China Centre; Dave Bull, Oxfam, Oxford; Terry Cannon, Thames Polytechnic; Ian Carter, World Health Organization, Geneva; Catherine Caufield, International Institute for Environment & Development; Clive Challis, D'Arcy McManus Masius; Fred Clairmonte, UN Conference on Trade and Development, Geneva; Roland Clarke, Ecology Party; Andrew Cornford, UNCTAD, Geneva; Pat Farquhar, UN Information Centre; Gerry Foley, IIED; F. John Frizell, Greenpeace International; Nicole Gallimore, Royal Institute of International Affairs; Dan Gallin, International Union of Foodworkers, Geneva; Maurice Goldsmith, Science Policy Foundation; Mark Halle, International Union for Conservation of Nature and Natural Resources, Gland; Nigel Harris, Development Planning Unit; Jerry Harrison, Protected Areas Data Unit, Kew; Richard Helmer, WHO, Geneva; Linda Holman, UN Information Centre; Don Holtum, formerly Morgan Guaranty Trust Company; Alfred Homberger, Blick Rothenberg and Noble; Mike Hopkins, ILO, Geneva; Martin Ince; Paul Jeorett, Zoological Society; Denis Jones, RIIA; Margaret Julian, RIIA; Michael Kaser, St Antony's College, Oxford; David Kewley, Pan Books; Henk de Koening, WHO, Geneva; Albert Köhler, World Meteorological Organization, Geneva; Joelle Kuntz, Geneva; Robert Lamb, IUCN, Gland; John Logue, Villanova University, Philadelphia; David Long, British Telecom; Jeffrey McNeely, IUCN, Gland; Alfred Meyer, Shearson/American Express, Geneva; John Montgomery, RIIA; François Nectoux; Kurt Noll, Union Bank of Switzerland, Vevey; Rhona O'Connell, Consolidated Goldfields; Janet Paice, UK Atomic Energy Authority; Walt Patterson, Oxford; Vela Pillay, Bank of China; Peter Richards, ILO, Geneva; Ms Saurwein, UN, New York; Joe Schwartzberg, University of Minnesota, Minneapolis; Clare Seabrook, International Tanker Owners Pollution Federation; Charles Secret, Friends of the Earth; Susan Segal, Walton-on-Thames; Judy Sharpe; A. Sivanandan, Institute of Race Relations; Dan Smith, Brighton; David Somerville, Scottish Campaign to Resist the Atomic Menace, Edinburgh; Malcolm Spaven, Armament and Disarmament Information Unit, University of Sussex; Kaye Spearman, Minority Rights Group; Odyer Sperandio, WHO, Geneva; H. Suzuki, ILO, Geneva; Malcolm Swanston, Derby; Jon Tinker, Earthscan; Basker Vashee, Transnational Institute, Amsterdam; Ruth Vermeer, International Organization of Consumer Unions, The Hague; Hazel Waters, IRR; Paul Wachtel, WWF, Gland; Ben Whitaker, MRG; Joseph Woodall, WHO, Geneva; Lissie Wright, Conservation Monitoring Centre, Cambridge.

The staffs of the following London libraries, public or with privileged access, have been gracious and willing collaborators: British Library Science Reference Library; Department of the Environment; Department of Transport; Family Planning Information Service; Foreign Office; Home Office; International Institute for Strategic Studies; International Labour Office; London Business School; London School of Economics; Morgan Guaranty Trust Company; Natural History Museum; Royal Aircraft Establishment (Farnborough); Royal Institute of International Affairs, Chatham House; St Pancras Reference Library; School of Oriental and African Studies; United Nations Information Centre; Westminster Reference Library; Women's Research and Resources Centre; Zoological Society.